The
Universal
Torah

Growth & Struggle in the
Five Books of Moses

GENESIS II

DR. PINCHAS POLONSKY

The Universal Torah

Growth & Struggle in the Five Books of Moses

GENESIS II

Originally Published as *Bible Dynamics: Contemporary Torah Commentary*

Following the Teaching of Rabbi Yehuda Leon ashkenazi (Manitou) and Rabbi Ouri Cherki

Translated from the Russian by Betzalel (Todd) Shandelman

5785 / 2025
Israel365

Contents

WEEKLY PORTION VAYETZE

Chapter 33: Jacob's Ladder 86

Weekly Portion
Toldot

Chapter 30

The Birth of Jacob and Esau

30.1. The Toldot ("Lineage") Portion

Toldot is the second of the two weekly portions that recount Isaac's life story. It consists of three parts: (1) the birth of Jacob and Esau and the sale of the birthright, (2) the interactions of Isaac and the Philistines, (3) Isaac's blessing of Jacob and Esau.

Thus, Isaac, the second of the Patriarchs, is considered in this portion from two different viewpoints: His external relations with the Philistines and his relationship with his own children.

The portion is called *Toldot*, but not merely because it opens with the words "These are the *toldot* (descendants) of Isaac." We noted (6:9) that the story of Noah likewise begins with the word *toldot*, "This is the ancestry of Noah," but that portion is nevertheless called "Noah," not *Toldot* as this one is. The difference is that the central figure of the "Noah" portion is Noah himself, while in this weekly portion the central figure is not Isaac, but the actual process of *toldot* – the personal development that occurs in the course of a generational transition.

In Isaac we see the beginning of a new kind of holiness, a holiness which is not only individual, but of an entire sequence of generations as a whole; that is, the holiness of all of human history. Isaac is correlated here to the historical process. Therefore, this *Toldot* portion deals with the question of how heritage is transmitted. Accordingly, its central themes will be birthright and blessing, two crucial aspects of inheritance.

30.2. Gevurah Must Acknowledge Itself a Continuation of Chesed (25:19)

יט וְאֵלֶּה תּוֹלְדֹת יִצְחָק בֶּן־אַבְרָהָם אַבְרָהָם הוֹלִיד אֶת־יִצְחָק:

[19] This is the story of Isaac, son of Abraham. Abraham begot Isaac.

We detect a redundancy in this verse: Twice we are told that Abraham is the father of Isaac. Which is why most likely *toldot* here means not pedigree, but offspring, or descendants. This verse can therefore be translated as follows: "These are the descendants born to Isaac, Abraham's son; [which became possible because] Abraham begot Isaac." In other words, Isaac could bear descendants only because Abraham first begot *him*. Only when Isaac, as *Gevurah* (strict judgment) acknowledges that he is the son of Abraham, *Chesed* (kindness), can Isaac beget descendants of his own.

A thirst for justice is in and of itself barren. Only when that desire feels that it is the offspring of *Chesed* – a facilitator in the implementation of mercy – will it be able to develop further, to create new structures in the universe.

30.3. The History of Mankind as a Path from Adam to the Messiah

The very idea of *toldot* – the transition from one generation to the next, but at the same time also the development of what came before – is unusually important in Judaism.

The word *toldot* appears ten times in Tanach. The first occurrence we encountered at 2:4: "Such is the story of heaven and earth" and the last in the book of Ruth at (4:18): "This is the line of Perez" which enumerates the lineage of David, or the forebears of the Messiah. When the Talmud deliberates on which verse in the Torah is the most "central," i.e., in which the essence of the Torah is most clearly expressed, the verse "Such is the story of heaven and earth" is proposed as one possibility – in the sense that a central idea of the Torah is the concept of *toldot*.

Rav I. L. Ashkenazi-Manitou notes that the idea of *toldot* is expressed in the fact that the Messiah is called *ben Adam*, "son of man" (Daniel 7:13, Psalms 80:18). The Messiah is of course a human being. The appellation "son of man" can therefore be understood in an additional sense. He is not only the "son of man," but also the "son of mankind." (The Hebrew word *Adam* can refer to a specific human being, and also to "man" as all of humanity.)

The Messiah is the offspring of mankind: God created man, and humanity itself begets the Messiah and brings him into the world. The Messiah does not come to humanity "from the outside" in order to "save" the human race, because they are not able to save themselves; on the contrary, humanity itself brings the Messiah into existence. The Messiah is a stage in the development of all mankind, when they enter the proper path on their own. From the point of view of the Torah, the meaning of history consists precisely in moving humanity along that path, through the mission entrusted to the Jewish people.

Thus, the idea of *toldot*, means understanding the path of humankind as the gradual transition from Adam to the Messiah. Thus, the Messiah arrives as the result of a synthesis of God's efforts and the efforts of humanity.

30.4. Jewishness and "Aramean-ness" (25:20)

> כ וַיְהִי יִצְחָק בֶּן־אַרְבָּעִים שָׁנָה בְּקַחְתּוֹ אֶת־רִבְקָה בַּת־
> בְּתוּאֵל הָאֲרַמִּי מִפַּדַּן אֲרָם אֲחוֹת לָבָן הָאֲרַמִּי לוֹ לְאִשָּׁה:

[20] Isaac was forty years old when he took to wife Rebekah, daughter of Bethuel the Aramean of Paddan-aram, sister of Laban the Aramean.

[20] Rebekah, daughter of Bethuel the Aramean of Paddan-aram, sister of Laban the Aramean: In this description of Rebekah, the root *Aram* is repeated three times: In the name of her place of birth and as a defining characteristic of both her father and her brother. One can then infer that this is a very significant point. It means that there is still much that is Aramean in Rebekah, and that Jacob and Esau come from the union of Isaac the Hebrew and Rebekah the Aramean.

As a people, the Arameans are completely different from the Jews. They too are descendants of Shem, but of a different lineage not connected with the Jews in any way (10:22). The Arameans were widely settled in the Middle East, and Aramaic was the universal language of communication. Nahor, Bethuel and Laban are scions of the Terah family, not Arameans by birth but Hebrews – descendants of Eber. But they assimilated among the Arameans, losing their Jewish identity and acquiring Aramean identity instead – the universal, cosmopolitan identity of that time. In their self-identification as Arameans we can detect the classical Jewish desire and temptation to become cosmopolitan, that is, the desire to forget their Jewish isolation and become "just normal people" by assimilating with other nations.

Rebekah brings this aspect of Aramean identity to Isaac's family. And this means that "cosmopolitan Judaism" must also have a place in the overall picture. It should not be dominant, of course, but it is important that it too be present. If Jews are too tightly confined only to their internal Jewish identity, discarding all elements of cosmopolitanism, this leads to the improper development of the Jewish people and makes fulfilling their universal mission impossible. The men of the house of Abraham therefore take wives from the daughters of the house of Nahor, so that the specifically Jewish component will be most important, but a measure of cosmopolitanism will be present as well.

30.5. God Accepts Isaac's Prayer (25:21)

כא וַיֶּעְתַּר יִצְחָק לַיי לְנֹכַח אִשְׁתּוֹ כִּי עֲקָרָה הִוא וַיֵּעָתֶר
לוֹ יי וַתַּהַר רִבְקָה אִשְׁתּוֹ:

[21] Isaac pleaded with the Lord on behalf of his wife, because she was barren; and the Lord responded to his plea, and his wife Rebekah conceived.

[21] The Lord responded to his plea: God answered *his* plea; that is, Isaac's, and not Rebekah's. The Midrash adds that Isaac's prayer, as he was "himself righteous, and a son of the righteous," was more efficacious than Rebekah's prayer, for she was "herself righteous, but the daughter of a villain." This is rather strange, however, for we would have expected exactly the opposite. A person who is "himself righteous, but the child of a villain" treads a longer, more difficult path than one born to an already righteous household and should therefore be deemed more worthy.

The point is that a child of the righteous will not become himself truly righteous if he simply continues on the path already blazed for him, but cannot tell the world anything new. To genuinely influence the world, he must become a righteous individual of a completely different type than his father. And Isaac was exactly that in relation to his father Abraham. It is much more difficult to achieve that than it is for the son of a villain to become righteous.

It is usually easiest for children to follow in the footsteps of their parents. Frequently, however, it also happens that children rebel against the ideology of their parents and head in the opposite direction. Instead of doing either of those things, it is much more important to maintain one's own independence and originality while also recognizing the importance of one's parents' path; to stay on our parents path and further their accomplishments while also moving in our own individual direction. This is precisely what a person who is "himself righteous, and also a child of the righteous" is able to accomplish. God will therefore favor him and answer his prayer.

30.6. Prayer-Request as Correction of the Righteous in Gevurah

[21] Isaac pleaded with the Lord on behalf of his wife: Literally translated, this verse means "Isaac prayed to the Lord *opposite* his wife." The Midrash understands that this means "*because* of his wife," that is, under the influence of his wife. The Midrash then adds that it was Rebekah who taught Isaac to employ prayer as a form of petition, whereas Isaac himself has previously used prayer only as Divine service.

There are two forms of religious devotion both of which have the purpose of actualizing man's dialogue with God: sacrifice and prayer. We find that in the beginning of *Bereshit* Cain, Abel, and Noah all brought sacrifices, and prayer began to appear only much later in the Torah, among the Patriarchs. The essence of sacrifice (and of prayer as Divine service) is our expression of gratitude to the Almighty for all that He bestows, and our attempt to preserve the status quo. In contrast, the essence of prayer as petition is the desire to effect productive change in the world, our desire to see the world develop.

When with the destruction of the Temple sacrifices were abolished, both of the functions just mentioned were assumed by daily prayer, and that is why today our prayers combine both petition and Divine service, two aspects that were initially distinct. Prayer as petition derives from the category of *Chesed*, and has the function of promoting peace, while prayer as Divine service, like sacrifice, is derived from the category of *Gevurah*, preservation of the universe.

The natural tendency of the righteous in the *Gevurah* category is to justify the existing state of affairs without asking God to change it. What can we possibly ask of God, Who has made the world such that all is for the best, and Who even without us knows what we need for our own good? Why bother Him with requests? If Rebekah happens to have no children, then surely that too is God's will.

But to a person in the category of *Chesed*, quite the contrary is true – it is essential that we ask for change. In my prayers I declare that the state of the world is not what it should be, and I therefore come to God asking Him to change the status quo.

Rebekah, who is *Chesed*, induces Isaac to begin praying in order to ask God to change His ways. Thus, "Isaac pleaded with the Lord on behalf of his wife" has an alternate meaning: "Isaac prayed *in the presence of* his wife," – that is, under her influence.

The position of *Gevurah*, unquestioningly justifying and accepting how God made the world, is correct in its own way, but its absolutization contradicts the Creator's desire to correct and improve the world in the process of human co-creation. For example, if a person is sick, we can say, "Since God has sent this person an illness, that is most likely how it has to be." But we can also see it another way. God wants us to make efforts, both spiritual and physical, to improve the world. He wants us to repent, to improve and to pray for healing. Yet He also wants us to develop science, technology and medicine in order to combat disease. Because, yes, the disease comes from God, but the physician's ability to treat and heal it also comes from God.

To correct those who are inclined to justify their own inaction by saying that everything is an act of God, He puts them in a situation in which they are nevertheless forced to turn to Him – not for their own sake, but for the sake of others. Rebekah influences Isaac to ask God for children, not for his own sake, but for the world's sake. How could it be that the wife of our patriarch Isaac was barren? After all, a patriarch must have offspring – without that he cannot possibly fulfill his mission. Therefore, we must not be satisfied with the current state of affairs; instead, we must strive to correct them. Isaac gradually comes to realize this and begins to pray.

For Isaac, prayer is a much more complicated thing than it is for Rebekah. Once he starts to pray, Isaac advances significantly. Because of prayer his *Gevurah* shifts towards *Chesed*, allowing the Patriarchs' process of purifying the *Sefirot* (the ten attributes of Divine Revelation) to take place. This is why Isaac's prayer is so important, and why "the Lord responded to his plea."

30.7. "But the Children Struggled in Her Womb" (25:22)

כב וַיִּתְרֹצֲצוּ הַבָּנִים בְּקִרְבָּהּ וַתֹּאמֶר אִם־כֵּן לָמָּה זֶּה אָנֹכִי וַתֵּלֶךְ לִדְרֹשׁ אֶת־יי:

[22] But the children struggled in her womb, and she said, "If so, why do I exist?" She went to inquire of the Lord.

[22] But the children struggled in her womb: The Midrash, in explaining this expression, describes in vivid terms how Rebekah would pass by the yeshivah of Shem and Eber, and would feel Jacob kicking and bursting forth from her womb. And when she passed a site of idolatry, Esau would likewise show his character. Thus, the Midrash sees in this "struggle" a conflict of the two realities of the unborn children inside Rebekah. (It is the conflict of the Jewish and Aramean influences within this family.)

Regarding the clash of Jacob and Esau, the Midrash explains that "they clashed and argued over who would take control of each of two worlds: this world and the World to Come." Each of them firmly owns one of these worlds, but wants to take possession of the other one too in order to rule over both. Jacob has a natural tendency to own the World to Come, but he lacks the stamina needed to exist in this world, and fights to gain stability in it. Esau, by his nature, dominates in this world, but he also wants to receive the World to Come.

The term "*olam ha-ba*," "The World to Come," does not mean "the other world" or "the world beyond the grave." It is a world of goals and aspirations that sits higher than our world. Jacob and Esau are competing for power and dominance both in this world and in that world of goals and aspirations. They clash with each other in the struggle for whose lineage will lead – who will drive the development of human society.

And she said, "If so, why do I exist?": The wording seems rather strange, and her commonplace perception of her predicament ("Why is this happening to me?") adds little to our understanding of the meaning of the passage. The Midrash therefore offers an alternate translation: "Why [is there a clash between] 'this' and 'I'?." In Kabbalistic terminology the concept of *Zeh*, "this," refers to God as the ruler of this world, while *Anochi*, "I," means God as the ruler of the World to Come.

Note that in Hebrew the pronoun "I" has two forms: the more common short form *ani* and the longer fuller form *anochi* which emphasizes the speaker as subject. The World to Come, i.e., the "goal," – spiritual aspirations, and ethical standards – are precisely represented by *anochi*, the full form of the word "I," which emphasizes the personal aspect, the personal God Who stands above this world. (We also note in passing that the Ten Commandments begin with the word *anochi*: "I the Lord am your God" [Exod. 20:2].)

Thus, the question facing Rebekah here is this: Who is the God of these children soon to be born? Is He *Zeh* or is He *Anochi*? Feeling a conflict within herself, Rebekah wants to know to which world her children will belong. And her question begins with the word *lamah*, "why." However, she is not asking about reasons, but about goals – why is this conflict necessary and what is its meaning.

30.8. The Connection of the Patriarchs to Noah, Shem, and Eber

[22] She went to inquire of the Lord: From the text that follows we see that prophecy as received by Rebekah was not known in her family. That is, she "went to inquire" not of Abraham or Isaac, but of some other "prophets of the Lord" of those times. The Midrash says that she went to Shem and Eber, who, according to the chronology given in the Torah (11:10-26), were still alive at that time.

The Midrash has much to say about the connection between the Jewish Patriarchs and the "original monotheists." Abraham studied with Noah, Shem, and Eber, Isaac studied with Shem and Eber, and even Jacob studied for several years in Eber's yeshivah. This emphasizes two essential aspects of Jewish tradition. First, that tradition begins not only with the Jewish Patriarchs but harks back to an earlier period of human history. Second, that each of the Jewish Patriarchs was an independent spiritual personality. It was not enough for Isaac to learn from Abraham; he required more study, which he did with Shem and Eber. And for Jacob too, the teachings of Abraham and Isaac alone were insufficient.

30.9. A Prophecy of Two Nations (25:23)

כג וַיֹּאמֶר יי לָהּ שְׁנֵי גֹיִים בְּבִטְנֵךְ וּשְׁנֵי לְאֻמִּים מִמֵּעַיִךְ
יִפָּרֵדוּ וּלְאֹם מִלְאֹם יֶאֱמָץ וְרַב יַעֲבֹד צָעִיר:

*[23] And the Lord answered her, "Two nations
are in your womb, two separate peoples shall
issue from your body; One people shall be
mightier than the other, and the older shall serve
the younger."*

In response to her question, Rebekah receives an important prophecy that speaks about the relationship between
Jacob and Esau, or even more broadly the relationship
between Jewish and European civilizations. It is a typical example of prophecy and we have several options for
understanding it.

**[23] Two nations are in your womb, Two separate peo-
ples shall issue from your body:** Each of the twins to be
born will manifest himself not only as a *goy*, a tribal ethnic
group, but as a *le'om*, nation – a particular people with its
own national consciousness, national character and national
ideas. Once the twins are born, they will be unable to remain
together and will necessarily be separated, because these
two national identities are in direct conflict.

**One people shall be mightier than the other, and the
older shall serve the younger":** The relationship between
these future peoples is expressed with very ambiguous
phrasing, which can be interpreted in opposite senses.
The translation given above is typical: "One people shall be

mightier than the other, and the older shall serve the younger."
But the Midrash adds to this: One of the nations will always
be stronger than the other. When Israel rises, Esau falls, and
vice versa – they cannot stand together. However, it is also
promised that the youngest, Israel, will be primarily stronger.

But this prophecy can also be translated and understood
in quite the opposite sense: "Each nation shall derive its
strength from the other, and the younger shall labor intensely."
That is, each of the two nations, Jacob and Esau, will have its
own form of power, which it will share with the other. Moreover, the younger, Jacob, will need to expend particularly great
effort for the success of this joint advancement.

Thus, Rebekah receives a highly ambiguous prophecy, which depends on both Jacob and Esau (the Jews and
Western civilization, respectively) for how it will play out,
whether their relationship will be one of conflict, or of
mutual assistance.

How this prophecy will be realized depends on the
humanity's level of maturity. In the initial stages of our development, each side sees the other as an enemy and a competitor who needs to be defeated. Initially, we cannot say
that that one or the other is wrong; on the contrary, development at the initial stages is possible only when each side
isolates itself from the other, each seeing an irreconcilable
element in the other.

But that kind of attitude must eventually be overcome. At a
higher level of understanding we are aware that our relationship should not be one of confrontation, but of mutual enrichment, with each side complementing the other ("each nation
shall derive its strength from the other"). This will require a
great deal of work, but in the end, success will be achieved.

Prophecy is always ambiguous, having not one, but several possible realizations. Prophecy determines the various

paths that the world can follow in order for it to develop, but the choice of a specific path depends on mankind itself.

We find a classic example of this, the dependence of the realization of a prophecy on people's behavior, in the book of Jonah: Nineveh was supposed to be "overturned" after forty days (Jonah 3:4), but its inhabitants turned themselves around through their repentance and brought about a spiritual revolution, after which a physical destruction was no longer necessary. (The Hebrew word of the prophecy, *neh-pechet*, can mean both "overturned" and "turned around.") This variability in the realization of prophecy is particularly important, because it is the reason that human destiny depends on people's actions.

Thus, Rebekah's prophecy does not determine the nature of the relationship between Jacob and Esau, it only establishes various possibilities for that relationship. Inevitably, it will be realized either the one way or the other, but it is we, humankind, who influence the outcome. Whether the Jewish and Western worlds, Jacob and Esau, will continue to perceive each other as competitors and enemies, or learn to cooperate and to complement each other, depends entirely on us.

30.10. The Birth of Esau (25:24-25)

כד וַיִּמְלְאוּ יָמֶיהָ לָלֶדֶת וְהִנֵּה תוֹמִם בְּבִטְנָהּ: כה וַיֵּצֵא הָרִאשׁוֹן אַדְמוֹנִי כֻּלּוֹ כְּאַדֶּרֶת שֵׂעָר וַיִּקְרְאוּ שְׁמוֹ עֵשָׂו:

[24] When her time to give birth was at hand, there were twins in her womb.
[25] The first one emerged red, like a hairy mantle all over; so they named him Esau.

[24] There were twins in her womb: An important introductory word in the Hebrew text, *ve-hinneh*, has not been rendered here at all, because its essence is difficult to capture in translation. *Hinneh* isoften approximated as *behold*. When it says, "her time to give birth was at hand, and, *behold*, there were twins in her womb," the word *hinneh* expresses surprise: Yes, despite Jacob and Esau's external dissimilarity, they are in fact twins, with all the closeness and deep connections that that entails.

In view of the confrontations and conflicts that will accompany Jacob, Esau, and their descendants, we are sometimes tempted to forget their brotherhood and to emphasize only their differences and rivalries. However, this approach is wrong for it is precisely the brotherhood of Jacob and Esau that will serve in the future as the foundation for correcting the world.

[25] Red, like a hairy mantle all over: Esau has two characteristics, which correspond to his two names: Edom and Esau. Edom from *adom* "red," (which linguistically also shares a root with *adamah* "earth," indicating a passion for this world), and Esau, "ready-made," from *aseh* "(to) make." His hairiness from birth symbolizes this. Esau likes wholeness and completeness, for in those, being a man of this world, he sees perfection. He receives the name "Esau" immediately, but acquires the name "Edom" only gradually – although its foundations too were laid from birth, at which time he is already called "red," beginning with the red lentil soup (v. 29 ff.) and continuing with his leaving the Land of Israel and creating his own state ("Esau – that is Edom" [35:1,9,19]). For only when we live in our own state does our spiritual essence reveal itself: Just as Jacob gradually becomes Israel, so does Esau become Edom.

In *gematria*, the numerical value of the name Esau (376) is equal to that of the word *shalom* "peace" which indicates the ability to maintain total calmness in a situation – completeness and perfection. But this is one of those situations where peace, *shalom*, is a state that is less than ideal, because one of the characteristics of such "completeness" is the absence of any further movement or development.

As we know, when one fails to advance, he eventually falls. And in falling, Esau becomes Edom; thus does his name, whose meaning is associated with *adamah*, earth, find its expression. (The name "Adam," which in its more general meaning refers to all of mankind, derives from the same root.) Even so, after his fall Esau can rise again, for this is the normal human process. But for that to happen, Esau will need Jacob's help.

Se'ar, "hair," the second characteristic of Esau mentioned at his birth, is revealed later in the name of the country, Seir, in which Esau's descendants will settle (36:8). Moreover, Jacob himself later calls his brother Esau *sa'ir*, "a hairy man" (27:11), but the very same word also means "goat" (i.e., "shaggy"). For that reason, Esau will later be connected, symbolically and mystically, with the scapegoat sent into the wilderness on Yom Kippur1 (Lev. 16:10).

30.11. The Birth of Jacob (25:26)

כו וְאַחֲרֵי־כֵן יָצָא אָחִיו וְיָדוֹ אֹחֶזֶת בַּעֲקֵב עֵשָׂו וַיִּקְרָא
שְׁמוֹ יַעֲקֹב וְיִצְחָק בֶּן־שִׁשִּׁים שָׁנָה בְּלֶדֶת אֹתָם:

[26] Then his brother emerged, holding on to the heel of Esau; so they named him Jacob. Isaac was sixty years old when they were born.

---

1   See also §43.4, "Arrival in Sukkot".

[26] His brother: In its first mention of Jacob, the Torah identifies him merely as "his (Esau's) brother." At birth Jacobs holds Esau by the *akev*, "heel," and he is therefore given the name *Ya'akov* (Jacob). Thus, his fundamental self-identification is determined not only by his relationship with his parents and the outside world, but also by how he behaves toward his brother, Esau. Jacob, "Yaakov," lives in a state of constant competition with Esau. (*Akov*, means to catch and overtake.)

Holding on to the heel of Esau: The heel is not a very significant part of the human body, which would seem to indicate that a person called by that name is likewise unimportant. Moreover, *akov* also means "indirect, curved, crooked" – in both the physical and ethical senses. (Cf. Jer. 17:9, *akov halev*, "The heart is deceitful.")

So they named him Jacob: Indeed, Jacob often acts indirectly, and it is no coincidence that Esau later says about his brother: "Was he, then, named Jacob that he might outsmart me (*vaya'kveni*) these two times? (27:36 [alternate translation]). The problem of curvature, indirectness, is indeed a significant problem of Jewish life in exile. However, Jacob (and the Jewish people) corrects that when he moves to the Land of Israel and receives the name "Israel" in the country which shares his name, which is linguistically associated with *yashar*, "straight, direct."

Jacob's great merit is that he is self-motivated to improve and "align," to become straight and direct where he was "curved" before. Jacob begins his life from a very subordinate position, grasping Esau's heel. Jacob is then forced to persuade his brother to sell him the birthright. Later, he must deceive his father, run away from home, and then work for Laban and submit to his whims.

Neither Abraham nor Isaac came from such a subordinate position; they were endowed with greatness from the very beginning. Surrounded by disciples and followers, Abraham was a recognized spiritual leader and "the elect of God" (23:6). His problem consisted merely in limiting his excessive *Chesed* (kindness). Isaac is likewise always successful and always his own boss. Although he chooses an inactive mode of behavior, preferring not to take initiative, but only to respond to circumstances, Isaac nevertheless follows that approach as a matter of his own free choice.

Abraham who is *Chesed*, and Isaac who is *Gevurah*, occupy the right and left sides of the *Sefirot* tree, respectively. Initially they are in the *gadlut* (greatness) category – a major stage in the development of the corresponding *Sefirah*. Each is assigned the task of shifting his *Sefirah* in the proper direction. In contrast, *Tiferet* (glory, splendor), Jacob's attribute, is on the median, central line of the tree from the beginning, and his task is not to shift his attribute, but to nurture it. Jacob is forced to obey by beginning with *katnut* (smallness), the smallest stage in development of the *Sefirah*, and he must raise it from *katnut* to *gadlut*. Jacob begins with a "small truth," and he must elevate it to become a "great truth."

Jacob is born a subordinate, but he will succeed in traversing the path from "Jacob" to "Israel" and becoming a leader, which in a sense is also the embodiment of the ascent from Exile to Redemption. It is a path that belongs to Jacob alone, a path that Abraham and Isaac did not have.

The story of Esau and Jacob parallels the story of Cain and Abel. Referring to the birth of Cain, her first son, Eve said: "I have gained (*kaniti*) a male child with the help of the Lord" (4:1, alternate translation: "I have acquired"). The Midrash understands this in the sense that "*kayin kullo kanui*," "Cain is fully acquired" or completed, just as Esau is born here "completed."

Then his brother emerged: Jacob's relationship to Esau is like that of Abel to Cain, where very similar wording is used (4:2). This indicates that from birth Abel's identity is defined by his being a brother to Cain. Although Abel could not influence Cain and was killed by him, Jacob is Abel's correction, and he will succeed at reforming Esau.

Isaac was sixty years old when they were born: Isaac married at age forty, and his sons were born when he was sixty years old. Twenty years had to pass for Isaac's initial correction – for him to be ready to become a father to Jacob and Esau.

As already discussed, the first stage in Isaac's correction was that he began to pray. This meant a shift toward the attribute of *Chesed*, thus faceting and reducing his *Gevurah*, eliminating some of its superfluous aspects. We also noted that Isaac was born when Abraham was one hundred years old, and Abraham was 175 years old when he died. Thus, Jacob and Esau (who were born when their father Isaac was sixty years old) were fifteen years old at the time of Abraham's death. This means that in their youth, Jacob and Esau must have received traditions and teachings not only from Isaac, but from Abraham as well. In fact, only after Abraham's death did Jacob's and Esau's paths diverge. For, according to the Midrash, the day of Abraham's death was the day of the birthright sale (v. 31 ff.).

30.12. Completion vs. Continuous Development

In connection with Esau's "completeness" and Jacob's dynamism, his constant movement and thirst for advancement, it is interesting for us to note the differences between the European and Jewish spiritual and philosophical paradigms.

European philosophy always strives for completeness, where all concepts are well-defined, everything is neatly laid out like the books on a library shelf and completeness is thought of as a necessary part of perfection.

But Jewish spiritual constructions, on the other hand – in both the Talmud and the Kabbalah – are always themselves unfinished, requiring further development. Only a general direction is given, after which the initial concepts of any such construction are determined and refined only in the process of its further use.

In general, it is a Jewish characteristic to be perpetually on the move (Europeans often perceive it as restlessness), demolishing standards and established concepts, constantly rethinking everything as one goes along.

The Germans, in particular, are the most precise and organized of all the European peoples. Their national character is the pinnacle of the European desire for "completeness." (Among the most prominent of German expressions is "*ordnung muss sein*," "there must be order.") Therefore, the Germans see the Jewish people as an anomaly and a disturbing element because Jews feel no need for such completeness. This is one of the root causes of German anti-Semitism.

30.13. The Illusory Stability of the Nations and Jacob's Real Endurance

Just as Jacob was born holding Esau by the heel, so too throughout his entire life he will be in pursuit of Esau, which shows that he is in a certain sense "dependent," and not entirely self-sufficient. Esau, on the other hand, with his feet planted firmly on the ground, considers his civilization very stable. Because of this he has no need to run anywhere, because he already has everything, and everything is just fine. But Jacob's status, on the other hand, is always "doubtful" and problematic.

Esau (who represents the peoples of the West) never questions his own existence. It would never occur to a Russian or a Frenchman to ask, "Why do Russians and Frenchmen exist in the world? Does our existence really make any sense?" They take their existence for granted and feel solidly self-sufficient in that existence.

For the Jewish people, however, the question of their continued existence never ceases to be relevant. This is because the reality for the Jewish people has always been that unless they take appropriate measures, every generation could be their last.

But Esau's people only *appear* to be stable. Viewing the history of mankind, we see dozens of nations that have ceased to exist. Their states were destroyed, after which they themselves disappeared among all the other nations, and their culture lives on only in museums. And all the while, the Jews, who often doubt the very meaning of their own existence, continue to live.

In other words, Jacob, whose existence is always in doubt, is more viable and stable than those nations whose existence seems solid. Jacob, always afraid of "running out of time," is running all the time. But he always catches up, which never fails to annoy Esau. Jacob is forever on the move, while Esau wants peace. But thanks to his perpetual motion, Jacob lives on.

30.14. Esau and Jacob as a Product of the Duality in Isaac and Rebekah

The source of the differences between Esau and Jacob is

the duality of Isaac and Rebekah: Isaac is a man of *Gevurah*, who, as he progresses, must correct and perfect that attribute. To do this he must separate the correct and proper "*Gevurah* of holiness" from the excessive "*Gevurah* of impurity." Rebekah, a representative of the Nahor family – i.e., Hebrews who assimilated in Aram – carries within herself a conflict between her "Jewishness" and her "Aramean-ness."

Rebekah's Jewishness is expressed in her *Chesed* (we have noted that offering hospitality to travelers is an essential practice of Abraham and of all Hebrews in general), while her Aramean element draws her toward cosmopolitanism; she thus avoids the limitations of an excessively narrow nationalist or clan-based framework. This quality, although, not dominant in Rebekah herself, manifests, first and foremost, in her father and brother, Bethuel and Laban. But given that Rebekah is so close to her immediate family, it is not by mere happenstance that she later sends Jacob to take a wife for himself from among Laban's daughters.

When we read them together, these two lines offer us two options for combining the qualities of Isaac and Rebekah. Isaac's purified *Gevurah* in conjunction with Rebekah's *Chesed* give us Jacob, who represents the *Sefirah* of *Tiferet*. But unpurified, excess *Gevurah*, combined with Aramean cosmopolitanism, gives rise to Esau. Excessive *Gevurah* will later be expressed in Roman imperial cruelty and a penchant for violence, which seeks to find balance in the adoption of Christianity, the religion of *Chesed*. Meanwhile, the Aramean component moves Esau towards imperial universalism.

As a result, Esau's Hebrew roots endure, albeit in a variation that is significantly diminished. But they can manifest nonetheless, and that gives Esau a path to improvement.

30.15. Field and Tent (25:27)

כז וַיִּגְדְּלוּ הַנְּעָרִים וַיְהִי עֵשָׂו אִישׁ יֹדֵעַ צַיִד אִישׁ שָׂדֶה
וְיַעֲקֹב אִישׁ תָּם יֹשֵׁב אֹהָלִים:

*[27] When the boys grew up, Esau became a
skillful hunter, a man of the outdoors; but Jacob
was a mild man who stayed in camp.*

**[27] Esau became a skillful hunter, a man of the outdoors;
but Jacob was a mild man who stayed in camp:** The literal
translation is "Jacob was a simple man dwelling in tents." As
children, the difference between the brothers was not too
apparent, but upon reaching adulthood they went their
different ways. Esau became a man of the field and open
spaces, actively working in the world around him. We should
recall here that Isaac too loved the field: "And Isaac went
out walking in the field toward evening…" (24:63). Isaac is a
farmer planting in the field (24:12), while Jacob is "a simple
man dwelling in tents." This is why Isaac feels that Esau is
spiritually and psychologically closer to him than Jacob is.

Isaac understands the birth of twins to mean that the
chosen people will consist of two tribes, the tribe of Esau
and the tribe of Jacob. Moreover, Isaac believes that Esau
should be the leader, as he is competent in practical matters,
and involved with the larger world. He is physically strong
and capable of sustained political power. Esau is even able
to kill and to conquer. And since Isaac's goal is to give rise
not only to a religion, but to a great nation, he of course
gives primacy to Esau.

The distinction that divides Jacob and Esau according to
the "tent vs. field" dichotomy is clearly associated with a very

similar distinction between two of Noah's sons, Shem and Japheth. Shem is the "tent," while Japheth is the "enlarged" space ("May God enlarge Japheth, and let him dwell in the tents of Shem" [9:27])2.* Accordingly, Jacob's essence is that of the Semitic world, while Esau will become the spiritual leader of the Japhetic world.

30.16. Isaac Favors Esau (25:28)

כח וַיֶּאֱהַב יִצְחָק אֶת־עֵשָׂו כִּי־צַיִד בְּפִיו וְרִבְקָה אֹהֶבֶת אֶת־יַעֲקֹב:

[28] Isaac favored Esau because he had a taste for game; but Rebekah favored Jacob.

[28] **Isaac favored Esau:** It is tempting to believe that Isaac, being blind, and thus unaware of Esau's unworthy deeds, favored the latter simply because of the victuals that he provided, whereas Rebekah had an accurate view of the reality and therefore favored Jacob. But to believe this would be a mistake. The origins of these preferences of Isaac and Rebekah actually lie much deeper. Isaac feels a psychological kinship with Esau, for both of them are men of the field.

Because he had a taste for game: We can understand this description of the relationship between Isaac and Esau in several ways. The very literal translation is "for it (or he) was prey in his mouth." This can be understood to mean that the game that Esau hunted became prey in Isaac's mouth.

---

2   See the detailed coverage in §12.5, "Noah and His Descendants After the Flood".

But it can also mean that Isaac himself was prey in Esau's mouth. That is, Esau used his mouth (speech) to "capture" his father Isaac.

The Midrash understands this to mean that Esau would pose difficult religious questions. For example, he would ask Isaac, "How does one tithe salt and straw?" With such questions, he "captured" (captivated) his father Isaac.

Typically, tithes are separated from harvested produce, but neither salt nor straw fall into that category. On the other hand, however, salt too is a "product of the earth"; perhaps then, said Esau, we would do well to tithe salt too? And straw, likewise, while not an edible harvest item for humans, serves as food for livestock. Perhaps, then, straw too should be tithed?

These were excellent questions that greatly pleased Isaac. He believed that Esau, given that he wanted to tithe even salt and straw, must have been, in his potential at least, an exceptionally righteous man. If Esau did bad things in life (and Isaac knew that to be the case, of course), well, those are the kind of mistakes that to just about anyone can make.

However, one ought not think that Esau was simply deceiving his father. Esau's questions derived not from any falsehood or hypocrisy whatsoever on his part. Rather, they were genuine questions, the expression of Esau's true essence.

What lies at the heart of the question of tithing salt and straw? When one separates tithes or sacrificial offerings from produce, it means that he wishes to reveal the holiness of a given thing by donating it to the Temple. Why is it so difficult to find the holiness of tithing in salt and straw? Salt is inanimate; it does not grow. The holiness of tithing is expressed only in things that live and grow. Straw too, although it is itself plant matter, becomes waste unsuitable for humans once the edible grains have been removed. There can be no holiness in that which is unfit for human consumption.

However, both salt and straw qualify as foodstuffs. Esau, in asking about the separation of tithes, adopts a comprehensive approach to revealing holiness: If we tithe at all, then all food in the world should be tithed. Esau is a maximalist, and this is an element of his greatness and his power. He aims to discover the holiness in all things.

Isaac is essentially satisfied. Of course he explains to Esau that there is no need to separate tithes from salt and straw. Nonetheless, he is impressed by this attribute in Esau, for it fully expresses the aspirations of a person such as Isaac, who is righteous in the category of strict legal justice. For him, there is no separation between the sacred and the profane. In principle, everything should be holy.

Indeed, Judaism believes that there is sanctity in all things. Actualizing that sanctity, however, is by far not always easy, or even possible.

Jacob is a man of compromise. Upon learning that salt and straw cannot be tithed, he will nonetheless tithe bread, wine, and olive oil; that is, he will do what is right, even if it is imperfect. But Esau, the man of extremes, in this same situation comes to a completely different decision. "If I cannot tithe everything," says he, "then I will tithe nothing!" Esau sees no reason to do anything half-heartedly. If it is impossible to fix everything, then let nothing be fixed!

This craving for total holiness, the desire to see holiness in everything without exception is also characteristic of Isaac. But Isaac, unlike Esau, is able to restrain himself. Fully aware that we live in an imperfect world, he avoids a breakdown and continues further along on his path, all of which is possible because Isaac limits his *Gevurah*. Esau is unable to do so, nor does he care to.

Isaac loves Esau most of all because of their psychological affinity. We have already noted that fathers are often mistaken in choosing their heirs. Very often a father wants his heir to be the son who is most like him, but another son who follows a different, non-paternal path then becomes the actual successor. If a father has been extraordinarily successful in his endeavors, then his heir must blaze a new trail, and not merely repeat what has already been accomplished. It is often difficult for a father to acknowledge and accept this reality.

30.17. Rebekah Favors Jacob

At that time neither Esau nor Jacob was close to qualifying for the role of leading the future people. Someone who has no spirituality, who has no "tent," cannot be the leader of the Chosen People. Nor can one who *only* dwells in tents qualify for this role. Given that their two sons were distinguished so starkly by this feature, what were Isaac and Rebekah to do?

In contemporary terms, Jacob, sitting at home, is the yeshivah student who does not engage with the surrounding world and has only a limited understanding of everyday life. And yet, from the next verse we see that there is a division of labor in the family, and that Jacob has other tasks apart from studying. Esau runs about the fields, catching and bringing home game, which Jacob then prepares for eating. Returning from the hunt, Esau is hardly surprised that Jacob has prepared a meal, because, so far as we can tell, this is the norm in their family. Jacob is also busy with his "homework," as is the lot of a family's younger members. In other words, his status in the family hierarchy is quite low. So far, all responsibility for maintaining the "world order" lies with Esau.

Isaac, being the man of *Gevurah*, evaluates and accepts the world as it is. In the current situation he therefore favors Esau, who is at least able to cope with everyday, real-life problems.

But Rebekah, a person of *Chesed*, has a different mindset. She does not want to remain stagnant; on the contrary, she wants to improve the world. Rebekah sees not only what each of her sons is today, but also their development potential – what they can become in the future.

Esau is content with his static self; he wants to remain as he is. But Jacob, a dynamic personality, strives to move forward – he is "holding on to the heel of Esau" – and has clear development potential.

Thus, Isaac, seeing his sons for what they are today, favors Esau. But Rebekah favors Jacob, for she sees what her sons will become tomorrow.

30.18. Esau's Fatigue and Downfall (25:29-30)

כט וַיָּזֶד יַעֲקֹב נָזִיד וַיָּבֹא עֵשָׂו מִן־הַשָּׂדֶה וְהוּא עָיֵף: ל
וַיֹּאמֶר עֵשָׂו אֶל־יַעֲקֹב הַלְעִיטֵנִי נָא מִן־הָאָדֹם הָאָדֹם
הַזֶּה כִּי עָיֵף אָנֹכִי עַל־כֵּן קָרָא־שְׁמוֹ אֱדוֹם:

[29] Once when Jacob was cooking a stew, Esau came in from the open, famished.
[30] And Esau said to Jacob, "Give me some of that red stuff to gulp down, for I am famished" – which is why he was named Edom.

[29] Esau came in from the open, famished: The literal meaning is: "Esau came from the field, and he was exhausted." Although the field is Esau's natural element, he returns from the field completely spent. This fatigue is not only physical (for in that case the Torah would not need to mention it); it is also spiritual. Being tired is a negative characteristic that indicates a problem. The Torah is telling us that Esau has come home on edge and impatient, ready to pounce on food, and unable to think of anything else.

Esau is spiritually tired, because he cannot find what he seeks: a way to tithe salt and straw and everything else in the world. The Midrash notes that "for I am famished" is expressed in the Torah with the long form of the pronoun "I," *anochi*. Thus, Esau's words can be understood as "I am tired [of seeking] *Anochi*" – the God of the World to Come. After these searches, Esau has decided that it is impossible to find Him. In other words, Esau is tired of his own futile search for absolute perfection. Esau's passion for totality is bringing him down. He concludes categorically that if God cannot be revealed in salt and straw, then His presence cannot be found anywhere.

The Midrash adds that this incident between Jacob and Esau takes place on the very day of Abraham's death. Because Isaac is in mourning for his father, he must not cook food for himself. Jacob, to whom, as a grandson, the laws of mourning do not apply, prepares the traditional funereal meal for his father. Abraham's death is obviously a moment of crisis for Esau. The great and righteous patriarch, who, by rights, should have lived forever, is suddenly found to be mortal – that is (as Esau perceives it), imperfect. This devastating realization demolishes Esau's worldview. Hence, Esau is "exhausted" – his world is disintegrating, and he ceases to strive for spirituality.

[30] Give me some of that red stuff to gulp down, for I am famished" – which is why he was named Edom: The literal translation is: "... of this red, red (stuff), for I am exhausted." As if guided by Nietzschean principles, Esau decides: "Since there is no God, I might as well just gulp down this supremely red – i.e., earthy – concoction. I've been searching for the very highest, but I have found nothing. The lowest is now more than good enough for me."

Which is why he was named Edom: Red is the color of lust, the color of passion. What Esau really wants is not to eat, but to fill his inner emptiness with bodily pleasures, to distract himself from thinking about the absurdity of existence. The potential of this "red approach," an integral part of Esau from birth, is now revealed, and Esau receives the name "Edom."

In the Jewish perception, red, at the lower end of the color spectrum, corresponds to the word *adamah*, "earth." Blue-violet, which is called *techelet*, is at the upper end of the spectrum. It is the color of the sky, associated with *tachlit*, a goal, aspiration, or mission. This color will later become a symbol of the Jewish nation.

The name "Edom," like *adom*, "red," is closely related to *adam*, "man." Edom-Esau is a normal, ordinary person. But Jacob-Israel must be somewhat abnormal if he is to have the strength and ability to bring all the rest of "normal" humanity to God. The Jewish people are therefore, from their very beginnings, an abnormal people.

30.19. The Sale of the Birthright (25:31)

לא וַיֹּאמֶר יַעֲקֹב מִכְרָה כַיּוֹם אֶת־בְּכֹרָתְךָ לִי:

[31] Jacob said, "First sell me your birthright."

Abraham's death produces an earthquake-like effect in the family, when all change becomes possible for them, and their inner human essence is manifested. Esau at this moment, disappointed in ideals, experiences a breakdown. But Jacob, on the contrary, decides at this critical juncture to move forward – to leave the tent and take responsibility for the future.

Esau's statement that he was exhausted, that he needed nothing more than "this red, red stuff," is a signal of danger – danger not only for Esau, but for the future of the entire family. In this kind of situation, Jacob's desire to possess the birthright is not at all a sign of callousness, or that he wishes to cash in on his brother's difficulties; rather, it means he is taking responsibility for his nearest of kin. An "exhausted" leader must step down. He is still deserving of respect, and to receive benefits (porridge), but he must be replaced. The purchase of the birthright – the bilateral agreement on the reversal of the brothers' status – therefore became a demonstration of Jacob's newfound sense of responsibility, his first step toward real leadership.

30.20. "Thus Did Esau Spurn the Birthright." (25:32-34)

לב וַיֹּאמֶר עֵשָׂו הִנֵּה אָנֹכִי הוֹלֵךְ לָמוּת וְלָמָּה־זֶּה לִי בְּכֹרָה: **לג** וַיֹּאמֶר יַעֲקֹב הִשָּׁבְעָה לִי כַּיּוֹם וַיִּשָּׁבַע לוֹ וַיִּמְכֹּר אֶת־בְּכֹרָתוֹ לְיַעֲקֹב: **לד** וְיַעֲקֹב נָתַן לְעֵשָׂו לֶחֶם וּנְזִיד עֲדָשִׁים וַיֹּאכַל וַיֵּשְׁתְּ וַיָּקָם וַיֵּלַךְ וַיִּבֶז עֵשָׂו אֶת־הַבְּכֹרָה:

[32] And Esau said, "I am at the point of death, so of what use is my birthright to me?"

[33] But Jacob said, "Swear to me first." So he swore to him, and sold his birthright to Jacob. [34] Jacob then gave Esau bread and lentil stew; he ate and drank, and he rose and went away. Thus did Esau spurn the birthright.

[32] Of what use is my birthright to me?: The birthright was associated with serving God, as practiced by the spiritual leader of the family. Esau denigrates this role, which to him has lost its meaning.

[33] Swear to me first: Since Isaac is alive, he alone remains the head of the family. Thus, the birthright cannot be transferred at this time. So Jacob demands of Esau an oath that will come into force only after the passing of their father – an oath that at that future time Esau will not lay claim to the birthright, and will instead cede it to Jacob.

Thus did Esau spurn the birthright: What matters is not only Jacob's desire to acquire the birthright, but also Esau's consent. It was Esau's denigration of the birthright that made its transfer to Jacob possible.

I am at the point of death: Here once again, the Torah uses the full form of "I" – *anochi*. Esau's words can therefore be translated as "The 'I,' (*Anokhi*, God of the World to Come) is at the point of death." When the loftiest of all goals dies, the birthright loses its meaning.

The birthright is not just personal property. First and foremost, it means taking responsibility for the direction in which the family, and the new nation now coming into existence, are headed. At this stage in the development of the

Patriarchs' family, the structure of the future chosen people was still unknown: Would it consist of two tribes, Jacob and Esau? Or the descendants of only one of them?

The situation is still undefined, and it remains so even after the sale of the birthright. But gradually, as Jacob takes possession of his birthright, he acquires more and more of Esau's characteristics, thus uniting within himself the attributes of both Jacob and Esau. This process will be completed upon Jacob's receipt of the name "Israel," at which time it shall be determined that the continuation of the Jewish nation will happen only through him.

Chapter 31

Isaac and Abimelech in Gerar and in Beer-Sheba

31.1. Chronology: Two Events in the Life of Isaac

The story of Isaac's relationship with Abimelech, and his stay in Gerar, where he calls Rebekah his sister, is told in the Torah after the story of the birth of Jacob and Esau. If the storyline of the Torah is linearly and chronologically sequential, it is not clear how Isaac could call Rebekah his sister when they already had grown children. But if the two events occurred in the reverse order, then why did the Torah rearrange their sequence?

In fact, both stories had a longer timeframe than it would initially seem. For example, the first story, which covers the period starting with the marriage of Isaac and Rebekah up to the sale of the birthright, covers an interval of more than thirty-five years. And the second story, which runs *in parallel to*, rather than following, that one, likewise recounts events that took place over many years: Isaac lives in Gerar for a long time, later finds himself in conflict with Abimelech, then the events transpire that took place only after Abraham's death, then Isaac moves to Beer-sheba, and so on.

Thus, Isaac settles in Gerar shortly after marrying Rebekah, when they are still childless. The two accounts then chronicle from two different vantage points what has been happening in parallel over several decades.

The Torah arranges the stories thematically rather than chronologically. It therefore first speaks of the family genealogy, the birth of Jacob and Esau, and the sale of the birthright, for those stories are the essence of Isaac's life as a transmitter of the Tradition. The Torah then moves on to an account of Isaac's life, and how his personality developed during his relations with Abimelech.

31.2. Isaac Continues His Father's Path (26:1)

א, וַיְהִי רָעָב בָּאָרֶץ מִלְּבַד הָרָעָב הָרִאשׁוֹן אֲשֶׁר הָיָה בִּימֵי
אַבְרָהָם וַיֵּלֶךְ יִצְחָק אֶל־אֲבִימֶלֶךְ מֶלֶךְ־פְּלִשְׁתִּים גְּרָרָה:

[1] There was a famine in the land–aside from the previous famine that had occurred in the days of Abraham – and Isaac went to Abimelech, king of the Philistines, in Gerar.

[1] Isaac went to Abimelech: "Abimelech," which means "my father is king," is the standard title of Philistine kings, just as "Pharaoh" is the standard title of the kings of Egypt. Thus, the Abimelech whom Isaac now has dealings with is not necessarily the Abimelech whom we read about during the Abraham narrative (20:1 ff.; 21:22 ff.).

There was a famine in the land–aside from the previous famine that had occurred in the days of Abraham: The

Torah draws our attention to parallels between events in the lives of Isaac and of Abraham. To perpetuate the path of his father, Isaac must first demonstrate that he is Abraham's son, by enduring many of the same hardships that Abraham did. However, Abraham overcame these problems while in the *Chesed* category, whereas Isaac does so while he is in the *Gevurah* category.

Isaac must preserve what Abraham started, because nothing can be perpetuated unless it is first preserved. This story of Isaac therefore began with the words "Abraham begot Isaac" (25:29), which we can also understand figuratively. With the threat of hunger looming, Isaac, as in "the previous famine that had occurred in the days of Abraham" (26:1), makes his way to Abimelech king of the Philistines in Gerar.

31.3. Isaac Remains in the Land of Israel (26:2-5)

ב וַיֵּרָא אֵלָיו יי וַיֹּאמֶר אַל־תֵּרֵד מִצְרָיְמָה שְׁכֹן בָּאָרֶץ אֲשֶׁר אֹמַר אֵלֶיךָ: ג גּוּר בָּאָרֶץ הַזֹּאת וְאֶהְיֶה עִמְּךָ וַאֲבָרְכֶךָּ כִּי־לְךָ וּלְזַרְעֲךָ אֶתֵּן אֶת־כָּל־הָאֲרָצֹת הָאֵל וַהֲקִמֹתִי אֶת־הַשְּׁבֻעָה אֲשֶׁר נִשְׁבַּעְתִּי לְאַבְרָהָם אָבִיךָ: ד וְהִרְבֵּיתִי אֶת־זַרְעֲךָ כְּכוֹכְבֵי הַשָּׁמַיִם וְנָתַתִּי לְזַרְעֲךָ אֵת כָּל־הָאֲרָצֹת הָאֵל וְהִתְבָּרֲכוּ בְזַרְעֲךָ כֹּל גּוֹיֵי הָאָרֶץ: ה עֵקֶב אֲשֶׁר־שָׁמַע אַבְרָהָם בְּקֹלִי וַיִּשְׁמֹר מִשְׁמַרְתִּי מִצְוֺתַי חֻקּוֹתַי וְתוֹרֹתָי:

[2] The Lord had appeared to him and said, "Do not go down to Egypt; stay in the land which I point out to you.
[3] Reside in this land, and I will be with you and bless you; I will assign all these lands to you and to your heirs, fulfilling the oath that I swore to your father Abraham.

[4] I will make your heirs as numerous as the
stars of heaven, and assign to your heirs all these
lands, so that all the nations of the earth shall
bless themselves by your heirs–
[5] inasmuch as Abraham obeyed Me and kept
My charge: My commandments, My laws, and
My teachings."

[2] Do not go down to Egypt: It is against that background of similarity that the differences between Abraham and Isaac come into focus. Unlike his father, Isaac does not go down to Egypt. Abraham, *Chesed*, was sent outward, to collect sparks of holiness from Babylon and Egypt. But Isaac, *Gevurah*, must preserve what has already been achieved. This requires him to spend his entire life within the Land of Israel.

The Midrash also associates this point with the *Akedah*, the Binding of Isaac. Although the sacrifice did not actually take place, Isaac, having been carried up to the altar, achieved a unique level of holiness. Thus, he is not allowed to leave the Holy Land.

Upon leaving Gerar, Isaac returns to live in the Beer-sheba region, following in the footsteps of his father Abraham. And from this same Beer-sheba Jacob will later go into exile (28:10). Upon returning to the Land of Israel and finding Isaac in Hebron, Jacob too will establish his residence there. Thus, Hebron will become a city of renown in Jewish history.

[3] I will assign all these lands to you and to your heirs, fulfilling the oath that I swore to your father Abraham. [4] ... so that all the nations of the earth shall bless themselves by your heirs: God's covenant with the Patriarchs speaks of the heritage of Abraham, of the founding of a nation, and of the Land of Israel; that is, the national-political aspect of life. The Patriarchal doctrine is more a system of values than a system of precepts; the formalized system of commandments will appear only through Moses after the Exodus from Egypt.

[3] Fulfilling the oath that I swore to your father Abraham: Isaac receives this blessing only because of Abraham. *Gevurah*, which itself produces nothing new, is charged with simply preserving what *Chesed* has previously created.

31.4. Isaac Calls Rebekah His Sister (26:6-11)

ו וַיֵּשֶׁב יִצְחָק בִּגְרָר: ז וַיִּשְׁאֲלוּ אַנְשֵׁי הַמָּקוֹם לְאִשְׁתּוֹ וַיֹּאמֶר אֲחֹתִי הִוא כִּי יָרֵא לֵאמֹר אִשְׁתִּי פֶּן־יַהַרְגֻנִי אַנְשֵׁי הַמָּקוֹם עַל־רִבְקָה כִּי־טוֹבַת מַרְאֶה הִוא: ח וַיְהִי כִּי אָרְכוּ־לוֹ שָׁם הַיָּמִים וַיַּשְׁקֵף אֲבִימֶלֶךְ מֶלֶךְ פְּלִשְׁתִּים בְּעַד הַחַלּוֹן וַיַּרְא וְהִנֵּה יִצְחָק מְצַחֵק אֵת רִבְקָה אִשְׁתּוֹ: ט וַיִּקְרָא אֲבִימֶלֶךְ לְיִצְחָק וַיֹּאמֶר אַךְ הִנֵּה אִשְׁתְּךָ הִוא וְאֵיךְ אָמַרְתָּ אֲחֹתִי הִוא וַיֹּאמֶר אֵלָיו יִצְחָק כִּי אָמַרְתִּי פֶּן־אָמוּת עָלֶיהָ: י וַיֹּאמֶר אֲבִימֶלֶךְ מַה־זֹּאת עָשִׂיתָ לָּנוּ כִּמְעַט שָׁכַב אַחַד הָעָם אֶת־אִשְׁתֶּךָ וְהֵבֵאתָ עָלֵינוּ אָשָׁם: יא וַיְצַו אֲבִימֶלֶךְ אֶת־כָּל־הָעָם לֵאמֹר הַנֹּגֵעַ בָּאִישׁ הַזֶּה וּבְאִשְׁתּוֹ מוֹת יוּמָת:

[6] So Isaac stayed in Gerar.
[7] When the men of the place asked him about his wife, he said, "She is my sister," for he was afraid to say "my wife," thinking, "The men of the place might kill me on account of Rebekah, for she is beautiful."
[8] When some time had passed, Abimelech king

of the Philistines, looking out of the window, saw
Isaac fondling his wife Rebekah.
[9] Abimelech sent for Isaac and said, "So she
is your wife! Why then did you say: 'She is my
sister?'" Isaac said to him, "Because I thought I
might lose my life on account of her."
[10] Abimelech said, "What have you done to
us! One of the people might have lain with your
wife, and you would have brought guilt upon us."
[11] Abimelech then charged all the people,
saying, "Anyone who molests this man or his
wife shall be put to death."

[7] When the men of the place asked him about his wife, he said, "She is my sister": Faced with excessive attention from the inhabitants of Gerar, Isaac behaves much as Abraham did in the same situation (20:2).

For he was afraid to say "my wife," thinking, "The men of the place might kill me": Is he doing the right thing here? Is his extra caution a good thing, or is that caution the very source of Isaac's conflict with Abimelech? Perhaps Isaac is simply unaware that circumstances have changed, and that there is no longer any threat of assault on his wife?

The fact that Isaac's behavior is determined by older, now obsolete standards can be understood as one of the problems of *Gevurah*, which fails to see in the world any development, or any change of circumstances. Because *Gevurah* believes that prior modes of behavior must be maintained, it is difficult for *Gevurah* to accept the need for change.

[10] Abimelech said, "What have you done to us! ... [11]

Abimelech then charged all the people: Do Abimelech's words demonstrate that Isaac's fears are unfounded? Or, on the contrary, did Isaac, from Abimelech's point of view, act hypocritically, which means that Isaac and Rebekah would have been in real danger if not for this royal proclamation?

The Torah offers no definite answer to this question. When such questions arise in life, as they often do, we have no choice but to rely on our own intuition. But we must always consider that either approach can lead to damage. Overestimating danger can be just as dangerous as underestimating it.

[8] Abimelech... saw Isaac fondling his wife Rebekah: In referring to marital relations between Isaac and Rebekah the Torah here uses the word *metzachek*, which literally means to laugh, play, or flirt. Isaac's holiness extends to his intimate relations with his wife, and those too are inseparable from laughter, as is Isaac's entire path in life. But when the same word is used (21:9) to describe Ishmael's behavior toward his brother, in that context it means mockery. (Relations with a brother are fundamentally different from relations with one's wife.)

31.5. Farming with Sanctity (26:12)

יב וַיִּזְרַע יִצְחָק בָּאָרֶץ הַהוּא וַיִּמְצָא בַּשָּׁנָה הַהוּא מֵאָה שְׁעָרִים וַיְבָרְכֵהוּ יי:

[12] Isaac sowed in that land and reaped a hundredfold the same year. The Lord blessed him,

[12] Isaac sowed in that land: Only Isaac of all the founders of the Jewish nation engaged in agriculture. Abraham, Jacob and his sons, and Moses were all shepherds. Only Isaac was a farmer.

As we noted much earlier3, farming and cattle breeding are conflicting professions. The history of mankind opened with the farmer Cain murdering his brother Abel, the cattle breeder.

Agriculture was initially a very difficult occupation. As he is driven out from the Garden of Eden, God tells Adam: "Cursed be the ground because of you ... Thorns and thistles shall it sprout for you" (3:17). That is, the earth will yield something other than what man has sown. Abel is therefore engaged in cattle breeding, which is easier work, while Cain is working much harder, trying to cope with the difficulties of agriculture. But he cannot withstand such a heavy burden.

The conflict between livestock breeding and farming was one of the causes of Joseph being sold into slavery. Joseph's brothers were cattle breeders, but Joseph, besides preferring to engage in farming himself, sought also to persuade his brothers to do the same. "There we were binding sheaves in the field." (37:7). For that reason he was sent to Egypt, to manage agriculture.

It is easier for a herder to be spiritual, than for a farmer. The very foundation of Jewish religious consciousness is the image of the herder: "Pastor," shepherd of his "flock."

A cattle breeder is a free man. He gazes at the sky and communicates with the entire world, not being attached to any particular place. He is constantly on the move and finds new places to be, unlike the farmer who but rarely lifts his head from his tract of land, sees nothing of his surroundings, and has no knowledge of other places, which makes him severely limited.

---

3   See §4.3, "The Conflict of the Farmer and the Herdsman".

The potential of agriculture, both materially and spiritually, is much greater than that of cattle breeding, but realizing that potential is incomparably more difficult. Therefore, only later, when the Jewish nation is coming into its own, and is prepared to assume tasks of greater complexity, will agriculture become the primary Jewish occupation.

It is the nature of the earth to attract humans to itself, and in the spiritual plane this is a very ambiguous process. It is no coincidence that the twentieth-century fascist movements of Europe arose from a romanticizing of nature, with the promoters marching around their land, singing praises of its "soul." Romancing the Land of Israel can also be dangerous. A society's soul must include a counterbalance, in order that that romance will not enslave them.

The earth affords enormous power, but it is dangerous. Among the Patriarchs, only Isaac was able to bear the heavy burden of agriculture, and through it to receive God's blessing. Isaac embodies the idea that there is holiness in all things: in agriculture, in digging wells, in "playing" with Rebekah, and in eating two kids for the sake of blessing of his son (27:9).

Isaac can cope with the greatness of the earth and remain spiritually correct, because his own holiness rules over nature. The Jewish people too must acquire this quality, so that they can later settle in the Land of Israel and engage in agriculture upon that land, while not becoming enslaved to the land.

And reaped a hundredfold: The name *Me'ah Sh'earim*, "Hundredfold," was given in 1874 to a new neighborhood of Jerusalem – one of the first outside the Old City – marking the onset of organized agricultural activity in the Land of Israel.

31.6. Philistine Hatred (26: 13-15)

יג וַיִּגְדַּל הָאִישׁ וַיֵּלֶךְ הָלוֹךְ וְגָדֵל עַד כִּי־גָדַל מְאֹד: יד
וַיְהִי־לוֹ מִקְנֵה־צֹאן וּמִקְנֵה בָקָר וַעֲבֻדָּה רַבָּה וַיְקַנְאוּ
אֹתוֹ פְּלִשְׁתִּים: טו וְכָל־הַבְּאֵרֹת אֲשֶׁר חָפְרוּ עַבְדֵי אָבִיו
בִּימֵי אַבְרָהָם אָבִיו סִתְּמוּם פְּלִשְׁתִּים וַיְמַלְאוּם עָפָר:

*[13] and the man grew richer and richer until he
was very wealthy:*
*[14] he acquired flocks and herds, and a large
household, so that the Philistines envied him.*
*[15] And the Philistines stopped up all the wells
which his father's servants had dug in the days
of his father Abraham, filling them with earth.*

**[13] and the man grew richer and richer until ... [14] he
acquired flocks and herds:** Any idealization of poverty is
foreign to the Torah. There is nothing wrong with accumu-
lating wealth through honest labor; Isaac's wealth, and the
efforts he expended to acquire it, were just another aspect
of his service to the Almighty. In the Divine there is the full-
ness of life, and never, as some would have it, a reduction of
life to purely "spiritual" aspects.

**The Philistines envied him. [15] And the Philistines
stopped up all the wells ... filling them with earth:** Isaac's
wealth arouses envy among the Philistines, who, besides
"stopping up the wells," also "fill them with earth," so that
even their location cannot be found later. The Philistines are
prepared to destroy even their own source of wealth, if that
is what it takes to hinder Isaac's advancement.

There is an important lesson here for the Jewish people.

The nations of the world so intensely hate the Jews for their successes, that there is no hope of coming to terms with them based on mutually beneficial cooperation (e.g., "As intelligent people, surely they will not work against their very own best interests"). Jews have made that mistake in every age, up to and including the era of modern-day Israel.

31.7. The Jews' Segregation from the Nations of the World (26:16)

טז וַיֹּאמֶר אֲבִימֶלֶךְ אֶל־יִצְחָק לֵךְ מֵעִמָּנוּ כִּי־עָצַמְתָּ מִמֶּנּוּ מְאֹד:

[16] And Abimelech said to Isaac, "Go away from us, for you have become far too big for us."

[16] You have become far too big for us: The literal translation is "You have become much stronger than us." But this does not mean that Isaac is stronger than the Philistines. A more correct rendering would be "You are too strong for us," i.e., you are stronger than we ourselves can allow.

The Hebrew word *mimennu,* besides meaning "than us," can also mean "from us." Thus, another possible translation is "for you are too strong – from us." That is, your wealth consists of what you have taken from us. Formally speaking, you have acquired your wealth by legal means. But since you've earned it in our country, you have in fact robbed us by taking what is ours. We therefore think it is best that you should leave.

It would be wrong, however, to understand Abimelech's words in a purely negative sense. In fact, for the nations of the world to embrace Jewish enlightenment, some distance between them is needed. The Jews must remain apart from them to some degree. Abimelech wants to expel Isaac because of the hostility that has arisen between them. But at a subconscious level, what is happening here is that there needs to be some distance between them if they are to have any sort of constructive interaction. Abimelech will later come to Isaac to forge an alliance, for he understands that Isaac is blessed. But this understanding cannot arise while Isaac lives so close by, in Gerar.

To properly influence the peoples of the world the Jews must remain separate from them. The nations will then seek out the Jews at their own initiative. But when the Jews try to live near them, passions rage and fuses blow. It is beyond the nations' tolerance, and conflict will inevitably arise.

31.8. Isaac Leaves the Philistines and Digs Wells (26: 17-22)

יז וַיֵּלֶךְ מִשָּׁם יִצְחָק וַיִּחַן בְּנַחַל־גְּרָר וַיֵּשֶׁב שָׁם: **יח** וַיָּשָׁב יִצְחָק וַיַּחְפֹּר ׀ אֶת־בְּאֵרֹת הַמַּיִם אֲשֶׁר חָפְרוּ בִּימֵי אַבְרָהָם אָבִיו וַיְסַתְּמוּם פְּלִשְׁתִּים אַחֲרֵי מוֹת אַבְרָהָם וַיִּקְרָא לָהֶן שֵׁמוֹת כַּשֵּׁמֹת אֲשֶׁר־קָרָא לָהֶן אָבִיו: **יט** וַיַּחְפְּרוּ עַבְדֵי־יִצְחָק בַּנָּחַל וַיִּמְצְאוּ־שָׁם בְּאֵר מַיִם חַיִּים: **כ** וַיָּרִיבוּ רֹעֵי גְרָר עִם־רֹעֵי יִצְחָק לֵאמֹר לָנוּ הַמָּיִם וַיִּקְרָא שֵׁם־הַבְּאֵר עֵשֶׂק כִּי הִתְעַשְּׂקוּ עִמּוֹ: **כא** וַיַּחְפְּרוּ בְּאֵר אַחֶרֶת וַיָּרִיבוּ גַּם־עָלֶיהָ וַיִּקְרָא שְׁמָהּ שִׂטְנָה: **כב** וַיַּעְתֵּק מִשָּׁם וַיַּחְפֹּר בְּאֵר אַחֶרֶת וְלֹא רָבוּ עָלֶיהָ וַיִּקְרָא שְׁמָהּ רְחֹבוֹת וַיֹּאמֶר כִּי־עַתָּה הִרְחִיב יי לָנוּ וּפָרִינוּ בָאָרֶץ:

[17] So Isaac departed from there and encamped in the wadi of Gerar, where he settled.

[18] Isaac dug anew the wells which had been dug in the days of his father Abraham and which the Philistines had stopped up after Abraham's death; and he gave them the same names that his father had given them.

[19] But when Isaac's servants, digging in the wadi, found there a well of spring water,

[20] the herdsmen of Gerar quarreled with Isaac's herdsmen, saying, "The water is ours." He named that well Esek, because they contended with him.

[21] And when they dug another well, they disputed over that one also; so he named it Sitnah.

[22] He moved from there and dug yet another well, and they did not quarrel over it; so he called it Rehoboth, saying, "Now at last the Lord has granted us ample space to increase in the land."

[18] And which the Philistines had stopped up after Abraham's death: Here we see the difference in the approaches of Abraham and Isaac. Unlike Abraham, Isaac's position among the local peoples is problematic, and after Abraham's death Isaac finds himself in contention with the Philistines. Jewish tradition considers the period of "they shall be enslaved and oppressed four hundred years" (15:13) to have begun from the moment of Isaac's birth. Although Isaac lives in the Land of Israel and not in exile, his status is no longer on the level of Abraham's, and the exile is therefore understood to begin with Isaac.

Isaac dug anew the wells ... and he gave them the same names: Wells (like rivers) are a source of spiritual, not only physical, hydration. The names of the wells are designed to reflect the dominant attributes of the surrounding world – life's goals and values.

And he gave them the same names that his father had given them: Isaac not only cares for the water itself, he restores the names that Abraham gave those wells, because *Gevurah* develops correctly only when it remembers that its source is *Chesed*. However, at this level Isaac only restores what Abraham has done previously; he does not carry it any further.

[19] But when Isaac's servants, digging in the wadi: The act of digging new wells (discovering new aspects of Tradition) are initiated not by Isaac himself, but by his servants (i.e., students, adherents).

[20] The herdsmen of Gerar quarreled with Isaac's herdsmen: The actions of Isaac's servants are at this stage unsuccessful, because the Philistines have now seized the water.

He named that well Esek, because they contended with him: Isaac behaves re-actively. Rather than planning development himself, he only reacts to current circumstances.

[22] He moved from there and dug yet another well, and they did not quarrel over it: At first, Isaac had no desire to go far, so he settled in the "wadi of Gerar." But the conflicts persisted. Even when Isaac's slaves find a well of "living water" (that is, the water in this well actively bubbles forth on its own), no peace results. Only when Isaac decides to move significantly further away, to distance himself from the Philistines, does the situation improve.

And dug yet another well, and they did not quarrel over it; so he called it Rehoboth: This time it is not Isaac's servants who dig the new well, but Isaac himself. He is then granted *Rehoboth*, "ample space to increase in the land." When we ourselves dig wells, whether physical or spiritual, rather than relying on our servants to do it, our position in the world improves.

When faced with conflict, Isaac departs. Thus, he demonstrates the attribute of *Gevurah*, which does not seek to expand, but only to maintain the status quo. The key to this approach is to not break down or despair, but rather to continue digging wells. Isaac does just that, and he therefore carries the day.

31.9. Isaac Leaves for Beer-Sheba (26:23-25)

כג וַיַּעַל מִשָּׁם בְּאֵר שָׁבַע: כד וַיֵּרָא אֵלָיו יי בַּלַּיְלָה
הַהוּא וַיֹּאמֶר אָנֹכִי אֱלֹהֵי אַבְרָהָם אָבִיךָ אַל־תִּירָא
כִּי־אִתְּךָ אָנֹכִי וּבֵרַכְתִּיךָ וְהִרְבֵּיתִי אֶת־זַרְעֲךָ בַּעֲבוּר
אַבְרָהָם עַבְדִּי: כה וַיִּבֶן שָׁם מִזְבֵּחַ וַיִּקְרָא בְּשֵׁם יי וַיֶּט־
שָׁם אָהֳלוֹ וַיִּכְרוּ־שָׁם עַבְדֵי־יִצְחָק בְּאֵר:

[23] From there he went up to Beer-sheba.
[24] That night the Lord appeared to him and said, "I am the God of your father Abraham. Fear not, for I am with you, and I will bless you and increase your offspring for the sake of My servant Abraham."
[25] So he built an altar there and invoked the Lord by name. Isaac pitched his tent there and his servants started digging a well.

[23] From there he went up to Beer-sheba: Isaac follows the path tread by his father Abraham, and he too gradually becomes a recognized teacher of spirituality living in a remote place.

[24] Fear Not: God now begins to address Isaac, as He had done for Abraham (15:1). He promises him His protection, not only from external threats (i.e., Isaac should not fear Abimelech), but, more fundamentally, from internal struggles, and from his fears of regressing from the level he had already attained due to potentially improper actions on his part. Abraham was afraid to fight, fearing any display of excessive aggression, *Gevurah*. But Isaac fears his own activity, his achievement of *Rehobot*, "ample spaces." Divine support is therefore at this moment so important to him.

[25] So he built an altar there and invoked the Lord by name: Having received the promise of Divine support, Isaac is now able to turn his attentions to engaging with the larger world, i.e., he begins to spread God's teachings.

Isaac pitched his tent there: He began inviting travelers to study with him, just as Abraham had done.

And his servants started digging a well: They, too, are now successfully disseminating God's teachings. Only when Isaac has risen to such a level, that his followers are now themselves successful teachers, does Abimelech visit Isaac to request a blessing.

31.10. Abimelech Visits Isaac (26:26-31)

כו וַאֲבִימֶלֶךְ הָלַךְ אֵלָיו מִגְּרָר וַאֲחֻזַּת מֵרֵעֵהוּ וּפִיכֹל
שַׂר־צְבָאוֹ: כז וַיֹּאמֶר אֲלֵהֶם יִצְחָק מַדּוּעַ בָּאתֶם אֵלַי

וְאַתֶּם שְׂנֵאתֶם אֹתִי וַתְּשַׁלְּחוּנִי מֵאִתְּכֶם: **כח** וַיֹּאמְרוּ
רָאוֹ רָאִינוּ כִּי־הָיָה יי | עִמָּךְ וַנֹּאמֶר תְּהִי נָא אָלָה
בֵּינוֹתֵינוּ בֵּינֵינוּ וּבֵינֶךָ וְנִכְרְתָה בְרִית עִמָּךְ: **כט** אִם־
תַּעֲשֵׂה עִמָּנוּ רָעָה כַּאֲשֶׁר לֹא נְגַעֲנוּךָ וְכַאֲשֶׁר עָשִׂינוּ עִמְּךָ
רַק־טוֹב וַנְּשַׁלֵּחֲךָ בְּשָׁלוֹם אַתָּה עַתָּה בְּרוּךְ יי: **ל** וַיַּעַשׂ
לָהֶם מִשְׁתֶּה וַיֹּאכְלוּ וַיִּשְׁתּוּ: **לא** וַיַּשְׁכִּימוּ בַבֹּקֶר וַיִּשָּׁבְעוּ
אִישׁ לְאָחִיו וַיְשַׁלְּחֵם יִצְחָק וַיֵּלְכוּ מֵאִתּוֹ בְּשָׁלוֹם:

[26] *And Abimelech came to him from Gerar,
with Ahuzzath his councilor and Phicol chief of
his troops.*
[27] *Isaac said to them, "Why have you come to
me, seeing that you have been hostile to me and
have driven me away from you?"*
[28] *And they said, "We now see plainly that the
Lord has been with you, and we thought: Let
there be a sworn treaty between our two parties,
between you and us. Let us make a pact with you*
[29] *that you will not do us harm, just as we have
not molested you but have always dealt kindly
with you and sent you away in peace. From now
on, be you blessed of the Lord!"*
[30] *Then he made for them a feast, and they
ate and drank.*
[31] *Early in the morning, they exchanged
oaths. Isaac then bade them farewell, and they
departed from him in peace.*

[29] That you will not do us harm: Now that Isaac has made
a life apart from the Philistines and proved his success to
them, his relationship with Abimelech changes. Abimelech
begins to fear Isaac.

Just as we … have always dealt kindly with you: Abimelech does not forget to present himself in a positive light.

From now on, be you blessed of the Lord!: Abimelech now acknowledges Isaac's status.

After separating ourselves from the nations of the world and achieving success, we are far more effective at glorifying the Divine name than we could have been had we been living among the nations.

The wealth Isaac had accumulated in Gerar was of no help to him: Abimelech still deemed his achievements illegitimate, and the Philistines stopped up his wells. Only when Isaac built his life separately from the surrounding nations did they recognize that what Isaac had achieved rightfully belonged to him, and that he was endowed with a Divine blessing. Only then did they seek to make peace and establish a union with him.

[27] Why have you come to me, seeing that you have been hostile to me and have driven me away from you?: Isaac's behavior during Abimelech's visit is different from Abraham's. Abraham mentioned the problem of the wells only after the conclusion of the treaty, which is why he received a rather evasive answer (21:26). But Isaac begins to make his grievances known to Abimelech straightaway. This is a manifestation of *Gevurah*.

[31] They exchanged oaths: Moreover, Isaac makes an oath to Abimelech that will remain in force only so long as Isaac is alive, but creates no alliance with him that would extend to future generations – as Abimelech had requested, and Abraham had done before. *Gevurah* contends with external conflict far more effectively than *Chesed* does.

31.11. "The Name of the City is Beer-Sheba." (26:32-33)

לב וַיְהִי | בַּיּוֹם הַהוּא וַיָּבֹאוּ עַבְדֵי יִצְחָק וַיַּגִּדוּ לוֹ עַל־
אֹדוֹת הַבְּאֵר אֲשֶׁר חָפָרוּ וַיֹּאמְרוּ לוֹ מָצָאנוּ מָיִם: **לג**
וַיִּקְרָא אֹתָהּ שִׁבְעָה עַל־כֵּן שֵׁם־הָעִיר בְּאֵר שֶׁבַע עַד
הַיּוֹם הַזֶּה:

*[32] That same day Isaac's servants came and
told him about the well they had dug, and said
to him, "We have found water!"*
*[33] He named it Shibah; therefore the name of
the city is Beer-sheba to this day.*

[32] That same day: Once Abimelech acknowledges Isaac's
greatness and honors him with a visit, Isaac's slaves' self-esteem increases, and this advances them forward.

**[32] Isaac's servants came and told him about the well
they had dug:** As his servant-disciples themselves develop
and advance God's teachings further, Isaac supports their
efforts by naming the well accordingly. Besides learning himself to embrace new paths of behavior, Isaac supports this
same approach in his students as well. For *Gevurah*, this is
an important advancement.

**[33] He named it Shibah; therefore the name of the city is
Beer-sheba to this day:** The names of the well and the city
are reinterpreted again here. Under Abraham, they were associated with an oath and with seven sheep (21:28). But now,
as the Midrash notes, the name of the well derives from its
being the seventh one dug by Isaac and his servants. (The
six previous wells were the three wells dug by Abraham, plus

three more: Esek, Sitnah and Rehoboth). The number seven completes the usefulness of the natural cycle of development. By so naming the well, Isaac emphasizes the integrity and completeness of his activities.

Chapter 32

Jacob and Esau Receive
Their Blessings

32.1. Esau's Wives (26:34-35)

לד וַיְהִי עֵשָׂו בֶּן־אַרְבָּעִים שָׁנָה וַיִּקַּח אִשָּׁה אֶת־יְהוּדִית
בַּת־בְּאֵרִי הַחִתִּי וְאֶת־בָּשְׂמַת בַּת־אֵילֹן הַחִתִּי: **לה**
וַתִּהְיֶיןָ מֹרַת רוּחַ לְיִצְחָק וּלְרִבְקָה:

*[34] When Esau was forty years old, he took to
wife Judith daughter of Beeri the Hittite, and
Basemath daughter of Elon the Hittite;
[35] and they were a source of bitterness to Isaac
and Rebekah.*

The story of the blessings is framed by the marriages of
Isaac's sons. First we are told about Esau's wives, and then,
at the end of the portion, about the plans for Jacob's marriage, and about Esau's new wives.

Isaac will be blessing his sons within the context of *toldot*,
the sequence of the generations. They are more than just

personal blessings; they are blessings for posterity. But for those blessings to be realized, their recipients must have suitable wives.

[34] When Esau was forty years old, he took to wife Judith daughter of Beeri the Hittite, and Basemath daughter of Elon the Hittite: Esau, in a superficial attempt to emulate his father Isaac, marries like him at age forty. But at the same time he violates his grandfather Abraham's traditions, by marrying local women instead of taking a wife from among the *ivrim* (Hebrews).

[35] And they were a source of bitterness to Isaac and Rebekah: It is not just that Esau's wives kept aloof from his parents, like strangers. Far worse, they behaved offensively toward Isaac and Rebekah. Esau's marriages were so improper, that they alone were a sufficient reason for him to forfeit his father's blessing.

32.2. Isaac's Old Age and Failing Eyesight (27:1)

א, וַיְהִי כִּי־זָקֵן יִצְחָק וַתִּכְהֶיןָ עֵינָיו מֵראֹת וַיִּקְרָא אֶת־עֵשָׂו ׀ בְּנוֹ הַגָּדֹל וַיֹּאמֶר אֵלָיו בְּנִי וַיֹּאמֶר אֵלָיו הִנֵּנִי:

[1] When Isaac was old and his eyes were too dim to see, he called his older son Esau and said to him, "My son." He answered, "Here I am."

[1] When Isaac was old: "Old age" usually means a loss of dynamics and a cessation of development. However, we will see here that even in his old age, Isaac will still need to perform a vital spiritual act of "faceting" his *Gevurah*, which is for him the central link in this story of the blessings. Having successfully coped with this challenge, Isaac does not stop, but moves from Beer-sheba to Hebron (35:27), thus completing his journey along Abraham's path.

His eyes were too dim to see: Literally, "his eyes dimmed from vision." The Midrash explains that when Isaac was lying upon the altar, tied up to become a sacrifice, the heavens opened. The sheer radiance of that "vision" overwhelmed his eyes, consequently weakening his eyesight.

A person who is too exalted, too close to higher worlds, looks and sees far afield, but, paradoxically, he often cannot make out what is happening right next to him.

We would be mistaken to think that Isaac, with his poor eyesight, simply did not realize that Esau was deceiving him. Of course Isaac knew what was going on. But "knowing" and correctly assessing the consequences are two very different things. Even highly righteous individuals will sometimes err, incorrectly evaluating the potentialities of events. Isaac, however, while mistaken in his actual relations with his two sons, nonetheless correctly perceived, in the abstract, the higher meaning of what was happening. And realizing his mistakes, he was able to advance himself, and also the world at large.

32.3. Isaac Chooses Esau (27:2-4)

ב וַיֹּאמֶר הִנֵּה־נָא זָקַנְתִּי לֹא יָדַעְתִּי יוֹם מוֹתִי: ג וְעַתָּה
שָׂא־נָא כֵלֶיךָ תֶּלְיְךָ וְקַשְׁתֶּךָ וְצֵא הַשָּׂדֶה וְצוּדָה לִּי צֵידה
(צָיִד): ד וַעֲשֵׂה־לִי מַטְעַמִּים כַּאֲשֶׁר אָהַבְתִּי וְהָבִיאָה לִּי
וְאֹכֵלָה בַּעֲבוּר תְּבָרֶכְךָ נַפְשִׁי בְּטֶרֶם אָמוּת:

[2] And he said, "I am old now, and I do not know how soon I may die.
[3] Take your gear, your quiver and bow, and go out into the open and hunt me some game.
[4] Then prepare a dish for me such as I like, and bring it to me to eat, so that I may give you my innermost blessing before I die."

[3] Take your gear, your quiver and bow, and go out into the open: God's covenant with the Patriarchs was aimed not only at creating a religious movement, but at creating a people living a full-fledged national life. To realize such an ideal, a man (or clan, or tribe) was needed who would be capable of maintaining political power. Understanding this, Isaac reasonably believes that Esau, who can cope with economic problems, and who "rules the field," is the one worthy of the blessing. Also, a state cannot survive without readiness to wage war, and Esau knows how to use weapons. And so, in anticipation of giving him the blessing, Isaac invites Esau to demonstrate these two qualities.

Isaac sees the future Jewish people as consisting of two tribes: the tribe of Esau, who will be occupied with the logistics of daily existence (which is why the blessing needs to be Esau's), and the tribe of Jacob, focused on spiritual life (like the tribe of Levi in the future). Isaac is aware of Esau's shortcomings: The Torah states plainly that Esau's wives "were a source of bitterness to Isaac and Rebekah." But he misjudges the relative potentials of Esau and Jacob. Rebekah could not hope to change his mind simply by bringing to his attention a few additional facts.

[4] So that I may give you my innermost blessing: Isaac believes that the blessing itself will be able to correct

Esau. Fundamentally, this was not a mistake on Isaac's part, because Isaac, although he errs in his assessment of the potentialities of current development, correctly perceives the world as a whole. The blessing can in fact correct Esau – but only if he receives it through Jacob and not directly. So to would be the future relationship of the Jews and Western civilization.

32.4. Rebekah Chooses Jacob (27: 5-10)

ה וְרִבְקָה שֹׁמַעַת בְּדַבֵּר יִצְחָק אֶל־עֵשָׂו בְּנוֹ וַיֵּלֶךְ עֵשָׂו
הַשָּׂדֶה לָצוּד צַיִד לְהָבִיא: ו וְרִבְקָה אָמְרָה אֶל־יַעֲקֹב
בְּנָהּ לֵאמֹר הִנֵּה שָׁמַעְתִּי אֶת־אָבִיךְ מְדַבֵּר אֶל־עֵשָׂו
אָחִיךָ לֵאמֹר: ז הָבִיאָה לִּי צַיִד וַעֲשֵׂה־לִי מַטְעַמִּים
וְאֹכֵלָה וַאֲבָרֶכְכָה לִפְנֵי יי לִפְנֵי מוֹתִי: ח וְעַתָּה בְנִי שְׁמַע
בְּקֹלִי לַאֲשֶׁר אֲנִי מְצַוָּה אֹתָךְ: ט לֶךְ־נָא אֶל־הַצֹּאן וְקַח־
לִי מִשָּׁם שְׁנֵי גְּדָיֵי עִזִּים טֹבִים וְאֶעֱשֶׂה אֹתָם מַטְעַמִּים
לְאָבִיךָ כַּאֲשֶׁר אָהֵב: י וְהֵבֵאתָ לְאָבִיךָ וְאָכָל בַּעֲבֻר אֲשֶׁר
יְבָרֶכְךָ לִפְנֵי מוֹתוֹ:

[5] Rebekah had been listening as Isaac spoke to his son Esau. When Esau had gone out into the open to hunt game to bring home,
[6] Rebekah said to her son Jacob, "I overheard your father speaking to your brother Esau, saying,
[7] 'Bring me some game and prepare a dish for me to eat, that I may bless you, with the Lord's approval, before I die.'
[8] Now, my son, listen carefully as I instruct you.
[9] Go to the flock and fetch me two choice kids, and I will make of them a dish for your father, such as he likes.

*[10] Then take it to your father to eat, in order
that he may bless you before he dies."*

**[5] Isaac spoke to his son Esau ... [6] Rebekah said to her
son Jacob:** The Torah emphasizes the contrast. Isaac considers Esau his son, but Rebekah's son is Jacob.

Isaac and Esau are both *Gevurah* personalities, but Isaac
can develop and remove from himself his "unclean *Gevurah*," which Esau on his own is not able to do. Rebekah and
Jacob, however, incline towards *Chesed*. Besides being able
to see the existing situation, they are also able to change it.

[6] Your father speaking to your brother Esau: Jacob is
capable of further development, but in this connection it is
important for him to remember that Esau is his brother, and
Rebekah reminds him of this. Jacob develops not only for his
own sake, but in order to change the world, which includes
advancing his brother Esau's descendants.

[8] Now, my son, listen carefully as I instruct you: The literal translation is: "Now my son, obey my voice, as to what
I am commanding you to do." If one's parents order him to
commit a crime, the son must not obey. Therefore, when
Rebekah proposes that Jacob deceive his father, Jacob, it
would seem, should refuse.

But instead of just saying, "Do what I am commanding
you," Rebekah adds the words "obey my voice." We have
already encountered this formulation in the Torah: "And
Abram heeded Sarai's request" (16:2); literally, "And Abram
obeyed Sarai's voice." This is no mere coincidence; Rebekah
words here are a prophecy, and Jacob therefore obeys her
decision. On the issue of *toldot* – successive generations and

determining the future nation's lineage – the opinion of the Matriarchs was always decisive, because in that aspect their prophetic spirit surpassed that of the Patriarchs.

Perhaps Rebekah was also relying on the prediction "And the older will serve the younger" (25:23), which can be understood in both senses: relative position within the hierarchy, and the enormous challenge of changing oneself. Jacob was weak in comparison to Esau; his own qualities alone would not have enabled him to create the Chosen People. But he is a dynamic personality who in the future will acquire some of Esau's attributes, thanks to which he will succeed at creating the Jewish nation.

For this advancement to begin, some change must occur in Jacob's personality to prove that he is worthy of the blessing. The most important the action needed to effect that change is for Jacob to appear before his father as Esau.

32.5. Removing the Threat of the Curse (27: 11-13)

יא וַיֹּאמֶר יַעֲקֹב אֶל־רִבְקָה אִמּוֹ הֵן עֵשָׂו אָחִי אִישׁ שָׂעִר
וְאָנֹכִי אִישׁ חָלָק: יב אוּלַי יְמֻשֵּׁנִי אָבִי וְהָיִיתִי בְעֵינָיו
כִּמְתַעְתֵּעַ וְהֵבֵאתִי עָלַי קְלָלָה וְלֹא בְרָכָה: יג וַתֹּאמֶר לוֹ
אִמּוֹ עָלַי קִלְלָתְךָ בְּנִי אַךְ שְׁמַע בְּקֹלִי וְלֵךְ קַח־לִי:

[11] Jacob answered his mother Rebekah, "But my brother Esau is a hairy man and I am smooth-skinned.

[12] If my father touches me, I shall appear to him as a trickster and bring upon myself a curse, not a blessing."

[13] But his mother said to him, "Your curse, my son, be upon me! Just do as I say and go fetch them for me."

[13] Just do as I say: Rebekah repeats the instruction to obey her "voice," i.e., her prophecies.

Your curse, my son, be upon me!: The meaning of this expression is not entirely clear. Rebekah could have said something like, "Do not be afraid, nothing bad will happen," or other such reassuring words. But how could she say, "your curse be upon me"?

In truth, perhaps she should not have said any such words. For as we learn later, after Jacob departed for Haran, Rebekah never saw her son again; she died before he returned.

But we can also understand Rebekah's words quite differently. I.e., not "may the curse fall upon me," but "responsibility for your curse is upon me," as if some part of the curse comes from within Rebekah herself. Being a product of the house of Laban the Aramean, Rebekah incorporates Aramean elements. And that is itself the source of the conflict between Jacob and Esau, and, consequently, the difficulties that have arisen in the family. Rebekah's Aramean component gives her both versatility and cunning (*Aram* is associated with *arum*, "cunning," and with *rama'ut*, "deception." It is these properties that enable Rebekah to develop a scheme for deceiving Isaac and to force Jacob to implement it. Having herself partly become a source of the family's problems, Rebekah must correct the situation in order to avert the "curse" that still lingers, if only in its potential.

In fact, Rebekah has a broader view of the problem than Jacob does. Jacob is troubled about what will become of him ("I shall bring upon myself a curse, not a blessing"), while Rebekah deals with the situation as a whole, in the context of the family's future. Jacob wants to be good, honest, and upright ("a blameless man," 25:27 [alternate translation]), but Rebekah understands that without conflict and crisis the situation cannot be resolved.

There is nothing good, of course, in this deception. But allowing the situation to develop in the wrong direction by allowing it to take its natural course would be catastrophic. Deception was a necessary expedient, and Rebekah herself saw it in just that light.

32.6. Rebekah Disguises Jacob (27:14-17)

יד וַיֵּלֶךְ וַיִּקַּח וַיָּבֵא לְאִמּוֹ וַתַּעַשׂ אִמּוֹ מַטְעַמִּים כַּאֲשֶׁר אָהֵב אָבִיו: טו וַתִּקַּח רִבְקָה אֶת־בִּגְדֵי עֵשָׂו בְּנָהּ הַגָּדֹל הַחֲמֻדֹת אֲשֶׁר אִתָּהּ בַּבָּיִת וַתַּלְבֵּשׁ אֶת־יַעֲקֹב בְּנָהּ הַקָּטָן: טז וְאֵת עֹרֹת גְּדָיֵי הָעִזִּים הִלְבִּישָׁה עַל־יָדָיו וְעַל חֶלְקַת צַוָּארָיו: יז וַתִּתֵּן אֶת־הַמַּטְעַמִּים וְאֶת־הַלֶּחֶם אֲשֶׁר עָשָׂתָה בְּיַד יַעֲקֹב בְּנָהּ:

[14] He got them and brought them to his mother, and his mother prepared a dish such as his father liked.
[15] Rebekah then took the best clothes of her older son Esau, which were there in the house, and had her younger son Jacob put them on;
[16] and she covered his hands and the hairless part of his neck with the skins of the kids.
[17] Then she put in the hands of her son Jacob the dish and the bread that she had prepared.

[15] Rebekah then took the best clothes of her older son Esau, which were there in the house, and had her younger son Jacob put them on: A different aspect is already being emphasized here: Both Esau and Jacob are Rebekah's sons, and Esau is the eldest. He stores in her house (not in his wives' houses!) his favorite clothing in which he attends to his father. Although Esau cannot become the leader of the people, he possesses some essential qualities that Jacob must adopt. Therefore, the goal of Rebekah's action is not merely to deceive Isaac, but to re-educate Jacob by dressing him up "in Esau."

32.7. Jacob Tries On "Esau-Ness" (27:18-20)

יח וַיָּבֹא אֶל־אָבִיו וַיֹּאמֶר אָבִי וַיֹּאמֶר הִנֶּנִּי מִי אַתָּה
בְּנִי: יט וַיֹּאמֶר יַעֲקֹב אֶל־אָבִיו אָנֹכִי עֵשָׂו בְּכֹרֶךָ עָשִׂיתִי
כַּאֲשֶׁר דִּבַּרְתָּ אֵלָי קוּם־נָא שְׁבָה וְאָכְלָה מִצֵּידִי בַּעֲבוּר
תְּבָרְכַנִּי נַפְשֶׁךָ: כ וַיֹּאמֶר יִצְחָק אֶל־בְּנוֹ מַה־זֶּה מִהַרְתָּ
לִמְצֹא בְּנִי וַיֹּאמֶר כִּי הִקְרָה יי אֱלֹהֶיךָ לְפָנָי:

[18] He went to his father and said, "Father." And he said, "Yes, which of my sons are you?"
[19] Jacob said to his father, "I am Esau, your first-born; I have done as you told me. Pray sit up and eat of my game, that you may give me your innermost blessing."
[20] Isaac said to his son, "How did you succeed so quickly, my son?" And he said, "Because the Lord your God granted me good fortune."

[19] I am Esau, your first-born: Jacob speaks these words not only to Isaac, but also to himself. He is altering his identity and trying on Esau's properties. But at the same time Jacob remains Jacob, speaking of God as the creator of events.

[20] God granted me good fortune: Jacob ascribes both of those circumstances to God – the possible reasons for his speedy capture of game, and his appearance to Isaac in the image of Esau.

32.8. The Voice is Jacob's, the Hands are Esau's (27:21-27)

כא וַיֹּאמֶר יִצְחָק אֶל־יַעֲקֹב גְּשָׁה־נָּא וַאֲמֻשְׁךָ בְּנִי הַאַתָּה זֶה בְּנִי עֵשָׂו אִם־לֹא: **כב** וַיִּגַּשׁ יַעֲקֹב אֶל־יִצְחָק אָבִיו וַיְמֻשֵׁהוּ וַיֹּאמֶר הַקֹּל קוֹל יַעֲקֹב וְהַיָּדַיִם יְדֵי עֵשָׂו: **כג** וְלֹא הִכִּירוֹ כִּי־הָיוּ יָדָיו כִּידֵי עֵשָׂו אָחִיו שְׂעִרֹת וַיְבָרְכֵהוּ: **כד** וַיֹּאמֶר אַתָּה זֶה בְּנִי עֵשָׂו וַיֹּאמֶר אָנִי: **כה** וַיֹּאמֶר הַגִּשָׁה לִּי וְאֹכְלָה מִצֵּיד בְּנִי לְמַעַן תְּבָרֶכְךָ נַפְשִׁי וַיַּגֶּשׁ־לוֹ וַיֹּאכַל וַיָּבֵא לוֹ יַיִן וַיֵּשְׁתְּ: **כו** וַיֹּאמֶר אֵלָיו יִצְחָק אָבִיו גְּשָׁה־נָּא וּשְׁקָה־לִּי בְּנִי: **כז** וַיִּגַּשׁ וַיִּשַּׁק־לוֹ וַיָּרַח אֶת־רֵיחַ בְּגָדָיו וַיְבָרְכֵהוּ וַיֹּאמֶר רְאֵה רֵיחַ בְּנִי כְּרֵיחַ שָׂדֶה אֲשֶׁר בֵּרֲכוֹ יי:

[21] Isaac said to Jacob, "Come closer that I may feel you, my son–whether you are really my son Esau or not."
[22] So Jacob drew close to his father Isaac, who felt him and wondered. "The voice is the voice of Jacob, yet the hands are the hands of Esau."
[23] He did not recognize him, because his hands were hairy like those of his brother Esau; and so he blessed him.
[24] He asked, "Are you really my son Esau?" And when he said, "I am,"
[25] he said, "Serve me and let me eat of my son's game that I may give you my innermost blessing." So he served him and he ate, and he

brought him wine and he drank.
[26] Then his father Isaac said to him, "Come
close and kiss me, my son";
[27] and he went up and kissed him. And he
smelled his clothes and he blessed him, saying,
"Ah, the smell of my son is like the smell of the
fields that the Lord has blessed.

[27] The smell of my son is like the smell of the fields that the Lord has blessed: Esau is a master of the field, but that is not enough to create a people, because his field is severed from contact with the Almighty. Only Jacob, by donning Esau's clothing, can create "the field that the Lord has blessed."

[22] The voice is the voice of Jacob, yet the hands are the hands of Esau: Neither Jacob nor Esau alone can receive the blessing. Only the "hybrid son" is worthy of that – the son who internally is Jacob, but can externally behave like Esau.

[23] He did not recognize him ... and so he blessed him: Isaac bestows the blessing while neither recognizing nor understanding just who stands before him. And this is itself Isaac's personal advancement – overcoming his excessive *Gevurah*.

32.9. The Blessing of Success and Power (27:28-29)

כח וְיִתֶּן־לְךָ הָאֱלֹהִים מִטַּל הַשָּׁמַיִם וּמִשְׁמַנֵּי הָאָרֶץ
וְרֹב דָּגָן וְתִירֹשׁ: **כט** יַעַבְדוּךָ עַמִּים וישתחו (וְיִשְׁתַּחֲווּ)
לְךָ לְאֻמִּים הֱוֵה גְבִיר לְאַחֶיךָ וְיִשְׁתַּחֲווּ לְךָ בְּנֵי אִמֶּךָ

אֹרְרֶיךָ אָרוּר וּמְבָרְכֶיךָ בָּרוּךְ:

*[28] "May God give you Of the dew of heaven
and the fat of the earth, Abundance of new grain
and wine.*
*[29] Let peoples serve you, And nations bow to
you; Be master over your brothers, And let your
mother's sons bow to you. Cursed be they who
curse you, Blessed they who bless you."*

[29] Be master: This is a blessing of strength, power, and success, but it is not the blessing of Abraham. It does not speak
of the Land, of communication with God, or of Abraham's
heritage. All these aspects, however, are mentioned later in
another blessing that Isaac will give Jacob before sending
him off to Laban (28:3).

By all appearances, Isaac from the very beginning was
planning to give his blessing for the family mission to Jacob.
The only question was whether Jacob needed to receive also
the "blessing of this-worldly success" in order to fulfill that
mission, or whether Esau could take that blessing for himself. Isaac wanted to separate them, but Rebekah decided
that Jacob must receive both blessings. And that is exactly
what happened.

32.10. The Faceting of Gevurah

The story of the blessings represents a great spiritual
achievement for Isaac. He had to realize his choice under
conditions of uncertainty, separating proper *Gevurah* from
its improper variant. Just as Abraham had to "facet" his *Chesed*

and give it the correct shape in order to be suitable as the foundation of the Jewish people, so too Isaac's task was to facet his *Gevurah*. Correctness and legitimacy, thoroughness and conscientiousness are all highly essential attributes, but they must not be allowed to overpower extra-systemic spontaneity. They must be restrained, so as not to hinder our ability to act freely in unpredictable situations.

Our world often develops along completely illogical lines, but in that illogic there is a greater harmony than in strict, causal regularity. In order to do the right thing even when everything going on around us is illogical and improper, we need to limit *Gevurah*. This is the task that Isaac is charged with accomplishing.

The attribute of *Gevurah* has a deep connection to the concepts of planning, causality, and order. Strict legality demands that we objectively consider each individual situation, and seek a clear, causal relationship between the intentions of the actors and their actions. The law itself also implements this cause-and-effect relationship in the form of a just sentence, when a good deed leads to a reward, and a bad one to retribution.

But at the same time, unclean, excessive *Gevurah* – a fanatical desire for the total application of law and deserved retribution – lead not to a correction of a problematic situation, but to its exacerbation and even its breakdown. Exaggerated application of any of the *Sefirot* attributes is antithetical to harmony and balance. Thus, the trials of our Patriarchs consisted in harmonizing the excesses of their personality traits.

But all that concerns *Gevurah* most of all, because excess *Gevurah* may turn out to be far more dangerous than excessive *Chesed*. There is even an idea in Kabbalah that the source of evil in our world is *Gevurah*, which has strayed from the equilibrium of the *Sefirot* tree and is now "swimming free-style." Since the world is imperfect, any attempt to implement everything too correctly, fairly, and juridically carries within it the seeds of destruction.

Isaac's truest test must be a situation in which events develop unplanned. When Jacob arrives to receive the blessing in Esau's place, Isaac senses that there is something abnormal happening. Standing before him is not the son he had expected to see, for he has "the voice of Jacob, but the hands of Esau." And although Isaac asks him time and again, "Are you really my son Esau?" he still cannot but doubt that there is someone strange standing before him.

Had Isaac acted "properly" then of course he should not have given the blessing to such a strange son. He should have said, "Something is wrong here. Let's just call off these blessings for now and open an investigation, so we can get to the bottom of who this person really is, who has Jacob's voice but Esau's hands." Isaac does otherwise, however. He overcomes his *Gevurah* and gives this strange son the blessing, thus proclaiming that logic, justice and the law are certainly important, but not absolute.

In giving a blessing to an unknown son in an unplanned situation, Isaac learns to "facet" excessive correctness, order, and rigidity brought on by pedantry and an over-demanding demeanor. Such faceting is necessary in order to properly build the future nation.

32.11 Isaac's Laugh

The name Isaac means "he will laugh" – in the grammatical future tense. When Isaac got his name, everyone laughed except for Isaac himself. Everyone else was laughing (albeit all of them differently) – Abraham, Sarah and Ishmael. But not Isaac. His time to laugh would come later.

As already noted, laughter expresses our joy over an unplanned development of events, when the level of harmony one experiences exceeds what was originally expected. Laughter is the recognition of a higher-order harmony in an external irregularity. Seeing such harmony, Isaac corrects his excess *Gevurah* and lays the foundation for Jewish laughter.

Laughter frees us from that which is mechanical and coerced, even if it is something experienced only internally. God is free, and, in acting freely, we feel that we too are approaching God. So we laugh for joy.

Now, a complete rejection of logic would of course destroy the universe, so most events obey the rules of logic. However, those events that do not obey logic are no less an essential part of the universe. At critical points the world develops unpredictably; to react properly to those events you need to be able to laugh at yourself – that is, to limit your own *Gevurah*, your ability to act "correctly."

The choice of the "abnormal son" – Jacob with Esau's hands – was Isaac's true laugh. (It is a laugh not in the sense of an external emotional reaction, but a laugh as an action, an act.) And in this, his most important test, Isaac realizes the true meaning of his name: "He who will laugh."

32.12. Divine Laughter

As we have already observed, Scripture teaches4 that God too laughs. The Midrash expands on this, telling us that God "plays with the Leviathan daily, and laughs with him." Thus, laughter is understood as an attribute of such importance,

---

4   Ps. 2:4, 37:13, 104:26.

that it is even among the attributes of the Divinity.

As expressed in the Psalms, God laughs first and foremost when He crushes evil designs. In a broader sense, however, the same applies to all human projects. This does not mean that God routinely hinders humans from realizing their plans. On the contrary, God will usually allow a person to fully execute his plan, except that the outcome is very often quite different from what was first conceived. Sometimes what results is even the very opposite of the original plan. And that is what we mean when we say that "God laughs."

Given that laughter is nothing less than a Divine attribute, it is vital that human beings too, created as they are in the image and likeness of God, will be able to laugh. Most important, however, is our ability to laugh at ourselves. We need this ability in order to overcome our limitations.

Indeed, because of our normal human limitations, any of our ideas can be erroneous and inaccurate, with the result that we cannot regard our ideas as of universal validity. We should not take ourselves too seriously. If we cannot laugh at ourselves, we become ridiculous to others. When a person takes himself too seriously, the effect is so utterly ridiculous that it is ludicrous even to mention it. Thus, by adopting an unexpected option that he himself had initially not foreseen, our laughing patriarch Isaac furthered both his own personal development and the creation of the Jewish nation.

32.13. Isaac's Extreme Trepidation (27:30-33)

ל וַיְהִי כַּאֲשֶׁר כִּלָּה יִצְחָק לְבָרֵךְ אֶת־יַעֲקֹב וַיְהִי אַךְ יָצֹא
יָצָא יַעֲקֹב מֵאֵת פְּנֵי יִצְחָק אָבִיו וְעֵשָׂו אָחִיו בָּא מִצֵּידוֹ:
לא וַיַּעַשׂ גַּם־הוּא מַטְעַמִּים וַיָּבֵא לְאָבִיו וַיֹּאמֶר לְאָבִיו
יָקֻם אָבִי וְיֹאכַל מִצֵּיד בְּנוֹ בַּעֲבֻר תְּבָרֲכַנִּי נַפְשֶׁךָ: **לב**

וַיֹּאמֶר לוֹ יִצְחָק אָבִיו מִי־אָתָּה וַיֹּאמֶר אֲנִי בִּנְךָ בְכֹרְךָ
עֵשָׂו: **לג** וַיֶּחֱרַד יִצְחָק חֲרָדָה גְּדֹלָה עַד־מְאֹד וַיֹּאמֶר מִי־
אֵפוֹא הוּא הַצָּד־צַיִד וַיָּבֵא לִי וָאֹכַל מִכֹּל בְּטֶרֶם תָּבוֹא
וָאֲבָרֲכֵהוּ גַּם־בָּרוּךְ יִהְיֶה:

[30] No sooner had Jacob left the presence of his father Isaac–after Isaac had finished blessing Jacob–than his brother Esau came back from his hunt.

[31] He too prepared a dish and brought it to his father. And he said to his father, "Let my father sit up and eat of his son's game, so that you may give me your innermost blessing."

[32] His father Isaac said to him, "Who are you?" And he said, "I am your son, Esau, your first-born!"

[33] Isaac was seized with very violent trembling. "Who was it then," he demanded, "that hunted game and brought it to me? Moreover, I ate of it before you came, and I blessed him; now he must remain blessed!"

[33] Isaac was seized with very violent trembling: Isaac's extreme trepidation was the result of the utter collapse of his worldview, as he realized the fallacy of his original plan for bestowing the blessings.

Now he must remain blessed!: Despite his trepidation, Isaac confirms his previous decision, thereby adding yet more force to the faceting of his *Gevurah*.

32.14. Esau's Anguish (27:34-38)

לד כְּשְׁמֹעַ עֵשָׂו אֶת־דִּבְרֵי אָבִיו וַיִּצְעַק צְעָקָה גְּדֹלָה
וּמָרָה עַד־מְאֹד וַיֹּאמֶר לְאָבִיו בָּרֲכֵנִי גַם־אָנִי אָבִי: לה
וַיֹּאמֶר בָּא אָחִיךָ בְּמִרְמָה וַיִּקַּח בִּרְכָתֶךָ: לו וַיֹּאמֶר
הֲכִי קָרָא שְׁמוֹ יַעֲקֹב וַיַּעְקְבֵנִי זֶה פַעֲמַיִם אֶת־בְּכֹרָתִי
לָקָח וְהִנֵּה עַתָּה לָקַח בִּרְכָתִי וַיֹּאמַר הֲלֹא־אָצַלְתָּ לִּי
בְּרָכָה: לז וַיַּעַן יִצְחָק וַיֹּאמֶר לְעֵשָׂו הֵן גְּבִיר שַׂמְתִּיו לָךְ
וְאֶת־כָּל־אֶחָיו נָתַתִּי לוֹ לַעֲבָדִים וְדָגָן וְתִירֹשׁ סְמַכְתִּיו
וּלְכָה אֵפוֹא מָה אֶעֱשֶׂה בְּנִי: לח וַיֹּאמֶר עֵשָׂו אֶל־אָבִיו
הַבְרָכָה אַחַת הִוא־לְךָ אָבִי בָּרֲכֵנִי גַם־אָנִי אָבִי וַיִּשָּׂא
עֵשָׂו קֹלוֹ וַיֵּבְךְּ:

[34] When Esau heard his father's words, he
burst into wild and bitter sobbing, and said to
his father, "Bless me too, Father!"
[35] But he answered, "Your brother came with
guile and took away your blessing."
[36] [Esau] said, "Was he, then, named Jacob that
he might supplant me these two times? First he
took away my birthright and now he has taken
away my blessing!" And he added, "Have you not
reserved a blessing for me?"
[37] Isaac answered, saying to Esau, "But I have
made him master over you: I have given him
all his brothers for servants, and sustained him
with grain and wine. What, then, can I still do
for you, my son?"
[38] And Esau said to his father, "Have you but
one blessing, Father? Bless me too, Father!" And
Esau wept aloud.

[34] **Bless me too, Father!:** Esau had offhandedly dispar-
aged the birthright, but now, tragically, he understands that

he has forfeited the blessing. The birthright was a responsibility of which he wished to be relieved, but the blessing is a gift of which he is now deprived.

[36] First he took away my birthright and now he has taken away my blessing!: Esau, in a fit of emotion, conflates the loss of the birthright with his loss of the blessing. In fact, at this moment he is informing his father of his transfer of the birthright. Esau apparently sees his sale of the birthright as legitimizing, in a certain sense, Jacob's receipt of the blessing. Therefore, rather than asking Isaac to return to him the blessing already given to Jacob, Esau asks for some other, different blessing.

Have you not reserved a blessing for me?: Esau had viewed the blessing from Isaac, an outstandingly righteous man, as his only hope of finding a place with God in the World to Come. Although Esau feels that he is the master in this world, he is not at all confident of what his destiny will be in the World to Come.

[37] But I have made him master over you: I have given him all his brothers for servants: Esau understands at this moment that since Jacob has already received the blessing, apparently he, Esau, must obtain his "salvation from hell" through Jacob (and the Western world through the adoption of the religion of the Jews). This is the cause of Esau's anguished wail.

[38] Have you but one blessing, Father?: Esau is not at all happy with the prospect of receiving his religion through Jacob. Only his fear of losing his place in the World to Come, and his realization that Jacob's blessings can at this point never be undone, allow him to be reconciled with such a fate.

But even now Esau is still hoping to receive an independent blessing from Isaac – his own path to the World to Come, not connected in any way with Jacob.

32.15. Esau Receives the Blessing of "Opposition to Jacob" (27: 39-40)

לט וַיַּעַן יִצְחָק אָבִיו וַיֹּאמֶר אֵלָיו הִנֵּה מִשְׁמַנֵּי הָאָרֶץ
יִהְיֶה מוֹשָׁבֶךָ וּמִטַּל הַשָּׁמַיִם מֵעָל: מ וְעַל־חַרְבְּךָ תִחְיֶה
וְאֶת־אָחִיךָ תַּעֲבֹד וְהָיָה כַּאֲשֶׁר תָּרִיד וּפָרַקְתָּ עֻלּוֹ מֵעַל
צַוָּארֶךָ:

[39] And his father Isaac answered, saying to him, "See, your abode shall enjoy the fat of the earth And the dew of heaven above.
[40] Yet by your sword you shall live, And you shall serve your brother; But when you grow restive, You shall break his yoke from your neck."

Esau's hopes for an independent blessing are not realized. He indeed receives a blessing, but it is again connected with his brother.

[39] See, your abode shall enjoy the fat of the earth And the dew of heaven above: This blessing is similar to Jacob's ("May God give you of the dew of heaven and the fat of the earth"), but the sources on which it draws are here enumerated in the opposite order. The starting point of Jacob's vitality is "the dew of heaven," but for Esau it is the "fat of the earth." This reciprocal relationship can easily develop into conflict, but it can also be a source of mutual enrichment.

[40] Yet by your sword you shall live: Esau's primary means of changing the world will be his sword, whereas Jacob was told (27:29): "Let peoples serve you, and nations bow to you"– with no need to wage war. Jacob's material well-being, and the admiration he receives from the nations, will be natural consequences of his spirituality, while Esau is characterized by his use of military means to subjugate humankind.

But when you grow restive, You shall break his yoke from your neck: Esau's most important function is to serve as opposition to Jacob. He will serve Jacob until he, Esau, "becomes restive"; that is, Esau will always provoke confrontation with Jacob, and be a source of trouble for him. Jacob therefore has no choice but to conduct himself properly with Esau, so as not to arouse Esau's "indignation," which would lead to disaster in their relationship.

32.16. Esau Threatens to Kill Jacob (27:41)

מא וַיִּשְׂטֹם עֵשָׂו אֶת־יַעֲקֹב עַל־הַבְּרָכָה אֲשֶׁר בֵּרְכוֹ אָבִיו
וַיֹּאמֶר עֵשָׂו בְּלִבּוֹ יִקְרְבוּ יְמֵי אֵבֶל אָבִי וְאַהַרְגָה אֶת־
יַעֲקֹב אָחִי:

[41] Now Esau harbored a grudge against Jacob because of the blessing which his father had given him, and Esau said to himself, "Let but the mourning period of my father come, and I will kill my brother Jacob."

[41] Now Esau harbored a grudge against Jacob: Esau now hated his brother for the blessing that Jacob had received, and also for his own blessing, which, as he believed, now bound him humiliatingly to Jacob.

And I will kill my brother Jacob: But why did Esau feel a need to talk about the murder, instead of just carrying it out straightaway? And why does he invoke their brotherhood? Unconsciously, it seems, Esau is not really interested in this murder, and he therefore poses his own psychological barriers to it. The first obstacle is temporary: So long as Isaac is alive, Jacob must not be killed. But the second barrier is a moral and ethical one: Esau calls Jacob his "brother." Esau understands that he and Jacob have common roots and a common source of vitality, and that their connection must therefore not be destroyed.

32.17. Rebekah Sends Jacob to Haran (27:42-46)

מב וַיֻּגַּד לְרִבְקָה אֶת־דִּבְרֵי עֵשָׂו בְּנָהּ הַגָּדֹל וַתִּשְׁלַח וַתִּקְרָא לְיַעֲקֹב בְּנָהּ הַקָּטָן וַתֹּאמֶר אֵלָיו הִנֵּה עֵשָׂו אָחִיךָ מִתְנַחֵם לְךָ לְהָרְגֶךָ: **מג** וְעַתָּה בְנִי שְׁמַע בְּקֹלִי וְקוּם בְּרַח־לְךָ אֶל־לָבָן אָחִי חָרָנָה: **מד** וְיָשַׁבְתָּ עִמּוֹ יָמִים אֲחָדִים עַד אֲשֶׁר־תָּשׁוּב חֲמַת אָחִיךָ: **מה** עַד־שׁוּב אַף־אָחִיךָ מִמְּךָ וְשָׁכַח אֵת אֲשֶׁר־עָשִׂיתָ לּוֹ וְשָׁלַחְתִּי וּלְקַחְתִּיךָ מִשָּׁם לָמָה אֶשְׁכַּל גַּם־שְׁנֵיכֶם יוֹם אֶחָד: **מו** וַתֹּאמֶר רִבְקָה אֶל־יִצְחָק קַצְתִּי בְחַיַּי מִפְּנֵי בְּנוֹת חֵת אִם־לֹקֵחַ יַעֲקֹב אִשָּׁה מִבְּנוֹת־חֵת כָּאֵלֶּה מִבְּנוֹת הָאָרֶץ לָמָּה לִי חַיִּים:

[42] When the words of her older son Esau were reported to Rebekah, she sent for her younger

son Jacob and said to him, "Your brother Esau is consoling himself by planning to kill you.

[43] Now, my son, listen to me. Flee at once to Haran, to my brother Laban.

[44] Stay with him a while, until your brother's fury subsides–

[45] until your brother's anger against you subsides–and he forgets what you have done to him. Then I will fetch you from there. Let me not lose you both in one day!"

[46] Rebekah said to Isaac, "I am disgusted with my life because of the Hittite women. If Jacob marries a Hittite woman like these, from among the native women, what good will life be to me?"

[42] The words of her older son Esau were reported to Rebekah ... [45] "Let me not lose you both in one day!": The Torah emphasizes here that because Esau too is Rebekah's son, she is acting in both their interests. Rebekah protects Esau from fratricide, because when one brother kills the other, it becomes impossible to maintain a relationship of any kind with even the surviving one.

She sent for her younger son Jacob and said to him: Rebekah again intervenes in the situation. We see here what a critical role the Matriarchs played in deciding along which lines the lineage of the Jewish people would be determined.

[45] Then I will fetch you from there: From verse 35:8 we may conclude that Rebekah at some point did send her nurse Deborah for Jacob (see also 24:59). But Jacob did not return immediately to his father's house, and Rebekah died, never seeing Jacob again.

[46] If Jacob marries a Hittite woman like these, from among the native women, what good will life be to me?: Besides wanting to put distance between him and Esau, Rebekah sends Jacob to Haran with the intent that he will marry Laban's daughters. This was apparently her plan from the very beginning; it did not arise only as a response to Esau's anger.

32.18. Jacob Receives the Blessing of Abraham (28: 1-4)

א וַיִּקְרָא יִצְחָק אֶל־יַעֲקֹב וַיְבָרֶךְ אֹתוֹ וַיְצַוֵּהוּ וַיֹּאמֶר לוֹ לֹא־תִקַּח אִשָּׁה מִבְּנוֹת כְּנָעַן: ב קוּם לֵךְ פַּדֶּנָה אֲרָם בֵּיתָה בְתוּאֵל אֲבִי אִמֶּךָ וְקַח־לְךָ מִשָּׁם אִשָּׁה מִבְּנוֹת לָבָן אֲחִי אִמֶּךָ: ג וְאֵל שַׁדַּי יְבָרֵךְ אֹתְךָ וְיַפְרְךָ וְיַרְבֶּךָ וְהָיִיתָ לִקְהַל עַמִּים: ד וְיִתֶּן־לְךָ אֶת־בִּרְכַּת אַבְרָהָם לְךָ וּלְזַרְעֲךָ אִתָּךְ לְרִשְׁתְּךָ אֶת־אֶרֶץ מְגֻרֶיךָ אֲשֶׁר־נָתַן אֱלֹהִים לְאַבְרָהָם:

[1] So Isaac sent for Jacob and blessed him. He instructed him, saying, "You shall not take a wife from among the Canaanite women.
[2] Up, go to Paddan-aram, to the house of Bethuel, your mother's father, and take a wife there from among the daughters of Laban, your mother's brother,
[3] May El Shaddai bless you, make you fertile and numerous, so that you become an assembly of peoples.
[4] May He grant the blessing of Abraham to you and your offspring, that you may possess

the land where you are sojourning, which God
assigned to Abraham."

[1] So Isaac sent for Jacob and blessed him: In this story, then, there are three different blessings that Isaac has given his sons. The first blessing Isaac gave Jacob, believing that it was Esau. The second blessing Isaac gave Esau, when he already knew that his first blessing had been given to Jacob. And the third blessing is given to Jacob here.

[3] May El Shaddai bless you … [4] May He grant the blessing of Abraham … that you may possess the land where you are sojourning, which God assigned to Abraham: Of those three blessings, only the last is the "blessing of the Covenant," mentioning the Land of Israel and Abraham. Thus, the legacy of the Covenant was from the very beginning intended for Jacob; only the "blessing of power" was at issue. At first Isaac had reserved that blessing for Esau, but in the end, through Rebekah's intervention, Jacob received both blessings.

[2] Up, go to Paddan-aram, to the house of Bethuel, your mother's father, and take a wife there from among the daughters of Laban, your mother's brother. [3] May El Shaddai bless you: The Blessing of the Covenant is associated with proper marriage. Only by marrying the daughters of Laban, rather than taking a wife from Egypt or Canaan, as Ishmael and Esau did, can Jacob be worthy of receiving the blessing of Abraham. Jacob's parents have brought him to a certain point of development, but now the process of his further education and advancement is no longer in their hands. From this point forward it is Jacob's wife who will determine to what level he will ultimately rise in life.

32.19. Rebekah, Mother of Jacob and Esau (28:5)

הַ וַיִּשְׁלַח יִצְחָק אֶת־יַעֲקֹב וַיֵּלֶךְ פַּדֶּנָה אֲרָם אֶל־לָבָן בֶּן־
בְּתוּאֵל הָאֲרַמִּי אֲחִי רִבְקָה אֵם יַעֲקֹב וְעֵשָׂו׃

[5] Then Isaac sent Jacob off, and he went to Paddan-aram, to Laban the son of Bethuel the Aramean, the brother of Rebekah, mother of Jacob and Esau.

Rebekah, mother of Jacob and Esau: Yet again the Torah emphasizes that Rebekah is the "mother of Jacob and Esau," i.e., she acts in the best interests of both. It was important not only for Jacob that he would receive the blessings, but for Esau as well. That is, it was important for the Western (Christian) world in the long run that both of those blessings went to Jacob. Indeed, Jacob will be able on that basis to create the Jewish nation, from which, in the end, Esau will also receive Divine light. For without the Jewish people, Esau cannot build his relationship with God.

32.20. Esau Takes a Wife from the Daughters of Ishmael (28:6-9)

וַ וַיַּרְא עֵשָׂו כִּי־בֵרַךְ יִצְחָק אֶת־יַעֲקֹב וְשִׁלַּח אֹתוֹ פַּדֶּנָה
אֲרָם לָקַחַת־לוֹ מִשָּׁם אִשָּׁה בְּבָרְכוֹ אֹתוֹ וַיְצַו עָלָיו
לֵאמֹר לֹא־תִקַּח אִשָּׁה מִבְּנוֹת כְּנָעַן׃ זַ וַיִּשְׁמַע יַעֲקֹב
אֶל־אָבִיו וְאֶל־אִמּוֹ וַיֵּלֶךְ פַּדֶּנָה אֲרָם׃ חַ וַיַּרְא עֵשָׂו כִּי
רָעוֹת בְּנוֹת כְּנָעַן בְּעֵינֵי יִצְחָק אָבִיו׃ טַ וַיֵּלֶךְ עֵשָׂו אֶל־
יִשְׁמָעֵאל וַיִּקַּח אֶת־מָחֲלַת ׀ בַּת־יִשְׁמָעֵאל בֶּן־אַבְרָהָם
אֲחוֹת נְבָיוֹת עַל־נָשָׁיו לוֹ לְאִשָּׁה׃

[6] When Esau saw that Isaac had blessed Jacob and sent him off to Paddan-aram to take a wife from there, charging him, as he blessed him, "You shall not take a wife from among the Canaanite women," [7] and that Jacob had obeyed his father and mother and gone to Paddan-aram, [8] Esau realized that the Canaanite women displeased his father Isaac. [9] So Esau went to Ishmael and took to wife, in addition to the wives he had, Mahalath the daughter of Ishmael son of Abraham, sister of Nebaioth.

[9] So Esau went … and took Mahalath the daughter of Ishmael: At the beginning of this chapter we noted that the narrative of the blessings is framed on both ends by the stories of Esau's wives. It begins with Esau taking Canaanite wives and ends with Esau marrying a girl from the Ishmaelite clan.

[8] Esau realized that the Canaanite women displeased his father Isaac: Esau respects his father. Seeing that Isaac wishes to marry off his children to *ivrim*, Hebrews, Esau wants to take a step in that direction.

[9] So Esau … took to wife, in addition to the wives he had: Nonetheless, we see neither remorse nor repentance from Esau. He marries Ishmael's daughter not *instead* of Canaanite wives, but *in addition* to them. His first two wives continue to be "a source of bitterness to Isaac and Rebekah," and it is possible that this was one of the reasons behind Esau's further separation from his family and his departure to Seir, even before Jacob had returned to the Land of Israel (32:4).

Weekly Portion
Vayetze

Chapter 33

Jacob's Ladder

33.1. Jacob Departs for Haran (28:10)

י וַיֵּצֵא יַעֲקֹב מִבְּאֵר שָׁבַע וַיֵּלֶךְ חָרָנָה׃

[10] Jacob left Beer-sheba, and set out for Haran.

Like our other Patriarchs, Jacob has two weekly portions devoted to his life story: *Vayetze* and *Vayishlach*. In both, he is the leading character.

Portion *Vayetze* (lit., "And he departed") tells the story of Jacob's exile, in which he acquires the character traits that he will need later, upon his return to the Land of Israel, for building his life there. The meaning of that exile for Jacob is that, upon his return, he shall have achieved a new level of personal development. It is this idea that Jacob envisions in his dream of the stairway (lit., "ladder").

The blessing that Isaac gave Jacob was preordained for his "hybrid" son – Jacob with Esau's hands. For that blessing to be realized, Jacob could not just remain himself; he had to gradually integrate the qualities of Esau into his own character.

This process began with Jacob's purchase of the birthright from Esau, after which Isaac's blessing then followed; then, in Haran, Jacob marries Leah, who was originally meant to marry Esau. And finally, Jacob's transformation becomes complete with his victory in his struggle with the angel.

The entire *Vayetze* portion is largely the story of the evolution of "Esau-ness" within Jacob. Jacob, once he has been augmented with those Esau characteristics, will receive the name "Israel," as described in weekly portion *Vayishlach*, which follows this one, and relates the story of Jacob's life in his own land.

Unlike Abraham and Isaac, each of whom had one son who continued the Covenant with God while the other son stepped aside, all of Jacob's children comprise the "chosen people." Thus, Jacob is a "nation in miniature," and his departure to Haran is a prototype of the Jewish *galut*, exile.

33.2. The Jewish Nation Takes Form in Exile

Jacob goes into exile in order to marry the daughters of Laban the Aramean, a necessary step for the formation of the Jewish people. Here we have a general principle: The Jewish nation takes form in exile, in the most prominent world centers. It must happen this way so that the Jews will be connected in close affinity with all of humankind by their unique spiritual threads, and thus be able to impart Divine light to the entire world.

As discussed earlier in this commentary, the Jewish people in the initial period of their history were in close contact with two great civilizations: Babylon and Egypt. Jacob now goes to Haran (Babylon), and will return from there after he has begotten children (that is, after he has become a family, "the house of Jacob"). He will then go down with all his descendants to Egypt, whence several centuries later the newly formed Jewish nation will emerge.

Babylon and Egypt are the two original branches of human culture that arose in the Garden of Eden (2:11). Using the synthesis of these two cultures as their foundation, the Jewish people "recreate" the Garden of Eden as a reference point for the further development of mankind.

Unlike other nations that are formed as a result of their historical development in their own territory, the Jewish nation arrives in its land as a ready-made people with its own character and teachings. Therefore, unlike other peoples for whom the relationship with their country is one of "child and parent" (enshrined in the terms "Motherland," "Vaterland," and the like), the relationship of the Jewish people to the Land of Israel is rather like that of husband and wife; that is, the union of two adults. The Jewish people must therefore take form first in Babylon (the paternal aspect), and then later in Egypt (the maternal aspect). Then, in a process that parallels human development, they "leave their father and mother" in order to contract a "marriage" with their land.

33.3. Jacob "Collides" with the Land (28:11)

יא וַיִּפְגַּע בַּמָּקוֹם וַיָּלֶן שָׁם כִּי־בָא הַשֶּׁמֶשׁ וַיִּקַּח מֵאַבְנֵי
הַמָּקוֹם וַיָּשֶׂם מְרַאֲשֹׁתָיו וַיִּשְׁכַּב בַּמָּקוֹם הַהוּא:

[11] He came upon a certain place and stopped there for the night, for the sun had set. Taking one of the stones of that place, he put it under his head and lay down in that place.

[11] He came upon a certain place: Literally, "he collided with the place." At the moment he parts with the Land of Israel, Jacob "collides" with it. It is essential that his passing into exile will not happen smoothly, but through a collision, a crisis. Before leaving the Land of Israel Jacob must recognize the importance of this Land, so that during his exile he will feel the need to return to it.

Says the Midrash: Jacob wanted to pass by this place, and continue further on his journey, but God said: "How can we allow him not to see just what kind of place this is?!" The sun then set unexpectedly, and Jacob was forced to spend the night.

Sometimes it happens in life that we want to push forward, but circumstances suddenly arise that detain and delay us. We ought not treat that kind of situation simply as a hindrance or obstacle. It just might be a signal from Above, telling us, as it were: Have a look around you, ponder the events, and try to figure out what new idea God is trying to tell you.

Jacob's dream and his actions upon awaking mark the inauguration of his unique approach to relating to God. And since all this happened with the setting of the sun, and concurrent with his going into "exile" (which is also called "night"), the Midrash sees in this verse an allusion to the traditional evening prayer, which Jacob instituted as a means of establishing contact with God in situations of darkness and exile.

We have already cited the Midrash that states that Abraham established the morning prayer service, *Shacharit*, because he related to God as the giver of life, an aspect most clearly manifested in the morning, when a person awakens from sleep. And Isaac established *Minchah*, the afternoon prayer service, at that time of day when one is expected to evaluate everything he has done in the course of the day, and to give an account of his actions. Finally, *Ma'ariv*, the evening prayer, was established by Jacob. It represents the idea that one can make contact with God at night when he feels most lonely and vulnerable, being at that time removed from life and from society.

The exile of the Jewish people from their Land took place in parallel with the exile of Divinity from the world. But the Jewish people continued to testify to the unity of the Creator even in exile, when the Divine presence was estranged from the world and direct Revelation ceased to occur. This is an important element of the role that the Jewish people have played in the history of mankind.

33.4. The Dream of the Stairway (28:12)

יב וַיַּחֲלֹם וְהִנֵּה סֻלָּם מֻצָּב אַרְצָה וְרֹאשׁוֹ מַגִּיעַ הַשָּׁמָיְמָה וְהִנֵּה מַלְאֲכֵי אֱלֹהִים עֹלִים וְיֹרְדִים בּוֹ:

[12] He had a dream; a stairway was set on the ground and its top reached to the sky, and angels of God were going up and down on it.

[12] A stairway ... and angels of God were going up and down on it: The word *vehinneh*, "and behold," which appears twice in the original Hebrew text, but is grammatically superfluous, interrupts the flow of the text, and is therefore indicative of some non-obvious meaning. The Midrash finds in this passage the idea that Jacob is himself the staircase between heaven and earth. Thus, *bo*, means not "on it," but, more literally, "in him" – Jacob. That is, the angels are ascending and descending inside Jacob himself.

Were going up and down on it: The angels first ascended the stairway from earth to heaven, and only after that did they descend on it back to earth. Thus, these are not angels who live in heaven, but angels living in the heart of man. First they ascend, and although they are tempted to seize the opportunity to remain there, at the top of the stairs, their actual goal is different. So they "descend" from Heaven back into this world, carrying with them what they have acquired in those upper realms.

Likewise, a human who rises into metaphysical worlds should not simply "dissolve in God." No, he must release that acquired light back into this material world. Man's divine task is not to "protect" his soul from this world, but on the contrary, to correct and improve this world. Only by doing so does the soul achieve the spiritual advancement that it needs in order to communicate with God.

Tradition says that "a dream is one sixtieth part of prophecy." Prophecy is very much associated with the Land of Israel. When the people of Israel go into *galut*, exile, into the "night," they utter the evening prayer and see prophetic dreams. Dreaming is a form of nostalgia. When a person is already far removed from some uplifting incident that he once experienced, he relives it in a dream. We will see later that prophecy comes to Jacob only in a dreaming state.

No such thing is found earlier in the Torah. Only once did God appear to Abraham while he slept. In all other instances He reveals himself to both Abraham and Isaac with no need for dreams of any kind. But to Jacob God appears only in dreams. Dreams are, in a certain sense, prophecy in exile.

33.5. God's Covenant with Jacob (28:13-15)

יג וְהִנֵּה יי נִצָּב עָלָיו וַיֹּאמַר אֲנִי יי אֱלֹהֵי אַבְרָהָם אָבִיךָ

וֵאלֹהֵי יִצְחָק הָאָרֶץ אֲשֶׁר אַתָּה שֹׁכֵב עָלֶיהָ לְךָ אֶתְּנֶנָּה
וּלְזַרְעֶךָ: **יד** וְהָיָה זַרְעֲךָ כַּעֲפַר הָאָרֶץ וּפָרַצְתָּ יָמָּה
וָקֵדְמָה וְצָפֹנָה וָנֶגְבָּה וְנִבְרְכוּ בְךָ כָּל־מִשְׁפְּחֹת הָאֲדָמָה
וּבְזַרְעֶךָ: **טו** וְהִנֵּה אָנֹכִי עִמָּךְ וּשְׁמַרְתִּיךָ בְּכֹל אֲשֶׁר־תֵּלֵךְ
וַהֲשִׁבֹתִיךָ אֶל־הָאֲדָמָה הַזֹּאת כִּי לֹא אֶעֱזָבְךָ עַד אֲשֶׁר
אִם־עָשִׂיתִי אֵת אֲשֶׁר־דִּבַּרְתִּי לָךְ:

*[13] And the Lord was standing beside him and
He said, "I am the Lord, the God of your father
Abraham and the God of Isaac: the ground on
which you are lying I will assign to you and to
your offspring.*
*[14] Your descendants shall be as the dust of the
earth; you shall spread out to the west and to
the east, to the north and to the south. All the
families of the earth shall bless themselves by
you and your descendants.*
*[15] Remember, I am with you: I will protect you
wherever you go and will bring you back to this
land. I will not leave you until I have done what
I have promised you."*

**[13] I am the Lord, the God of your father Abraham and
the God of Isaac: the ground on which you are lying I will
assign to you and to your offspring:** Having acquired the
birthright and received his father's blessing, Jacob enters
into a Covenant with God. The covenant begins by mentioning Abraham and Isaac. Since this is the covenant of the
Patriarchs, its essence is a connection with God through the
Jewish people and the Land of Israel.

Jacob is very doubtful of the path he is taking. On his
own initiative he has embarked on the path of acquiring

the characteristics of Esau (which began the moment that he bought the birthright from him), but under pressure from outside he is now moving even further in that direction. His mother forces him to receive a blessing. Laban forces him to marry Leah. An angel forces him to fight. An encounter with Esau forces Jacob to rebuild his relationship with him. And the incident with Shechem forces Jacob's children to fight. Thus, Jacob is constantly being pushed towards becoming *Israel*. Evidently, following this path is for Jacob himself highly problematic, and in this he is vastly different from Abraham and Isaac.

Even after receiving his father's blessing, Jacob is still in doubt, and, in a certain sense, almost his entire life can be seen as a process of ridding himself of these doubts. The process begins with God promising to support him and confirming his status.

Abraham and Isaac follow their own paths. As leaders within their system, they lead Jacob, who is their subordinate and underling. Thus, Abraham and Isaac show the *gadlut*, "greatness," of their attributes, *Chesed* and *Gevurah*, while Jacob represents the *katnut*, "smallness," of his category, which is *Tiferet*, adornment. The *gadlut* of the *Sefirah* of *tiferet* is Israel.

[14] Your descendants shall be as the dust of the earth: Speaking with Abraham, God compared his future descendants with the stars in the sky (15:5), while in this conversation with Jacob the Jewish people are likened to the dust of the earth. Both of those are innumerable quantities – something eternal that cannot be destroyed. But stars represent a state of greatness, while dust is insignificant. Thus, God tells Abraham about the Jews' status in the Land of Israel, of heaven and of *geulah* (redemption). But to Jacob He speaks of the dust of the earth and *galut* (exile).

The blessing that Abraham receives describes an ideal state. The stars in the sky can be neither touched nor harmed. But Jacob's blessing describes the reality. In order to survive their long history of exile, the Jewish people must have the property of sand. Even when trampled underfoot, they will neither die nor disappear.

[15] I will protect you wherever you go: Jacob had to follow the path of exile so that later he could not only return to his prior level, but also rise above it.

The nature and characteristics of Jacob (Jacob, who is not yet Israel) gives rise to *Exilic* Jewry, who are perpetually dependent on others and forced to live in submission to them. The Jews are subordinated physically, politically, and spiritually. Their political circumstances, their surrounding culture, and their whole way of life in the Diaspora are determined not by the Jews themselves, but by the surrounding nations. In this sense, the Jews in exile are an "object," not "subject," of history.

When Jacob receives the name "Israel," although he appears to be mastering Esau's qualities, he is integrating the paths traveled by Abraham, Isaac, and Jacob.

33.6. Possessing the Land

The promise of "The ground on which you are lying I will assign to you and to your offspring" is directly related to the Jewish mission: "All the families of the earth shall bless themselves by you and your descendants" (v. 13 and 14).

In seven places in the book of *Bereshit* (Genesis) the Almighty makes a covenant with the Patriarchs, and in all of those the covenant speaks of the Land. Not only of Jewish life in the Land, but of Jewish political authority there ("I will give you the land"). This is the central principle of the Divine promise.

In the traditional Western view, "political" considerations are incompatible with "spiritual" ones, and the two are often regarded as even antithetical. But here we see that the Book of Genesis understands things differently. By virtue of their state the Jewish people become a historical entity, realizing their pan-national existence in the Holy Land. As a result, a nationwide dialogue begins with God, thanks to which the nations of the world also receive Divine light. (It is therefore no coincidence that the history of the ancient Jewish state – the books of Joshua, Judges, Samuel, and Kings – were included in the Holy Scriptures. That is, they are a part of the Divine revelation.)

The central position that the Land occupies in God's covenant with the Patriarchs, but with no specific mention of any commandments, demonstrates that Jewish life in the Land of Israel is primary, while the commandments are only secondary to it, i.e., they are only a tool for securing life in the Land of Israel. The giving of the commandments is itself only secondary to the giving of the Land.

33.7. The Covenant Concerning the Return from Exile

God concludes an accord with Jacob regarding his return from exile. A people that goes into a long exile will most often not return. They will either find a new place to settle or disperse and disappear. God here promises that besides not allowing the Jewish people to disappear, He will also return them to their land, along with the wealth they have accumulated during their exile. For this scheme, which later in Jewish history was realized repeatedly, the Patriarchs were intended to serve as the first prototype. But neither Abraham nor Isaac was a nation – the nation begins with Jacob. Jacob's exile therefore represents the first exile of the Jewish nation.

Jacob, forced to leave the land, is feeling significant apprehension. Will his departure destroy his connection with his family and his legacy? Will Esau, who remains behind, take possession of the Land, which will then become Esau's country? God therefore promises Jacob that this will not happen.

The essence of Jacob is the Judaism of *galut*, of exile. And it is therefore Jacob with whom God makes a covenant for his preservation in exile, and his eventual return to his land.

33.8. "The Lord is Present in This Place" (28:16)

טז וַיִּיקַץ יַעֲקֹב מִשְּׁנָתוֹ וַיֹּאמֶר אָכֵן יֵשׁ יי בַּמָּקוֹם הַזֶּה וְאָנֹכִי לֹא יָדָעְתִּי:

> *[16] Jacob awoke from his sleep and said, "Surely the Lord is present in this place, and I did not know it!"*

[16] Surely the Lord is present in this place, and I did not know it: As already noted, the Kabbalah interprets the word *Zeh*, "this," as meaning the God of this world, and *Anochi*, emphatic "I," as referring to the God of the World to Come.

In other words, until now Jacob was not aware that *Anochi*, the God of the World to Come, can be revealed in "this" world, and that there is even a particular place uniquely designated for connecting the two worlds. That place is critically important for the Jewish people because it serves precisely that purpose: Integrating the *Anochi* and the *Zeh* into a single, unified whole.

Many people consider the idea that God's special presence would inhabit a particular place unacceptable or "primitive." Those people find it much easier to assert that God is present everywhere, because acknowledging His special Divine presence in a specific place is for them problematic. This is because their sense of God's transcendence, universality, and absolute nature implies to them that the idea that God would occupy a "distinct and definite location" is unacceptable. This problem of perception bears a certain similarity to the attitude regarding the idea of a Chosen People, which is likewise deemed problematic.

In both cases, however, the "choosing" is carried out not for the sake of the particular place or people *per se*, but in order to transmit Divine light through them to the rest of the world and the rest of humanity. The notion of the holiness of a particular place, as discovered by Jacob, contradicts neither the concept of God's transcendence nor the idea of His manifestation in the rest of the world, for, in fact, it only supplements and reinforces them.

Thus, before departing from the Land of Israel, Jacob must receive some additional "piece of Zionism," so as not to succumb to the great cosmopolitan temptation to remain in the Diaspora instead of returning to the Land. It is essential that Jacob be firmly tied to the Land, and to this end God makes a Covenant with him, thus uniting the *Anochi* and the *Zeh*.

We have already noted that from the point of view of Judaism, this world we live in is no less Divine than the World to Come, and God's presence in this world is no less significant than His presence in that other one. The very first chapter of our book, Genesis, repeats again and again, at each stage of the Creation, that "God saw that it was good."

Man's purpose by no means consists in allowing his soul to flee from this world into the World to Come (as Gnostic religious systems, for example, like to tell us). Rather, man's purpose is to effect the unification of this world and the World to Come. What Jacob understood upon awakening was precisely that.

33.9. The Trepidation of Experiencing Holiness (28:17)

יז וַיִּירָא וַיֹּאמַר מַה־נּוֹרָא הַמָּקוֹם הַזֶּה אֵין זֶה כִּי אִם־
בֵּית אֱלֹהִים וְזֶה שַׁעַר הַשָּׁמָיִם:

[17] Shaken, he said, "How awesome is this place! This is none other than the abode of God, and that is the gateway to heaven."

[17] Shaken, he said, "How awesome is this place!: Instead of "shaken," a more literal translation of *va-yee-rah* would be "he was overcome with fear." We have encountered the Hebrew root *Y-R-'* – "(to) fear" – previously, in the story of the *Akedah* (ch. 22). Both *va-yee-rah* and *no-ra* ("awesome") of this verse derive from that root.

This is none other than the abode of God, and that is the gateway to heaven: Jacob's fervor is here directed equally to this particular place, Bethel, and to the country as a whole. It is brought on by a sense of the grandeur of the Land of Israel, and the understanding that living there is truly difficult, because of the Divinity that manifests so powerfully there, and therefore demands so much from its residents. Because Jacob, by his inner nature, is a Jew of the Diaspora, he finds the Land of Israel rather frightening, even as he is, at the same time, inexorably drawn to it.

For classical Diaspora Jewry, the idea that a place is holy can be a source of internal conflict. Certain Diaspora Jews will therefore fail to notice this type of holiness at all. That is, they will say that there is no concept of "sanctity of place" in Judaism, but only "sanctity of time," as expressed through the Sabbath and the Jewish festivals. But some will go so far as to do battle even with that idea – under the guise of militant Jewish anti-Zionism, for example.

The fact is, however, that the true life force of the Jewish Diaspora community derives precisely from actualizing its connection with the Land of Israel, and "plugging into" it. In our times especially, the most important and effective means of preserving the vitality of the Jewish Diaspora communities is their direct involvement in Israeli current affairs, their maintaining an emotionally personal and vital connection with the State of Israel, and their participation in Israel-oriented projects. Jacob likewise, notwithstanding that he must go into exile, revives his connection with the land and draws his vitality from it.

33.10. Stone as Monument (28:18)

יח וַיַּשְׁכֵּם יַעֲקֹב בַּבֹּקֶר וַיִּקַּח אֶת־הָאֶבֶן אֲשֶׁר־שָׂם מְרַאֲשֹׁתָיו וַיָּשֶׂם אֹתָהּ מַצֵּבָה וַיִּצֹק שֶׁמֶן עַל־רֹאשָׁהּ:

[18] Early in the morning, Jacob took the stone that he had put under his head and set it up as a pillar and poured oil on the top of it.

[18] Jacob took the stone that he had put under his head: For the monument he is about to create, Jacob takes none other than the stone on which he's been sleeping. Essentially, he wishes to construct a monument to the "stairway reaching to the sky" of which he has dreamt.

And poured oil on the top of it: In such contexts "oil" always means olive oil. Here, the libation itself constitutes the consecration of the monument. We encounter this form of worship for the first time in this passage, but later in the Torah such libations of oil are the accepted method of all consecrations – of the Temple vessels, for example, as well as the anointing of priests and kings. In fact, the very word "messiah" (Hebr. *mashiach*) means "the anointed one" – that is, the king.

In ancient times olive oil was a primary source of illumination. Anointing with olive oil thus symbolized that the person or vessel being anointed – or the stone, as in this story – is acknowledged as a source of light to others.

And set it up as a pillar: Constructing any such stone monument (*matzevah*) was later strictly forbidden to the Children of Israel (Deut. 16:22). Only altars consisting of many stones were allowed. The Talmud notes in this connection: "What was beloved to God in the times of the Patriarchs (e.g., the stone here erected by Jacob) became hateful to Him and prohibited in the era of their descendants." A monolith symbolizes Divine Providence as directed toward the individual, whereas an altar, a single structure of many stones, represents God's Providence with respect to the entire nation. After the birth of the Jewish nation it was forbidden to erect a "monument," because an individual Jew could no longer have that kind of direct communication with God. Thenceforth, such communication could only happen within the context of the nation as a whole.

33.11. Bethel Had Previously Been Called "Luz" (28:19)

יט וַיִּקְרָא אֶת־שֵׁם־הַמָּקוֹם הַהוּא בֵּית־אֵל וְאוּלָם לוּז
שֵׁם־הָעִיר לָרִאשֹׁנָה:

[19] He named that site Bethel; but previously the name of the city had been Luz.

[19] **Bethel:** We have met Bethel earlier in the Torah. It was one of Abraham's stopovers during his southbound migration. (12:8). But here Jacob reimagines that place and updates its name.

Previously the name of the city had been Luz: The Torah's mention of the former name is important not only for its historical value, for it has a metaphysical meaning as well. There is a Jewish idea that *luz* is the name of a certain tiny but indestructible bone in the human body. (It cannot be burned, wear out, or the like.) And from just this bone humans will be resurrected at the end of time. The city of Bethel and Jacob's Ladder are a *luz* bone for the Jewish nation as a whole – an indestructible point from which the national presence of Jews in the Land of Israel will at the proper time be resurrected.

33.12. Mountain, Field, and House (28:20-22)

כ וַיִּדַּר יַעֲקֹב נֶדֶר לֵאמֹר אִם־יִהְיֶה אֱלֹהִים עִמָּדִי
וּשְׁמָרַנִי בַּדֶּרֶךְ הַזֶּה אֲשֶׁר אָנֹכִי הוֹלֵךְ וְנָתַן־לִי לֶחֶם
לֶאֱכֹל וּבֶגֶד לִלְבֹּשׁ: כא וְשַׁבְתִּי בְשָׁלוֹם אֶל־בֵּית אָבִי
וְהָיָה יי לִי לֵאלֹהִים: כב וְהָאֶבֶן הַזֹּאת אֲשֶׁר־שַׂמְתִּי
מַצֵּבָה יִהְיֶה בֵּית אֱלֹהִים ...

[20] Jacob then made a vow, saying, "If God remains with me, if He protects me on this journey that I am making, and gives me bread to eat and clothing to wear,
[21] and if I return safe to my father's house – the Lord shall be my God.
[22] And this stone, which I have set up as a pillar, shall be God's abode; ...

[22] And this stone ... shall be God's abode: In Abraham's encounter with God, the place of their meeting is called a "mountain" (i.e., Mount Moriah, 22:2). Isaac's place of meeting God is a "field" (24:63). But Jacob experiences the meeting place as "God's abode," a whole new level of awareness in the encounter.

Abraham's "mountain" rises above everyone and everything; it dominates, thus representing *Chesed*, which diffuses widely. Isaac's "field" is the object of an action: plowing. It symbolizes the role of a subordinate, which is *Gevurah* – conserving the *status quo*. In both cases, however, it is nature in all its majesty, *gadlut* – its own category of greatness.

Here, "God's abode" (lit., "God's house") of Jacob is something completely different – it represents not nature, but society. Jacob is the first of the Patriarchs to be aware of God's dialogue with society, which is why he becomes the progenitor of the Twelve Tribes that comprise the structure of the people. In this house a person must find his connection with God, first and foremost through relationships of mutual understanding that he shares with other people.

[22] And this stone, which I have set up as a pillar: A monument is an object surrounded by people from every direction, but always from the outside. A house, on the other hand, represents the opposite idea. Its walls are outside, and the people are inside. Jacob's category is *Tiferet*: beauty and balance. Every person who gathers inside that house is an independent – and therefore complex – individual. The relationships among those individuals will sometimes involve conflict, giving rise to the ambiguity and confusion that are typical of Jacob's story.

In the lives of Abraham and Isaac the proper course of action is usually clear. Their problem is to transcend their natural inclinations and find the strength to take the necessary action. But in Jacob's narrative it is often not clear to us how we think he should proceed, and on what basis to decide which behavior will be correct.

And so, Jacob frequently finds himself in complex and "improper" situations. He receives a blessing intended for his brother Esau. When he finally marries at an advanced age after working seven years for the woman he loves, on his wedding night he receives not her, but a different woman. His wives are in constant conflict. His own sons sell their little brother Joseph – Jacob's favorite son – into slavery.

And yet, only as the result of a personal development like Jacob's can a nation be created. Since the goal of Judaism is to consecrate society, and not only the individual, the necessary advancement would not be possible without severe internal conflicts and the efforts to find their resolution.

Shall be God's abode: If there is a place for all inside the common house, then the quarrels are neither extrinsic and random, but an inevitable and indispensable part of life. Since they cannot be avoided, they must be overcome. Any such conflict will then be not an obstacle on the path to God, but the foundation on which such a path can and will be constructed.

33.13. Tithing (28:22)

כב ... וְכֹל אֲשֶׁר תִּתֶּן־לִי עַשֵּׂר אֲעַשְּׂרֶנּוּ לָךְ:

[22] "... and of all that You give me, I will set aside a tithe for You."

Jacob's declaration here explicates the idea of tithing, an important commandment in Judaism. In a later era (after the giving of the Torah at Mount Sinai) tithing became obligatory, but here the Torah refers to it as only a general principle.

The essence of the revelation that Jacob has received is the unification of Heaven and Earth, based on the idea that the spiritual and material aspects of life are inseparable. This time that principle has been revealed to Jacob in clear terms, but later, throughout his life and the lives of his descendants, this fundamental idea will manifest itself only covertly. Therefore, Jacob needs a token to serve as a reminder.

Were God to bestow his His gifts in an obvious manner, man would always be aware of their miraculous character. But those gifts normally come to us instead through "natural" means. For example, a person labors, and in exchange he reaps a harvest or collects wages. The natural cause and effect of that process hinders our realization that we are receiving all those benefits only from God. When one tithes his earnings, he proclaims to God, as it were: "I know well that all I have acquired has come to me only through Your benevolent assistance, and not as the result of my own efforts."

Chapter 34

Jacob and Laban's Daughters

34.1. A Journey to the East in Search of the Unity of Mankind (29:1)

א וַיִּשָּׂא יַעֲקֹב רַגְלָיו וַיֵּלֶךְ אַרְצָה בְנֵי־קֶדֶם:

[1] Jacob resumed his journey and came to the land of the Easterners.

In the Torah the east is called *kedem*, which means, literally, "primordial" – something that was in the universe *ab initio*. The same word is used with reference to the Garden of Eden: "The Lord God planted a garden in Eden, in the east (*mi-kedem*)" (2:8), which is of course telling us not just a fact of geography, but something about the essence of the Garden. In the Torah, the concept of "east" refers not only to relative geographical position, but also to intrinsic value.

Geographically, Jacob's destination is Haran. But *substantively*, he seeks to travel to the "east," to a rebirth of the Divine image that was primordially invested in man. A dream of a stairway changes Jacob. If his original goal in departing

for Haran was to hide from Esau's wrath, he is now searching for origins, for he is aware of his mission (and that of the
future Jewish people) with respect to humanity. This is an
essential step on the path of his transformation from Jacob
to Israel.

34.2. Three Flocks of Sheep at the Well (29:2)

‏ב וַיַּרְא וְהִנֵּה בְאֵר בַּשָּׂדֶה וְהִנֵּה־שָׁם שְׁלֹשָׁה עֶדְרֵי־
צֹאן רֹבְצִים עָלֶיהָ כִּי מִן־הַבְּאֵר הַהִוא יַשְׁקוּ הָעֲדָרִים
וְהָאֶבֶן גְּדֹלָה עַל־פִּי הַבְּאֵר:

[2] There before his eyes was a well in the open.
Three flocks of sheep were lying there beside it,
for the flocks were watered from that well. The
stone on the mouth of the well was large.

[2] Three flocks of sheep: Such details do not seem all that
relevant to Jacob's life story. The approach of our Jewish
tradition to such passages that seem "extraneous" to the
narrative is to seek and find their allegorical significance.

Thus, in this case the Midrash identifies the three herds
with the three races of mankind – the descendants of Shem,
Ham, and Japheth. (In Scripture the nations of the world are
often called "flocks," and their kings – "shepherds.") Meta-
physically, Jacob meets these three categories of humanity
at a well in the East, which are meant to become an object
of careful deliberation on his part.

34.3. Mutual Distrust and Water Shortage (29:3)

ג וְנֶאֶסְפוּ־שָׁמָּה כָל־הָעֲדָרִים וְגָלְלוּ אֶת־הָאֶבֶן מֵעַל פִּי
הַבְּאֵר וְהִשְׁקוּ אֶת־הַצֹּאן וְהֵשִׁיבוּ אֶת־הָאֶבֶן עַל־פִּי
הַבְּאֵר לִמְקֹמָהּ:

*[3] When all the flocks were gathered there, the
stone would be rolled from the mouth of the well
and the sheep watered; then the stone would be
put back in its place on the mouth of the well.*

One of potential allegoric interpretation of this verse can
be the following: the peoples of the world lack water – both
materially and spiritually. Here the well's orifice is secured
with a heavy stone, indicating great concern for water; only
after it is rolled away through joint communal effort will it
then be possible to water the sheep. But because water is in
short supply, the stone must then be also rolled back into
place, to assure that no one will draw water in excess of his
allotted quantity. Thus, while a pragmatic peace among the
nations (accord among the shepherds) can guarantee that
none of them will die of thirst, it cannot provide any of those
nations with enough drinking water.

There is no mutual trust among the shepherds of the
flocks, and each one fears not receiving his fair share. All this
illustrates mankind's principal problem; its distortion of the
concept of brotherhood. The shepherds believe that the
existing system allows each of them to safeguard his guar-
anteed ration of water. But exactly the opposite is true: The
absence of true brotherhood is itself the reason that there
is a water shortage at all.

34.4. Jacob Brings News of Brotherhood (29:4)

ד וַיֹּאמֶר לָהֶם יַעֲקֹב אֲחַי מֵאַיִן אַתֶּם וַיֹּאמְרוּ מֵחָרָן
אֲנָחְנוּ:

[4] Jacob said to them, "My friends, where are you from?" And they said, "We are from Haran."

[4] Jacob said to them, "My friends, where are you from?":
The literal translation is, "My brothers, where are you from?"

Jacob goes into exile toward the East in order to beget the Jewish people, but at the same time he strives to make contact with the origins of all mankind, in order to understand their essential problems. Jacob's descendants, after all, will need to solve those same problems in the future.

Jacob believes that humanity's most pressing problem is their violation of the tenets of fraternity. Jacob's flight from Esau, his twin brother who has threatened to kill him, inspires Jacob to search for the brotherhood in humanity. In the stone that seals the opening to the well Jacob sees a problem. And so, when Jacob greets the strangers, his first words to them are *Achai!*, "My brothers!"

As do the Jewish people, Jacob brings the message of brotherhood to the nations of the world, while also pointing to its origins. His question, "Where are you from?" is not about geography (for isn't it clear that the shepherds hail from nearby Haran?), but an invitation to those shepherds to contemplate their own essence. "Just think about it, guys – how did all of you get here? Since we are all created by God, we all have one Father. And that means that we are brothers."

It is these very ideas that the Torah will later proclaim, and that the Jews will proffer to humanity: If we are to feel a sense of universal brotherhood, we must acknowledge that everything in the universe shares the same, identical origins. But for now, at least, the "shepherds" – leaders of the three major branches of humanity – are not very attentive to his call. With their response "we are from Haran" they go no further than the question of their physical location, the natural order of things. At this early stage of human history, Jacob's uniquely Jewish approach is too visionary for the peoples of the world, and it therefore remains alien to them.

34.5. Deficient Brotherhood: An Ancient Problem

Relations between brothers are a central topic in the book of Genesis. Throughout this rather long book, we repeatedly encounter conflicts between brothers: Cain and Abel, Isaac and Ishmael, Jacob and Esau, Joseph and his brothers. Like civil war, such conflicts are always difficult to resolve.

A primary cause of these conflicts is that brothers lay claim to a common inheritance, needing to share it among themselves. But this applies especially to the twins Esau and Jacob.

The biblical commandment (Lev. 19:18) "Love your fellow as yourself" primarily concerns close relatives, such as brothers. Peace among brothers is the basis of human progress, its foundation. The problems of brotherhood are most acutely felt in the story of Joseph, and they receive true resolution in the story of Moses and Aaron, who shared no inheritance, but attained the level of a mutually complementary relationship.

34.6. Rachel Actualizes Jacob's Intervention in the Life of Haran (29:5-10)

ה וַיֹּאמֶר לָהֶם הַיְדַעְתֶּם אֶת־לָבָן בֶּן־נָחוֹר וַיֹּאמְרוּ
יָדָעְנוּ: ו וַיֹּאמֶר לָהֶם הֲשָׁלוֹם לוֹ וַיֹּאמְרוּ שָׁלוֹם וְהִנֵּה
רָחֵל בִּתּוֹ בָּאָה עִם־הַצֹּאן: ז וַיֹּאמֶר הֵן עוֹד הַיּוֹם גָּדוֹל
לֹא־עֵת הֵאָסֵף הַמִּקְנֶה הַשְׁקוּ הַצֹּאן וּלְכוּ רְעוּ: ח
וַיֹּאמְרוּ לֹא נוּכַל עַד אֲשֶׁר יֵאָסְפוּ כָּל־הָעֲדָרִים וְגָלְלוּ
אֶת־הָאֶבֶן מֵעַל פִּי הַבְּאֵר וְהִשְׁקִינוּ הַצֹּאן: ט עוֹדֶנּוּ
מְדַבֵּר עִמָּם וְרָחֵל | בָּאָה עִם־הַצֹּאן אֲשֶׁר לְאָבִיהָ כִּי
רֹעָה הִוא: י וַיְהִי כַּאֲשֶׁר רָאָה יַעֲקֹב אֶת־רָחֵל בַּת־לָבָן
אֲחִי אִמּוֹ וְאֶת־צֹאן לָבָן אֲחִי אִמּוֹ וַיִּגַּשׁ יַעֲקֹב וַיָּגֶל אֶת־
הָאֶבֶן מֵעַל פִּי הַבְּאֵר וַיַּשְׁקְ אֶת־צֹאן לָבָן אֲחִי אִמּוֹ:

[5] He said to them, "Do you know Laban the son of Nahor?" And they said, "Yes, we do."

[6] He continued, "Is he well?" They answered, "Yes, he is; and there is his daughter Rachel, coming with the flock."

[7] He said, "It is still broad daylight, too early to round up the animals; water the flock and take them to pasture."

[8] But they said, "We cannot, until all the flocks are rounded up; then the stone is rolled off the mouth of the well and we water the sheep."

[9] While he was still speaking with them, Rachel came with her father's flock; for she was a shepherdess.

[10] And when Jacob saw Rachel, the daughter of his uncle Laban, and the flock of his uncle Laban, Jacob went up and rolled the stone off the mouth of the well, and watered the flock of his uncle Laban.

[7] Water the flock and take them to pasture: Seeing Rachel and sensing his deep connection with her, Jacob suddenly feels himself involved in the affairs of Haran. This city is now becoming for him not just a refuge from his brother's vengeance, but a home, if only a temporary one. Jacob then takes to intervening in the situation, to such an extent that he even asks the shepherds why they are not properly tending to their work, why they are not taking their sheep to graze.

[8] But they said: The shepherds react to the intervention quite calmly and constructively, which seems to indicate their willingness to listen to Jacob's message.

We cannot, until all the flocks are rounded up; then the stone is rolled off the mouth of the well and we water the sheep: The shepherds agree that affairs in their country are being improperly handled. However, they attribute the problem not to their lack of brotherhood, but to objective, situational difficulties – in this case, the water shortage.

[10] Jacob went up and rolled the stone off the mouth of the well, and watered the flock of his uncle Laban: With no hesitation whatsoever, Jacob takes up the problem and immediately solves it. Firstly, his own strength is sufficient to roll away the stone, which normally yields only to a concerted communal effort. Secondly, according to the Midrash, there is suddenly enough water for everyone, and there is no longer any need to reseal the mouth of the well with the stone.

Jacob is the Jewry of the Diaspora, who undertake the task of transforming the world around them and are phenomenally successful.

Only later does it become clear that the problem was not

one of objective, physical limitations at all, but only a lack of fraternity. And therefore, despite the blessing that Jacob has brought to the inhabitants of Haran, they (in the person of "Laban's sons," [31:1]) despise him. This, of course, also quite accurately reflects the situation of the Jewish people in exile.

[9] Rachel came with her father's flock: In the Torah's value system, the fact that Rachel herds the sheep testifies to her qualities as a leader, a "pastor." And that is why Rachel's opinion will carry so much weight in determining the family's future direction.

34.7. Jacob's Tears (29: 11-12)

יא וַיִּשַּׁק יַעֲקֹב לְרָחֵל וַיִּשָּׂא אֶת־קֹלוֹ וַיֵּבְךְּ: יב וַיַּגֵּד יַעֲקֹב לְרָחֵל כִּי אֲחִי אָבִיהָ הוּא וְכִי בֶן־רִבְקָה הוּא וַתָּרָץ וַתַּגֵּד לְאָבִיהָ:

[11] Then Jacob kissed Rachel, and broke into tears.
[12] Jacob told Rachel that he was her father's kinsman, that he was Rebekah's son; and she ran and told her father.

[11] Then Jacob kissed Rachel: The grammatical construction of the Hebrew here is not *et rachel,* "(he kissed) Rachel," but *le-rachel,* which means that he kissed Rachel's hand. It would be quite inaccurate to imagine Jacob forcing his kisses on a total stranger.

And broke into tears: The Midrash explains that Jacob cried because he called to mind the matchmaking events that led to his own parents' marriage. Those events apparently took place at this same Haran well. Eliezer, Abraham's steward, had brought an entire caravan of camels, and "all the bounty of his master" (23:10), when he came to find a wife for Isaac. But Jacob, hastily fleeing his brother's wrath, has come to meet his bride completely empty-handed.

Note, by contrast, that Eliezer did not communicate with the local residents. He had only one objective: to collect Rebekah and bring her home to Isaac, for at Isaac's stage of development, *Gevurah*, the Jews are still withdrawn within themselves and are not trying to influence the world. But Jacob enters into dialogue with the shepherds, because he is planning to live in this place, and he wants to improve it.

The Midrash adds that Isaac was by no means poor. When Jacob's parents sent him off to Laban for the purpose of marriage, they provided him with gifts for the bride and for her father. But Eliphaz, Esau's son, attacked Jacob en route and threatened to kill him.

Jacob bought him off with all available property, explaining that "being poor is like being dead." Eliphaz assented and let Jacob be. But now, Jacob is distressed that having come to get married, he has no gifts to offer his bride.

In fact, Jacob tends to downplay his attainments, accomplishments, and status (see for example 47:9). But this feeling of "not quite measuring up" does not depress Jacob; rather, it motivates him to "take the situation by the heel" and run with it.

34.8. Jacob's Agreement with Laban for Marrying Rachel (29: 13-20)

יג וַיְהִי כִשְׁמֹעַ לָבָן אֶת־שֵׁמַע ׀ יַעֲקֹב בֶּן־אֲחֹתוֹ וַיָּרָץ לִקְרָאתוֹ וַיְחַבֶּק־לוֹ וַיְנַשֶּׁק־לוֹ וַיְבִיאֵהוּ אֶל־בֵּיתוֹ

וַיְסַפֵּר לְלָבָן אֵת כָּל־הַדְּבָרִים הָאֵלֶּה: **יד** וַיֹּאמֶר לוֹ לָבָן
אַךְ עַצְמִי וּבְשָׂרִי אָתָּה וַיֵּשֶׁב עִמּוֹ חֹדֶשׁ יָמִים: **טו** וַיֹּאמֶר
לָבָן לְיַעֲקֹב הֲכִי־אָחִי אַתָּה וַעֲבַדְתַּנִי חִנָּם הַגִּידָה לִּי
מַה־מַּשְׂכֻּרְתֶּךָ: **טז** וּלְלָבָן שְׁתֵּי בָנוֹת שֵׁם הַגְּדֹלָה לֵאָה
וְשֵׁם הַקְּטַנָּה רָחֵל: **יז** וְעֵינֵי לֵאָה רַכּוֹת וְרָחֵל הָיְתָה
יְפַת־תֹּאַר וִיפַת מַרְאֶה: **יח** וַיֶּאֱהַב יַעֲקֹב אֶת־רָחֵל
וַיֹּאמֶר אֶעֱבָדְךָ שֶׁבַע שָׁנִים בְּרָחֵל בִּתְּךָ הַקְּטַנָּה: **יט**
וַיֹּאמֶר לָבָן טוֹב תִּתִּי אֹתָהּ לָךְ מִתִּתִּי אֹתָהּ לְאִישׁ אַחֵר
שְׁבָה עִמָּדִי: **כ** וַיַּעֲבֹד יַעֲקֹב בְּרָחֵל שֶׁבַע שָׁנִים וַיִּהְיוּ
בְעֵינָיו כְּיָמִים אֲחָדִים בְּאַהֲבָתוֹ אֹתָהּ:

[13] On hearing the news of his sister's son Jacob,
Laban ran to greet him; he embraced him and
kissed him, and took him into his house. He told
Laban all that had happened,
[14] and Laban said to him, "You are truly my
bone and flesh." When he had stayed with him
a month's time,
[15] Laban said to Jacob, "Just because you are a
kinsman, should you serve me for nothing? Tell
me, what shall your wages be?"
[16] Now Laban had two daughters; the name
of the older one was Leah, and the name of the
younger was Rachel.
[17] Leah had weak eyes; Rachel was shapely
and beautiful.
[18] Jacob loved Rachel; so he answered, "I will
serve you seven years for your younger daughter
Rachel."
[19] Laban said, "Better that I give her to you
than that I should give her to an outsider. Stay
with me."
[20] So Jacob served seven years for Rachel and

*they seemed to him but a few days because of
his love for her.*

[14] You are truly my bone and flesh: There is a clear allusion here to the story of Adam and Eve (2:23). Laban's words
are an indication not only of his familial kinship with Jacob,
but of his consent to let Jacob marry Rachel.

He had stayed with him a month's time: Laban at first
tests Jacob. In order to determine the seriousness of his
intentions, Laban accommodates Jacob in his house for a
full month.

**Just because you are a kinsman, should you serve me for
nothing?**: From these words we understand that this first
month Jacob not only lived with Laban, but worked for him,
and, moreover, received no compensation. Laban poses the
question "Tell me, what shall your wages be?" to determine
the magnitude of Jacob's pretensions, and to learn how he,
Jacob, views the situation.

[16] Now Laban had two daughters: The Midrash adds that
Leah and Rachel were twins, like Esau and Jacob, but ten
years younger than them.

**[17] Leah had weak eyes; Rachel was shapely and beauti-
ful:** It is not entirely clear at first why Rachel's beauty and
Leah's weak eyes are being contrasted here. The meaning of
this contrast finds full expression not so much in the story of
Rachel and Leah as in the dynamics of the relations of their
children, Joseph and Judah. But in general terms, Leah's weak
eyes represent a view of eternity that pays no attention to

ephemeral trifles, while Rachel's beauty is the transience that is realized in the richness of a this-worldly existence. Later we will consider in more detail the entire complex of these relationships.

[18] Jacob loved Rachel: Jacob fell in love with Rachel because of the affinity he felt with her as *Jacob* – his level of development at that moment. But it is from Leah that the primary spiritual forces of the Jewish nation will later be born, namely: the Levites (the priesthood and the Temple) and the dynasty of King David and the Messiah. Moreover, Leah's final resting place will be alongside Jacob in the cave of Machpelah, the nation's preeminent tomb, while Rachel will be buried on the road leading to Bethlehem. Thus, Leah is Jacob's wife "in perpetuity," after he is already *Israel*, but Rachel is his "interim" wife, while he is still *Jacob*.

Jacob loved: It is interesting to observe how the Torah represents the different attitude of each Patriarch toward his choice of a wife. Nothing at all is said about how Abraham came to marry Sarah. About Isaac, however, we know that Abraham's servant chose his wife, while Isaac himself had no say of his own in that process. Only at the level of Jacob do we see not only his exercise of independent choice, but a genuine struggle to find a wife whom he considers suitable to himself.

I will serve you seven years for ... Rachel: Jacob himself offers to work seven years for Laban in exchange for Rachel, rather than asking to marry her immediately. By all appearances, this was a mistake on his part. Jacob feels his poverty too keenly, with the result that he must pay for his low self-esteem and inadequate expectations. Instead, he should have merely communicated to Laban his wish to marry Rachel, offering no payment at all, and then waited to see how his future father-in-law would respond. Perhaps Laban would have demanded a lower price, or would himself have proposed that Jacob marry Rachel first and work for him afterwards. But now Laban accepts Jacob's highly attractive offer: His daughter will be married with no dowry, while he, meanwhile, will receive at no cost to himself the services of a laborer now highly motivated by the promise of his future reward.

[20] So Jacob served seven years for Rachel and they seemed to him but a few days because of his love for her: Indeed, these seven years pass imperceptibly to Jacob, because he is energized by love and romance. But he finds the next seven years, during which he suddenly finds himself working for his second wife, not nearly so romantic. And Rachel too, we can imagine, was less than thrilled to have had to wait so many years to marry Jacob.

When we compare all this with the story of his mother Rebekah's betrothal, when Eliezer refused to wait at all, and carried off the bride forthwith, we see that Jacob's expectations are very significantly understated. Later, however, over the course of his long-standing relationship with Laban, Jacob will learn to act more staunchly and directly. Thus, Jacob gradually continues to develop into Israel.

34.9. Jacob Marries Leah (29:21-25)

כא וַיֹּאמֶר יַעֲקֹב אֶל־לָבָן הָבָה אֶת־אִשְׁתִּי כִּי מָלְאוּ יָמָי וְאָבוֹאָה אֵלֶיהָ: **כב** וַיֶּאֱסֹף לָבָן אֶת־כָּל־אַנְשֵׁי הַמָּקוֹם וַיַּעַשׂ מִשְׁתֶּה: **כג** וַיְהִי בָעֶרֶב וַיִּקַּח אֶת־לֵאָה בִתּוֹ וַיָּבֵא

אֹתָהּ אֵלָיו וַיָּבֹא אֵלֶיהָ: **כד** וַיִּתֵּן לָבָן לָהּ אֶת־זִלְפָּה שִׁפְחָתוֹ לְלֵאָה בִתּוֹ שִׁפְחָה: **כה** וַיְהִי בַבֹּקֶר וְהִנֵּה־הִוא לֵאָה ...

[21] Then Jacob said to Laban, "Give me my wife, for my time is fulfilled, that I may cohabit with her."
[22] And Laban gathered all the people of the place and made a feast.
[23] When evening came, he took his daughter Leah and brought her to him; and he cohabited with her. –
[24] Laban had given his maidservant Zilpah to his daughter Leah as her maid. –
[25] When morning came, there was Leah! ...

[21] Give me my wife ... that I may cohabit with her: The Midrash remarks: "But even a simpleton would not speak so crudely!" (That is, directly and frankly.) It then adds: "Because Jacob knew that he had to beget twelve sons, he felt that he must hurry."

Over the course of his seven years working for Laban, Jacob learned to be tougher than he had been when he left his parental home. But as it turned out, even that was not enough.

[25] When morning came, there was Leah!: The Midrash adds that Jacob indeed suspected that Laban might deceive him. He therefore arranged with Rachel in advance that just before the wedding ceremony she would give him certain signals they had agreed upon, in order to confirm that the bride he was about to marry was in fact Rachel. (Her identity could otherwise not be known, because of the established custom that a bride's face would always be concealed with a veil.) But Rachel, upon learning that her father had decided to deceive Jacob, and not wanting to disgrace and expose her sister, shared those signs with Leah, who did everything just as Jacob and Rachel had agreed. Jacob therefore did not suspect the deception.

All that was a major display of generosity on Rachel's part, thanks to which she eventually assumed the role of a senior wife in the family. Jacob's marriage to Leah turned out to be a necessary element for his further development, as we shall see.

34.10. Jacob Marries Rachel (29:25-30)

כה ... וַיֹּאמֶר אֶל־לָבָן מַה־זֹּאת עָשִׂיתָ לִּי הֲלֹא בְרָחֵל עֲבַדְתִּי עִמָּךְ וְלָמָּה רִמִּיתָנִי: **כו** וַיֹּאמֶר לָבָן לֹא־יֵעָשֶׂה כֵן בִּמְקוֹמֵנוּ לָתֵת הַצְּעִירָה לִפְנֵי הַבְּכִירָה: **כז** מַלֵּא שְׁבֻעַ זֹאת וְנִתְּנָה לְךָ גַּם־אֶת־זֹאת בַּעֲבֹדָה אֲשֶׁר תַּעֲבֹד עִמָּדִי עוֹד שֶׁבַע־שָׁנִים אֲחֵרוֹת: **כח** וַיַּעַשׂ יַעֲקֹב כֵּן וַיְמַלֵּא שְׁבֻעַ זֹאת וַיִּתֶּן־לוֹ אֶת־רָחֵל בִּתּוֹ לוֹ לְאִשָּׁה: **כט** וַיִּתֵּן לָבָן לְרָחֵל בִּתּוֹ אֶת־בִּלְהָה שִׁפְחָתוֹ לָהּ לְשִׁפְחָה: **ל** וַיָּבֹא גַּם אֶל־רָחֵל וַיֶּאֱהַב גַּם־אֶת־רָחֵל מִלֵּאָה וַיַּעֲבֹד עִמּוֹ עוֹד שֶׁבַע־שָׁנִים אֲחֵרוֹת:

[25] ... So he said to Laban, "What is this you have done to me? I was in your service for Rachel! Why did you deceive me?"
[26] Laban said, "It is not the practice in our place to marry off the younger before the older.
[27] Wait until the bridal week of this one is over and we will give you that one too, provided you serve me another seven years."

[28] Jacob did so; he waited out the bridal week of the one, and then he gave him his daughter Rachel as wife. –

[29] Laban had given his maidservant Bilhah to his daughter Rachel as her maid. –

[30] And Jacob cohabited with Rachel also; indeed, he loved Rachel more than Leah. And he served him another seven years.

[26] It is not the practice in our place to marry off the younger before the older: The literal translation is "to marry off the younger before the firstborn." Laban's choice of words recalls Jacob's declaration to his father: "I am your son Esau, your firstborn" (27:32). As Jacob deceived his father, so does Laban deceive Jacob.

It is not the practice in our place: The emphasis is on "our." Laban seems to be saying: "I suppose that in Canaan, where *you* come from, such impudence – a younger brother usurping his father's blessing by means of a deception – is considered perfectly normal. But here in Haran we are a decent folk, and we always act responsibly. We would never marry off the younger before the older.

[28] Jacob did so: Jacob chooses to not respond to Laban's argument, because he feels that it is to a certain extent defensible. However, the question of why Jacob would think so – that is, on what basis Laban's position can be justified – is in fact far from simple. The essence of the situation, which is more complicated than mere "measure-for-measure" retribution, is as follows. Jacob, having received Esau's blessing, should also – as a kind of "package deal" – get Leah, the woman originally intended for Esau.

The Midrash explains: Because Rebekah had twin sons, and her brother Laban had twin daughters, the people of the community used to say: "The two pairs of twins are well-suited: the elder (Leah) to the elder (Esau), and the younger to the younger." The Midrash then adds, that Leah was so distressed by all the talk of her being expected to marry the villain Esau, that she cried her eyes out. Hence: "Leah had weak eyes" (v. 17).

However, Leah was not the "revenge" taken on Jacob for having deceived his father, but on the contrary, it helped him to reveal his potential and achieve greatness. But Jacob at the time of his marriage still does not understand this. The situation seems unfair to him, but he remains silent, because, from a moral perspective, there is no valid objection that he can possibly raise.

[27] Wait until the bridal week of this one is over: Jacob marries Rachel immediately after the seven-day wedding feast for him and Leah. (We note that the Jewish people still observe the same seven-day wedding celebration even today.) Then, after consummating this second marriage, Jacob works for Laban yet another seven years. Regarding Bilhah and Zilpah, the Tradition tells us that they, too, were the daughters of Laban, born to him from his maidservant, however, and not his wife. Thus, all four wives of Jacob were Laban's daughters.

34.11. The Problem of Jacob Marrying Two Sisters

Although polygamy is not prohibited by the Torah, neither is it encouraged. Judaism deems monogamous marriage the ideal. (Throughout Jewish history, the practice of polygamy was always rare, even before it was finally prohibited outright much later, in the Middle Ages.)

On the other hand, the Torah very explicitly forbids marrying two sisters. And furthermore, even after a divorce, one is forbidden to marry his ex-wife's sister so long as the divorced sister is still alive (Lev. 18:18). Thus, according to Torah law, after he married Leah it was forbidden for Jacob to marry Rachel, *even* if he were to divorce Leah. How, then, could Jacob enter into such a marriage with Rachel?

The explanation is that before the giving of the Torah, the doctrines of Judaism were not yet established law, and the Patriarchs were not obliged to observe the laws of the Torah, which would be formalized only in the future. Of course, spiritual and moral principles, which in the future would become laws, were known and recognized by the Patriarchs, and in this sense, "the Patriarchs observed the Torah even before it was given."

But those principles at that time had the status of "desirable but not binding." Had Jacob originally intended to marry two sisters, that would have been wrong. But since the situation arose *post factum*, Jacob had the right to decide (and did decide) that the undesirability of marrying two sisters was in this case far less than the enormous damage that refraining from marrying Rachel would have caused.

Had this happened after the giving of the Torah, Jacob could not have married Rachel, irrespective of that "damage." But because doing so was at that time only undesirable, but not forbidden, Jacob was within his rights to evaluate the undesirability versus the damage, and to choose whichever he deemed the lesser of the two evils.

This is not the only instance in the Torah where the Patriarchs violated a prohibition that would become formalized only later. For example, as noted earlier (28:18) Jacob erected a "stone pillar," notwithstanding that the Torah explicitly forbids it, in unusually strong terms, as abhorrent to God (Deut. 16:22). This is a clear illustration of the principle that "the Teachings given to the forefathers are not the same as the Teachings given to their descendants." In those two fundamentally different eras, the Torah is likewise realized in different ways.

Another important aspect of this story is that the Torah's prohibition of marrying sisters can be seen as itself a consequence of Jacob's difficult relationship with his wives. Those complications would lead to conflict between brothers, the sale of Joseph, and other unfortunate consequences. The point here is that the absolute meaning of a commandment in no way negates the historical nature of its formalization. For example, the commandment to eat matzah during Passover has, simultaneously, both an absolute, moral significance and a philosophical, concretely historical one (namely, the Israelites' hasty departure from Egypt, which left them no time to prepare leavened bread).

In other words, certain fundamental principles do exist in the universe, but these descend into the world in the form of specific events in the lives of the Patriarchs and the Jewish nation, through whom fundamental principles of the universe are then realized in this lower world.

Says the Talmud: "The affairs of the Patriarchs serve as future indicators for their descendants." In other words, what for posterity would be realized as law was for the Patriarchs merely an aspect of their life story. Thus, as concerns the prohibition of marrying sisters, we can suggest that Jacob had to experience his ordeal concerning Rachel and Leah in order that, as a result, the law that banned marrying sisters would be formulated.

(See also the discussion of this topic below in portion 36.17, "Events in the Life of the Patriarchs as a Source of the Commandments.")

Chapter 35

The Birth of Rachel's and Leah's Children

35.1. Leah's First Children Are Born (29:31-35)

לא וַיַּרְא יי כִּי־שְׂנוּאָה לֵאָה וַיִּפְתַּח אֶת־רַחְמָהּ וְרָחֵל
עֲקָרָה: **לב** וַתַּהַר לֵאָה וַתֵּלֶד בֵּן וַתִּקְרָא שְׁמוֹ רְאוּבֵן
כִּי אָמְרָה כִּי־רָאָה יי בְּעָנְיִי כִּי עַתָּה יֶאֱהָבַנִי אִישִׁי: **לג**
וַתַּהַר עוֹד וַתֵּלֶד בֵּן וַתֹּאמֶר כִּי־שָׁמַע יי כִּי־שְׂנוּאָה אָנֹכִי
וַיִּתֶּן־לִי גַּם־אֶת־זֶה וַתִּקְרָא שְׁמוֹ שִׁמְעוֹן: **לד** וַתַּהַר עוֹד
וַתֵּלֶד בֵּן וַתֹּאמֶר עַתָּה הַפַּעַם יִלָּוֶה אִישִׁי אֵלַי כִּי־יָלַדְתִּי
לוֹ שְׁלֹשָׁה בָנִים עַל־כֵּן קָרָא־שְׁמוֹ לֵוִי: **לה** וַתַּהַר עוֹד
וַתֵּלֶד בֵּן וַתֹּאמֶר הַפַּעַם אוֹדֶה אֶת־יי עַל־כֵּן קָרְאָה
שְׁמוֹ יְהוּדָה וַתַּעֲמֹד מִלֶּדֶת:

*[31] The Lord saw that Leah was unloved and he
opened her womb; but Rachel was barren.*
*[32] Leah conceived and bore a son, and named
him Reuben; for she declared, "It means: 'The
Lord has seen my affliction'; it also means: 'Now
my husband will love me."*
[33] She conceived again and bore a son, and

declared, "This is because the Lord heard that
I was unloved and has given me this one also";
so she named him Simeon.
[34] Again she conceived and bore a son and
declared, "This time my husband will become
attached to me, for I have borne him three sons."
Therefore he was named Levi.
[35] She conceived again and bore a son, and
declared, "This time I will praise the Lord."
Therefore she named him Judah. Then she
stopped bearing.

[31] The Lord saw that Leah was unloved and he opened her womb; but Rachel was barren: The Torah essentially holds Jacob responsible for Rachel's childlessness. Jacob should have understood that since, however unexpectedly, Leah had become his wife, it was not mere happenstance, but the Divine will, and he should have tried to love Leah more. But he did not. God therefore intervened in order to balance the situation, and Leah gave birth, while Rachel remained childless.

When we shy away from a challenge that life places in our path, then besides leaving it to God to compensate for our failures, we also run the risk of paying a steep price for them.

[32] Reuben – The Lord has seen my affliction ... the Lord heard that I was unloved and has given me this one also ... – Simeon. [34] ... This time my husband will become attached to me, for I have borne him three sons. ... – Levi: The names of Leah's first three children reflect her passionate desire to win Jacob's love by bearing him children.

This time I will praise the Lord. Therefore she named him Judah: Only after giving birth to a fourth son, Leah begins to feel that she is an independent, autonomous personality. She therefore gives him a name that expresses her personal relationship with God but has no direct connection with Jacob.

Leah's sons' names speak of her gradual personal growth. The name of her firstborn, Reuben (from *ra'oh*, "(to) see,"), tells of her difficult marriage. She hopes that God will see her distress, having been forced to marry Jacob through a deception, and that Jacob will therefore soften his attitude towards her.

Leah's distress is, in a sense, a reflection of Jacob's own distress over having received his father's blessing through a deception. It is striking that, evidently, Jacob himself cannot see this profound parallelism in their destinies. We have already noted that it is Leah who is Jacob's wife "in perpetuity," for she is his *gadlut*, his greatness. But Jacob, who has not yet become Israel, is at first completely unaware of that.

The name of Leah's second son, "Simon," is this time formed not from "God sees," but from *shamo'a*, "(to) hear: "God hears." Even after Leah has given birth to Jacob's firstborn, his love for her remains constrained. The name she gives her son this time is a reproach to Jacob (and not to her father Laban, as was the name of her first son). To hear means to evaluate, to make a careful assessment (as opposed to vision, which indicates only a general, high-level view of a situation). Leah continues to love Jacob, but gradually learns to view him more critically.

The name of Leah's third son, "Levi," is formed from the root *hilaveh*, "(to) accompany": my husband will now cling to me. Having despaired of any hope of influencing Jacob at a deeper level, Leah now hopes for his "mechanical" attachment to her through their children.

Only when all that fails does Leah finally free herself of her complexes with respect to Jacob and Rachel, and turn to a personal dialogue with God. The name of her fourth son speaks of this: "Judah," from the root (le)hodot,"(to) give thanks."

35.2. Rachel's Envy and Jacob's Anger (30:1-2)

א וַתֵּרֶא רָחֵל כִּי לֹא יָלְדָה לְיַעֲקֹב וַתְּקַנֵּא רָחֵל בַּאֲחֹתָהּ וַתֹּאמֶר אֶל־יַעֲקֹב הָבָה־לִּי בָנִים וְאִם־אַיִן מֵתָה אָנֹכִי: **ב** וַיִּחַר־אַף יַעֲקֹב בְּרָחֵל וַיֹּאמֶר הֲתַחַת אֱלֹהִים אָנֹכִי אֲשֶׁר־מָנַע מִמֵּךְ פְּרִי־בָטֶן:

[1] When Rachel saw that she had borne Jacob no children, she became envious of her sister; and Rachel said to Jacob, "Give me children, or I shall die."
[2] Jacob was incensed at Rachel, and said, "Can I take the place of God, who has denied you fruit of the womb?"

[1] Rachel ... became envious of her sister; and ... said to Jacob, "Give me children, or I shall die": The literal translation is: "Give me children, for without [children] I die" (that is, I am as good as dead). Rachel is quite clear in expressing her feelings that being childless is for her a fate equivalent to death. But we also know that what she is "dying" from more than anything else is envy – from the fact that her sister has children, but she does not.

This approach to dealing with life's problems is of course completely wrong. But we must not judge Rachel too harshly for saying such things. In life, it often happens that even improper motives can prod us to ask the right questions. Rachel's envy leads her to a realization of the crisis, and to register complaints that are not entirely unjustified. And that is because the source of the problem here is not Rachel, the problem is Jacob.

[2] Jacob was incensed at Rachel: Leah loves Jacob, Jacob loves Rachel, and Rachel envies Leah. Strictly speaking, Jacob in this kind of situation has every reason to be dissatisfied with Rachel, and to tell her so, for she demands of him something that only God can grant. But in fact, it is Jacob here who is in the wrong for not loving Leah enough, and he knows that. Jacob's underlying sense of guilt, his attempt to protect himself from that feeling, exasperates him.

35.3. Jacob Marries Bilhah, Rachel's Handmaiden (30:3-4)

ג וַתֹּאמֶר הִנֵּה אֲמָתִי בִלְהָה בֹּא אֵלֶיהָ וְתֵלֵד עַל־בִּרְכַּי וְאִבָּנֶה גַם־אָנֹכִי מִמֶּנָּה׃ ד וַתִּתֶּן־לוֹ אֶת־בִּלְהָה שִׁפְחָתָהּ לְאִשָּׁה וַיָּבֹא אֵלֶיהָ יַעֲקֹב׃

[3] She said, "Here is my maid Bilhah. Consort with her, that she may bear on my knees and that through her I too may have children."
[4] So she gave him her maid Bilhah as concubine, and Jacob cohabited with her.

Having purchased the birthright from Esau, and then received the blessing previously designated for Esau, Jacob still did not realize how heavy the burden he had taken upon himself was. Perhaps this was for the best. By knowing in advance what difficulties lie ahead, we might abandon our chosen path, and our lost opportunities could be considerable.

But now Jacob must solve the problem of his marriage with Leah, who was originally supposed to be Esau's wife, but who ended up married to him. For now he is not able to love Leah as much as he loves Rachel, because so far he is only Jacob, not yet having integrated enough of Esau's qualities into his own.

Because he could not sufficiently love his two wives, Jacob gets a third, and then a fourth wife. He must learn to properly apportion his feelings among them, which is precisely the path he must follow in order to acquire Esau's qualities.

Needless to say, it is impossible to force oneself to love a stranger. But Jacob's situation is rather different. He is close to both wives – as they, too, are to him. They bear him children, and he willingly also accepts his marriage to Leah. The only problem is the level of attention that he pays to each of them. It is truly difficult to behave properly under such conditions, and this is one of the reasons that Jewish tradition did not recommend polygamy, and subsequently prohibited it outright.

The troubled relations between Jacob's wives affected his family for a very long time. After Rachel's death, these problems led to a conflict with Reuben over Bilhah (35:22). But in the end a resolution was achieved, and it was Leah who then became Jacob's "wife for all eternity." She was buried with him in the cave of Machpelah, and the descendants of her sons Judah and Levi received the kingship and the priesthood in Israel, respectively.

[3] That she may bear on my knees and that through her I too may have children: These words recall the story of Sarah and Hagar (16:2). But Rachel is not afraid that she will have issues with Bilhah – perhaps because, in view of the conflict with Leah, each handmaiden, unlike Hagar, remains loyal to her mistress. Because Bilhah and Zilpah conduct themselves with dignity in this situation, as did their children later, their descendants will be fully included in the framework of the Jewish people. This contrasts even more starkly with the behavior of Ishmael, who was expelled from Abraham's family, because he was unwilling to be satisfied with a subordinate position.

35.4. Children of Bilhah (30: 5-8)

ה וַתַּהַר בִּלְהָה וַתֵּלֶד לְיַעֲקֹב בֵּן: ו וַתֹּאמֶר רָחֵל דָּנַנִּי אֱלֹהִים וְגַם שָׁמַע בְּקֹלִי וַיִּתֶּן־לִי בֵּן עַל־כֵּן קָרְאָה שְׁמוֹ דָּן: ז וַתַּהַר עוֹד וַתֵּלֶד בִּלְהָה שִׁפְחַת רָחֵל בֵּן שֵׁנִי לְיַעֲקֹב: ח וַתֹּאמֶר רָחֵל נַפְתּוּלֵי אֱלֹהִים ׀ נִפְתַּלְתִּי עִם־אֲחֹתִי גַּם־יָכֹלְתִּי וַתִּקְרָא שְׁמוֹ נַפְתָּלִי:

[5] Bilhah conceived and bore Jacob a son.
[6] And Rachel said, "God has vindicated me; indeed, He has heeded my plea and given me a son." Therefore she named him Dan.
[7] Rachel's maid Bilhah conceived again and bore Jacob a second son.
[8] And Rachel said, "A fateful contest I waged with my sister; yes, and I have prevailed." So she named him Naphtali.

[5] Bilhah ... bore ... a son. [6] And Rachel said: It is Rachel who names Bilhah's children, which shows that she considers them her own.

[6] God has vindicated me; ... she named him Dan. [8] A fateful contest I waged with my sister ... she named him Naphtali: Rachel sees the rivalry with her sister as *din*, judgment and *naftulim*, struggle. From these words she creates names for the newborns. Her perception of life as a rivalry with her sister continues to be the source of Rachel's problems. Only when she abandons the conflict with her sister, and focuses instead on her relationship with Jacob and with God, can she then give birth.

One of the central internal tasks of Jacob's family is to address the problem of conflict between brothers, in order to achieve unity even while experiencing crisis. (In the book of Genesis, as we have already mentioned, this is mankind's primary problem.) To reinforce the potentialities of the tension of this confrontation, four firstborns must be born in Jacob's family. The birth of each will become a step on the path to constructing an effective system of "moral birthright."

Bilhah's firstborn son Dan is pivotal in this system, because he is "the firstborn who lays no claim to the right of the firstborn." He perfects the concept of brotherhood, and thus facilitates – indeed makes possible – the birth of Joseph.

35.5. Jacob's Marriage to Zilpah, Leah's Maidservant, and His Children from Her (30:9-13)

ט וַתֵּרֶא לֵאָה כִּי עָמְדָה מִלֶּדֶת וַתִּקַּח אֶת־זִלְפָּה שִׁפְחָתָהּ
וַתִּתֵּן אֹתָהּ לְיַעֲקֹב לְאִשָּׁה: י וַתֵּלֶד זִלְפָּה שִׁפְחַת לֵאָה

לְיַעֲקֹב בֵּן: יא וַתֹּאמֶר לֵאָה בגד (בָּא גָד) וַתִּקְרָא אֶת־
שְׁמוֹ גָּד: יב וַתֵּלֶד זִלְפָּה שִׁפְחַת לֵאָה בֵּן שֵׁנִי לְיַעֲקֹב:
יג וַתֹּאמֶר לֵאָה בְּאָשְׁרִי כִּי אִשְּׁרוּנִי בָּנוֹת וַתִּקְרָא אֶת־
שְׁמוֹ אָשֵׁר:

*[9] When Leah saw that she had stopped bearing,
she took her maid Zilpah and gave her to Jacob
as concubine.
[10] And when Leah's maid Zilpah bore Jacob
a son,
[11] Leah said, "What luck!" So she named him
Gad.
[12] When Leah's maid Zilpah bore Jacob a
second son,
[13] Leah declared, "What fortune!" meaning,
"Women will deem me fortunate." So she named
him Asher.*

[9] Leah saw that she had stopped bearing: At first Leah
was hoping that the huge preponderance in the number of
her children would gradually make her more attractive to
Jacob. But now, with the weight of her advantage at risk, she
is still receiving insufficient attention from him. She therefore resolves to improve her status.

[11] Leah said, "What luck!": When Rachel gave her handmaiden to Jacob, she was motivated by a sense of tragedy.
But Leah's problems are not as great as Rachel's, and the
birth of additional children therefore seems to her in some
sense a bonus. But it is, in fact, a "needed bonus," because
her feeling of happiness depends on it.

Gad ... Asher: From the names of the sons (*Gad*, "luck, happiness"; *Asher*, "bliss"), we see that although in Leah's actions too there is an element of competition with Rachel, Leah is not fixated on this conflict. She rejoices in what she has, which testifies to her higher spiritual level, and corresponds to Jacob's status in his further development as Israel.

35.6. Hierarchy in Jacob's Family and in the Jewish People

Bilhah and Zilpah gradually became Jacob's full-fledged wives, and their sons too were an essential component of the Jewish people, unlike Ishmael in his time, who had been expelled. In the patriarchal family there is always a hierarchy – some family members are higher and some lower. But the sons of Bilhah and Zilpah placidly accept their lesser status. They do not try to break the system, as Hagar and Ishmael did, and their status therefore becomes normalized over time. At first, the sons of Leah are primary, and the other brothers are subordinate to them. But after Jacob blesses each of his sons (ch. 49) – and Moses will later do likewise (Deut. 33) – the unified mosaic of the Jewish people will consist of all twelve sons, each becoming a tribe in every sense.

When we try to demolish a naturally occurring structure, and mechanically replace it with one that is supposedly more correct and more just, nothing good will usually come of that. First we need to grow correctly within the existing, fundamental structure, and to assure our proper development in our elemental state. Only then can we introduce changes and improvements for our own benefit, and the benefit of the system as a whole.

35.7. The Story of the Mandrakes (30:14-16)

יד וַיֵּלֶךְ רְאוּבֵן בִּימֵי קְצִיר־חִטִּים וַיִּמְצָא דוּדָאִים
בַּשָּׂדֶה וַיָּבֵא אֹתָם אֶל־לֵאָה אִמּוֹ וַתֹּאמֶר רָחֵל אֶל־לֵאָה
תְּנִי־נָא לִי מִדּוּדָאֵי בְּנֵךְ: טו וַתֹּאמֶר לָהּ הַמְעַט קַחְתֵּךְ
אֶת־אִישִׁי וְלָקַחַת גַּם אֶת־דּוּדָאֵי בְּנִי וַתֹּאמֶר רָחֵל לָכֵן
יִשְׁכַּב עִמָּךְ הַלַּיְלָה תַּחַת דּוּדָאֵי בְנֵךְ: טז וַיָּבֹא יַעֲקֹב מִן־
הַשָּׂדֶה בָּעֶרֶב וַתֵּצֵא לֵאָה לִקְרָאתוֹ וַתֹּאמֶר אֵלַי תָּבוֹא
כִּי שָׂכֹר שְׂכַרְתִּיךָ בְּדוּדָאֵי בְּנִי וַיִּשְׁכַּב עִמָּהּ בַּלַּיְלָה הוּא:

*[14] Once, at the time of the wheat harvest,
Reuben came upon some mandrakes in the field
and brought them to his mother Leah. Rachel
said to Leah, "Please give me some of your son's
mandrakes."*
*[15] But she said to her, "Was it not enough for
you to take away my husband, that you would
also take my son's mandrakes?" Rachel replied,
"I promise, he shall lie with you tonight, in return
for your son's mandrakes."*
*[16] When Jacob came home from the field in the
evening, Leah went out to meet him and said, "You
are to sleep with me, for I have hired you with my
son's mandrakes." And he lay with her that night.*

[14] Give me some of your son's mandrakes: Rachel is still
childless. Neither Jacob's love nor the birth of children by
her maidservant can help her. She therefore tries to exploit
every means at her disposal. When Reuben goes walking
in the fields and finds the berries of *duda'im* (mandrakes),
considered conducive to conception, Rachel asks Leah for
those, and agrees to her conditions.

[15] Rachel replied, "I promise, he shall lie with you tonight, in return for your son's mandrakes": This was not Leah's condition, but Rachel's offer. Rachel offers as payment something that is very dear to her.

It would be completely wrong, however, to imagine that this was the only option available to Leah for bringing Jacob into her tent. Jacob all these years had of course not left Leah, notwithstanding that Rachel's residence is his primary home.

It should be noted that a man who has two or more wives is required by Torah law to live regularly with each of them. The very fact that Leah, having ceased to give birth, gives Jacob her handmaiden shows the degree of connection and trust that existed between them. But even one night spent with Jacob is precious to Leah, and she agrees to hand over the mandrakes in exchange for that. Leah is therefore rewarded with her next child.

35.8. The Birth of the Youngest Sons of Leah (30: 17-20)

יז וַיִּשְׁמַע אֱלֹהִים אֶל־לֵאָה וַתַּהַר וַתֵּלֶד לְיַעֲקֹב בֵּן
חֲמִישִׁי: יח וַתֹּאמֶר לֵאָה נָתַן אֱלֹהִים שְׂכָרִי אֲשֶׁר־
נָתַתִּי שִׁפְחָתִי לְאִישִׁי וַתִּקְרָא שְׁמוֹ יִשָּׂשכָר: יט וַתַּהַר
עוֹד לֵאָה וַתֵּלֶד בֵּן־שִׁשִּׁי לְיַעֲקֹב: כ וַתֹּאמֶר לֵאָה זְבָדַנִי
אֱלֹהִים | אֹתִי זֶבֶד טוֹב הַפַּעַם יִזְבְּלֵנִי אִישִׁי כִּי־יָלַדְתִּי
לוֹ שִׁשָּׁה בָנִים וַתִּקְרָא אֶת־שְׁמוֹ זְבֻלוּן:

[17] God heeded Leah, and she conceived and bore him a fifth son.
[18] And Leah said, "God has given me my reward for having given my maid to my husband." So

she named him Issachar.
[19] When Leah conceived again and bore Jacob
a sixth son,
[20] Leah said, "God has given me a choice gift;
this time my husband will exalt me, for I have
borne him six sons." So she named him Zebulun.

[18] Issachar: "Reward." **[20] Zevulun:** "My husband will exalt me." These names too show that Leah views the situation not as a conflict with Rachel, but as an element of her relationship with Jacob and with God.

[17] God heeded Leah: When Leah finally turns to God, He hears her.

[18] God has given me my reward for having given my maid to my husband: While Rachel relies on technical solutions, Leah views the situation from a moral perspective. Leah sees her merit not in the fact that she has bought a night with Jacob for the price of mandrakes, but that, having ceased to give birth, she has given her handmaiden to her husband, thereby sacrificing some of her own intimate relations for the good of both Jacob and her own inner family. And so she receives another child as compensation.

35.9. The Birth of Dinah (30:21)

כא וְאַחַר יָלְדָה בַּת וַתִּקְרָא אֶת־שְׁמָהּ דִּינָה:

[21] Last, she bore him a daughter, and named
her Dinah.

The Torah mentions the birth of a daughter rather infrequently, and even when it does so here, the meaning of the name "Dinah" ("judgment") is nonetheless not explained. However, immediately after Dinah's birth we are informed of the birth of Joseph. The Midrash offers the following elaboration.

Everyone in the family knew that Jacob could have a maximum of twelve sons. Leah already had six sons, and the two maidservants each had two. Thus, Jacob already had ten sons. Were Leah now to give birth to another boy, Rachel could have only one son; that is, even fewer than either maidservant. According to the Midrash, Leah was now supposed to give birth to a boy. But Leah, wanting Rachel to have at least two sons, prayed to God to change the sex of her child, and Dinah was born.

Leah's submitting to "self-judgment" made it possible for Rachel to give birth to Joseph and Benjamin, and also afforded Leah herself an opportunity to attain yet one more level of spiritual growth. Leah therefore names her daughter "Dinah," from *din*, "judgment."

35.10. The Dynamics of Leah's Development

The dynamics of Leah's development and correction consist in her gradually coming to understand and acknowledge that Rachel, not Leah, is Jacob's foundational wife.

Technically, Leah was Jacob's wife before Rachel was, and her words to Rachel "Was it not enough for you to take away my husband?" (30:15) demonstrate the tension of their conflict. It is quite difficult for Leah to acknowledge her sister's primacy. Recall that according to the Midrash, it was Rachel who acted nobly and helped Leah get married by passing to her sister the signs that she and Jacob had agreed upon, whereas Leah asked God to give her sister Rachel children only after she already had six children of her own.

But Leah does gradually yield to Rachel's primacy. This is evident from their relationship at the family conclave (31:14). Many centuries later, in the era of the Judges, when Boaz took Ruth as his wife, the inhabitants of Beit-Lechem (Bethlehem), who are the descendants of Leah's son Judah, proclaimed "May the Lord make the woman who is coming into your house like Rachel and Leah." (Ruth 4:11) Thus, Scripture puts Rachel ahead of Leah and establishes the fixed relative positions of the two Matriarchs within the Jewish people. Rachel comes first, although her legacy is transitory, and Leah follows, although her legacy is eternal.

The significance of this relative placement of the sisters is that "eternity," or Leah's weak eyes, must acknowledge that certain primacy of "transience," or Rachel's beauty. Transience goes first, paving the way for eternity. The same is true of the monarchy. Rachel's son Joseph's kingdom must come first, and only then the kingdom of Leah's son Judah.

When Joseph's brothers initially refused to recognize his supremacy, it was the sin of Leah not accepting Rachel's primacy. Later, however, Leah and her children will acknowledge the errors of their approach, and this will be their correction.

35.11. The Status of Women in Jacob's Family

Wives occupy a leading position in Jacob's family. Jacob's wives decide with whom he will spend the night, what names to give his children, and when their family should return to Canaan. Although the elevated status of wives is typical of the Jewish Patriarchs, this is especially evident in the Jacob narrative. But Jacob's wives' influence is particularly strong for yet another reason: they are native citizens in their home country, while Jacob is their "guest."

With rare exceptions among the peoples of the world, patrilocal settlement has always been the norm. A man brings his wife to his parents' home; son and daughter-in-law and their young family then live with the husband's parents. A husband in this situation continues to live in the place where he was raised, where everything is familiar to him. He feels that he is the master of his domain, while his wife for a long time feels like a stranger. The position of the daughter-in-law in this situation is of course not simple: she often disagrees with her mother-in-law on how to run the household, and her status overall is rather low.

Contrarily, in the case of matrilocal settlement of a new family, the wife continues to live in the house in which she grew up, and she feels she is the mistress of her own domain. This approach is exactly the one that was accepted over the centuries among Ashkenazi Jews, thus providing Ashkenazi women with an incomparably higher social status than women of other nations routinely had.

The position that his wives occupied was a serious challenge for Jacob himself, but greatly advanced the Jewish people. In general, the elevated status of a woman is a challenge for her husband in and of itself. The higher her status, the higher the man's level must be to accept and successfully deal with the challenge, and the more difficult it will be for him. But this is also a condition of his proper development.

The social-familial structure of Ashkenazi communities, which were based on matrilocal settlement, created especially salutary conditions for significant intellectual and socio-psychological growth among Ashkenazi men.

35.12. The Birth of Joseph (30:22-24)

כב וַיִּזְכֹּר אֱלֹהִים אֶת־רָחֵל וַיִּשְׁמַע אֵלֶיהָ אֱלֹהִים וַיִּפְתַּח אֶת־רַחְמָהּ: כג וַתַּהַר וַתֵּלֶד בֵּן וַתֹּאמֶר אָסַף אֱלֹהִים אֶת־חֶרְפָּתִי: כד וַתִּקְרָא אֶת־שְׁמוֹ יוֹסֵף לֵאמֹר יֹסֵף יי לִי בֵּן אַחֵר:

[22] Now God remembered Rachel; God heeded her and opened her womb.
[23] She conceived and bore a son, and said, "God has taken away my disgrace."
[24] So she named him Joseph, which is to say, "May the Lord add another son for me."

[22] God heeded her: This is the first time the Torah mentions that Rachel prayed. Rachel at first relied on technical methods for solving the problem of her infertility: on Jacob's miraculous intervention, on her maidservant Bilhah, and on the mandrakes. But the situation is now changing. Rachel bears Jacob a son only after she herself begins to pray, relying on her own dialogue with God.

[23] God has taken away my disgrace: Although Rachel still speaks of her disgrace that has been removed (for she perceives childlessness as something shameful), she gives her son the positive name Joseph, from the Hebrew root *Y-S-P*, "(to) add, continue," expressing her confidence that she will continue to bear yet more children.

[24] May the Lord add another son for me: Rachel has moved beyond the stage of competing with Leah, and is now seeking solutions to her own internal problems. This is the basis for repairing relations in their family.

Chapter 36

Jacob and Laban's Sheep

36.1. The Birth of Joseph, and the Opportunity to Return to the Land of Israel (30:25-26)

כה וַיְהִי כַּאֲשֶׁר יָלְדָה רָחֵל אֶת־יוֹסֵף וַיֹּאמֶר יַעֲקֹב אֶל־
לָבָן שַׁלְּחֵנִי וְאֵלְכָה אֶל־מְקוֹמִי וּלְאַרְצִי: **כו** תְּנָה אֶת־
נָשַׁי וְאֶת־יְלָדַי אֲשֶׁר עָבַדְתִּי אֹתְךָ בָּהֵן וְאֵלֵכָה כִּי אַתָּה
יָדַעְתָּ אֶת־עֲבֹדָתִי אֲשֶׁר עֲבַדְתִּיךָ:

[25] After Rachel had borne Joseph, Jacob said to Laban, "Give me leave to go back to my own homeland.
[26] Give me my wives and my children, for whom I have served you, that I may go; for well you know what services I have rendered you."

[25] After Rachel had borne Joseph, Jacob said to Laban, "Give me leave": We understand from the context that Jacob's seven years of working for Rachel are now ending. The end of Jacob's agreed term of service for his wives could also be a reason for him to leave his father-in-law. However, the Torah does not mention this explicitly, citing only the birth of Joseph as the signal to Jacob that he should leave Laban, because it was precisely Joseph's birth that served as a major turning point in Jacob's life. After all, Jacob came to Laban to marry and have children, and he considers Rachel his first and primary wife. When Rachel gives birth to Joseph, the original task is deemed complete.

The birth of Joseph was also necessary for balancing relations within the family. So long as Rachel had no children, she could not take her rightful, first place among Jacob's wives. Jacob's family is finally achieving balance and they are now ready to return to the Land of Israel.

Moreover, Joseph is Esau's antipode, his opposition. Because Joseph, like Esau, rules over the material world, he can be positioned as Esau's antithesis. Neither in war, nor in economics, nor in politics can Jewish spirituality or the priesthood (i.e., Jews like Judah) be used to counter hostile forces. For that we need Joseph, whose knowledge and skill are a match for Esau himself. In the person of Joseph, a Jewish personality has at last been born who can cope with Esau. There is no need for Jacob to remain in exile any longer; he can return home and engage in settling the land.

It is interesting to note that in *gematria* (the sum of the numerical values of the letters in a word), the names "Joseph" and "Zion" share the same value (156). As concerns modern-day Israel, this equivalence alludes to the fact that only Jews like Joseph can become the core of the Zionist movement that builds the Jewish state. Jews like Judah are unable to create such a movement – although it is they who in the future will fill the Jewish state with spiritual content.

In other words, Zionism cannot survive as a purely religious movement. It must have a connection with the material world, and it must be able to manage it. In its first stage,

Zionism therefore manifests as *Mashiach ben Yosef*, i.e., the kingdom of Joseph's descendants. Only at the next stage, the era of *Mashiach ben David*, can purely spiritual aspects become the foundation of Jewish statehood.

[26] Give me my wives and my children, for whom I have served you, that I may go; for well you know what services I have rendered you: Jacob's appeal to Laban has the character of a request, not a demand. Jacob is now waiting to be allowed to depart, but later he will leave without any permission, because it is life's problems themselves that give him his staunch resolve and independence, and the ability to become a leader. Only by taking a stand against Laban can Jacob acquire those qualities of Esau that are so important for him to advance to the status of Israel.

36.2. Jacob Lingers with Laban for the Receipt of His Wages (30:27-31)

כז וַיֹּאמֶר אֵלָיו לָבָן אִם־נָא מָצָאתִי חֵן בְּעֵינֶיךָ נִחַשְׁתִּי וַיְבָרֲכֵנִי יי בִּגְלָלֶךָ: **כח** וַיֹּאמַר נָקְבָה שְׂכָרְךָ עָלַי וְאֶתֵּנָה: **כט** וַיֹּאמֶר אֵלָיו אַתָּה יָדַעְתָּ אֵת אֲשֶׁר עֲבַדְתִּיךָ וְאֵת אֲשֶׁר־הָיָה מִקְנְךָ אִתִּי: **ל** כִּי מְעַט אֲשֶׁר־הָיָה לְךָ לְפָנַי וַיִּפְרֹץ לָרֹב וַיְבָרֶךְ יי אֹתְךָ לְרַגְלִי וְעַתָּה מָתַי אֶעֱשֶׂה גַם־אָנֹכִי לְבֵיתִי: **לא** וַיֹּאמֶר מָה אֶתֶּן־לָךְ וַיֹּאמֶר יַעֲקֹב לֹא־תִתֶּן־לִי מְאוּמָה אִם־תַּעֲשֶׂה־לִּי הַדָּבָר הַזֶּה אָשׁוּבָה אֶרְעֶה צֹאנְךָ אֶשְׁמֹר:

[27] But Laban said to him, "If you will indulge me, I have learned by divination that the Lord has blessed me on your account."
[28] And he continued, "Name the wages due from me, and I will pay you."

[29] But he said, "You know well how I have served you and how your livestock has fared with me.
[30] For the little you had before I came has grown to much, since the Lord has blessed you wherever I turned. And now, when shall I make provision for my own household?"
[31] He said, "What shall I pay you?" And Jacob said, "Pay me nothing! If you will do this thing for me, I will again pasture and keep your flocks:

[27] If you will indulge me: Jacob wishes to take his family and depart. He asks no additional compensation from Laban for his many years of work. In response, Laban persuades Jacob to continue working for him, and proposes that Jacob himself should name his price.

I have learned by divination that the Lord has blessed me on your account: By emphasizing that he knows that God's blessing came to him through Jacob, Laban creates the illusion of mutual understanding.

[31] If you will do this thing for me, I will again pasture and keep your flocks: For Jacob, any delay in departure is undesirable. Joseph has already been born, which means it is time to return home. But despite all this, Jacob agrees to postpone his departure. The Torah deems this delay so significant that it devotes two chapters to describing Jacob's six years of efforts to receive payment for his years of service to Laban.

The longer Jacob drags out his return, the more dangerous it will be. But Jacob does not wish to return, if it means leaving behind even the smallest particle of the Jewish heritage he has acquired in exile. He must find the "golden mean," so as not to spend too much time with Laban, but also not to forfeit what is rightfully his due. And in this he is treading a very fine line. Tradition tells us that Jacob stayed on with Laban longer than he should have, which is the reason he eventually had to flee under life-threatening conditions.

Throughout history, even after thousands of years of negative experiences, Diaspora Jews continue to deceive themselves concerning the good graces of neighboring peoples, and overshoot their chances for a peaceful, uneventful departure. Tragically, they must again and again extricate themselves from the claws of the surrounding world, paying with their very flesh for the opportunity to return to their Land.

36.3. Spotted, Speckled, and Mottled (30:32-33)

לב אֶעֱבֹר בְּכָל־צֹאנְךָ הַיּוֹם הָסֵר מִשָּׁם כָּל־שֶׂה ׀ נָקֹד וְטָלוּא וְכָל־שֶׂה־חוּם בַּכְּשָׂבִים וְטָלוּא וְנָקֹד בָּעִזִּים וְהָיָה שְׂכָרִי: **לג** וְעָנְתָה־בִּי צִדְקָתִי בְּיוֹם מָחָר כִּי־תָבוֹא עַל־שְׂכָרִי לְפָנֶיךָ כֹּל אֲשֶׁר־אֵינֶנּוּ נָקֹד וְטָלוּא בָּעִזִּים וְחוּם בַּכְּשָׂבִים גָּנוּב הוּא אִתִּי:

[32] let me pass through your whole flock today, removing from there every speckled and spotted animal – every dark-colored sheep and every spotted and speckled goat. Such shall be my wages. [33] In the future when you go over my wages, let my honesty toward you testify for me: if there are among my goats any that are not speckled or

spotted or any sheep that are not dark-colored, they got there by theft."

[32] Removing from there every speckled and spotted animal – every dark-colored sheep and every spotted and speckled goat. Such shall be my wages: In formal terms, Jacob was proposing to take for himself the lower-grade animals having speckles and spots. Such wool is more difficult to process, which would make it easier for Jacob to obtain Laban's consent for dividing the livestock.

Every speckled and spotted animal: The Torah is essentially a book of moral and ethical teachings. Thus, since the Torah makes a point to relate the episode of Jacob and the sheep, its significance must go beyond the merely historical. But that said, it is not easy to find the spiritual meaning of this story. This is therefore one of those passages of the Torah in which we feel the Kabbalistic (mystical) aspects begging to be included in the primary meaning of the text. According to this Kabbalistic approach, Laban, whose name means "white," is associated with the *Ein Sof*, the "Divine Infinity," because white light includes every other color of the visible color spectrum.

Laban, violating the moral standards of social relations, is understood as representing "an unclean (immoral) attempt to connect with the *Ein Sof*." He wants to devour Jacob, to see him dissolve and disappear into the endless Aramean universality, while Jacob's task is to break free, finding his own specific color. Jacob therefore needs neither pure white nor pure black; he needs "black on white," i.e., unique shades of "spotted, speckled, and mottled." In other words, Jewish specificity must break free of Aramean universality.

36.4. Laban Leaves Jacob with White Sheep (30: 34-36)

לד וַיֹּאמֶר לָבָן הֵן לוּ יְהִי כִדְבָרֶךָ׃ לה וַיָּסַר בַּיּוֹם הַהוּא
אֶת־הַתְּיָשִׁים הָעֲקֻדִּים וְהַטְּלֻאִים וְאֵת כָּל־הָעִזִּים
הַנְּקֻדּוֹת וְהַטְּלֻאֹת כֹּל אֲשֶׁר־לָבָן בּוֹ וְכָל־חוּם בַּכְּשָׂבִים
וַיִּתֵּן בְּיַד־בָּנָיו׃ לו וַיָּשֶׂם דֶּרֶךְ שְׁלֹשֶׁת יָמִים בֵּינוֹ וּבֵין
יַעֲקֹב וְיַעֲקֹב רֹעֶה אֶת־צֹאן לָבָן הַנּוֹתָרֹת׃

[34] And Laban said, "Very well, let it be as you say."
[35] But that same day he removed the streaked and spotted he-goats and all the speckled and spotted she-goats – every one that had white on it – and all the dark-colored sheep, and left them in the charge of his sons.
[36] And he put a distance of three days' journey between himself and Jacob, while Jacob was pasturing the rest of Laban's flock.

[34] Very well, let it be as you say: Laban has received an attractive offer that he cannot refuse.

[35] But that same day he removed the streaked and spotted he-goats and all the speckled and spotted she-goats ... and left them in the charge of his sons: Moreover, Laban immediately takes to deceiving Jacob. He goes through the herd and culls all the colored sheep, so that the only spotted sheep that Jacob can hope to get are the ones that will be born to the whites. Jacob, however, does not protest Laban's actions.

Jacob allows Laban to take those sheep not because he needs no payment, but because he did not raise those sheep himself. When Jacob himself will later breed sheep of motley shades, the herd will then unquestionably belong to him. From Babylon's extensive cultural wealth Jacob selects only those components that are suitable for building the future Jewish people. He selects only the sheep that serve his needs. And "sheep" here refers also to spiritual, not only material property.

Jacob had two tasks to accomplish in Haran: creating a family and acquiring wealth. These two aspects, children and wealth, together comprise a people and its culture. At the next stage of Jewish history, as they are leaving Egypt, our ancestors too will need to take with them a "mixed multitude" (Exodus 12:38), and gold and silver – the wealth of Egypt.

Much earlier in Jewish history, Abraham was promised that his descendants "in the end shall go free with great wealth" (15:14), and these words, although directly related to the Exodus from Egypt, apply to Jacob as well. Of course, wealth is not given away for free, and Jacob – like the Jews in Egypt – works hard, first for his wives (i.e., for the sake of creating a nation), and then to amass property (i.e. so that that nation will be wealthy). But it is also important for Jacob to take from Babylon the wealth that is his own, and not anyone else's.

Thus, the Jews must likewise bring back from their exile something valuable – the spiritual achievements of other nations, the sparks that are contained there, which they must then correctly process and integrate into the Land of Israel. Without that the world cannot function correctly, nor will the Jews be able to influence mankind. To a large extent, it was for just this purpose that that they were sent into exile.

36.5. Jacob Affects the Suit of Sheep (30: 37-43)

לז וַיִּקַּח־לוֹ יַעֲקֹב מַקַּל לִבְנֶה לַח וְלוּז וְעַרְמוֹן וַיְפַצֵּל
בָּהֵן פְּצָלוֹת לְבָנוֹת מַחְשֹׂף הַלָּבָן אֲשֶׁר עַל־הַמַּקְלוֹת: **לח**
וַיַּצֵּג אֶת־הַמַּקְלוֹת אֲשֶׁר פִּצֵּל בָּרְהָטִים בְּשִׁקֲתוֹת הַמָּיִם
אֲשֶׁר תָּבֹאןָ הַצֹּאן לִשְׁתּוֹת לְנֹכַח הַצֹּאן וַיֵּחַמְנָה בְּבֹאָן
לִשְׁתּוֹת: **לט** וַיֵּחֱמוּ הַצֹּאן אֶל־הַמַּקְלוֹת וַתֵּלַדְןָ הַצֹּאן
עֲקֻדִּים נְקֻדִּים וּטְלֻאִים: **מ** וְהַכְּשָׂבִים הִפְרִיד יַעֲקֹב
וַיִּתֵּן פְּנֵי הַצֹּאן אֶל־עָקֹד וְכָל־חוּם בְּצֹאן לָבָן וַיָּשֶׁת־לוֹ
עֲדָרִים לְבַדּוֹ וְלֹא שָׁתָם עַל־צֹאן לָבָן: **מא** וְהָיָה בְּכָל־
יַחֵם הַצֹּאן הַמְקֻשָּׁרוֹת וְשָׂם יַעֲקֹב אֶת־הַמַּקְלוֹת לְעֵינֵי
הַצֹּאן בָּרְהָטִים לְיַחְמֵנָּה בַּמַּקְלוֹת: **מב** וּבְהַעֲטִיף הַצֹּאן
לֹא יָשִׂים וְהָיָה הָעֲטֻפִים לְלָבָן וְהַקְּשֻׁרִים לְיַעֲקֹב: **מג**
וַיִּפְרֹץ הָאִישׁ מְאֹד מְאֹד וַיְהִי־לוֹ צֹאן רַבּוֹת וּשְׁפָחוֹת
וַעֲבָדִים וּגְמַלִּים וַחֲמֹרִים:

[37] *Jacob then got fresh shoots of poplar, and of almond and plane, and peeled white stripes in them, laying bare the white of the shoots.*
[38] *The rods that he had peeled he set up in front of the goats in the troughs, the water receptacles, that the goats came to drink from. Their mating occurred when they came to drink,*
[39] *and since the goats mated by the rods, the goats brought forth streaked, speckled, and spotted young.*
[40] *But Jacob dealt separately with the sheep; he made these animals face the streaked or wholly dark-colored animals in Laban's flock. And so he produced special flocks for himself, which he did not put with Laban's flocks.*
[41] *Moreover, when the sturdier animals were mating, Jacob would place the rods in the*

troughs, in full view of the animals, so that they
mated by the rods;
[42] but with the feebler animals he would not
place them there. Thus the feeble ones went to
Laban and the sturdy to Jacob.
[43] So the man grew exceedingly prosperous,
and came to own large flocks, maidservants and
menservants, camels and asses.

[37] Jacob then got fresh shoots: Jacob learns from Laban
an Aramean ploy: how to prevent yourself from being eaten
alive by using legal means to turn a situation to your own
advantage.

[39] The goats brought forth streaked, speckled, and spotted young: Jacob invokes the aid of a certain system of mystical selection, while at the same time also hoping for Divine
Providence ("And in the dream an angel of God said to me,
'Jacob!' 'Here,' I answered." – 31:11). In the end, he manages to
extract from the white sheep the mutations that he needs.

**[42] Thus the feeble ones went to Laban and the sturdy to
Jacob:** On the one hand, Laban wants to exploit the blessing that comes to him through Jacob, but on the other, he
does not want to pay Jacob for his work. Jacob therefore
leaves Laban whatever sheep are born naturally. Jacob does
not actually select the weak animals to be Laban's; he simply makes no special effort to breed variegated specimens
when the sheep are weak.

[43] So the man grew exceedingly prosperous: Jacob is
right both legally and morally. He does nothing illicit, and

acts with cunning in response to the behavior of Laban, who is doing his utmost to assure that Jacob will be left with nothing. When Jacob, in violation of all norms of proper conduct and family values, later flees from Laban, he will be justified in that too, because Laban's behavior with Jacob has also been unworthy. The Torah is teaching us that while we are living with "Labans" in their countries we cannot afford to be childishly innocent and naive, for it will be impossible for us then to survive.

36.6. Faceting the Attribute of Tiferet

We have noted earlier that Jacob is in the category of *Tiferet*, "glory, splendor," which is also *emet*, "truth." Its essence is in the balance between *Chesed* and *Gevurah*; that is, in understanding when to use *Chesed*'s mercy, and when, on the contrary, to use the harshness of *Gevurah*. Jacob by means of his tests, like Abraham and Isaac before him, successfully facets his attribute. In particular, he must realize that not always by far is the truth expressed through the direct and candid delivery of complete information. Sometimes it is a truly worthy deed simply not to be a sucker.

Jacob, who inclines to honesty ("a blameless man" – 25:27 [alternate translation]), must all his life balance himself on the edge of truthfulness – and sometimes even cross that line – so that his attribute of "truth" will receive the necessary faceting, in order to serve as the basis for the future survival of the Jewish people. Living with Laban in Haran is for Jacob a "higher education." Time and again they try to deceive him, and Jacob, while always acting honestly (albeit often not in the most exemplary manner), must be cunning simply to survive.

Jacob leaves not when he notices the change in Laban's attitude, but when God directly orders him to leave without delay. Thus, by his nature, Jacob (even in his relations with Laban) demonstrates a less harsh approach to the world around him than the world truly deserves.

36.7. Jacob's Rods and the Tefillin

The rods that Jacob set before the sheep are associated, according to the Midrash, with tefillin – phylacteries. These are leather boxes containing excerpts from the Five Books of the Torah, written on narrow strips of parchment, which Jewish men don on their upper arm and above the forehead during morning prayers. At the same time, the Midrash notes the "temporal" nature of the functioning of the rods as tefillin. When Jacob uses those rods to create the desired breed of sheep, there is a sanctity on the rods similar to that of tefillin, and therefore "those rods were Jacob's tefillin." But when Jacob removes the rods, for he no longer has any use for them, they again become ordinary branches.

As we have already had occasion to mention, sanctity in the era of the Patriarchs did not adhere to material objects. It remained for only a specified time, and then departed from the object that had received it. Only after the giving of the Torah did sanctity achieve a quality of permanence. Today, if sacred objects such as tefillin or a mezuzah become unusable, they retain their full sanctity, and such objects must therefore, rather than being summarily discarded, be placed in a *genizah*, a special place of protected storage.

Similarly, in the era of the Patriarchs the Chosen People was not yet a fixed concept. An individual who remained within Abraham's family belonged to that people, while those who left it ceased to be Jewish. Only after the Exodus and the giving of the Torah did Jewishness become a lasting and permanent attribute. Still in the same vein, the laws of Judaism took on the form of a fixed system of commandments only after the giving of the Torah. Until that time, only ideals, but not duties, were the basis of the teachings of the Patriarchs.

Returning, then, to the rods as tefillin: The midrash notes that in all tefillin there is "black and white" – the text written in black ink, and the white (i.e., blank) expanses of parchment, respectively. But Jacob's rods too have a kind of "black and white." There is black material covered with a *kelippah* ("shell," the bark that covers the rods), and we need to reveal the white *Or Ein Sof*, the light of Divine Infinity that is hidden inside it. The strippable bark and the visible white strip correspond to the tefillin, for both represent transcendence beyond the strictly material essence.

Moreover, Jacob's rods, like the tefillin, are perfectly even and straight. In referring to the head tefillin the Torah uses an unusual word, *totafot*, that derives from no known Hebrew root. One interpretation of this word is "that which is a replacement for the god Thoth." The traditional headdress of the pharaohs was the *uraeus*, an image of a cobra attached to the forehead, a symbol of wisdom associated with the god Thoth.

(Laban said: "I have learned by divination that the Lord has blessed me on your account." (30:27). The Hebrew is *nichashti*, which can be rendered as "I have become snakelike.")

It is this serpent of Egyptian royal garb that is transformed at the Exodus into Jewish tefillin. (*Totafot*, "that which replaces the god Thoth.")

The serpent coils itself into circles – a symbol of nature, in which there are no straight lines or sharp angles. (In the

Kabbalah too, a circle is symbolic of nature.) Tefillin must be square in shape, with sharply delineated right angles. A straight, direct ray of light (contrasting with everything that is natural and round) symbolizes Divine Providence, morality, meaning. When the square, angular tefillin replaces the circular snake, this symbolizes the victory of moral imperatives over nature, in which no morals intrinsically exist.

Jacob's straight rods express that same idea – the sovereignty of Divine Providence over the forces of nature, which will later be symbolized by the tefillin.

36.8. Jacob's Sheep as the Stages of Descent of the Sefirot from the Ein Sof

(In this portion we offer an overview of the Kabbalistic interpretation of the episode of Jacob's sheep, which sees it as representing stages in the creation of the universe. Readers who find this portion too difficult may skim or skip it. Comprehension of later chapters will not be affected in any way.)

Jacob receives a white herd of sheep for grazing (since Laban has taken all the spotted sheep). By breeding that herd, he must obtain for himself three types of sheep: *akudim* (streaked), *nekudim* (speckled), and *berudim* (mottled). More precisely, *akudim* means "bound," as in *la'akod*, "to hitch (an animal)," from the same root as *Akedat Yitzchak*, "the Binding of Isaac." When used with reference to the pigmentation of sheep it means animals marked with a pattern on their legs in the form of ringlets. Those sheep are, as it were, hobbled by rings, "ringed." *Nekudim* is a pattern of distinct dots, and *berudim* means spots intersecting one another.

White, as already noted, represents Laban (whose name literally means "white"), and the birth of colored sheep from

white ones represents the birth of Jacob's diverse children –
"streaked, speckled, and mottled" – from the daughters of
Laban. White is clear parchment, the universal, and black is
the written letters, the specific. Laban's intentions, like white,
which absorbs all other colors (i.e., it wants to "swallow"
everything), are to devour Jacob without letting go of him.

According to the kabbalah of Rabbi Isaac Luria (d. 1572,
Safed), Jacob's three types of sheep are interpreted as the
three stages of the descent of the *Sefirot* from the *Or Ein
Sof*, "The Light of Divine Infinity." This scheme can be elab-
orated as follows:

(1) Before the Creation, there is only infinite light, *Or Ein
Sof*. For the world to come into existence, that light
must give it space, and it therefore "self-constricts,"
it recedes to its edges, leaving a round, empty space
within. (In the Kabbalah this process is called *tzimtzum*, "self-constriction.") In this empty space the universe can now be constructed.

(2) After that *tzimtzum* (self-constriction of the *Or Ein
Sof*) happened, a *reshimo*, "imprint," remained in the
resulting empty space – a reflection of the original
Divine light that had now retreated. It is also called
avir, "air." This empty space (the *reshimo*, *avir*) has no
"corners," that is, it is entirely without heterogene-
ities of any kind, and is therefore called *agul*, "round."

This aspect of the universe is further responsible for the ongoing, uniform operation of the laws
of nature, which are dispassionate and impartial –
there is no defined direction or aspiration. The laws
of nature know no concept of freedom or purpose,
good or bad; those laws only maintain the order of
the universe, but do not themselves strive toward
anything. The coercion that exists in the world is a

consequence of the *agul* (that which is round or circular) as manifested in the cyclical laws of nature.

(3) Further into this space (which is a *round*, wide, uniform, and weak reflection), a *kav* – "direct ray, beam" is allowed to enter – a strong, narrow directed beam of light from the *Or Ein Sof*. In contrast to the *round* "off-reflection" that represents the cyclic, non-directional and causative laws of nature, the direct ray represents teleological Providence, which has its purpose and carries meaning.

(4) The point at which this direct ray enters the circular reflection is hereinafter referred to as the "top," meaning that in empty space there now arises an orientation of top and bottom. Beginning from the top, the ray advances to the bottom, the center of the empty space, and through this ray the formation and development of worlds takes place. The *round* connects with the Almighty through all that is natural, and the direct ray connects with the Almighty through Providence. The development and advancement of worlds does not occur naturally; rather, it is a manifestation of striving for the goal that God has established in the universe.

(5) From the *reshimo* ("imprint") the *Sefirot* are the first to be formed, under the influence of the ray. They then undergo a process of gradual transformation. The white light of the *Or Ein Sof* (it is white in the sense that it absorbs everything into itself), when passed through the "color filters" of the *Sefirot*, identifies individual lines of the Divine regulation of the world, which are further intertwined, forming a colored image of the universe that is filled with independence and dialogue.

The *Sefirot* can also be understood as "vessels of light," categories through which particular, specific aspects of Divinity become manifest – such as, for example, *Chochmah, Binah, Da'at, Chesed, Gevurah,* and *Tiferet*, all of which we have examined earlier.

The idea that "the *Sefirot* are formed from the *reshimo* under the influence of the ray" can also be formulated as "the *Sefirot* descend from the *Or Ein Sof* into empty space, spreading from top to bottom along this ray."

(6) The structure of the *Sefirot* is further reduplicated down, forming *worlds*. This reduplication is the reason for the similarity of the higher and lower in those worlds. Their sequence is more semantic than chronological: they descend from the higher-spiritual to the lower-material.

(7) And at the very top of this system of worlds (i.e., at the very root of the semantic and causal relationships that exist in the universe that surrounds us), are located those three stages of the descent of the *Sefirot* from the *Or Ein Sof*, that correspond to the colors of the Jacob's sheep – *akudim, nekudim* and *berudim*. Jacob's straight rods (and much later, the tefillin) represent the *ray*, because it is those very rods that are an instrument for breeding sheep, the source of the formation of the *Sefirot* and their development.

(8) At the threshold of the starting point at which the ray from the *Or Ein Sof* is just about to begin, everything is one, and nothing distinct can exist there. (Such absolute unity can exist only inside the Light of Infinity.) But in the process of the ray entering the empty space, when the *Sefirot* are supposed to appear, at the first stage of their development they initially appear

as *akudim*, "hobbled," i.e., they are at that point still rigidly bound into a single, inseparable unit.

(9) On the one hand, the unity of the *Sefirot* reflects the Divine unity, and to that extent it is both good and correct. But on the other hand, when all extremities are bound up into a single whole, advancement becomes impossible, and the entire process is thus deprived of its meaning. The Divine purpose, after all, is not to remain ever stagnant, but to advance the world. Remaining stuck at the first stage, *akudim*, when everything is connected and united, would be inconsistent with the Divine Plan.

Unity is important, but this unity must be achieved at the next level, as free unification that follows separation (we have touched on this issue earlier in this work, in our discussion of the transition from unity "back to back" to unity "face to face"). Having "untied," "unhobbled" the *Sefirot*, they are given their freedom: Each becomes independent of all the others and can now advance. They then move from the *akudim* stage to the *nekudim* stage – the "points" located lower down, along the ray. At this stage the *Sefirot* are represented as separate points not connected with one another.

(10) When the *Sefirot* become independent of each other, the opportunity then arises for development and advancement, and this is essential. However, a new problem arises: the problem of concentrating only on oneself. Having become independent, each *Sefirah* now sees only itself. Each exists entirely on its own and does not correlate with the others. In this situation, the *Sefirah* inevitably begins to absolutize itself. It deems itself is so important and all-embracing

that it believes it can contain all the Divine light in its entirety.

(11) The *Sefirot* are Divine categories. However, each Sefirah represents a very narrow part of Divinity, a limited vessel for the manifestation of one or another shade of Divine light. When a *Sefirah* tries to absorb all the Divine Light in its entirety (thus declaring itself the primary category of Divinity), then it tries to contain more than can fit into it, and it therefore bursts. Thus, the *Sefirot* at the *nekudim* stage "shatter from within," and a *shevirat keilim*, "shattering of vessels" occurs, after which the fragments of light, the "sparks," fall downward, where they are captured by the *kelippah* (outer shell).

(11a) The state in which the vessels are shattered is called olam tohu, "the world of chaos." Thus, the world of chaos and destruction arises when certain positive ideas are trying to contain more than they can.

(11b) Any positive and correct idea that proclaims itself the essence of Divinity will burst and break, because, no matter how good the idea may be, it is necessarily limited, and the attempt to "fit everything into it" will lead to its collapse. For example, the demand for complete and absolute justice destroys justice. Implementing a policy of universal mercy only degrades the recipients of that mercy (that is, what they will receive is "*anti*-mercy"). A desire to do everything very rationally leads to completely irrational behavior. A declaration that "God is love" in practice only primitivizes God. As a general principle, then, any idea of goodness that tries to realize only itself by discarding everything else will necessarily lead to the collapse of the system. This is the realization in our world of the idea of *shevirat keilim,* "shattering of the vessels."

(12) The next stage after *shevirat keilim* is the *tikkun* ("correction") stage, represented by the color of *berudim,* "mottled sheep" (in spots that intersect one another, just as all individual spots on modern camouflage clothing form a certain unified, complex spot). That is exactly what the *Sefirot* must become in the process of *tikkun,* "correction." At that point they have again become a vessel capable of receiving and containing the Divine light and transmitting it to us. In order to facilitate that *tikkun* process, we must remove the sparks from the outer shell, and glue them together to again become vessels. We can compare this to a radio receiver that has gone to pieces and its components tossed into the trash. After cleaning those components and properly rewiring their connections, we will again have a device capable of receiving Divine "radio broadcasts."

(13) Thus, the *Sefirot* can exist in three different states: *akudim,* streaked, then *nekudim,* speckled, when each exists on its own and there is a *shevirah,* shattering, and, finally, *berudim,* mottled, when the *Sefirot* are elaborately interconnected as the result of correction, *tikkun.* The *Sefirot* at this stage are no longer positioned independently of one another, but form an interconnected structure, the classical *Sefirot* tree (see the illustrations in portion 5.6). The equilibrium represented by that tree provides the foundation for a mended world.

(14) The progression from *akudim* to *nekudim* to *berudim* is a universal scheme that repeats itself in all elements of the universe. And, of course, the system of

the *Sefirot* can be observed at every level, essentially articulating the fundamental principle of mysticism, which asserts that the structure of higher worlds is repeated (reproduced) in lower ones. Thus, anything that happened once in higher worlds, when the universe was created, must later be realized again in lower worlds. Every concept that comes into the world must pass through these three stages, just like the stages of the descent of the *Sefirot*.

Thus, Jacob's breeding sheep of different stripes is regarded in Kabbalistic terms as representing the creation of the world, paralleling the stages of the descent of the *Sefirot*. By breeding sheep while at the same time moving away from Laban, Jacob creates worlds – he creates coloreds from whites, and the variegated from the infinitely uniform *Or Ein Sof*. A multicolored world then appears, in which all the colors of the spectrum have been separated out, and each is individually manifested.

Accordingly, each of the twelve sons of Jacob (each tribe of the Jewish people), has his own character, which must then be united with the all-encompassing scheme.

* * *

Of course, the Kabbalistic reading of the story of Jacob and his sheep in no way negates its simple meaning, namely, that Jacob is engaged in breeding sheep of whatever colors allow him to maximize his compensation for the labor he performs, in order to properly support his family. The

Kabbalah adds another layer to this reading, but only so as to complement, but not supplant, the simple reading of the Torah text.

Any story in the Torah, not only the story of Jacob's sheep, can sustain a Kabbalistic dimension of reading. The Kabbalah, an integral part of Judaism, enables us to better understand the commandments, study the Torah, and serve the Almighty. The above lengthy commentary was intended to open for the reader only a small window onto that world.

Chapter 37

Jacob Flees Laban's Home

37.1. Jacob Pulls Away (31:1-3)

א וַיִּשְׁמַע אֶת־דִּבְרֵי בְנֵי־לָבָן לֵאמֹר לָקַח יַעֲקֹב אֵת כָּל־
אֲשֶׁר לְאָבִינוּ וּמֵאֲשֶׁר לְאָבִינוּ עָשָׂה אֵת כָּל־הַכָּבֹד הַזֶּה:
ב וַיַּרְא יַעֲקֹב אֶת־פְּנֵי לָבָן וְהִנֵּה אֵינֶנּוּ עִמּוֹ כִּתְמוֹל
שִׁלְשׁוֹם: ג וַיֹּאמֶר יי אֶל־יַעֲקֹב שׁוּב אֶל־אֶרֶץ אֲבוֹתֶיךָ
וּלְמוֹלַדְתֶּךָ וְאֶהְיֶה עִמָּךְ:

[1] Now he heard the things that Laban's sons were saying: "Jacob has taken all that was our father's, and from that which was our father's he has built up all this wealth."
[2] Jacob also saw that Laban's manner toward him was not as it had been in the past.
[3] Then the Lord said to Jacob, "Return to the land of your fathers where you were born, and I will be with you."

[1] Jacob has taken all that was our father's: When Laban asked Jacob to stay on with him, he spoke of the blessing that the Lord had bestowed on him through Jacob. But now the situation has changed, and Jacob is seen as a thief.

In countries of the Jewish exile, there very often comes a moment when the local population decides that the new-comers – who were initially just weak and oppressed refu-gees, but have now become an active, economically viable stratum of society – have seized all the key positions, and now only profit at the expense of the local residents. It is best not to prolong one's stay in a foreign country long enough for that moment to arrive. But Jacob missed that moment.

Now he heard the things that Laban's sons were saying: The "sons of Laban" in this case are the local population, and "Laban" is its leadership. A change in public opinion (as expressed here by Laban's sons) occasions a change in the direction of public policy ("Laban's manner toward him"). Jacob has prolonged his stay with Laban to the point of put-ting himself at risk of persecution.

[3] Then the Lord said to Jacob, "Return to the land of your fathers: Jacob still tarries, not leaving until God directly and urgently tells him to do so. It is an eternal Jewish prob-lem to ignore the fact that the living in the country of exile is only temporary; they desire to remain there yet longer, still hoping that constructive interaction with the surrounding foreign culture remains possible.

These six years that Jacob worked for Laban to increase his holdings were for Jacob the most dangerous period of all those twenty years. Because, although he realized that the time had come to return to his ancestral land, Jacob lingered on, unsure whether he had already collected every possible "sheep." That is, Jacob worried about leaving behind some element of Babylonian civilization that would be needed for the future development of the Jewish people. Doing so might result in damage later and could even force a return to Babylon to retrieve whatever had been forgotten.

And I will be with you: This promise gives Jacob the courage to leave Laban without asking his permission.

37.2. Jacob Consults with Rachel and Leah (31:4-16)

ד וַיִּשְׁלַח יַעֲקֹב וַיִּקְרָא לְרָחֵל וּלְלֵאָה הַשָּׂדֶה אֶל־צֹאנוֹ: ה וַיֹּאמֶר לָהֶן רֹאֶה אָנֹכִי אֶת־פְּנֵי אֲבִיכֶן כִּי־אֵינֶנּוּ אֵלַי כִּתְמֹל שִׁלְשֹׁם וֵאלֹהֵי אָבִי הָיָה עִמָּדִי: ו וְאַתֵּנָה יְדַעְתֶּן כִּי בְּכָל־כֹּחִי עָבַדְתִּי אֶת־אֲבִיכֶן: ז וַאֲבִיכֶן הֵתֶל בִּי וְהֶחֱלִף אֶת־מַשְׂכֻּרְתִּי עֲשֶׂרֶת מֹנִים וְלֹא־נְתָנוֹ אֱלֹהִים לְהָרַע עִמָּדִי: ח אִם־כֹּה יֹאמַר נְקֻדִּים יִהְיֶה שְׂכָרֶךָ וְיָלְדוּ כָל־הַצֹּאן נְקֻדִּים וְאִם־כֹּה יֹאמַר עֲקֻדִּים יִהְיֶה שְׂכָרֶךָ וְיָלְדוּ כָל־הַצֹּאן עֲקֻדִּים: ט וַיַּצֵּל אֱלֹהִים אֶת־מִקְנֵה אֲבִיכֶם וַיִּתֶּן־לִי: י וַיְהִי בְּעֵת יַחֵם הַצֹּאן וָאֶשָּׂא עֵינַי וָאֵרֶא בַּחֲלוֹם וְהִנֵּה הָעַתֻּדִים הָעֹלִים עַל־הַצֹּאן עֲקֻדִּים נְקֻדִּים וּבְרֻדִּים: יא וַיֹּאמֶר אֵלַי מַלְאַךְ הָאֱלֹהִים בַּחֲלוֹם יַעֲקֹב וָאֹמַר הִנֵּנִי: יב וַיֹּאמֶר שָׂא־נָא עֵינֶיךָ וּרְאֵה כָּל־הָעַתֻּדִים הָעֹלִים עַל־הַצֹּאן עֲקֻדִּים נְקֻדִּים וּבְרֻדִּים כִּי רָאִיתִי אֵת כָּל־אֲשֶׁר לָבָן עֹשֶׂה לָּךְ: יג אָנֹכִי הָאֵל בֵּית־אֵל אֲשֶׁר מָשַׁחְתָּ שָּׁם מַצֵּבָה אֲשֶׁר נָדַרְתָּ לִּי שָׁם נֶדֶר עַתָּה קוּם צֵא מִן־הָאָרֶץ הַזֹּאת וְשׁוּב אֶל־אֶרֶץ מוֹלַדְתֶּךָ: יד וַתַּעַן רָחֵל וְלֵאָה וַתֹּאמַרְנָה לוֹ הַעוֹד לָנוּ חֵלֶק וְנַחֲלָה בְּבֵית אָבִינוּ: טו הֲלוֹא נָכְרִיּוֹת נֶחְשַׁבְנוּ לוֹ כִּי מְכָרָנוּ וַיֹּאכַל גַּם־אָכוֹל אֶת־כַּסְפֵּנוּ: טז כִּי כָל־הָעֹשֶׁר אֲשֶׁר הִצִּיל אֱלֹהִים מֵאָבִינוּ לָנוּ הוּא וּלְבָנֵינוּ וְעַתָּה כֹּל אֲשֶׁר אָמַר אֱלֹהִים אֵלֶיךָ עֲשֵׂה:

[4] Jacob had Rachel and Leah called to the field, where his flock was,

[5] and said to them, "I see that your father's manner toward me is not as it has been in the past. But the God of my father has been with me.

[6] As you know, I have served your father with all my might;

[7] but your father has cheated me, changing my wages time and again. God, however, would not let him do me harm.

[8] If he said thus, 'The speckled shall be your wages,' then all the flocks would drop speckled young; and if he said thus, 'The streaked shall be your wages,' then all the flocks would drop streaked young.

[9] God has taken away your father's livestock and given it to me.

[10] "Once, at the mating time of the flocks, I had a dream in which I saw that the he-goats mating with the flock were streaked, speckled, and mottled.

[11] And in the dream an angel of God said to me, 'Jacob!' 'Here,' I answered.

[12] And he said, 'Note well that all the he-goats which are mating with the flock are streaked, speckled, and mottled; for I have noted all that Laban has been doing to you.

[13] I am the God of Beth-el, where you anointed a pillar and where you made a vow to Me. Now, arise and leave this land and return to your native land.'"

[14] Then Rachel and Leah answered him, saying, "Have we still a share in the inheritance of our father's house?

[15] Surely, he regards us as outsiders, now that
he has sold us and has used up our purchase
price.
[16] Truly, all the wealth that God has taken
away from our father belongs to us and to our
children. Now then, do just as God has told you."

[4] Jacob had Rachel and Leah called to the field: When
Jacob summons his wives to a conference out of doors (the
Midrash explains that "walls have ears"), he gives Rachel pri-
ority over Leah. But Leah does not protest (v. 14).

[16] Belongs to us and to our children: Rachel and Leah
say, "our children," thus emphasizing unity. We see here a
clear indication that relations have now been harmonized
within Jacob's family.

**[6] As you know, I have served your father with all my
might:** Rather than simply informing them of his decision
as a *fait accompli*, Jacob explains the situation to his wives in
detail. He needs their support and strives for mutual understanding within the family. Once again this underscores the
wives' exalted status in the families of the Patriarchs.

**[3] Return to the land of your fathers where you were
born:** In departing from Laban's house, Jacob is returning
home, but Rachel and Leah will be abandoning their home
and their country. It is less than obvious that they understood when they married Jacob that at some point they
would have to relocate to Canaan, to which at that time
they had no connection. Jacob in his monologue therefore
emphasizes three points:

(1) Laban's unworthy behavior and the danger he poses to Jacob and his family;

(2) Divine intervention: Protection from Laban, the order to leave, and God's message to Jacob that his work in Paddan-aram is now complete (all the "streaked, speckled, and mottled" sheep have already been born);

(3) The Divine support is related to the Beit-El covenant, and the return to Canaan is an integral part of that covenant.

This lengthy elaboration by Jacob was important for severing Rachel and Leah spiritually from Paddan-aram, and to prepare them for forging their connection with the Land of Israel. But Jacob only partially achieves his goal. Although Rachel and Leah acknowledge that Laban's behavior is unworthy in the material plane, their response shows that they are still not able to make a clean break with Paddan-aram, and to create a connection with the Land of Israel. Because of this, Rachel cannot restrain herself from stealing Laban's *teraphim* (idols, 31:34), and this will result in tragedy.

37.3. Escape (31:17-21)

יז וַיָּקָם יַעֲקֹב וַיִּשָּׂא אֶת־בָּנָיו וְאֶת־נָשָׁיו עַל־הַגְּמַלִּים: יח וַיִּנְהַג אֶת־כָּל־מִקְנֵהוּ וְאֶת־כָּל־רְכֻשׁוֹ אֲשֶׁר רָכָשׁ מִקְנֵה קִנְיָנוֹ אֲשֶׁר רָכַשׁ בְּפַדַּן אֲרָם לָבוֹא אֶל־יִצְחָק אָבִיו אַרְצָה כְּנָעַן: יט וְלָבָן הָלַךְ לִגְזֹז אֶת־צֹאנוֹ וַתִּגְנֹב רָחֵל אֶת־הַתְּרָפִים אֲשֶׁר לְאָבִיהָ: כ וַיִּגְנֹב יַעֲקֹב אֶת־לֵב לָבָן הָאֲרַמִּי עַל־בְּלִי הִגִּיד לוֹ כִּי בֹרֵחַ הוּא: כא וַיִּבְרַח הוּא וְכָל־אֲשֶׁר־לוֹ וַיָּקָם וַיַּעֲבֹר אֶת־הַנָּהָר וַיָּשֶׂם אֶת־פָּנָיו הַר הַגִּלְעָד:

[17] Thereupon Jacob put his children and wives on camels;

[18] and he drove off all his livestock and all the wealth that he had amassed, the livestock in his possession that he had acquired sin Paddan-aram, to go to his father Isaac in the land of Canaan.

[19] Meanwhile Laban had gone to shear his sheep, and Rachel stole her father's household idols.

[20] Jacob kept Laban the Aramean in the dark, not telling him that he was fleeing,

[21] and fled with all that he had. Soon he was across the Euphrates and heading toward the hill country of Gilead.

[20] Jacob kept Laban the Aramean in the dark: Literally, "Jacob stole the heart of Laban the Aramean." The Torah here emphasizes the Aramean in Laban, his cunning, which serves as additional justification for Jacob to respond in kind.

[18] And he drove off all his livestock and all the wealth that he had amassed: Jacob takes "his livestock" (what belonged to him originally, and what he has acquired through skillful breeding). He has no need, however, for anything belonging to Laban, for he is now making a clean break from Paddan-aram.

[19] Rachel stole her father's household idols: Rachel, however, who still fails to understand the need for a clean break, steals the teraphim, Laban's household idols, the "guardian angels" of her parental home. We see here a clear parallel to Lot's wife, who looked back at Sodom and turned into a pillar of salt (19:26). In both of these cases there is a reluctance to break one's spiritual connection with a former world that must now be fully abandoned.

Household idols: Such are Laban's spirituality and aesthetics. The teraphim are to him nothing more than "domestic religious sculpture." His daughters, however, have a rather different relationship with those teraphim. Leah has "weak eyes," and is thus relatively indifferent to aesthetics. (Leah, in fact, sees farther and higher than ordinary beauty, because her connection is with eternity rather than temporality.) But for Rachel, who is "shapely and beautiful," aesthetics and family spirituality are paramount, and so she cannot resist the temptation to take the teraphim with her.

Such "excessive spirituality" will actually prevent the future Jewish nation from developing normally in the Land of Israel. Jacob by this time felt no temptation to take any further spirituality from Laban, but Rachel had not yet come to that level. She is still too attached to the house of Lavan, which was important only at earlier stage in the development of the Jewish people. In the end, this will directly lead to Raqchel's death while giving birth to Benjamin.

Today, too, as we, Jewish nation, return from the countries of our Exile carrying with us the "spiritual gold of Egypt", we must exercise extreme care not to bring with us into the Land of Israel elements of excessive, improper spirituality.

37.4. Laban Chases Down Jacob (31:22-29)

כב וַיֻּגַּד לְלָבָן בַּיּוֹם הַשְּׁלִישִׁי כִּי בָרַח יַעֲקֹב: **כג** וַיִּקַּח אֶת־אֶחָיו עִמּוֹ וַיִּרְדֹּף אַחֲרָיו דֶּרֶךְ שִׁבְעַת יָמִים וַיַּדְבֵּק

אֹתוֹ בְּהַר הַגִּלְעָד: **כד** וַיָּבֹא אֱלֹהִים אֶל־לָבָן הָאֲרַמִּי
בַּחֲלֹם הַלָּיְלָה וַיֹּאמֶר לוֹ הִשָּׁמֶר לְךָ פֶּן־תְּדַבֵּר עִם־יַעֲקֹב
מִטּוֹב עַד־רָע: **כה** וַיַּשֵּׂג לָבָן אֶת־יַעֲקֹב וְיַעֲקֹב תָּקַע
אֶת־אָהֳלוֹ בָּהָר וְלָבָן תָּקַע אֶת־אֶחָיו בְּהַר הַגִּלְעָד: **כו**
וַיֹּאמֶר לָבָן לְיַעֲקֹב מֶה עָשִׂיתָ וַתִּגְנֹב אֶת־לְבָבִי וַתְּנַהֵג
אֶת־בְּנֹתַי כִּשְׁבֻיוֹת חָרֶב: **כז** לָמָּה נַחְבֵּאתָ לִבְרֹחַ וַתִּגְנֹב
אֹתִי וְלֹא־הִגַּדְתָּ לִּי וָאֲשַׁלֵּחֲךָ בְּשִׂמְחָה וּבְשִׁרִים בְּתֹף
וּבְכִנּוֹר: **כח** וְלֹא נְטַשְׁתַּנִי לְנַשֵּׁק לְבָנַי וְלִבְנֹתָי עַתָּה
הִסְכַּלְתָּ עֲשׂוֹ: **כט** יֶשׁ־לְאֵל יָדִי לַעֲשׂוֹת עִמָּכֶם רָע וֵאלֹהֵי
אֲבִיכֶם אֶמֶשׁ ׀ אָמַר אֵלַי לֵאמֹר הִשָּׁמֶר לְךָ מִדַּבֵּר עִם־
יַעֲקֹב מִטּוֹב עַד־רָע:

[22] On the third day, Laban was told that Jacob
had fled.

[23] So he took his kinsmen with him and
pursued him a distance of seven days, catching
up with him in the hill country of Gilead.

[24] But God appeared to Laban the Aramean
in a dream by night and said to him, "Beware of
attempting anything with Jacob, good or bad."

[25] Laban overtook Jacob. Jacob had pitched his
tent on the Height, and Laban with his kinsmen
encamped in the hill country of Gilead.

[26] And Laban said to Jacob, "What did you
mean by keeping me in the dark and carrying
off my daughters like captives of the sword?

[27] Why did you flee in secrecy and mislead me
and not tell me? I would have sent you off with
festive music, with timbrel and lyre.

[28] You did not even let me kiss my sons and
daughters good-by! It was a foolish thing for
you to do.

[29] I have it in my power to do you harm; but

the God of your father said to me last night,
'Beware of attempting anything with Jacob,
good or bad.'

[29] I have it in my power to do you harm: Laban's words clearly indicate that he has pursued Jacob with hostile, not at all peaceful, intentions.

But the God of your father said to me last night: Only Heavenly intervention saves Jacob from death.

Beware of attempting anything with Jacob, good or bad: You must not try to kill him, nor to persuade him to stay.

As already mentioned, the internecine conflict between Abraham and Nahor had to do with their different views on the future of the *ivrim* (Hebrews). But more specifically, whether they should separate themselves from the nations of the world, or would they do better to assimilate among those peoples, spreading spirituality and ethical monotheism.

Bethuel and Laban were descended from the Nahor line, as were also the Matriarchs Rebekah, Rachel, and Leah. Not by chance were the tribes of Israel born from them, for this line carries important sparks of holiness. Indeed, the Jews exist only to facilitate the correction of the entire world, and without the ideas of universalism the existence of the Jewish people becomes meaningless. Even so, the line of Abraham claims that in order to correct the peoples of the world, it is first necessary to separate from them and to build a nation that lives its own independent life. But the Nahor family strongly disagrees with this idea.

Jacob arrived in the house of Laban as a poor fugitive from Canaan. He then married Laban's daughters, and lived with him and worked for him many more years, thereby demonstrating the apparent correctness of the Nahor approach.

But when Jacob now flees, the situation becomes diametrically reversed. Jacob is now demonstrating the correctness of Abraham's ideas rather than Nahor's. And Laban, who formerly wanted only to keep Jacob at home, is now ready to kill him. Jacob's return to Canaan "steals the heart of Laban" (31:20, alternate translation). That is, Jacob destroys Laban's worldview and leaves him bereft of a future by finally resolving the dispute of the *ivrim* in favor of the Land of Israel.

Zionism wrests the very heart from the Jewish Diaspora, which is one of the main reasons that even today the State of Israel provokes such strong ideological and even religious opposition among many Jews living beyond its borders.

37.5. Laban Searches Jacob's Tents (31:30-35)

לְ וְעַתָּה הָלֹךְ הָלַכְתָּ כִּי־נִכְסֹף נִכְסַפְתָּה לְבֵית אָבִיךָ לָמָּה גָנַבְתָּ אֶת־אֱלֹהָי: **לֹא** וַיַּעַן יַעֲקֹב וַיֹּאמֶר לְלָבָן כִּי יָרֵאתִי כִּי אָמַרְתִּי פֶּן־תִּגְזֹל אֶת־בְּנוֹתֶיךָ מֵעִמִּי: **לֹב** עִם אֲשֶׁר תִּמְצָא אֶת־אֱלֹהֶיךָ לֹא יִחְיֶה נֶגֶד אַחֵינוּ הַכֶּר־לְךָ מָה עִמָּדִי וְקַח־לָךְ וְלֹא־יָדַע יַעֲקֹב כִּי רָחֵל גְּנָבָתַם: **לֹג** וַיָּבֹא לָבָן בְּאֹהֶל יַעֲקֹב | וּבְאֹהֶל לֵאָה וּבְאֹהֶל שְׁתֵּי הָאֲמָהֹת וְלֹא מָצָא וַיֵּצֵא מֵאֹהֶל לֵאָה וַיָּבֹא בְּאֹהֶל רָחֵל: **לֹד** וְרָחֵל לָקְחָה אֶת־הַתְּרָפִים וַתְּשִׂמֵם בְּכַר הַגָּמָל וַתֵּשֶׁב עֲלֵיהֶם וַיְמַשֵּׁשׁ לָבָן אֶת־כָּל־הָאֹהֶל וְלֹא מָצָא: **לֹה** וַתֹּאמֶר אֶל־אָבִיהָ אַל־יִחַר בְּעֵינֵי אֲדֹנִי כִּי לוֹא אוּכַל לָקוּם מִפָּנֶיךָ כִּי־דֶרֶךְ נָשִׁים לִי וַיְחַפֵּשׂ וְלֹא מָצָא אֶת־הַתְּרָפִים:

[30] Very well, you had to leave because you were longing for your father's house; but why did you steal my gods?

[31] Jacob answered Laban, saying, "I was afraid because I thought you would take your daughters from me by force.

[32] But anyone with whom you find your gods shall not remain alive! In the presence of our kinsmen, point out what I have of yours and take it." Jacob, of course, did not know that Rachel had stolen them.

[33] So Laban went into Jacob's tent and Leah's tent and the tents of the two maidservants; but he did not find them. Leaving Leah's tent, he entered Rachel's tent.

[34] Rachel, meanwhile, had taken the idols and placed them in the camel cushion and sat on them; and Laban rummaged through the tent without finding them.

[35] For she said to her father, "Let not my lord take it amiss that I cannot rise before you, for the period of women is upon me." Thus he searched, but could not find the household idols.

[30] Why did you steal my gods?: Although it is obvious from Jacob's answer in the next verse that Laban posed a real danger, Laban, after receiving the Divine warning, cannot mention his daughters or property. All he can do is to demand the return of the teraphim.

[32] But anyone with whom you find your gods shall not remain alive!: Jacob believes that all the members of his family relate to Laban just the same as he himself does, and thus none of them could have appropriated those idols for themselves. He swears a hasty oath, which will later lead to tragic consequences.

Excessive confidence in one's rightness, even with the best intentions, is very dangerous, and awareness of this is an important aspect of faceting Tiferet, "truth," Jacob's attribute.

[35] I cannot rise before you: Notwithstanding how badly Laban wants to find the teraphim, he will not ask Rachel to change her seat. The Torah mandates that a place where a woman has sat during her menstrual period is "unclean," and this was apparently the commonly held view also in the general culture of those times. Laban will therefore not search for the teraphim where Rachel is sitting.

37.6. Jacob Responds to Laban's Accusation (31:36-43)

לו וַיִּחַר לְיַעֲקֹב וַיָּרֶב בְּלָבָן וַיַּעַן יַעֲקֹב וַיֹּאמֶר לְלָבָן מַה־פִּשְׁעִי מַה חַטָּאתִי כִּי דָלַקְתָּ אַחֲרָי: **לז** כִּי־מִשַּׁשְׁתָּ אֶת־כָּל־כֵּלַי מַה־מָּצָאתָ מִכֹּל כְּלֵי־בֵיתֶךָ שִׂים כֹּה נֶגֶד אַחַי וְאַחֶיךָ וְיוֹכִיחוּ בֵּין שְׁנֵינוּ: **לח** זֶה עֶשְׂרִים שָׁנָה אָנֹכִי עִמָּךְ רְחֵלֶיךָ וְעִזֶּיךָ לֹא שִׁכֵּלוּ וְאֵילֵי צֹאנְךָ לֹא אָכָלְתִּי: **לט** טְרֵפָה לֹא־הֵבֵאתִי אֵלֶיךָ אָנֹכִי אֲחַטֶּנָּה מִיָּדִי תְּבַקְשֶׁנָּה גְּנֻבְתִי יוֹם וּגְנֻבְתִי לָיְלָה: **מ** הָיִיתִי בַיּוֹם אֲכָלַנִי חֹרֶב וְקֶרַח בַּלָּיְלָה וַתִּדַּד שְׁנָתִי מֵעֵינָי: **מא** זֶה־לִּי עֶשְׂרִים שָׁנָה בְּבֵיתֶךָ עֲבַדְתִּיךָ אַרְבַּע־עֶשְׂרֵה שָׁנָה בִּשְׁתֵּי בְנֹתֶיךָ וְשֵׁשׁ שָׁנִים בְּצֹאנֶךָ וַתַּחֲלֵף אֶת־מַשְׂכֻּרְתִּי עֲשֶׂרֶת מֹנִים: **מב** לוּלֵי אֱלֹהֵי אָבִי אֱלֹהֵי אַבְרָהָם וּפַחַד יִצְחָק הָיָה לִי כִּי עַתָּה רֵיקָם שִׁלַּחְתָּנִי אֶת־עָנְיִי וְאֶת־יְגִיעַ כַּפַּי רָאָה אֱלֹהִים וַיּוֹכַח אָמֶשׁ: **מג** וַיַּעַן לָבָן וַיֹּאמֶר אֶל־יַעֲקֹב הַבָּנוֹת בְּנֹתַי וְהַבָּנִים בָּנַי וְהַצֹּאן צֹאנִי וְכֹל אֲשֶׁר־אַתָּה רֹאֶה לִי־הוּא וְלִבְנֹתַי מָה־אֶעֱשֶׂה לָאֵלֶּה הַיּוֹם אוֹ לִבְנֵיהֶן אֲשֶׁר יָלָדוּ:

[36] Now Jacob became incensed and took up his

grievance with Laban. Jacob spoke up and said to Laban, "What is my crime, what is my guilt that you should pursue me?

[37] You rummaged through all my things; what have you found of all your household objects? Set it here, before my kinsmen and yours, and let them decide between us two.

[38] "These twenty years I have spent in your service, your ewes and she-goats never miscarried, nor did I feast on rams from your flock.

[39] That which was torn by beasts I never brought to you; I myself made good the loss; you exacted it of me, whether snatched by day or snatched by night.

[40] Often, scorching heat ravaged me by day and frost by night; and sleep fled from my eyes.

[41] Of the twenty years that I spent in your household, I served you fourteen years for your two daughters, and six years for your flocks; and you changed my wages time and again.

[42] Had not the God of my father, the God of Abraham and the Fear of Isaac, been with me, you would have sent me away empty-handed. But God took notice of my plight and the toil of my hands, and He gave judgment last night."

[43] Then Laban spoke up and said to Jacob, "The daughters are my daughters, the children are my children, and the flocks are my flocks; all that you see is mine. Yet what can I do now about my daughters or the children they have borne?

[36] Now Jacob became incensed and took up his grievance with Laban: One of the stages in Jacob's development as he returns to his country is that he learns to exercise his right to speak freely. Having reached the border of Canaan, Jacob is increasingly becoming Israel. He freely speaks his mind, despite the strength and support that Laban has behind him. Jacob, besides addressing the baseless accusations of theft, also advances counterclaims for his twenty years of service. Only now do we learn that he has been receiving less than the going rate, even while working harder and more effectively than a typical shepherd.

[39] That which was torn by beasts I never brought to you: According to the laws of the Torah (Ex. 22:12), and also the Code of Hammurabi, a shepherd is not obliged to compensate for this kind of loss, and must only show the torn remains to the owner. But Jacob declined to invoke that escape clause.

[43] The daughters are my daughters, the children are my children, and the flocks are my flocks; all that you see is mine: Jacob's monologue makes not the slightest impression on Laban. Laban brazenly asserts that everything that Jacob has – his wives, his children, and his herds – belongs to him, Laban, and that only a Divine order is preventing him from reclaiming it all from Jacob.

This is an important lesson for the Jews: No matter how honorably they behave in the Diaspora, there is a high probability that they will eventually be accused of "robbing the local population." And no reasonable argument will be effective to clear them of this charge.

Although Laban finds Jacob's talk not the least convincing, it is important in a different way, namely, it enables Jacob to correctly perceive and position himself. Although the Jews should not hope to easily persuade "Laban," or expect that the surrounding nations will readily yield to their arguments, the ability to freely formulate and express their position is indispensable, most of all for the Jews themselves. It is an integral part of the sense of inner freedom that is necessary for their proper development.

37.7. Laban and Jacob Part Company (31:44-54)

מד וְעַתָּה לְכָה נִכְרְתָה בְרִית אֲנִי וָאָתָּה וְהָיָה לְעֵד בֵּינִי וּבֵינֶךָ: מה וַיִּקַּח יַעֲקֹב אָבֶן וַיְרִימֶהָ מַצֵּבָה: מו וַיֹּאמֶר יַעֲקֹב לְאֶחָיו לִקְטוּ אֲבָנִים וַיִּקְחוּ אֲבָנִים וַיַּעֲשׂוּ־גָל וַיֹּאכְלוּ שָׁם עַל־הַגָּל: מז וַיִּקְרָא־לוֹ לָבָן יְגַר שָׂהֲדוּתָא וְיַעֲקֹב קָרָא לוֹ גַּלְעֵד: מח וַיֹּאמֶר לָבָן הַגַּל הַזֶּה עֵד בֵּינִי וּבֵינֶךָ הַיּוֹם עַל־כֵּן קָרָא־שְׁמוֹ גַּלְעֵד: מט וְהַמִּצְפָּה אֲשֶׁר אָמַר יִצֶף יי בֵּינִי וּבֵינֶךָ כִּי נִסָּתֵר אִישׁ מֵרֵעֵהוּ: נ אִם־תְּעַנֶּה אֶת־בְּנֹתַי וְאִם־תִּקַּח נָשִׁים עַל־בְּנֹתַי אֵין אִישׁ עִמָּנוּ רְאֵה אֱלֹהִים עֵד בֵּינִי וּבֵינֶךָ: נא וַיֹּאמֶר לָבָן לְיַעֲקֹב הִנֵּה | הַגַּל הַזֶּה וְהִנֵּה הַמַּצֵּבָה אֲשֶׁר יָרִיתִי בֵּינִי וּבֵינֶךָ: נב עֵד הַגַּל הַזֶּה וְעֵדָה הַמַּצֵּבָה אִם־אָנִי לֹא־אֶעֱבֹר אֵלֶיךָ אֶת־הַגַּל הַזֶּה וְאִם־אַתָּה לֹא־תַעֲבֹר אֵלַי אֶת־הַגַּל הַזֶּה וְאֶת־הַמַּצֵּבָה הַזֹּאת לְרָעָה: נג אֱלֹהֵי אַבְרָהָם וֵאלֹהֵי נָחוֹר יִשְׁפְּטוּ בֵינֵינוּ אֱלֹהֵי אֲבִיהֶם וַיִּשָּׁבַע יַעֲקֹב בְּפַחַד אָבִיו יִצְחָק: נד וַיִּזְבַּח יַעֲקֹב זֶבַח בָּהָר וַיִּקְרָא לְאֶחָיו לֶאֱכָל־לָחֶם וַיֹּאכְלוּ לֶחֶם וַיָּלִינוּ בָּהָר:

[44] Come, then, let us make a pact, you and I, that there may be a witness between you and me."
[45] Thereupon Jacob took a stone and set it up as a pillar.

[46] And Jacob said to his kinsmen, "Gather stones." So they took stones and made a mound; and they partook of a meal there by the mound.
[47] Laban named it Yegar-sahadutha, but Jacob named it Gal-ed.
[48] And Laban declared, "This mound is a witness between you and me this day." That is why it was named Gal-ed;
[49] And [it was called] Mizpah, because he said, "May the Lord watch between you and me, when we are out of sight of each other.
[50] If you ill-treat my daughters or take other wives besides my daughters – though no one else be about, remember, God Himself will be witness between you and me."
[51] And Laban said to Jacob, "Here is this mound and here the pillar which I have set up between you and me:
[52] this mound shall be witness and this pillar shall be witness that I am not to cross to you past this mound, and that you are not to cross to me past this mound and this pillar, with hostile intent.
[53] May the God of Abraham and the god of Nahor – their ancestral deities – judge between us." And Jacob swore by the Fear of his father Isaac.
[54] Jacob then offered up a sacrifice on the Height, and invited his kinsmen to partake of the meal. After the meal, they spent the night on the Height.

[44] Come, then, let us make a pact: It is no longer possible for Laban to recover the fugitives, nor can he any longer rob Jacob. He thus has no choice but to conclude an alliance with Jacob, a friendship treaty.

[50] If you ... take other wives besides my daughters: Laban understands that the further development of the Jewish people no longer depends on him. He wants only a guarantee that Jacob will not marry other wives, so that all subsequent generations will be descendants only of his daughters.

There is a significant amount of hypocrisy in all this. Originally, Jacob had no need at all for more than just one wife – he initially sought to marry Rachel alone. Even so, this is a positive desire on Laban's part, which is aroused in him, however, only because Jacob now holds all the cards.

[51] This mound: The Torah gives the names of this "Mound of Testimony" in two languages. In Aramaic it is "*Yegar-sahadutha*," and in Hebrew, *Gal-Ed*. Jacob, now returning to the Land of Israel, reverts to speaking Hebrew, while Laban remains an Aramaean speaking the *lingua franca* of that era.

Jewish self-expression cannot be complete unless Hebrew is a living language. It is no coincidence that in the modern era, the resurrection of Hebrew occurred contemporaneously with the rise of the Zionist movement that revived Jewish national life in its ancient homeland. The mound here erected serves not only as the geographical boundary separating Laban from Jacob, but also as the sign of our internal chronological and linguistic "boundary" separating Jacob of the Diaspora from the future nation – Israel in the Holy Land.

37.8. The Angels Meet Jacob at Mahanaim (32:1-3)

א וַיַּשְׁכֵּם לָבָן בַּבֹּקֶר וַיְנַשֵּׁק לְבָנָיו וְלִבְנוֹתָיו וַיְבָרֶךְ
אֶתְהֶם וַיֵּלֶךְ וַיָּשָׁב לָבָן לִמְקֹמוֹ: ב וְיַעֲקֹב הָלַךְ לְדַרְכּוֹ
וַיִּפְגְּעוּ־בוֹ מַלְאֲכֵי אֱלֹהִים: ג וַיֹּאמֶר יַעֲקֹב כַּאֲשֶׁר רָאָם
מַחֲנֵה אֱלֹהִים זֶה וַיִּקְרָא שֵׁם־הַמָּקוֹם הַהוּא מַחֲנָיִם:

*[1] Early in the morning, Laban kissed his sons
and daughters and bade them good-by; then
Laban left on his journey homeward.*
*[2] Jacob went on his way, and angels of God
encountered him.*
*[3] When he saw them, Jacob said, "This is God's
camp." So he named that place Mahanaim.*

**Laban ... left on his journey homeward. [2] Jacob went on
his way:** The literal translation is "Laban went and returned
to his place, and Jacob went on his way." Laban retreats backward, while Jacob advances forward.

[2] Angels of God encountered him: Just as Jacob had seen
angels when he was leaving the Land of Israel (28:12), so
does he meet them now again upon his return. When he was
departing, however, the angels were on the stairway and in
heaven. But now Jacob meets them down on earth. And he
names the place *Mahanaim*, "Two Camps."

According to the Midrash, the angels who accompanied
Jacob to Paddan-aram leave him, and the angels of the Land
of Israel take over for them. There is an important difference
between these two groups of angels. Because the Land of
Israel is under the direct control of the Almighty, the angels
play only a subsidiary role in it – they "live on the land." But

the inhabitants of lands outside the borders of Israel are governed by the leading angels of their respective regions, who
exercise their control from heaven. Each such angel is called
Sar, the "minister" of the given country (see Daniel, ch. 10).

Weekly Portion
Vayishlach

Chapter 38

Jacob Battles the Angel

38.1. Jacob's Transition to "Israel"

These two portions of the Torah – the one just completed, and this one now beginning – recount the life story of the third of our three Patriarchs. The two portions are associated, respectively, with his two names, "Jacob" and "Israel." The first portion, *Vayetze*, tells about his life in exile, where his name is Jacob, while the second, *Vayishlach*, describes his life in his own land, where he is called "Israel." Receiving the name "Israel" is connected with the return to the Land, where Jacob begins to exist as an independent, national-political entity.

Earlier in this book, Genesis, we have seen a very similar situation with the first of the three Patriarchs, whose life story, likewise under two different names, is told in the two weekly Torah portions *Lech Lecha* and *Vayera*. His name is "Abram" in the first of those portions, but "Abraham" in the second.

As already noted, Israel is actually Jacob who has acquired some of Esau's qualities, a synthesis that results in a "hybrid" of Isaac's two sons, who has "Jacob's voice but Esau's hands"

(27:22). Although originally intended to confuse their father, this synthesis was needed for further personal development. Jacob had to learn how to behave in the manner of his older brother Esau: to fight, to hunt, to manage wildlife, and so on.

Jacob must master Esau's qualities in order to achieve "Esau-ness" in all aspects relating to hands. But Jacob's voice (that is, what he proclaims to the world) must always remain "the voice of Jacob."

For that voice to be heard by mankind, *Jacob* must become *Israel*, for the Jewish people can influence the world only as an independent people and state. Only in their Land and in connection with it can the Jewish people create biblical texts that change the course of human history. In isolation from that Land the Jews can create only Talmudic texts, which are highly important for them, but not compelling enough to influence the rest of mankind.

38.2. The Nations of the World Sanction Israel's Return to Its Land (32:4)

ד וַיִּשְׁלַח יַעֲקֹב מַלְאָכִים לְפָנָיו אֶל־עֵשָׂו אָחִיו אַרְצָה שֵׂעִיר שְׂדֵה אֱדוֹם:

[4] Jacob sent messengers ahead to his brother Esau in the land of Seir, the country of Edom,

[4] Jacob sent messengers ahead: Jacob is now returning from the northeast, from Haran, to his father Isaac in Hebron. Seir and Edom are south of Hebron and south of the Dead Sea, a region that stretches down to Eilat. Why is Jacob sending messengers to Esau (who lives, as can be seen from this verse, apart from Isaac), instead of proceeding directly to his father in Hebron? Jacob had fled from Esau because he was threatening to kill him. Why would Jacob now, as the Midrash puts it, "wake a sleeping dog by yanking its tail"?

Apparently, seeking permission from Edom to return from exile makes historical sense. "Jacob" must keep "Esau" in the loop because the Jews' return to their Land will likewise affect other world nations.

In that era, Esau was just Jacob's brother. But as already noted, Jewish tradition identifies Esau with the Roman Empire and all of Western Christian civilization. Edom is king of this world, a superpower, an international authority. Israel's return to its land causes upheaval on the world map, and human ethical norms therefore require the Jews to inform Esau – i.e., the nations of the world – that it is imminent. The peoples of the world should be deeply involved in this process. The revival of Jewish life in the Land of Israel must receive their sanction.

Geulah, Redemption, the Messianic return of the people of Israel to their Land, is a *geulah* for the entire world as well. Israel must grant the peoples of the world the opportunity to participate in their return, so that that event can become a beacon for them too.

Establishing statehood is a complex process for any nation, but for the Jewish people it is even more difficult and problematic. The mission of the Jewish people is to influence humanity. Were it otherwise, they would long ago have left the stage of history, like so many other peoples of antiquity. The Jewish state is an essential element of influence. The peoples of the world must acknowledge this fact and assent to it.

And that is why Moses, in the events leading up to the Exodus from Egypt, repeatedly asks Pharaoh's permission for the Jews to leave his country. (God could have led the Jews out of Egypt with or without such permission from Pharaoh.)

Likewise, Cyrus King of Persia authorizes the building of the Second Temple, and the creation of the modern State of Israel drew its authority from the relevant decisions of the League of Nations and the United Nations. From a religious perspective, this is a critical point.

Of course, the Jews' right to their Land in no way depends on the nations of the world. But the exercise of that right must find support in legitimization by those nations.

38.3. Jacob Addresses Esau (32:5-6)

ה וַיְצַו אֹתָם לֵאמֹר כֹּה תֹאמְרוּן לַאדֹנִי לְעֵשָׂו כֹּה אָמַר
עַבְדְּךָ יַעֲקֹב עִם־לָבָן גַּרְתִּי וָאֵחַר עַד־עָתָּה: ו וַיְהִי־לִי
שׁוֹר וַחֲמוֹר צֹאן וְעֶבֶד וְשִׁפְחָה וָאֶשְׁלְחָה לְהַגִּיד לַאדֹנִי
לִמְצֹא־חֵן בְּעֵינֶיךָ:

[5] and instructed them as follows, "Thus shall you say, 'To my lord Esau, thus says your servant Jacob: I stayed with Laban and remained until now;
[6] I have acquired cattle, asses, sheep, and male and female slaves; and I send this message to my lord in the hope of gaining your favor.'"

[5] And remained until now: More literally, "And I have tarried until now." Jacob believes that he stayed too long with Laban and should have returned earlier.

[6] Cattle, asses, sheep, and male and female slaves: This enumeration of property in no way accords with Isaac's blessing that Jacob preempted from Esau. That blessing promised "the dew of heaven and the fat of the earth" (27:28), that is, land that yields a bountiful harvest. But cattle, asses, sheep, and slaves have nothing to do with the land or its produce.

Jacob is trying to convince Esau that Isaac's blessing has not had its desired effect, and that Esau therefore has no reason to be angry. This of course demonstrates that Jacob continues to have issues with Isaac's blessing. He still feels that he should not have received that blessing, that it is not rightfully his.

38.4. Jacob Fears Being Killed, but Also Having to Kill (32:7-8)

ז וַיָּשֻׁבוּ הַמַּלְאָכִים אֶל־יַעֲקֹב לֵאמֹר בָּאנוּ אֶל־אָחִיךָ
אֶל־עֵשָׂו וְגַם הֹלֵךְ לִקְרָאתְךָ וְאַרְבַּע־מֵאוֹת אִישׁ עִמּוֹ: ח
וַיִּירָא יַעֲקֹב מְאֹד וַיֵּצֶר לוֹ ...

[7] The messengers returned to Jacob, saying, "We came to your brother Esau; he himself is coming to meet you, and there are four hundred men with him."
[8] Jacob was greatly frightened; in his anxiety, ...

[7] And there are four hundred men with him: An entourage of four hundred men clearly shows that Esau is not preparing for a peaceful meeting with his brother. Jacob has spent twenty years in exile, during which time Esau has apparently amassed a powerful army.

[8] Jacob was greatly frightened; in his anxiety ...: The Torah here uses two related terms to describe Jacob's internal condition: fright, and anxiety. Rather than understanding these terms as synonymous, the Midrash takes their meanings as complementarily opposite. Jacob is frightened that Esau would kill *him*, but anxious at the thought that he himself might have to kill *others*. And he dreads both of those equally.

Jacob is afraid of killing his enemies. What if those soldiers are completely innocent? What if they are good people who have gone to war not by choice? We see here that Jacob is not prepared to build a state. How can one do battle with one's enemies while fearing that someone having no inimical intentions might get hurt?

Jacob's reluctance to fight and kill is a perfectly normal human emotion, but it means that Jacob has not yet become Israel. War is bad in and of itself, but to create a people, Jacob must learn to fight, which includes overcoming his own fear of having to fight.

The Midrash explains that Jacob's dread of killing Esau is his fear of extinguishing any sparks of goodness and holiness within Esau that were destined to be revealed only in the future through Esau's descendants. Indeed, among Esau's descendants (and, in principle, among the descendants of any of the enemies of the Jews today) there may be good people, even truly righteous individuals, whose later appearance will be impossible if their wicked ancestors are eliminated now.

What Jacob is here experiencing is a natural and very characteristically Jewish feeling. In today's Arab-Israeli conflict, the number of Jewish peacekeepers who deem it a priority to refrain from killing Arabs is incommensurably greater than in any comparable situation where a people is in a state of war threatening its very existence. And although these Jews' position is of course completely indefensible, we must admit that this too is typically "Jewish" behavior.

Each element within the Jewish people sees its own aspect of truth and is prepared to fight for that truth. There is an aspect of the highest truth in the idea that even in our enemies "on the other side," and in the forces of evil generally, there are sparks of holiness and correctness. Thus, the "Jewish peacekeepers," even while they speak out against Israel, are motivated by a proper Jewish sentiment.

This feeling, however, is in them not correctly realized, for it has been elevated to the level of an absolute, which means it is trying to embody the whole ideal of justice, while it is in fact only a limited part of it. (This mechanism was explained in detail earlier [§34.8], in the context of the process of *shevirat keilim*, the "shattering of vessels.")

The balanced and correct approach would be to adopt a humane attitude toward the enemy, but with the understanding that under conditions of danger threatening the very existence of the Jewish people, self-preservation must always remain the highest priority. Risking the lives of our own citizens and soldiers while we defend our enemies who fight against us and kill us is self-destructive behavior and represents a gross distortion of reality.

But what about those potentially righteous individuals who will never be born from the villain whom we kill today? The answer is that we leave it to God himself to devise a plan for preserving the sparks of holiness that need to come from there. We can only act as our situation today requires; all the rest is hidden from us. We must move past our fear of destroying the spark of future good that might be hiding in today's evil. We must fight – neither demonizing the enemy, nor being afraid to destroy him.

38.5. Jacob's Prayer (32:8-13)

ח ... וַיַּחַץ אֶת־הָעָם אֲשֶׁר־אִתּוֹ וְאֶת־הַצֹּאן וְאֶת־הַבָּקָר
וְהַגְּמַלִּים לִשְׁנֵי מַחֲנוֹת: ט וַיֹּאמֶר אִם־יָבוֹא עֵשָׂו אֶל־
הַמַּחֲנֶה הָאַחַת וְהִכָּהוּ וְהָיָה הַמַּחֲנֶה הַנִּשְׁאָר לִפְלֵיטָה:
י וַיֹּאמֶר יַעֲקֹב אֱלֹהֵי אָבִי אַבְרָהָם וֵאלֹהֵי אָבִי יִצְחָק יי
הָאֹמֵר אֵלַי שׁוּב לְאַרְצְךָ וּלְמוֹלַדְתְּךָ וְאֵיטִיבָה עִמָּךְ: יא
קָטֹנְתִּי מִכֹּל הַחֲסָדִים וּמִכָּל־הָאֱמֶת אֲשֶׁר עָשִׂיתָ אֶת־
עַבְדֶּךָ כִּי בְמַקְלִי עָבַרְתִּי אֶת־הַיַּרְדֵּן הַזֶּה וְעַתָּה הָיִיתִי
לִשְׁנֵי מַחֲנוֹת: יב הַצִּילֵנִי נָא מִיַּד אָחִי מִיַּד עֵשָׂו כִּי־
יָרֵא אָנֹכִי אֹתוֹ פֶּן־יָבוֹא וְהִכַּנִי אֵם עַל־בָּנִים: יג וְאַתָּה
אָמַרְתָּ הֵיטֵב אֵיטִיב עִמָּךְ וְשַׂמְתִּי אֶת־זַרְעֲךָ כְּחוֹל הַיָּם
אֲשֶׁר לֹא־יִסָּפֵר מֵרֹב:

[8] ... he divided the people with him, and the
flocks and herds and camels, into two camps,
[9] thinking, "If Esau comes to the one camp
and attacks it, the other camp may yet escape."
[10] Then Jacob said, "O God of my father
Abraham and God of my father Isaac, O Lord,
who said to me, 'Return to your native land and
I will deal bountifully with you'!
[11] I am unworthy of all the kindness that You
have so steadfastly shown Your servant: with my
staff alone I crossed this Jordan, and now I have
become two camps.
[12] Deliver me, I pray, from the hand of my
brother, from the hand of Esau; else, I fear, he
may come and strike me down, mothers and
children alike.
[13] Yet You have said, 'I will deal bountifully
with you and make your offspring as the sands
of the sea, which are too numerous to count.'"

In his youth, Jacob would intentionally avoid engaging with his brother Esau. Now, too, Jacob continues to fear Esau, but he will need to negotiate with him.

For Jacob, meeting with Esau will be a meeting with God as well. It is the most important encounter of Jacob's life. The Talmud notes that Jacob prepared for the event in three ways: gifts for Esau, prayers for deliverance, and readiness for war. Jacob's personal advancement in these aspects also marked the completion of his transformation to *Israel*, thus serving as a watershed between the two major periods of his life.

38.6. Gifts for Esau (32:14-21)

יד וַיָּלֶן שָׁם בַּלַּיְלָה הַהוּא וַיִּקַּח מִן־הַבָּא בְיָדוֹ מִנְחָה לְעֵשָׂו אָחִיו: טו עִזִּים מָאתַיִם וּתְיָשִׁים עֶשְׂרִים רְחֵלִים מָאתַיִם וְאֵילִים עֶשְׂרִים: טז גְּמַלִּים מֵינִיקוֹת וּבְנֵיהֶם שְׁלֹשִׁים פָּרוֹת אַרְבָּעִים וּפָרִים עֲשָׂרָה אֲתֹנֹת עֶשְׂרִים וַעְיָרִם עֲשָׂרָה: יז וַיִּתֵּן בְּיַד־עֲבָדָיו עֵדֶר עֵדֶר לְבַדּוֹ וַיֹּאמֶר אֶל־עֲבָדָיו עִבְרוּ לְפָנַי וְרֶוַח תָּשִׂימוּ בֵּין עֵדֶר וּבֵין עֵדֶר: יח וַיְצַו אֶת־הָרִאשׁוֹן לֵאמֹר כִּי יִפְגָשְׁךָ עֵשָׂו אָחִי וּשְׁאֵלְךָ לֵאמֹר לְמִי־אַתָּה וְאָנָה תֵלֵךְ וּלְמִי אֵלֶּה לְפָנֶיךָ: יט וְאָמַרְתָּ לְעַבְדְּךָ לְיַעֲקֹב מִנְחָה הִוא שְׁלוּחָה לַאדֹנִי לְעֵשָׂו וְהִנֵּה גַם־הוּא אַחֲרֵינוּ: כ וַיְצַו גַּם אֶת־הַשֵּׁנִי גַּם אֶת־הַשְּׁלִישִׁי גַּם אֶת־כָּל־הַהֹלְכִים אַחֲרֵי הָעֲדָרִים לֵאמֹר כַּדָּבָר הַזֶּה תְּדַבְּרוּן אֶל־עֵשָׂו בְּמֹצַאֲכֶם אֹתוֹ: כא וַאֲמַרְתֶּם גַּם הִנֵּה עַבְדְּךָ יַעֲקֹב אַחֲרֵינוּ כִּי־אָמַר אֲכַפְּרָה פָנָיו בַּמִּנְחָה הַהֹלֶכֶת לְפָנָי וְאַחֲרֵי־כֵן אֶרְאֶה פָנָיו אוּלַי יִשָּׂא פָנָי:

[14] After spending the night there, he selected from what was at hand these presents for his brother Esau:

[15] 200 she-goats and 20 he-goats; 200 ewes and 20 rams;

[16] 30 milch camels with their colts; 40 cows and 10 bulls; 20 she-asses and 10 he-asses.

[17] These he put in the charge of his servants, drove by drove, and he told his servants, "Go on ahead, and keep a distance between droves."

[18] He instructed the one in front as follows, "When my brother Esau meets you and asks you, 'Whose man are you? Where are you going? And whose [animals] are these ahead of you?'

[19] you shall answer, 'Your servant Jacob's; they are a gift sent to my lord Esau; and [Jacob] himself is right behind us.'"

[20] He gave similar instructions to the second one, and the third, and all the others who followed the droves, namely, "Thus and so shall you say to Esau when you reach him.

[21] And you shall add, 'And your servant Jacob himself is right behind us.'" For he reasoned, "If I propitiate him with presents in advance, and then face him, perhaps he will show me favor."

[14] He selected from what was at hand these presents for his brother Esau: From the list of Jacob's gifts to Esau we can surmise how very extensive must have been the property that Jacob brought with him when he left Laban.

[17] Go on ahead, and keep a distance between droves: This was done in order to satisfy the eye (the greed) of Esau and to amaze him with the size of the gift.

[21] If I propitiate him with presents in advance, and then face him, perhaps he will show me favor: Literally, "... and after that I will see his face, perhaps he will lift my face (i.e., forgive me)." These lofty turns of phrase are far more appropriate for addressing celestial beings, such as angels, than a creature of flesh and blood like Esau, as Jacob does here. Thus, we see that Jacob, besides fearing Esau, also genuinely reveres him.

38.7. Jacob Battles the Angel (32:22-25)

כב וַתַּעֲבֹר הַמִּנְחָה עַל־פָּנָיו וְהוּא לָן בַּלַּיְלָה־הַהוּא
בַּמַּחֲנֶה: כג וַיָּקָם | בַּלַּיְלָה הוּא וַיִּקַּח אֶת־שְׁתֵּי נָשָׁיו
וְאֶת־שְׁתֵּי שִׁפְחֹתָיו וְאֶת־אַחַד עָשָׂר יְלָדָיו וַיַּעֲבֹר אֵת
מַעֲבַר יַבֹּק: כד וַיִּקָּחֵם וַיַּעֲבִרֵם אֶת־הַנָּחַל וַיַּעֲבֵר אֶת־
אֲשֶׁר־לוֹ: כה וַיִּוָּתֵר יַעֲקֹב לְבַדּוֹ וַיֵּאָבֵק אִישׁ עִמּוֹ עַד
עֲלוֹת הַשָּׁחַר:

[22] And so the gift went on ahead, while he remained in camp that night.
[23] That same night he arose, and taking his two wives, his two maidservants, and his eleven children, he crossed the ford of the Jabbok.
[24] After taking them across the stream, he sent across all his possessions.
[25] Jacob was left alone. And a man wrestled with him until the break of dawn.

[23] That same night he arose: Jacob can find no peace. He vacillates between his wish to return to his country and his desire to flee from Esau.

He crossed the ford of the Jabbok. [24] After taking them across the stream, he sent across all his possessions: Unlike other crossings (Abraham crossing the Euphrates, and the Israelites crossing the Red Sea and, later, the Jordan River), this crossing is carried out in two stages. Jacob first transfers his family and property but remains himself on the opposite shore. The reason is that there are two "crossings" that need to be made here – an external crossing and an internal one. Jacob needs to transition from living in exile to living independently in his own land. And in order to achieve that, he must now also defeat the angel.

The description of Jacob's struggle with the angel (or, possibly, with God Himself) is a story about a mystical experience that is beyond our understanding, and whose details are largely hidden from us. But its essence, apparently, is that Jacob does not automatically inherit God's promise given to Abraham and Isaac. Rather, he must earn that Covenant as the result of a struggle. Jacob is not born into the Covenant, but acquires it.

[25] Jacob was left alone: The translation of *levado* as "alone" is not entirely accurate. *Levad* means "in private (with)," but not necessarily "alone." (*Lavud*, for example, is derived similarly, and means "joined to another.") In other words, there is someone else with Jacob who shares a very tight connection with him.

Jacob harbors a deep-seated fear of Esau, and lives his entire life "in private company" with the angel of Esau. Thus, before the reunion with his brother Jacob must defeat the angel within himself. As we shall see below, Jacob's struggle with the angel of Esau is simultaneously a "struggle with God."

During this struggle Jacob is promised that he will receive the name "Israel," because he has finally gained the "Esau-ness" in his own soul by defeating the angel. However, he does not receive his new name immediately after the victory. That will happen only after the incident of Dinah in Shechem.

38.8. The Dislocation of Jacob's Thigh (32:26)

כו וַיַּרְא כִּי לֹא יָכֹל לוֹ וַיִּגַּע בְּכַף־יְרֵכוֹ וַתֵּקַע כַּף־יֶרֶךְ
יַעֲקֹב בְּהֵאָבְקוֹ עִמּוֹ:

[26] When he saw that he had not prevailed against him, he wrenched Jacob's hip at its socket, so that the socket of his hip was strained as he wrestled with him.

[26] He wrenched Jacob's hip at its socket: The angel cannot defeat Jacob, but it can inflict injury upon him by dislocating his hip. According to the Midrash, this dislocation, which occurred before dawn had broken, symbolizes all those Jews (descendants of Jacob) who departed from the Jewish people during the long night of exile without waiting for the "light of day." (The hip here symbolizes intimate relations and the birth of children.)

The dislocation of Jacob's hip means that the struggle took place on an actual physical level. But even so, this in no way contradicts the view that the struggle was a spiritual one within Jacob himself, and the dislocation of his hip was its psychosomatic consequence. Either way, the important thing here is that the struggle was real (even if it was only Jacob's own, internal struggle). And the wounds and losses that Jacob sustained from it were both substantial and appreciable.

38.9. The Angel's Blessing (32:27)

כז וַיֹּאמֶר שַׁלְּחֵנִי כִּי עָלָה הַשָּׁחַר וַיֹּאמֶר לֹא אֲשַׁלֵּחֲךָ כִּי
אִם־בֵּרַכְתָּנִי׃

[27] Then he said, "Let me go, for dawn is breaking." But he answered, "I will not let you go, unless you bless me."

[27] Let me go, for dawn is breaking: The struggle continues until dawn breaks, i.e., until the coming of the Messianic Redemption, when the Divine light will illuminate the world.

As Jacob went into exile, we read: "He ... stopped there for the night, for the sun had set" (28:11). Exile is called "night." But here, sunrise too is mentioned, for the return of the Jewish people to the Land of Israel marks the onset of day, the advent of light.

I will not let you go, unless you bless me: Despite the sun rising, Jacob refuses to let go of the angel until he receives a blessing from him. This means that even when the time has come for the Jews to return to their land, they need Esau's blessing.

In the history of modern-day Israel we see this point in the fact that the Jewish state was created on a foundation of the knowledge and skills that the Jews had learned from Esau, i.e., from the peoples of Europe (in the fields of government, social sciences, the military, and economics, among others). The political design of the Zionist movement could have arisen only in Western Europe, where the Jews were sufficiently assimilated to absorb the social, scientific, and technical knowledge of the broader culture. Theodore Herzl is a prime example of this idea. Thanks to Herzl's assimilation, he was able to promote a practical program for creating a modern state.

38.10. Jacob's Name Change to "Israel" is Proclaimed (32:28-29)

כח וַיֹּאמֶר אֵלָיו מַה־שְּׁמֶךָ וַיֹּאמֶר יַעֲקֹב: כט וַיֹּאמֶר
לֹא יַעֲקֹב יֵאָמֵר עוֹד שִׁמְךָ כִּי אִם־יִשְׂרָאֵל כִּי־שָׂרִיתָ עִם־
אֱלֹהִים וְעִם־אֲנָשִׁים וַתּוּכָל:

[28] Said the other, "What is your name?" He replied, "Jacob."
[29] Said he, "Your name shall no longer be Jacob, but Israel, for you have striven with beings divine and human, and have prevailed."

[28] What is your name?: The angel asks Jacob his name not because the angel does not know it himself, but to make Jacob aware of the change. In this it is similar to God's question to Adam: "Where are you?" (3:9).

[29] Your name shall no longer be Jacob: Although proclaimed here, the actual name change will occur only later (35:10). Jacob is not quite ready at this moment to become *Israel*.

Israel: Here the etymology of the name Israel is from *Sar-El*, "he who does battle with an angel" (or "with God"). It also can be derived from *Yashar-El*, "direct to God."

For you have striven with beings divine and human: The

expression *sarita 'im elohim* can be understood as either "striven with God" or "striven with an angel".

Jacob was embattled on many fronts. He faced constant pressure exerted on him by others, which he needed to resist in order to prevail. He fought with people (Esau and Laban) and with the angel of Esau, overcoming his fear of him. He also "fought with God", transcending the category of *Elohim*, which in this verse can be understood as judgment and predestination. The greatness of Jacob-Israel as the "God Fighter" is that he does not merely accept the "fate" that Heaven initially allots to him. Rather, he claims and takes for himself that which was intended by Isaac for Esau. Thus, he acquires for himself an even more exalted mission.

38.11. Israel as "He Who Struggles with God"

To understand the meaning of "struggling with God," and the idea of Israel as a "God-fighting" people, we must bear in mind that the two most common names of God, *Adonai*[5] (the Tetragrammaton, God's four-letter name) and *Elohim*, have completely different meanings in Hebrew. These names are usually translated as "the Lord" and "God," respectively. However, because the meanings of these words in the English language, when applied to the Deity, are almost identical, many fundamental Torah texts – including, for example, the famous *Shema' Yisrael* – lose important shades of meaning in translation.

---

5   By long-standing Jewish religious tradition, God's four-letter name, pronounced "*Adonai*," is represented in informal writing (and speaking) by only the placeholder "*Ha-Shem*," which means, literally, "The Name." Henceforth in the book we too will follow that practice. Only in this first instance of its appearance have we, for the sake of clarity, spelled out that name in writing in its full form, as it is actually pronounced during prayer and obligatory communal readings of Scripture (and often in formal private study as well).

Ha-Shem ("the Lord") is the manifestation of God in His true essence, the personal God Who stands above nature. But *Elohim* ("God") is God's manifestation in the form of world harmony, the soul of nature, which is the "veil" that conceals Him from this world.

Thus, "to struggle with God (*Elohim*)" means to glimpse the Divine behind the mask of nature, to see *Ha-Shem* behind the mask of *Elohim*, to resist the natural course of events, so as to achieve instead a direct dialogue with God at the level that He is *Ha-Shem* (God beyond nature). And in that process to transcend even that which Heaven seems to have preordained.

Throughout their very long history the Jewish people have staunchly opposed any concept of nature that obscures the *"transcendental, personal Divinity."* From the point of view of nature and naturalness alone, the Jews should have disappeared long ago, as did so many other peoples, their contemporaries in every age. But Israel, the "God-Fighter," refuses to come to terms with the natural course of history. And he therefore lives on forever.

38.12. The Difference Between Israel and Jacob in Character and Status

Jacob is forced to be cunning not only because of his difficult external circumstances. He has certain complexes regarding Esau, and still feels that he has received his father's blessing, originally intended for Esau, undeservedly.

Modern-day Jews, his descendants, have likewise a certain aspect of "resourcefulness" that is especially evident among the Jews of the Diaspora. This skill is of course indispensable for surviving in exile. But among the peoples of the world this typically Jewish attribute arouses significant hostility.

Israel, however, is of a completely different character. Living in his own country, and having a strong sense of his inalienable right to it, he is frank and direct. His actions are sometimes even crude. But in the eyes of the peoples of the world Israel seems much more natural and correct than Jacob does. The world's attitude toward Israel is far more respectful than it is toward Jacob.

On the other hand, however, Israel has a new and different problem. Jacob is used to seeing Esau behave in a belligerent manner, but when the tables are turned, and Israel in war exhibits "Esau-like" behavior, Esau is shocked, because he does not expect this from the Jews at all. The European nations are content to endure Jacob in his state of debasement, but when suddenly the Jews achieve the status of *Israel* and break free from the familiar hierarchy, this elicits outrage among the Esau peoples.

And yet, Esau can receive spirituality only from Israel, but not from Jacob. The Jewish (biblical) influence on the world from the Land of Israel is therefore incomparably greater than that of the Diaspora.

38.13. Jacob and Israel as a Dual Lineage Within the Jewish People

So, our third Patriarch has two names, "Jacob" and "Israel." The name Jacob derives from "'-k-v," from which root comes the noun *ekev*, "heel." As a verb, this root means "to follow behind (someone)," but also denotes the quality of being "indirect" or "crooked," or hindering another's progress by bypassing him. ("[Esau] said, 'Was he, then, named Jacob that he might supplant me [*vayakveni*] these two times?'" [27:36]).

Contrarily, the name Israel is derived from the root *yashar*, "straight, direct." Thus, these two names, "Jacob" and "Israel," have opposite meanings.

We have seen these two aspects – "to be direct" and "to overtake" – in the history of the Creation. The first chapter of this book, Genesis, describes God's contact with man through nature: a connection with God is achieved by man through his power over nature, matter. The Holy One Blessed be He appears there as the God of nature, and is called *Elohim*. But in the second chapter of Genesis, "Ha-Shem," the Tetragrammaton, is used, because the Holy One Blessed be He there reveals Himself to Adam by "overtaking nature" – as the God of the Covenant.

A covenant is a special relationship between God and man that bypasses the natural order of things. The names "Jacob" and "Israel" directly correspond to these two Adams. God connects with the first of those through nature, but to the second directly, without resorting to nature. Jacob corresponds to Adam of the first creation story, to Adam of the "indirect" connection with God through nature. And Israel corresponds to Adam of the second story, the Adam of direct connection.

Accordingly, Jacob's wife is Rachel, who has beauty, because beauty is one of the aspects of power over matter. Their son Joseph is also "beautiful" (39: 6), he rules over matter and is therefore able to rebuild Egypt.

But Israel's wife is Leah, with her "weak eyes" that are indifferent to the material world, because when one has a direct connection with God this world is not all that interesting; Leah's most prominent son Judah is able to overpower nature and rise above it. (We will examine this aspect in more detail below.)

In other words, the two wives of our Patriarch Jacob /

Israel reflect his essential dichotomy: Jacob is married to Rachel, and Israel to Leah. While he is only Jacob, he loves Rachel but not Leah. But Rachel dies soon after his change of name, and Leah remains Israel's only wife.

Leah was originally meant to marry Esau. Only by assimilating Esau's qualities and becoming Israel could Jacob understand her. (It is even possible that had he loved Leah enough from the very beginning, Jacob could have become Israel sooner than he did.)

The descendant of Jacob and Rachel is the *Messiah, the son of Joseph*, who realizes his mission by transforming nature. The descendant of Israel and Leah is the *Messiah, the son of David*, who achieves direct contact with God, and teaches the same to all of humanity. The task of all Messianic aspiration is to advance the world toward the integration of those two.

Summarized in comprehensive table format, the scheme just described looks like this:

JACOB	ISRAEL
Rachel	Leah
Beauty, ephemerality	Weak eyes, eternity
Leading son: Joseph	**Leading son:** Judah
Characteristic story: Joseph in command in Egypt	**Characteristic story:** The Tamar incident, teshuvah (repentance and correction)
Power to reform and control materiality	Transcending, rising above materiality

"Indirect" connection with God, serving God by reforming nature	Direct connection with God, serving God from beyond nature
Joshua son of Nun King Saul Mashiach ben Yosef	King David King Solomon Mashiach ben David
Capital: Shechem	**Capital:** Hebron
Jerusalem as their unification	
First Adam's Creation Story	Second Adam's Creation Story
Administrative professionals and scientists: Engineers, managers, financiers	Spiritual leaders and artists, philosophers and mystics
Modern-day Israel	The future State of Israel
Dynamics: Diaspora Jewry becomes a united, nationalist-political movement in the Land of Israel	**Dynamics:** Holy Land Jewry transcends the nationalist structure in order to exert a universalist influence on humankind

The Messianic process consists of the unification of Joseph and Judah, as made clear by the prophet Ezekiel (37:1528):

> [15] *"The word of the Lord came to me:*
> [16] *And you, O mortal, take a stick and write on*

*it, "Of Judah and the Israelites associated with
him"; and take another stick and write on it, "Of
Joseph – the stick of Ephraim – and all the House
of Israel associated with him.*

*[17] Bring them close to each other, so that they
become one stick, joined together in your hand. ...*

*[21] ... Thus said the Lord God: I am going to take
the Israelite people from among the nations
they have gone to, and gather them from every
quarter, and bring them to their own land.*

*[22] I will make them a single nation in the land,
on the hills of Israel, and one king shall be king of
them all. Never again shall they be two nations,
and never again shall they be divided into two
kingdoms. ...*

*[27] My Presence shall rest over them; I will be
their God and they shall be My people.*

*[28] And when My Sanctuary abides among
them forever, the nations shall know that I the
Lord do sanctify Israel."*

* * *

Unlike Abraham and Sarah, whose former names became
entirely obsolete after they were given new ones, Jacob
receives a new name, but still also retains his former name.
Thus, even as he attains the level of *Israel* (a direct connection to God), he must not surrender the name "Jacob" (having a connection with God by transforming the world). In
becoming *Mashiach ben David*, he must not lose his *Mashiach ben Yosef*.

38.14. Rachel and Leah in the Perspective of Sacred History

Apropos of Jacob's two names, which, as we have seen, correspond to his dual hypostases, we should address in more detail the differences and similarities of Jacob's two wives. Because in Jacob's two wives we again see a one-to-one correspondence to his two names.

Leah, wife of Israel, and mother of the lines of kingdom and priesthood (Judah and Levi, respectively) thus symbolizes the future, eternity, and *gadlut*, the category of greatness. And Rachel, the wife of Jacob, mother of the preliminary kingdom (Joseph and Saul) represents the present, temporality, and *katnut*, smallness – the Jewish people in their lesser form.

Rachel represents beauty, and power over matter. Her son Joseph is extraordinarily handsome and dominates Egypt. His kingdom, although temporary, comes first. And in future Jewish history too, the kingdom of Judah and *Mashiach ben David* cannot be built "from naught"; the kingdom of Joseph and *Mashiach ben Yosef* must precede it. Even so, Rachel, temporality, was buried in *Beit Lechem* (Bethlehem), separate from Jacob, while Leah, eternity, was buried with him in the Cave of Machpelah, the tomb of the patriarchs in Hebron (49:31).

It so happened that Jacob married the two sisters in close succession. (Divine Providence had determined that this was necessary in order for Jacob to acquire certain characteristics of Esau.) Although Jacob wanted and intended to marry only Rachel, Leah too became his wife – "perforce." Leah at first was not well-suited to Jacob, being a match only for Jacob's alter ego, Israel, and only after he had acquired some of Esau's qualities.

Rachel and Leah are different also in that they correspond to the categories of Exile (Diaspora) and the Land of Israel, respectively. In Rachel is expressed the idea that the Jewish nation were connected to their land even during the Exile. When the First Temple was destroyed and the Jews went into exile to Babylonia, the prophet Jeremiah exclaims (31:15): "Thus said the Lord: A cry is heard in Ramah – wailing, bitter weeping – Rachel weeping for her children. She refuses to be comforted for her children, who are gone."

But Leah, during the Exile, cries for no one, for she is simply nowhere to be found. Leah will awaken only upon returning to the Land. Therefore, with the birth of Benjamin and the death of Rachel, the period of exile ends completely. From the moment that Jacob, Jew of the Exile, buries Rachel, the preliminary stage of the birth of the Jewish people has reached completion. When Jacob then moves on to Hebron, he is already not Jacob, but Israel.

At the same time, from a historical perspective there is an important contrast between the nationalist and personal realizations of Rachel and Leah.

At the national level, the victory is Leah's. Jacob at first prefers Rachel, but gradually Leah seizes more and more important positions. Both the priesthood and the kingdom come from her, as do most of Jacob's children, the tribes of the Jewish people. And she is buried with Jacob in the cave of Machpelah. Leah loves Jacob, and gradually this love conquers all.

On the other hand, in the course of future Jewish history Rachel is personally self-sufficient, which Leah is not. We get the feeling that all of Leah has gone into being Jacob's wife and the mother of his children, that Leah's realization happens exclusively through her descendants. Leah's image is not highlighted, while Rachel is seen as a personality in her own right.

Rachel's grave in Beit Lechem (Bethlehem) is located a considerable distance from the Tomb of the Patriarchs in Hebron. On the one hand, this could be a shortcoming, but on the other hand, it emphasizes that Rachel's burial place is special. Numerous people come to pray at Rachel's Tomb. Rachel's *yahrtzeit* (anniversary of death), which falls on the eleventh day of the month of Heshvan, is an important date on the Jewish calendar, whereas Tradition has not recorded the dates of the deaths of our other Patriarchs and Matriarchs. No special dates in the Jewish calendar honor the memory of Abraham, Isaac, Jacob, Sarah, Rebekah, or Leah. But for Rachel such a day is annually observed.

If we were to try to pinpoint Leah's influence on Jacob, we could say that she taught Jacob directness – the ability to express, candidly and in plain terms, her problems and demands. Leah goes out to meet Jacob (30:16) and immediately, without any tinge of bashfulness, informs him that she has "hired" (purchased) his intimacy for herself that night.

One of the most important milestones on Jacob's path to becoming Israel is that he acquires the ability to speak openly about his problems. For example, when Esau levels an accusation, "First he took away my birthright and now he has taken away my blessing!," Jacob cannot bring himself to say: "Well, actually, you sold me that birthright yourself." Jacob is embarrassed by his own position, a major flaw that is characteristic also of Diaspora Jews. On his way to becoming Israel – on the way to becoming a self-sufficient nation living in its own land – Jacob needs to learn to overcome this shyness and to assert his own presence. Leah teaches Jacob this quality, the same one that we later witness in Judah, Leah's descendant, who is not too shy to admit publicly that he is the father of Tamar's unborn child (38:26).

But Leah puts her entire self into influencing Jacob. She

therefore never figures as an autonomous personality in subsequent Jewish history, nor is she ever specifically mentioned in the books of the Prophets either by name or allusion. But Rachel, as it turns out, is seen in the historical perspective as very much her own person. She is specifically mentioned by name and plays a unique role.

Rachel and Leah had to face different types of challenges. Leah felt a constant need to win over Jacob, whom Rachel, in her opinion, had taken from her. And she achieved that objective, by and large. But since this was Leah's ultimate and only goal, once it had been realized she left no additional imprint.

Rachel's problem was her lack of children, and in a sense this problem never found its resolution. When Joseph is born, Rachel prays for her next child, but then she dies in the process of giving birth to Benjamin. Rachel's lifelong issues relating to children remained unrealized.

This lack of fulfillment became for Rachel a kind of desperate melancholy, which gave rise to her uncommonly plaintive appeal to God – a cry for help. And that is precisely the reason that Rachel will later exert such a unique influence on the Jewish people. Even in a seemingly unsolvable situation, the "children of Rachel" never lose hope, and life goes on. It is therefore Rachel who prays for her children, i.e., for the Jewish people as they go into exile.

Other nations who were expelled from their country never returned to it. After several centuries of living in a foreign land, such return was for them no longer possible. But the Jews set a highly unique precedent. The return of the Jewish people to their land contravenes every law of social history.

In a hopeless situation it is Rachel who is the author of an impassioned plea to God to let her children return. In the end, her prayer is realized, and the Jewish people do return. In this does Rachel's unusual power consist.

38.15. The Angel's Hidden Name (32:30)

לֹ וַיִּשְׁאַל יַעֲקֹב וַיֹּאמֶר הַגִּידָה־נָּא שְׁמֶךָ וַיֹּאמֶר לָמָּה זֶּה
תִּשְׁאַל לִשְׁמִי וַיְבָרֶךְ אֹתוֹ שָׁם:

[30] Jacob asked, "Pray tell me your name." But he said, "You must not ask my name!" And he took leave of him there.

[30] You must not ask my name!: There are other instances in Tanakh where an angel will not reveal his name to humans. The story of Samson's parents is one such example. "The angel said to him, 'You must not ask for my name; it is unknowable!'" (Judges 13:18).

As already noted, in Jewish culture a name reflects not the essence of an object, but its purpose. Our correct relationship with the angels, manifestations of the Divine will, is often possible only if the purpose of the Divine intervention we are experiencing remains unknown to us (just as a teacher must not fully reveal his methods to his students, because doing so would undermine the educational process).

Such secrecy is typical of angels who make an appearance to humans. But it is especially true of "malevolent angels" – because an awareness of the positive, providential role of evil would prevent people from properly responding to it.

In a sense, from the global-mystical point of view no evil exists as an "independent entity." What appears to us as evil is an element in the enigmatic nature of the universe that is necessary for the realization of good. But as soon as we descend from that certain "global-mystical," abstract level of eternity to the level of operational views and decisions, an approach such as "evil does not actually exist" becomes destructive. We must feel that evil *does* exist, and we must fight it, because only when we struggle with evil and vanquish it does that evil become "a necessary component for the realization of good."

In order to find the strength and the energy needed for that struggle and its ensuing victory, one often needs to "not understand" why that evil exists at all – to "not know the name of the angel." Only a very select group of people of the highest spiritual attainments are able to realize the meaning of evil while also at the same time vigorously fighting it, and even they understand the meaning of evil only in the general sense; the details are hidden from them. The name of an angel with whom Jacob struggles is therefore unknown even to him.

We note as a general truth that there must be things in the world that are incomprehensible to us, whose meaning we are not privy to. Otherwise, we could never achieve the purpose for which these things could descend into the world. In religious discourse there are always questions that must remain unanswered – for the time being, at least. For example, in our times there remains the unanswered question of why God saw fit to allow the Holocaust to happen, and other similar questions whose answers we shall never know.

Had Jacob known from the outset that the angel existed expressly to enable him, by virtue of their struggle, to triumph in his relationship with Esau, Jacob would have felt no urgency in the situation, nor would he have had the strength to fight a battle of that kind. Jacob must therefore receive a blessing from an angel whose name he will never learn, because that knowledge would only have hindered him.

Because the blessing comes to him through the angel of Esau, Jacob achieves control over the "Esau-ness" within himself, and he feels no further shame in that. Or, to put it differently, Jacob now understands (i.e., the angel he has fought has now acknowledged) that the blessings he received from his father were indeed rightfully his.

Unless one does battle with God there can be no blessing. Israel's chutzpah, the "boldness of Zionism" (the notorious Israeli "impudence") is especially pronounced "at sunrise" (32:27), i.e., at the onset of the process of Messianic Redemption. And that "impudence" is the most important guarantee of Israel's advancement and survival.

38.16. To See God and Remain Alive (32:31-32)

לא וַיִּקְרָא יַעֲקֹב שֵׁם הַמָּקוֹם פְּנִיאֵל כִּי־רָאִיתִי אֱלֹהִים
פָּנִים אֶל־פָּנִים וַתִּנָּצֵל נַפְשִׁי: לב וַיִּזְרַח־לוֹ הַשֶּׁמֶשׁ
כַּאֲשֶׁר עָבַר אֶת־פְּנוּאֵל וְהוּא צֹלֵעַ עַל־יְרֵכוֹ:

[31] So Jacob named the place Peniel, meaning, "I have seen a divine being face to face, yet my life has been preserved."
[32] The sun rose upon him as he passed Penuel, limping on his hip.

(31, 32) Peniel, ... Penuel: "To God face to face."

[31] I have seen a divine being face to face: As already noted, the words *Elohim* and *El* used in these verses, and throughout this story, can refer either to God (in the category of *Elohim*, "the God of nature") or to an angel. Thus, it is possible to interpret the text in two different ways.

Jacob understood that his struggle was with both of those: with the angel of Esau and with God. He recognized this meeting as a spiritual and mystical experience of utmost significance – a new birth, the emergence of Israel.

Yet my life has been preserved: The idea of expecting death after one has an encounter with God is found many times in Tanakh (e.g., Ex. 24:11, Jud. 6:22-23, 13:22, Isa. 6:5). Meeting the Supreme Harmony of the universe face to face makes a person want to "dissolve" into the Divine by departing this world. But Judaism considers that attraction nothing more than a temptation that must be resisted and overcome. We must strive not only to see God, but to remain alive; not only to rise to the Supreme Harmony, but to bring His light into this world, and down to this earth.

[32] The sun rose upon him as he passed Penuel: In order to attain the radiance of the sun, the Messianic liberation, one must pass through Penuel, a face-to-face struggle in which our life itself is in true peril from our encounter with an angel. However, when we recognize that struggle as an encounter with God that enables us to transcend the category of *Elohim* (the Divine system of nature and its laws), then the sun will indeed rise upon us.

As he passed Penuel: Jacob's victory was not absolute. His hip was dislocated in the process of achieving that victory. But the goal of that struggle, receiving a blessing from God by vanquishing the angel of Esau, was achieved. And so Jacob successfully "passes Penuel," i.e., he acquires the strength he needs to ascend to the Holy Land.

38.17. Commandments Derived from Events in the Lives of the Patriarchs (32:33)

לג עַל־כֵּן לֹא־יֹאכְלוּ בְנֵי־יִשְׂרָאֵל אֶת־גִּיד הַנָּשֶׁה אֲשֶׁר
עַל־כַּף הַיָּרֵךְ עַד הַיּוֹם הַזֶּה כִּי נָגַע בְּכַף־יֶרֶךְ יַעֲקֹב בְּגִיד
הַנָּשֶׁה:

[33] That is why the children of Israel to this day do not eat the thigh muscle that is on the socket of the hip, since Jacob's hip socket was wrenched at the thigh muscle.

By instituting a new commandment as a remembrance of what befell Jacob, The Torah posits his meeting with the angel and with God as a key archetypal event for the future history of the Jewish people.

And yet, the connection between the angel's having injured Jacob's tendon and the commandment that all Jews must refrain from eating a certain tendon in the hindquarters of a cow is of course not direct but symbolic. The Torah is merely providing an example of how the meaning of the commandments can be revealed.

Many of the Torah's commandments are reminders of moments in Jewish history. The text of the Torah is divided, as it were, into portions. Some of those acquaint us with the commandments, while others recount historical events. But those stories too pertain to the commandments, in that they provide an historical basis for them.

For example, the commandment to tie *tzitzit* (fringes) on four-cornered garments is associated with Abraham's words to the king of Sodom: "I will not take so much as a *thread* or a sandal strap of what is yours" (14:23).

And as previously noted, the tefillin (phylacteries), which the Torah calls *totafot*, symbolize the Jewish victory over Egypt. The Torah prescribes that the image of the Egyptian god Thoth, which had the form of a curved snake attached to the foreheads of the pharaohs, is to be replaced by the square tefillin that Jewish men wear above their foreheads.

And as one final example, the prohibition of marrying two sisters is based on the story of Jacob and his family. (This point too has been mentioned previously.)

But even so, the symbolism of the many commandments that derive from historical events related in the Torah in no way negates our understanding of them as something fundamentally metaphysical, having roots in the transcendental. The origins of the Torah's commandments belong to the category of the eternal that has now descended from Heaven. The commandments belong to higher worlds, but to find their way into our world they need to be embodied in history, acquiring their earthly form through those historical events.

Chapter 39

The Reunion of
Jacob and Esau

39.1. The Reunion (33:1-4)

א וַיִּשָּׂא יַעֲקֹב עֵינָיו וַיַּרְא וְהִנֵּה עֵשָׂו בָּא וְעִמּוֹ אַרְבַּע
מֵאוֹת אִישׁ וַיַּחַץ אֶת־הַיְלָדִים עַל־לֵאָה וְעַל־רָחֵל וְעַל
שְׁתֵּי הַשְּׁפָחוֹת: ב וַיָּשֶׂם אֶת־הַשְּׁפָחוֹת וְאֶת־יַלְדֵיהֶן
רִאשֹׁנָה וְאֶת־לֵאָה וִילָדֶיהָ אַחֲרֹנִים וְאֶת־רָחֵל וְאֶת־
יוֹסֵף אַחֲרֹנִים: ג וְהוּא עָבַר לִפְנֵיהֶם וַיִּשְׁתַּחוּ אַרְצָה
שֶׁבַע פְּעָמִים עַד־גִּשְׁתּוֹ עַד־אָחִיו: ד וַיָּרָץ עֵשָׂו לִקְרָאתוֹ
וַיְחַבְּקֵהוּ וַיִּפֹּל עַל־צַוָּארָו וַיִּשָּׁקֵהוּ וַיִּבְכּוּ:

*[1] Looking up, Jacob saw Esau coming,
accompanied by four hundred men. He divided the
children among Leah, Rachel, and the two maids,
[2] putting the maids and their children first,
Leah and her children next, and Rachel and
Joseph last.
[3] He himself went on ahead and bowed low
to the ground seven times until he was near his
brother.*

[4] Esau ran to greet him. He embraced him and,
falling on his neck, he kissed him; and they wept.

[2] And Rachel and Joseph last: Those who are most import-ant to him Jacob puts furthest from danger.

[3] And bowed low to the ground seven times: A more pre-cise translation is "and he prostrated himself unto the earth." Jacob's seven bows demonstrate his complete recognition of Esau's seniority. (The number seven represents the full-ness of nature.)

[4] He embraced him and, falling on his neck, he kissed him: Contrary to Jacob's expectations, Esau, rather than attacking him, hugs and kisses him. Perhaps this is because Jacob is still limping.

A limping Jacob is no rival. Your brother the loser won't be causing you any headaches. Just pity the poor guy.

[4] And they wept: Consider this historical parallel: After a third of the Jewish people died in the Holocaust, the world community – in a sudden fit of compassion – even agreed to grant the Jews the right to create the State of Israel, endow-ing them with a scrap of land that was already puny even before it was divided into three fragments.

But a strong, proud, and independent Israel that occupies the full extent of its biblical borders poses a problem for Esau.

39.2. Jacob Prostrates Himself Before Esau (33:5-11)

ה וַיִּשָּׂא אֶת־עֵינָיו וַיַּרְא אֶת־הַנָּשִׁים וְאֶת־הַיְלָדִים

וַיֹּאמֶר מִי־אֵלֶּה לָּךְ וַיֹּאמַר הַיְלָדִים אֲשֶׁר־חָנַן אֱלֹהִים
אֶת־עַבְדֶּךָ: ו וַתִּגַּשְׁןָ הַשְּׁפָחוֹת הֵנָּה וְיַלְדֵיהֶן וַתִּשְׁתַּחֲוֶיןָ:
ז וַתִּגַּשׁ גַּם־לֵאָה וִילָדֶיהָ וַיִּשְׁתַּחֲווּ וְאַחַר נִגַּשׁ יוֹסֵף
וְרָחֵל וַיִּשְׁתַּחֲווּ: ח וַיֹּאמֶר מִי לְךָ כָּל־הַמַּחֲנֶה הַזֶּה אֲשֶׁר
פָּגָשְׁתִּי וַיֹּאמֶר לִמְצֹא־חֵן בְּעֵינֵי אֲדֹנִי: ט וַיֹּאמֶר עֵשָׂו
יֶשׁ־לִי רָב אָחִי יְהִי לְךָ אֲשֶׁר־לָךְ: י וַיֹּאמֶר יַעֲקֹב אַל־נָא
אִם־נָא מָצָאתִי חֵן בְּעֵינֶיךָ וְלָקַחְתָּ מִנְחָתִי מִיָּדִי כִּי עַל־
כֵּן רָאִיתִי פָנֶיךָ כִּרְאֹת פְּנֵי אֱלֹהִים וַתִּרְצֵנִי: יא קַח־נָא
אֶת־בִּרְכָתִי אֲשֶׁר הֻבָאת לָךְ כִּי־חַנַּנִי אֱלֹהִים וְכִי יֶשׁ־
לִי־כֹל וַיִּפְצַר־בּוֹ וַיִּקָּח:

[5] Looking about, he saw the women and the children. "Who," he asked, "are these with you?" He answered, "The children with whom God has favored your servant."

[6] Then the maids, with their children, came forward and bowed low;

[7] next Leah, with her children, came forward and bowed low; and last, Joseph and Rachel came forward and bowed low;

[8] And he asked, "What do you mean by all this company which I have met?" He answered, "To gain my lord's favor."

[9] Esau said, "I have enough, my brother; let what you have remain yours."

[10] But Jacob said, "No, I pray you; if you would do me this favor, accept from me this gift; for to see your face is like seeing the face of God, and you have received me favorably.

[11] Please accept my present which has been brought to you, for God has favored me and I have plenty." And when he urged him, he accepted.

[5] The children with whom God has favored your servant: When Jacob sent messengers to Esau, he ordered them: "Thus shall you say, 'To my lord Esau, thus says your servant Jacob'" (32:5). This form of address can hardly be regarded as ordinary politeness. But here we read that Jacob even prostrated himself on the ground seven times while approaching his brother. The point is not only that Jacob seeks to appease Esau, as an attempt to avoid a confrontation. The situation is more complicated. We see this most clearly in Jacob's reply when Esau refuses his gifts: "No, I pray you, ... accept from me this gift; for to see your face is like seeing the face of God."

[8] To gain my lord's favor: Jacob has so clearly exceeded all reasonable limits of politeness, that we are puzzled by his highly obsequious posturing toward Esau. But the explanation is that Jacob is still Jacob, and not yet Israel. Jacob does not just bow to Esau – he *prostrates* himself before him. The turns of phrase that Jacob uses – "To gain my lord's favor," "for to see your face is like seeing the face of God" – are normally reserved in the Torah for addressing a Divine being, not mere mortals.

Jacob, it would seem, truly sees Esau as a higher reality, and well-nigh worships him. He is not cowering before Esau nor is he engaging in mere flattery, for in fact Jacob truly and sincerely acknowledges Esau's greatness, and feels that he lacks much of what Esau has. Jacob's behavior is not motivated by any fear of Esau, but by trepidation born of reverence. Jacob is afraid to enter into a conflict with his illustrious brother, because he is still in the process of acquiring the qualities of *Israel*. For now, he has received only a promise of that name.

[10] To see your face is like seeing the face of God: (Alternate translation: "... like seeing the face of an angel.") The Midrash concludes from these words that Jacob fought with none other than Esau's angel himself. Jacob's victory over the angel, i.e., his victory over his own internal "Esau," was of utmost importance. Without it, Jacob could not have even dared a reunion Esau. But until a spiritual victory is actualized in the material world, it has not yet been realized, and the process of Jacob becoming Israel was as yet incomplete.

Although Jacob's admiration for him is of course exaggerated, Esau has an important positive core within him. Jacob has much to learn from Esau (that is, the Jews must learn from Western civilization), and that course of study is still today far from complete.

Esau is not a righteous man; he had even threatened in as many words to kill Jacob. Nevertheless, Jacob sincerely admires his brother, because only through that admiration can he adopt from Esau those qualities that he needs for his own personal development.

Although he acknowledges his own imperfections and still lags Esau, Jacob by no means suffers from an inferiority complex, for that would be disastrous. On the contrary, he demonstrates his true admiration for his brother, and seeks to acquire his own missing qualities that Esau possesses.

It would be completely wrong for the Jewish people to disparage or even neglect Esau's culture. The creation of Israel, the synthesis of Jacob and Esau, happens with Jacob, not Esau serving as its foundation – precisely because Jacob shows a desire for such synthesis and mutual self-examination with his brother, while Esau does not. If one or another group within the Jewish people, as has been known to happen, decides to wave the flag of "isolationism," arguing that there is no need to adopt anything from Esau nor to admire the achievements of a foreign culture, then Israel runs the risk of never becoming Israel at all.

Although he prostrates himself before Esau, Jacob has battled Esau's angel, thereby defeating the very essence of Esau within himself. He has defeated, but not destroyed. On the contrary – Jacob needs a blessing from the angel he has just defeated. Jacob seeks not to destroy the power of Esau, but to achieve the proper integration of that power within himself. Only thus can Jacob become Israel.

The victory in the end will be Jacob's. Esau by his own choice will cede the central place in the Holy Land to Jacob, and relocate himself to Seir.

39.3. Jacob Distances Himself from Esau (33:12-15)

יב וַיֹּאמֶר נִסְעָה וְנֵלֵכָה וְאֵלְכָה לְנֶגְדֶּךָ: יג וַיֹּאמֶר אֵלָיו
אֲדֹנִי יֹדֵעַ כִּי־הַיְלָדִים רַכִּים וְהַצֹּאן וְהַבָּקָר עָלוֹת עָלָי
וּדְפָקוּם יוֹם אֶחָד וָמֵתוּ כָּל־הַצֹּאן: יד יַעֲבָר־נָא אֲדֹנִי
לִפְנֵי עַבְדּוֹ וַאֲנִי אֶתְנַהֲלָה לְאִטִּי לְרֶגֶל הַמְּלָאכָה אֲשֶׁר־
לְפָנַי וּלְרֶגֶל הַיְלָדִים עַד אֲשֶׁר־אָבֹא אֶל־אֲדֹנִי שֵׂעִירָה:
טו וַיֹּאמֶר עֵשָׂו אַצִּיגָה־נָּא עִמְּךָ מִן־הָעָם אֲשֶׁר אִתִּי
וַיֹּאמֶר לָמָּה זֶּה אֶמְצָא־חֵן בְּעֵינֵי אֲדֹנִי:

[12] And [Esau] said, "Let us start on our journey, and I will proceed at your pace."
[13] But he said to him, "My lord knows that the children are frail and that the flocks and herds, which are nursing, are a care to me; if they are driven hard a single day, all the flocks will die.
[14] Let my lord go on ahead of his servant, while I travel slowly, at the pace of the cattle before

*me and at the pace of the children, until I come
to my lord in Seir."*
*[15] Then Esau said, "Let me assign to you some
of the men who are with me." But he said, "Oh
no, my lord is too kind to me!"*

**[14] Let my lord go on ahead of his servant ... [15] Then
Esau said, "Let me assign to you some of the men who are
with me." But he said, "Oh no":** As much as Jacob admires
Esau, he prudently refuses not only his company, but also his
protection. (Esau's folk are handy for keeping you safe for a
while, but in the end they are bound to become a thorn in
your side.) Jacob needs to have proper relations with Esau,
but he must not rely on Esau's direct support.

39.4. Arrival in Succoth (33:16-17)

טז וַיָּשָׁב בַּיּוֹם הַהוּא עֵשָׂו לְדַרְכּוֹ שֵׂעִירָה: יז וְיַעֲקֹב נָסַע
סֻכֹּתָה וַיִּבֶן לוֹ בָּיִת וּלְמִקְנֵהוּ עָשָׂה סֻכֹּת עַל־כֵּן קָרָא
שֵׁם־הַמָּקוֹם סֻכּוֹת:

*[16] So Esau started back that day on his way
to Seir.*
*[17] But Jacob journeyed on to Succoth, and built
a house for himself and made stalls for his cattle;
that is why the place was called Succoth.*

[17] But Jacob journeyed on to Succoth: Succoth for Jacob
means building a home (*sukkah*, "hut") for both his family
and his livestock. In these two verses, which *prima facie*

speak only of geographical peregrinations, the Kabbalah sees an allusion to the structure of the universe as expressed in the Jewish holidays. ("Succoth," here the name of a place, is also a major Jewish festival that follows immediately after Jewish New Year and the Day of Atonement. See Lev. 23:33 ff.).

Before Jacob enters Succoth, Esau has already departed for the land of Seir. (The name "Seir" is very close to *sa'ir*, "goat." Moreover, the same word *sa'ir* also means "hairy," and when Jacob calls Esau "a hairy man" (27:11), he uses that exact word.) Esau's departure to Seir is symbolized by the "scapegoat" of Yom Kippur. Succoth – finding a home – is preceded by the elimination of evil, sending into the wilderness the *sa'ir la'azazel*, the "Scapegoat of Azazel" (Lev. 16:8).

Jacob tells Esau, "until I come to my lord in Seir," but in reality, he is not going there, nor has he any intention of doing so. The Midrash says that Jacob will come to Seir only in the Messianic era, when "liberators shall march up on Mount Zion to wreak judgment on Mount Esau; and dominion shall be the Lord's" (Obadiah v. 21). After the world finds its correction, Jacob too will come to Seir, which by then shall have ceased to be the abode of Esau alone. The "scapegoat," *sa'ir* / Seir, which symbolizes the Evil Inclination, will then no longer need to be sent away into the wilderness. It will instead take its rightful place within the structures of holiness.

The festival of Succoth is associated with the Exodus from Egypt: "The Israelites journeyed from Raamses to Succoth .... in the first month, on the fifteenth day of the first month ... and encamped at Succoth." (Exodus 12:37, Numbers 33:3-5). From here we see that the festival of Succoth should really be annexed to Passover, and immediately follow it. But the ideal plans of the Exodus were not realized. Not all goals are achieved immediately, some are left for the future.

Therefore, Succoth is a symbol of the Messianic era, for on that holiday all the nations of the world will come to the Temple in Jerusalem (Zechariah 14:16). For this reason, the festival of Succoth was postponed until the autumn, and its observance follows Yom Kippur, the sending of the Scapegoat, and the correction of all the nations of the world.

Chapter 40

The Incident of Dinah in Shechem

40.1. Jacob Arrives in Shechem (33:18-20)

יח וַיָּבֹא יַעֲקֹב שָׁלֵם עִיר שְׁכֶם אֲשֶׁר בְּאֶרֶץ כְּנַעַן בְּבֹאוֹ מִפַּדַּן אֲרָם וַיִּחַן אֶת־פְּנֵי הָעִיר: יט וַיִּקֶן אֶת־חֶלְקַת הַשָּׂדֶה אֲשֶׁר נָטָה־שָׁם אָהֳלוֹ מִיַּד בְּנֵי־חֲמוֹר אֲבִי שְׁכֶם בְּמֵאָה קְשִׂיטָה: כ וַיַּצֶּב־שָׁם מִזְבֵּחַ וַיִּקְרָא־לוֹ אֵל אֱלֹהֵי יִשְׂרָאֵל:

[18] Jacob arrived safe in the city of Shechem which is in the land of Canaan – having come thus from Paddan-aram – and he encamped before the city.
[19] The parcel of land where he pitched his tent he purchased from the children of Hamor, Shechem's father, for a hundred kesitahs.
[20] He set up an altar there, and called it El-elohe-yisrael.

[18] Jacob arrived: Scripture now again calls him Jacob, after it just said: "You shall be called Jacob no more, but Israel shall be your name" (35:10). Because even now it is still only a promise. Jacob must endure yet another crisis in Shechem before he can truly become Israel.

Safe in the city of Shechem: Jacob's arrival in Shechem goes well. He is now out of danger and has also to a large extent freed himself from his complexes with respect to Esau. He has not yet, however, overcome his insecurities concerning the locals who continued to live in the Land while Jacob was in exile.

[19] The parcel of land where he pitched his tent he purchased from the children of Hamor, Shechem's father, for a hundred kesitahs: Jacob is hoping for constructive cooperation with his Canaanite neighbors, and buys a plot of land at full price to serve as his home. The purpose of this purchase was to legitimize and reinforce his status there. (This is the second Jewish purchase in the Land of Israel, the first being the Cave of Machpelah.) On this site near Shechem the tomb of Joseph still stands today.

Jacob erects an altar, thereby proclaiming his cultural and ethical values, and calls it *El-elohe-yisrael*. But we shall soon see how Jacob's hopes for peaceful co-existence will be shattered.

It is no coincidence that Jacob chooses Shechem for implementing his plan of integrating himself peacefully and constructively into the life of the Land. From a geographical point of view, crossing the Jordan in the Penuel area (this is where the Jabbok [32:23] flows into the Jordan), Jacob, it would seem, is supposed to go south, to Hebron, to his father, but for some reason he heads instead toward the northeast, to Shechem.

We have previously cited the opinion that Shechem was founded by Abraham, which would mean that the inhabitants of Shechem are the descendants of Abraham's disciples. Jacob believed that he could find Abraham's monotheism and spiritual values in Shechem, and he hoped that with just such people he could establish a working relationship.

[18] Jacob arrived safe in the city of Shechem ... and he encamped before the city: *Vayichan*, "he encamped," is understood in the Midrash as related to *chen*, "kindness, mercy, favor." The Midrash tells us that Jacob worked to establish a civilized society in Shechem by endowing it with three things: A market complex, minted coinage, and communal baths.

(Those three things were the hallmarks of Hellenic civilization in the era when this Midrash was compiled. But for Jacob's times, ca. 18th century BCE, this is of course an anachronism.)

The Midrash means to say that upon returning from Paddan-aram (Babylonia), one of the world's leading cultural centers of that period, Jacob sought to bring civilization to Shechem. He believed that since its inhabitants had a connection to monotheism, fostering their advancement would be a worthwhile endeavor.

And he encamped before the city: "Before" in the Torah's usual geographical orientation means "from the east." The Shechem of the Canaanite era was located on the site which is today the Tell Balata mound. During archaeological excavations on this site during the nineteenth century, the ruins of a city of that same era were discovered, including its eastern gate. The story that is told in the next chapter of the Torah unfolds close to that gate.

[20] And called it "El-elohe-yisrael": This name reflects Jacob's genuine desire to be acknowledged as Israel, an essential prerequisite for his achieving that.

40.2. Dinah Visits the Daughters of the Land (34:1)

א, וַתֵּצֵא דִינָה בַּת־לֵאָה אֲשֶׁר יָלְדָה לְיַעֲקֹב לִרְאוֹת
בִּבְנוֹת הָאָרֶץ:

[1] Now Dinah, the daughter whom Leah had borne to Jacob, went out to visit the daughters of the land.

[1] Now Dinah ... went out to visit the daughters of the land: Perhaps it was Jacob's desire to establish positive relations with Shechem that led to Dinah's going out "to visit the daughters of the land." When one's desire for amicable relations with the neighbors is not tempered with caution and keeping a healthy distance, tragic consequences may ensue.

But it is also possible that even from the very beginning Jacob had considered marrying off Dinah to some resident of Shechem. When Dinah picked up on her father's idea, albeit in a distorted form, this led to a careless act on her part.

In a certain sense, the birth of a daughter posed a serious problem for Jacob. The tribes of Israel were supposed to descend from his sons, who would influence and reform humanity. The birth of a daughter could have been understood to mean that there would now be an additional, thirteenth tribe serving a similar purpose, but in reverse – for the peoples of the world to influence the Jews. In the Kabbalah, the male attribute is always understood as actively effecting change, and the female one as being a passive receiver.

For effective communication with the peoples of the world, the influence must go in both directions, because without the receiving aspect, neither can the giver's potential be realized. Dinah was supposed to be the progenitor of Israel's "female" tribe, which would receive the very best that the peoples of the world had to offer. This tribe's purpose would be to compensate for the attributes that were lacking in Israel's identity. Thus, Jacob had to find among the nations of the world one people that would represent all the positive qualities of humanity, through which Israel's foundation of universalism would find completion.

Jacob believed that the best society for creating that additional, thirteenth tribe of Israel was in Shechem.

According to the Midrash, Jacob was originally supposed to give Dinah to Esau as a wife. Leah, Dinah's mother, was herself meant to be Esau's wife, but Jacob, upon receiving Esau's blessing, also received the wife who had been pre-ordained for Esau. It was correct and necessary that Jacob would marry Leah for the sake of his personal development, but it also meant that Esau had been deprived.

Thus, Dinah could have filled in that gap. It is no coincidence that once again the Torah says here, "Dinah, the daughter whom Leah had borne to Jacob." By marrying Dinah, Esau would quite possibly have found his own correction, and introduced into the family of Jacob, the Jewish people, their missing components.

But Jacob was afraid to allow that. The Midrash says that Jacob, when he was about to meet Esau, hid Dinah in a wooden chest so that Esau would not be attracted to her. Jacob fears too strong a connection with Esau. He wants to find someone for Dinah who, if less imposing, is still their relative in some sense, and Jacob believes that he can find such a person in Shechem, the city of Abraham's students. Jacob therefore changes direction after crossing the Jordan, and goes not to his father in Hebron, but to Shechem.

40.3. The Rape of Dinah (34:2-4)

ב וַיַּרְא אֹתָהּ שְׁכֶם בֶּן־חֲמוֹר הַחִוִּי נְשִׂיא הָאָרֶץ וַיִּקַּח
אֹתָהּ וַיִּשְׁכַּב אֹתָהּ וַיְעַנֶּהָ: ג וַתִּדְבַּק נַפְשׁוֹ בְּדִינָה בַּת־יַעֲקֹב
וַיֶּאֱהַב אֶת־הַנַּעֲרָ וַיְדַבֵּר עַל־לֵב הַנַּעֲרָ: ד וַיֹּאמֶר שְׁכֶם אֶל־
חֲמוֹר אָבִיו לֵאמֹר קַח־לִי אֶת־הַיַּלְדָּה הַזֹּאת לְאִשָּׁה:

[2] Shechem son of Hamor the Hivite, chief of the country, saw her, and took her and lay with her by force.
[3] Being strongly drawn to Dinah daughter of Jacob, and in love with the maiden, he spoke to the maiden tenderly.
[4] So Shechem said to his father Hamor, "Get me this girl as a wife."

[2] Shechem ... saw her: The prince of Shechem bears the same name as his city. The Midrash believes that Jacob could have seen in that a positive sign, for it might have meant that Shechem had a ruler who would take personal responsibility for the fate of his city and its inhabitants. The rulers of Shechem were Hivites, one of the prominent Canaanite nations (10:17), but this does not necessarily imply that the same was true of the entire population of the city. The Canaanites in Shechem might have been a newer ethnic group superimposed on a more ancient substrate.

Jacob was hoping that the fundamental ethical norms that

Shechem had received from Abraham still remained, and that some limited additional influence on his part would be enough to allow him to live near them, and perhaps even to intermarry with them. But the behavior of the inhabitants of Shechem showed that he was mistaken. Jacob's sons decided that because Shechem had rejected the moral standards already instilled in him, they had no hope of correction, and had to be destroyed for the crime they had committed.

[4] So Shechem said to his father Hamor, "Get me this girl as a wife": Shechem acts quite prudently. Rather than renouncing his barbaric act there and then, he wants to give it legitimacy.

[3] He spoke to the maiden tenderly: That is, he was able to convince her that in view of the rape already committed, she would do better to agree to marry him.

In Shechem's actions we see no desire to improve. He continues to hold Dinah in his home and has no intention of releasing her. Shechem must obtain the consent of Jacob's family to marry Dinah only to normalize her status, because he will not be able to establish a normal relationship with her otherwise.

40.4. Jacob Remains Silent (34:5)

ה וְיַעֲקֹב שָׁמַע כִּי טִמֵּא אֶת־דִּינָה בִתּוֹ וּבָנָיו הָיוּ אֶת־ מִקְנֵהוּ בַּשָּׂדֶה וְהֶחֱרִשׁ יַעֲקֹב עַד־בֹּאָם:

[5] Jacob heard that he had defiled his daughter Dinah; but since his sons were in the field with his cattle, Jacob kept silent until they came home.

[5] Jacob kept silent: Jacob's silence is dual, not only physical but also emotional. He is genuinely bewildered, because his plan for integrating with Shechem is failing, and he himself cannot find a way out of the crisis

[5] But since his sons were in the field with his cattle, Jacob kept silent until they came home: This critical moment in Jacob's life story represents the transfer of his initiative, including the spiritual, to his sons. As we shall soon see, this moment will become one of the most highly decisive for the formation of Jacob's *Israel* attribute.

40.5. Jacob's Sons Recognize Themselves as Israel (34:6-7)

ו וַיֵּצֵא חֲמוֹר אֲבִי־שְׁכֶם אֶל־יַעֲקֹב לְדַבֵּר אִתּוֹ: ז וּבְנֵי
יַעֲקֹב בָּאוּ מִן־הַשָּׂדֶה כְּשָׁמְעָם וַיִּתְעַצְּבוּ הָאֲנָשִׁים וַיִּחַר
לָהֶם מְאֹד כִּי־נְבָלָה עָשָׂה בְיִשְׂרָאֵל לִשְׁכַּב אֶת־בַּת־יַעֲקֹב
וְכֵן לֹא יֵעָשֶׂה:

[6] Then Shechem's father Hamor came out to Jacob to speak to him.
[7] Meanwhile Jacob's sons, having heard the news, came in from the field. The men were distressed and very angry, because he had committed an outrage in Israel by lying with Jacob's daughter – a thing not to be done.

[6] Then Shechem's father Hamor came out to Jacob to speak to him: Hamor wants to speak with Jacob, but Jacob's sons take the lead.

[7] The men were ... very angry, because he had committed an outrage in Israel: This is the second place in the Torah that the name "Israel" is used. (The first was in the angel's proclamation itself of Jacob's impending name change.) The name "Israel" refers to the Jewish people living their self-sufficient national life in their own land. The sons of Jacob must not allow Shechem to hush up the rape incident, because that would humiliate the entire Jewish people, and would also serve as an excuse for the nations in the future to always regard Israel as occupying the lowest position in the social hierarchy.

An individual is integrated into the larger society at three primary levels: his family, his nationality, and humanity as a whole. But these three levels are by their nature all quite different.

The foundation of family relationships is love. Without love a family disintegrates. Thus, love is primary, while marital dynamics play only a secondary role in family life.

At the national level things are different. Relations are regulated primarily by the law, as adjudicated by the courts. Conflicts between citizens are resolved judicially, and the penal system too is administered through the courts.

At the international level, however, the judiciary is largely ineffective, and the law plays only a secondary role. At this level, conflict resolution is based primarily on raw power.

A nation's status is largely determined by how much its people allow themselves to be pushed around. Jacob has still not internalized this lesson. But his sons *are* already Israel, for they understand that the future existence of the Jewish nation depends precisely on how they posture themselves now.

British Prime Minister Winston Churchill once remarked, "When a nation that needs to choose between shame and war chooses shame, in the end it will get both."

Had the citizens of Shechem perceived the actions of their prince as a crime that demanded correction, they would have said: "We are guilty. We are returning Dinah to you, and we want to make amends." But nothing like that happens. Thus, Jacob's sons are left with no option but to go to war.

40.6. Jacob's Sons Negotiate with Hamor and Shechem (34:8-24)

ח וַיְדַבֵּר חֲמוֹר אִתָּם לֵאמֹר שְׁכֶם בְּנִי חָשְׁקָה נַפְשׁוֹ בְּבִתְּכֶם תְּנוּ נָא אֹתָהּ לוֹ לְאִשָּׁה: ט וְהִתְחַתְּנוּ אֹתָנוּ בְּנֹתֵיכֶם תִּתְּנוּ־לָנוּ וְאֶת־בְּנֹתֵינוּ תִּקְחוּ לָכֶם: י וְאִתָּנוּ תֵּשֵׁבוּ וְהָאָרֶץ תִּהְיֶה לִפְנֵיכֶם שְׁבוּ וּסְחָרוּהָ וְהֵאָחֲזוּ בָּהּ: יא וַיֹּאמֶר שְׁכֶם אֶל־אָבִיהָ וְאֶל־אַחֶיהָ אֶמְצָא־חֵן בְּעֵינֵיכֶם וַאֲשֶׁר תֹּאמְרוּ אֵלַי אֶתֵּן: יב הַרְבּוּ עָלַי מְאֹד מֹהַר וּמַתָּן וְאֶתְּנָה כַּאֲשֶׁר תֹּאמְרוּ אֵלָי וּתְנוּ־לִי אֶת־הַנַּעֲרָ לְאִשָּׁה: יג וַיַּעֲנוּ בְנֵי־יַעֲקֹב אֶת־שְׁכֶם וְאֶת־חֲמוֹר אָבִיו בְּמִרְמָה וַיְדַבֵּרוּ אֲשֶׁר טִמֵּא אֵת דִּינָה אֲחֹתָם: יד וַיֹּאמְרוּ אֲלֵיהֶם לֹא נוּכַל לַעֲשׂוֹת הַדָּבָר הַזֶּה לָתֵת אֶת־אֲחֹתֵנוּ לְאִישׁ אֲשֶׁר־לוֹ עָרְלָה כִּי־חֶרְפָּה הִוא לָנוּ: טו אַךְ־בְּזֹאת נֵאוֹת לָכֶם אִם תִּהְיוּ כָמֹנוּ לְהִמֹּל לָכֶם כָּל־זָכָר: טז וְנָתַנּוּ אֶת־בְּנֹתֵינוּ לָכֶם וְאֶת־בְּנֹתֵיכֶם נִקַּח־לָנוּ וְיָשַׁבְנוּ אִתְּכֶם וְהָיִינוּ לְעַם אֶחָד: יז וְאִם־לֹא תִשְׁמְעוּ אֵלֵינוּ לְהִמּוֹל וְלָקַחְנוּ אֶת־בִּתֵּנוּ וְהָלָכְנוּ: יח וַיִּיטְבוּ דִבְרֵיהֶם בְּעֵינֵי חֲמוֹר וּבְעֵינֵי שְׁכֶם בֶּן־חֲמוֹר: יט וְלֹא־אֵחַר הַנַּעַר לַעֲשׂוֹת הַדָּבָר כִּי חָפֵץ בְּבַת־יַעֲקֹב וְהוּא נִכְבָּד מִכֹּל בֵּית אָבִיו: כ וַיָּבֹא חֲמוֹר וּשְׁכֶם בְּנוֹ אֶל־שַׁעַר עִירָם וַיְדַבְּרוּ אֶל־אַנְשֵׁי עִירָם לֵאמֹר: כא הָאֲנָשִׁים הָאֵלֶּה שְׁלֵמִים הֵם אִתָּנוּ וְיֵשְׁבוּ בָאָרֶץ וְיִסְחֲרוּ אֹתָהּ וְהָאָרֶץ הִנֵּה רַחֲבַת־יָדַיִם לִפְנֵיהֶם אֶת־בְּנֹתָם נִקַּח־לָנוּ לְנָשִׁים וְאֶת־בְּנֹתֵינוּ נִתֵּן לָהֶם: כב אַךְ־בְּזֹאת יֵאֹתוּ לָנוּ הָאֲנָשִׁים לָשֶׁבֶת אִתָּנוּ לִהְיוֹת לְעַם אֶחָד בְּהִמּוֹל לָנוּ

כָּל־זָכָר כַּאֲשֶׁר הֵם נִמֹּלִים: **כג** מִקְנֵהֶם וְקִנְיָנָם וְכָל־
בְּהֶמְתָּם הֲלוֹא לָנוּ הֵם אַךְ נֵאוֹתָה לָהֶם וְיֵשְׁבוּ אִתָּנוּ:
כד וַיִּשְׁמְעוּ אֶל־חֲמוֹר וְאֶל־שְׁכֶם בְּנוֹ כָּל־יֹצְאֵי שַׁעַר
עִירוֹ וַיִּמֹּלוּ כָּל־זָכָר כָּל־יֹצְאֵי שַׁעַר עִירוֹ:

[8] And Hamor spoke with them, saying, "My son Shechem longs for your daughter. Please give her to him in marriage.

[9] Intermarry with us: give your daughters to us, and take our daughters for yourselves:

[10] You will dwell among us, and the land will be open before you; settle, move about, and acquire holdings in it."

[11] Then Shechem said to her father and brothers, "Do me this favor, and I will pay whatever you tell me.

[12] Ask of me a bride-price ever so high, as well as gifts, and I will pay what you tell me; only give me the maiden for a wife."

[13] Jacob's sons answered Shechem and his father Hamor – speaking with guile because he had defiled their sister Dinah –

[14] and said to them, "We cannot do this thing, to give our sister to a man who is uncircumcised, for that is a disgrace among us.

[15] Only on this condition will we agree with you; that you will become like us in that every male among you is circumcised.

[16] Then we will give our daughters to you and take your daughters to ourselves; and we will dwell among you and become as one kindred.

[17] But if you will not listen to us and become circumcised, we will take our daughter and go."

[18] Their words pleased Hamor and Hamor's son Shechem.

[19] And the youth lost no time in doing the thing, for he wanted Jacob's daughter. Now he was the most respected in his father's house.

[20] So Hamor and his son Shechem went to the public place of their town and spoke to their fellow townsmen, saying,

[21] "These people are our friends; let them settle in the land and move about in it, for the land is large enough for them; we will take their daughters to ourselves as wives and give our daughters to them.

[22] But only on this condition will the men agree with us to dwell among us and be as one kindred: that all our males become circumcised as they are circumcised.

[23] Their cattle and substance and all their beasts will be ours, if we only agree to their terms, so that they will settle among us."

[24] All who went out of the gate of his town heeded Hamor and his son Shechem, and all males, all those who went out of the gate of his town, were circumcised.

[8] My son Shechem longs for your daughter. Please give her to him in marriage: There is no mention of a crime, and Shechem's passionate attachment to Dinah is advanced as the argument for justifying the marriage.

[9] Intermarry with us: Hamor and Shechem are confident that they will be able to assimilate the Jacob family into their people. It never occurs to them to condemn Shechem's crime, not to mention punishing him for it. And this means that notwithstanding their peace proposals today, they can in the future perpetrate any violence at all against Jacob's family.

[13] Jacob's sons answered Shechem and his father Hamor – speaking with guile because he had defiled their sister Dinah: It is the position of Jacob's sons that in the absence of remorse and correction on the part of the inhabitants of Shechem, their prince's crime becomes nothing less than an act of war. And in a situation of war, no act of deception is out of bounds.

[17] But if you will not listen to us and become circumcised, we will take our daughter and go: So as not to arouse suspicion, Jacob's sons say only "we will take our daughter" (although it is not obvious how they could do so, seeing that Dinah is held captive in the royal residence). Nor do they mention punishing Shechem for his crime.

[18] Their words pleased Hamor and Hamor's son Shechem: The inhabitants of Shechem base their decisions and actions only on economic considerations.

[23] Their cattle and substance and all their beasts will be ours: The wealth and herds of Jacob and his family are apparently so extensive that they are an ample enticement for the entire population of the city.

[24] All ... heeded Hamor and his son Shechem, and all males, all those who went out of the gate of his town, were circumcised: The inhabitants of Shechem agree to be circumcised only so that they can take possession of the riches of Jacob's family; they have no intention of entering into a covenant with God. Moreover, they fail to voice any condemnation whatsoever of Shechem's crime, thus sharing responsibility for it.

40.7. The Destruction of Shechem (34:25-29)

כה וַיְהִי בַיּוֹם הַשְּׁלִישִׁי בִּהְיוֹתָם כֹּאֲבִים וַיִּקְחוּ שְׁנֵי־בְנֵי־
יַעֲקֹב שִׁמְעוֹן וְלֵוִי אֲחֵי דִינָה אִישׁ חַרְבּוֹ וַיָּבֹאוּ עַל־הָעִיר
בֶּטַח וַיַּהַרְגוּ כָּל־זָכָר: כו וְאֶת־חֲמוֹר וְאֶת־שְׁכֶם בְּנוֹ הָרְגוּ
לְפִי־חָרֶב וַיִּקְחוּ אֶת־דִּינָה מִבֵּית שְׁכֶם וַיֵּצֵאוּ: כז בְּנֵי
יַעֲקֹב בָּאוּ עַל־הַחֲלָלִים וַיָּבֹזּוּ הָעִיר אֲשֶׁר טִמְּאוּ אֲחוֹתָם:
כח אֶת־צֹאנָם וְאֶת־בְּקָרָם וְאֶת־חֲמֹרֵיהֶם וְאֵת אֲשֶׁר־
בָּעִיר וְאֶת־אֲשֶׁר בַּשָּׂדֶה לָקָחוּ: כט וְאֶת־כָּל־חֵילָם וְאֶת־
כָּל־טַפָּם וְאֶת־נְשֵׁיהֶם שָׁבוּ וַיָּבֹזּוּ וְאֵת כָּל־אֲשֶׁר בַּבָּיִת:

[25] On the third day, when they were in pain, Simeon and Levi, two of Jacob's sons, brothers of Dinah, took each his sword, came upon the city unmolested, and slew all the males.
[26] They put Hamor and his son Shechem to the sword, took Dinah out of Shechem's house, and went away.
[27] The other sons of Jacob came upon the slain and plundered the town, because their sister had been defiled.
[28] They seized their flocks and herds and asses, all that was inside the town and outside;
[29] all their wealth, all their children, and their wives, all that was in the houses, they took as captives and booty.

[25] Simeon and Levi ... slew all the males. [26] They put Hamor and his son Shechem to the sword: To reach Hamor, Shechem, and Dinah, they had to first kill all the men. The Midrash takes this as evidence that Simeon and Levi originally intended only to kill Shechem and take Dinah. But the inhabitants of the city rose up to defend their ruler, and they too therefore had to be killed.

[27] And plundered the town, because their sister had been defiled: Maimonides notes that every nation has an obligation, as one of the Seven Noahide Laws, to establish laws and courts of justice, and that any society that covers for its criminals bears collective guilt *ipso facto* for the offenses of those individuals. Thus, all the citizens of Shechem are held responsible for the crime committed against Dinah.

When a nation perpetrates violence against you, this must be seen not merely as a personal vendetta, but as outright war, and different standards of behavior therefore apply than would be otherwise assumed in peacetime. Acts that would be completely outside consideration in peacetime becomes permissible (and even necessary) in war.

Had Shechem repented by returning Dinah and admitting to his crime (even while continuing to ask for her hand in marriage), the attitude toward him might have been completely different. But Shechem was proposing to marry Dinah while all the while still holding her hostage. And the inhabitants of the city fully supported him in this.

All this implies a state of war, and in war we do not seek out the guilty party directly; everyone is held responsible. The rules of war in those times also included the right to capture and plunder everything that belonged to the enemy.

If the citizens of Shechem were indeed descendants of

Abraham's disciples, then their first duty was hospitality, Abraham's most important ethical principle. For having violated that principle they must be held to a higher standard than other nations, and their punishment must be more severe.

40.8. Did Simeon and Levi Act Properly? (34:30-31)

ל וַיֹּאמֶר יַעֲקֹב אֶל־שִׁמְעוֹן וְאֶל־לֵוִי עֲכַרְתֶּם אֹתִי
לְהַבְאִישֵׁנִי בְּיֹשֵׁב הָאָרֶץ בַּכְּנַעֲנִי וּבַפְּרִזִּי וַאֲנִי מְתֵי
מִסְפָּר וְנֶאֶסְפוּ עָלַי וְהִכּוּנִי וְנִשְׁמַדְתִּי אֲנִי וּבֵיתִי: **לא**
וַיֹּאמְרוּ הַכְזוֹנָה יַעֲשֶׂה אֶת־אֲחוֹתֵנוּ:

[30] Jacob said to Simeon and Levi, "You have brought trouble on me, making me odious among the inhabitants of the land, the Canaanites and the Perizzites; my men are few in number, so that if they unite against me and attack me, I and my house will be destroyed." [31] But they answered, "Should our sister be treated like a whore?"

[30] You have brought trouble on me, making me odious among the inhabitants of the land: Note that Jacob does not accuse his sons of immoral behavior or of having committed an injustice. He only expresses pragmatic concern about the possible consequences of their actions. Jacob fears war, because he is not yet Israel, but his sons understand that in international relations, violence is the only way to respond to an attack if one wishes to not be utterly decimated. This, unfortunately, remains the guiding principle of relations between nations even in our enlightened times.

If they unite against me and attack me, I and my house will be destroyed: Jacob's reaction is an expression of the *galut* mentality of survival: "Do not respond to the attack, or they will come and kill everyone!" But the brothers' response to him reflects the *modus operandi* of an autonomous Jewish nation living in its own land.

[31] Should our sister be treated like a whore?: The dialogue ends with a question. The Torah gives no answer to it, nor does it record Jacob's own response. It remains an open question.

Later, when blessing his sons on his deathbed, Jacob will level a sharp criticism against Simeon and Levi (49:5), ostensibly for their actions in this incident of Dinah and Shechem. But the Midrash understands that criticism as referring to the behavior of the brothers in the story of the sale of Joseph (37:19).

Chapter 41

Jacob Becomes Israel

41.1. Jacob Goes Up to Bethel (35:1-8)

א וַיֹּאמֶר אֱלֹהִים אֶל־יַעֲקֹב קוּם עֲלֵה בֵית־אֵל וְשֶׁב־
שָׁם וַעֲשֵׂה־שָׁם מִזְבֵּחַ לָאֵל הַנִּרְאֶה אֵלֶיךָ בְּבָרְחֲךָ מִפְּנֵי
עֵשָׂו אָחִיךָ: ב וַיֹּאמֶר יַעֲקֹב אֶל־בֵּיתוֹ וְאֶל כָּל־אֲשֶׁר עִמּוֹ
הָסִרוּ אֶת־אֱלֹהֵי הַנֵּכָר אֲשֶׁר בְּתֹכְכֶם וְהִטַּהֲרוּ וְהַחֲלִיפוּ
שִׂמְלֹתֵיכֶם: ג וְנָקוּמָה וְנַעֲלֶה בֵּית־אֵל וְאֶעֱשֶׂה־שָּׁם
מִזְבֵּחַ לָאֵל הָעֹנֶה אֹתִי בְּיוֹם צָרָתִי וַיְהִי עִמָּדִי בַּדֶּרֶךְ
אֲשֶׁר הָלָכְתִּי: ד וַיִּתְּנוּ אֶל־יַעֲקֹב אֵת כָּל־אֱלֹהֵי הַנֵּכָר
אֲשֶׁר בְּיָדָם וְאֶת־הַנְּזָמִים אֲשֶׁר בְּאָזְנֵיהֶם וַיִּטְמֹן אֹתָם
יַעֲקֹב תַּחַת הָאֵלָה אֲשֶׁר עִם־שְׁכֶם: ה וַיִּסָּעוּ וַיְהִי |
חִתַּת אֱלֹהִים עַל־הֶעָרִים אֲשֶׁר סְבִיבֹתֵיהֶם וְלֹא רָדְפוּ
אַחֲרֵי בְּנֵי יַעֲקֹב: ו וַיָּבֹא יַעֲקֹב לוּזָה אֲשֶׁר בְּאֶרֶץ כְּנַעַן
הוּא בֵּית־אֵל הוּא וְכָל־הָעָם אֲשֶׁר־עִמּוֹ: ז וַיִּבֶן שָׁם
מִזְבֵּחַ וַיִּקְרָא לַמָּקוֹם אֵל בֵּית־אֵל כִּי שָׁם נִגְלוּ אֵלָיו
הָאֱלֹהִים בְּבָרְחוֹ מִפְּנֵי אָחִיו: ח וַתָּמָת דְּבֹרָה מֵינֶקֶת
רִבְקָה וַתִּקָּבֵר מִתַּחַת לְבֵית־אֵל תַּחַת הָאַלּוֹן וַיִּקְרָא
שְׁמוֹ אַלּוֹן בָּכוּת:

*[1] God said to Jacob, "Arise, go up to Bethel and
remain there; and build an altar there to the God*

*who appeared to you when you were fleeing from
your brother Esau."*

*[2] So Jacob said to his household and to all who
were with him, "Rid yourselves of the alien gods
in your midst, purify yourselves, and change
your clothes.*

*[3] Come, let us go up to Bethel, and I will build
an altar there to the God who answered me
when I was in distress and who has been with
me wherever I have gone."*

*[4] They gave to Jacob all the alien gods that they
had, and the rings that were in their ears, and
Jacob buried them under the terebinth that was
near Shechem.*

*[5] As they set out, a terror from God fell on the
cities round about, so that they did not pursue
the sons of Jacob.*

*[6] Thus Jacob came to Luz – that is, Bethel – in
the land of Canaan, he and all the people who
were with him.*

*[7] There he built an altar and named the site
El-bethel, for it was there that God had revealed
Himself to him when he was fleeing from his
brother.*

*[8] Deborah, Rebekah's nurse, died, and was
buried under the oak below Bethel; so it was
named Allon-bacuth.*

[1] Arise, go up to Bethel and remain there: With Jacob's
return to Bethel the cycle of his exile is now complete, and
the fulfillment of the promises made when he left for Haran
has reached its logical conclusion. It is there that Jacob will

finally receive the name "Israel." This change of name happens only after the incident of Dinah and Shechem, in which Jacob's children demonstrated that they had moved beyond their father, and already felt that they were *Israel*.

[2] Rid yourselves of the alien gods in your midst: After taking Shechem, Jacob's sons now have "alien gods" that they could preserve as relics. But since these are the gods of peoples who were living in the land before Jacob and his family arrived, there was a danger that someone might begin to regard those idols as the "authentic culture" of the land to which they had now come. This potential hazard needed to be addressed.

It should be noted that Jacob buried those idols under a tree, rather than destroying them, because ancient idolatry, in principle, contains certain correct and valid elements. These will be revealed in the future, to become an important component of mankind's heritage.

[5] A terror from God fell on the cities round about, so that they did not pursue the sons of Jacob: The Torah here confirms the pragmatic correctness of Simeon and Levi, whose acts terrified the inhabitants of Canaan. It turned out that taking proactive measures by intimidating potential enemies provided maximum security, even if it was of course unpleasant for Jacob to have to acknowledge that.

[8] Deborah, Rebekah's nurse, died: The Midrash sees a rebuke to Jacob in this report of Deborah's death, and adds that at some point during Jacob's stay with Laban, Rebekah had sent her nurse Deborah to Jacob with a message that it was now safe for him to return to Canaan. But Jacob was then in no hurry, and even now, when he finally returns, he does not go immediately to his parents in Hebron. The Midrash avers that because Jacob was taking his time, Rebekah died before his return.

41.2. Jacob Becomes Israel (35:9-10)

ט וַיֵּרָא אֱלֹהִים אֶל־יַעֲקֹב עוֹד בְּבֹאוֹ מִפַּדַּן אֲרָם וַיְבָרֶךְ
אֹתוֹ: י וַיֹּאמֶר־לוֹ אֱלֹהִים שִׁמְךָ יַעֲקֹב לֹא־יִקָּרֵא שִׁמְךָ עוֹד
יַעֲקֹב כִּי אִם־יִשְׂרָאֵל יִהְיֶה שְׁמֶךָ וַיִּקְרָא אֶת־שְׁמוֹ יִשְׂרָאֵל:

*[9] God appeared again to Jacob on his arrival
from Paddan-aram, and He blessed him.
[10] God said to him, "You whose name is Jacob,
You shall be called Jacob no more, But Israel
shall be your name." Thus He named him Israel.*

[10] Thus He named him Israel: The interval from Penuel (32:31) where the angel promised Jacob that his name would be "Israel," and to Bethel when this renaming actually took place, was a transitional stage. During that period Jacob already felt himself Israel in relation to Esau and was already able to cope with Esau's guardian angel, but he still felt that he had no right to do battle with the inhabitants of the Land. He has now finally learned that lesson. It is this ability that naturally distinguishes the Jews living in the Land of Israel from Diaspora Jews.

41.3. Renewal of the Covenant (35:11-15)

יא וַיֹּאמֶר לוֹ אֱלֹהִים אֲנִי אֵל שַׁדַּי פְּרֵה וּרְבֵה גּוֹי וּקְהַל
גּוֹיִם יִהְיֶה מִמֶּךָּ וּמְלָכִים מֵחֲלָצֶיךָ יֵצֵאוּ: יב וְאֶת־הָאָרֶץ

אֲשֶׁר נָתַתִּי לְאַבְרָהָם וּלְיִצְחָק לְךָ אֶתְּנֶנָּה וּלְזַרְעֲךָ אַחֲרֶיךָ אֶתֵּן אֶת־הָאָרֶץ: **יג** וַיַּעַל מֵעָלָיו אֱלֹהִים בַּמָּקוֹם אֲשֶׁר־דִּבֶּר אִתּוֹ: **יד** וַיַּצֵּב יַעֲקֹב מַצֵּבָה בַּמָּקוֹם אֲשֶׁר־דִּבֶּר אִתּוֹ מַצֶּבֶת אָבֶן וַיַּסֵּךְ עָלֶיהָ נֶסֶךְ וַיִּצֹק עָלֶיהָ שָׁמֶן: **טו** וַיִּקְרָא יַעֲקֹב אֶת־שֵׁם הַמָּקוֹם אֲשֶׁר דִּבֶּר אִתּוֹ שָׁם אֱלֹהִים בֵּית־אֵל:

[11] And God said to him, "I am El Shaddai. Be fertile and increase; A nation, yea an assembly of nations, Shall descend from you. Kings shall issue from your loins.
[12] The land that I assigned to Abraham and Isaac I assign to you; And to your offspring to come Will I assign the land."
[13] God parted from him at the spot where He had spoken to him;
[14] and Jacob set up a pillar at the site where He had spoken to him, a pillar of stone, and he offered a libation on it and poured oil upon it.
[15] Jacob gave the site, where God had spoken to him, the name of Bethel.

[11] And God said to him: God's promise to Jacob in Bethel as he was leaving for exile is now realized. The first stage of the Covenant is now complete, and the Torah moves on to the second phase of the promises. The name *El Shaddai*, "God Almighty," means the Almighty as guarantor, which corresponds to the name "God of the Covenant," and also to the blessings received by Abraham (17:1) and transmitted to Isaac and Jacob (28:3).

A nation, yea an assembly of nations, shall descend from you. Kings shall issue from your loins: Here we see not only the promise of progeny and the Land, but an indicator of the versatility and importance of the Jewish people. Each of the twelve tribes of Israel will be, in a sense, its own nation. The Jewish people unite those tribes in their diversity (rather than striving for uniformity); thus the Jewish people are a microcosm of the diversity that is seen in all of humanity, and which is reflected in them.

[14] Jacob set up a pillar: The erection of this monument and confirmation of the name of this place as "Bethel" completes the cycle of exile (see 28:18).

Chapter 42

The Birth of Benjamin and the Return to Hebron

42.1. The Birth of Benjamin (35:16-18)

טז וַיִּסְעוּ מִבֵּית אֵל וַיְהִי־עוֹד כִּבְרַת־הָאָרֶץ לָבוֹא
אֶפְרָתָה וַתֵּלֶד רָחֵל וַתְּקַשׁ בְּלִדְתָּהּ: יז וַיְהִי בְהַקְשֹׁתָהּ
בְּלִדְתָּהּ וַתֹּאמֶר לָהּ הַמְיַלֶּדֶת אַל־תִּירְאִי כִּי־גַם־זֶה לָךְ
בֵּן: יח וַיְהִי בְּצֵאת נַפְשָׁהּ כִּי מֵתָה וַתִּקְרָא שְׁמוֹ בֶּן־
אוֹנִי וְאָבִיו קָרָא־לוֹ בִנְיָמִין:

[16] They set out from Bethel; but when they were still some distance short of Ephrath, Rachel was in childbirth, and she had hard labor.
[17] When her labor was at its hardest, the midwife said to her, "Have no fear, for it is another boy for you."
[18] But as she breathed her last – for she was dying – she named him Ben-oni; but his father called him Benjamin.

[16] They set out from Bethel: Since the cycle of exile is now complete, Jacob leaves Bethel and goes to Hebron, back to his father Isaac.

[18] But as she breathed her last – for she was dying – she named him Ben-oni; but his father called him Benjamin: All of Jacob's sons are named by his wives; Jacob has no active role in that process. Rachel too, as she lies dying on the birthstool, names her newborn baby *Ben-Oni*, "son of my grief." But Jacob changes the name to *Binyamin*, "son of my right hand." Even in the face of Rachel's tragic death, life must go on.

Benjamin opens a new chapter in the formation of Israel's identity. As Jacob's youngest son, he is the first to be born in the Land of Israel. And concurrently with his birth, Jacob's passivity ceases, and he now fully becomes Israel. We can say that Benjamin, the first of Jacob's children born to *Israel*, is truly Israel.

From now on, all the tribes of Israel are determined by their relation to Benjamin, who is Israel by birth, and these relationships form the background of the upcoming story of Joseph and his brothers. When Joseph and Judah during their confrontation in Egypt debate Benjamin's fate – with which of the two is their youngest brother to remain – it is actually a debate about which of them represents the true continuation of the Patriarchs.

Benjamin has a great many essential qualities. Because he was not involved in the conflict of Joseph and the brothers, he can unite the Jewish nation. His future inheritance in the Land of Israel is at the very center of it, between the territories of Judah and Joseph. The Temple is located in his inheritance (i.e., the Temple Mount, while the rest of ancient Jerusalem belongs to the tribe of Judah). And from the tribe of Benjamin will also come Saul, the first of the kings of Israel, who united the tribes into one unified state.

At the same time, Benjamin, being the youngest, is overly obsessed with his independence, always suspecting other tribes of trying to displace him by occupying a more dominant position. This sometimes led to grave consequences, and once even to a war, in which the tribe of Benjamin nearly perished (Judges 20:13).

42.2. Rachel's Death and Burial (35:19-21)

יט וַתָּמָת רָחֵל וַתִּקָּבֵר בְּדֶרֶךְ אֶפְרָתָה הִוא בֵּית לָחֶם: כ וַיַּצֵּב יַעֲקֹב מַצֵּבָה עַל־קְבֻרָתָהּ הִוא מַצֶּבֶת קְבֻרַת־רָחֵל עַד־הַיּוֹם: כא וַיִּסַּע יִשְׂרָאֵל וַיֵּט אָהֳלֹה מֵהָלְאָה לְמִגְדַּל־עֵדֶר:

[19] Thus Rachel died. She was buried on the road to Ephrath – now Bethlehem.
[20] Over her grave Jacob set up a pillar; it is the pillar at Rachel's grave to this day.
[21] Israel journeyed on, and pitched his tent beyond Migdal-eder.

[19] Thus Rachel died. She was buried on the road to Ephrath – now Bethlehem: The Tomb of Rachel is still today one of the most important Jewish shrines and pilgrimage destinations.

[20] Jacob set up a pillar ... [21] Israel journeyed on: It is *Jacob* who erects the monument to Rachel. But when he journeys on to Hebron, he is already *Israel*.

Two decades earlier, when Jacob went into exile, it happened in two stages: First he was exiled from his family (from Hebron), and then from the Land (from Bethel). So now he returns from exile also in two stages: first to Bethel (after receiving the name "Israel"), and then to his father in Hebron.

On his way from Bethel to Hebron, Jacob must experience the crisis of Rachel's death, and the restructuring of family relations.

42.3. The Incident of Reuben and Bilhah (35:22-26)

כב וַיְהִי בִּשְׁכֹּן יִשְׂרָאֵל בָּאָרֶץ הַהִוא וַיֵּלֶךְ רְאוּבֵן וַיִּשְׁכַּב
אֶת־בִּלְהָה פִּילֶגֶשׁ אָבִיו וַיִּשְׁמַע יִשְׂרָאֵל וַיִּהְיוּ בְנֵי־יַעֲקֹב
שְׁנֵים עָשָׂר: כג בְּנֵי לֵאָה בְּכוֹר יַעֲקֹב רְאוּבֵן וְשִׁמְעוֹן וְלֵוִי
וִיהוּדָה וְיִשָּׂשכָר וּזְבֻלוּן: כד בְּנֵי רָחֵל יוֹסֵף וּבִנְיָמִן:
כה וּבְנֵי בִלְהָה שִׁפְחַת רָחֵל דָּן וְנַפְתָּלִי: כו וּבְנֵי זִלְפָּה
שִׁפְחַת לֵאָה גָּד וְאָשֵׁר אֵלֶּה בְּנֵי יַעֲקֹב אֲשֶׁר יֻלַּד־לוֹ בְּפַדַּן
אֲרָם:

[22] While Israel stayed in that land, Reuben went and lay with Bilhah, his father's concubine; and Israel found out. Now the sons of Jacob were twelve in number.
[23] The sons of Leah: Reuben – Jacob's first-born – Simeon, Levi, Judah, Issachar, and Zebulun.
[24] The sons of Rachel: Joseph and Benjamin.
[25] The sons of Bilhah, Rachel's maid: Dan and Naphtali.
[26] And the sons of Zilpah, Leah's maid: Gad and Asher. These are the sons of Jacob who were born to him in Paddan-aram.

[22] Reuben went and lay with Bilhah, his father's concubine ... Now the sons of Jacob were twelve in number: The report that Reuben "lay with Bilhah" is followed immediately, in the very same verse and without interruption, by the words "Now the sons of Jacob were twelve in number." The Torah is emphasizing that Reuben is excluded neither from the count of Jacob's sons nor from the list of the progenitors of the Tribes of Israel. According to tradition, this means that his crime is not as serious as might seem to us from a simple reading of the Torah text.

The Midrash asserts that Reuben did not engage in intimate relations with Bilhah, but merely rearranged his father's bed, and lay down where it is not a son's place to be. This kind of behavior is viewed as a serious sin on par with adultery. But, of course, in fact it is not.

If Reuben had actually committed adultery, then later, after entering the Land of Israel, the Reuben tribe could not have participated in the Covenant on Mount Gerizim and Ebal, nor responded with "Amen!" as the Torah requires there: "Cursed be he who lies with his father's wife ... And all the people shall say, Amen." (Deut. 27:20)

In human terms, Reuben is the most simple-minded of all of Jacob's sons. His praiseworthy acts and his missteps are equally naive. So, what actually happened here between Reuben and Bilhah? The Midrash explains the situation as follows.

While Rachel was alive, Jacob's bed, i.e., his personal sleeping quarters, was in Rachel's tent. Leah and her sons all respected the established family hierarchy, according to which Rachel occupied first place within the family.

But after Rachel's death, Jacob, instead of transferring his bed to Leah's tent, moved it to the tent of Bilhah, Rachel's maidservant. As if to say that the memory of his dead wife

Rachel was more precious to him than even his surviving wife Leah.

Reuben, Leah's eldest son was outraged by Jacob's actions, for he could not bear to see his father so humiliate his mother Leah. He therefore rearranged his father's bed by removing it from Bilhah's tent. And because Reuben dared to intervene in his father's intimate life, the Torah accuses him of (an act equivalent to) having committed adultery.

Jacob, because of this act, although he did not deprive Reuben and his tribe of their rightful place among the Jewish people, did deprive Reuben of his primacy (49:4). Leadership must remain in the hands of cool-headed, even-tempered individuals. Those who display unbridled emotionality and lack of restraint should not be allowed to wield power.

Nevertheless, Reuben's maneuver made a positive impression on his father. After learning of the incident, Jacob reacted as Israel (v. 22); that is, as required by the laws of political authority. And Reuben therefore retained his position among the tribes.

By enumerating Jacob's children, the Torah here (and in the following verses) outlines the structure of Jacob's family. Within that family, Jacob remains Jacob, his children are from Paddan-aram (i.e., descendants of Laban), and Jacob acknowledges that the primacy remains, for now, with Esau. The real Israel is not Jacob, but only his descendants.

42.4. The Return to Hebron, and the Death of Isaac (35: 27-29)

כז וַיָּבֹא יַעֲקֹב אֶל־יִצְחָק אָבִיו מַמְרֵא קִרְיַת הָאַרְבַּע
הִוא חֶבְרוֹן אֲשֶׁר־גָּר־שָׁם אַבְרָהָם וְיִצְחָק: כח וַיִּהְיוּ
יְמֵי יִצְחָק מְאַת שָׁנָה וּשְׁמֹנִים שָׁנָה: כט וַיִּגְוַע יִצְחָק

וַיָּמָת וַיֵּאָסֶף אֶל־עַמָּיו זָקֵן וּשְׂבַע יָמִים וַיִּקְבְּרוּ אֹתוֹ
עֵשָׂו וְיַעֲקֹב בָּנָיו:

[27] And Jacob came to his father Isaac at Mamre, at Kiriath-arba – now Hebron – where Abraham and Isaac had sojourned.
[28] Isaac was a hundred and eighty years old
[29] when he breathed his last and died. He was gathered to his kin in ripe old age; and he was buried by his sons Esau and Jacob.

[27] And Jacob came to his father Isaac at Mamre, at Kiriath-arba – now Hebron: Jacob went into exile from Beer-sheba (28:10), but now returns to Hebron. This is because Isaac, sometime during the twenty years of Jacob's absence, had relocated from Beer-Sheba to Hebron.

Where Abraham and Isaac had sojourned: From this verse we can infer that Abraham too spent the end of his life in Hebron.

(29) He was buried by his sons Esau and Jacob: Esau remains Isaac's eldest son. Because Jacob has ceded the leading position within the family to Esau, here he is again called Jacob. Only when Esau finally moves to Mount Seir does Jacob come to the fore.

Chapter 43

Jacob and Esau Part Ways

43.1. Esau Departs from the Land of Canaan (36:6)

ו וַיִּקַּח עֵשָׂו אֶת־נָשָׁיו וְאֶת־בָּנָיו וְאֶת־בְּנֹתָיו וְאֶת־כָּל־
נַפְשׁוֹת בֵּיתוֹ וְאֶת־מִקְנֵהוּ וְאֶת־כָּל־בְּהֶמְתּוֹ וְאֵת כָּל־קִנְיָנוֹ
אֲשֶׁר רָכַשׁ בְּאֶרֶץ כְּנָעַן וַיֵּלֶךְ אֶל־אֶרֶץ מִפְּנֵי יַעֲקֹב אָחִיו:

[6] Esau took his wives, his sons and daughters, and all the members of his household, his cattle and all his livestock, and all the property that he had acquired in the land of Canaan, and went to another land because of his brother Jacob.

[6] Esau took his wives: As already noted, the story of Jacob's blessings (ch. 27) is framed, on either end, by the accounts of Esau's marriages (26:34 and 28:9). The implication is that Esau is being excluded from the Covenant because he has married improperly. Here too, the description of Esau's departure from Canaan begins with a description of his wives, because it was his wives, apparently, who significantly influenced that decision.

And went to another land because of his brother Jacob:
When Jacob returns to the future Land of Israel, his predominance is so evident that Esau now departs entirely of his own initiative, without war and without struggle. Jacob has now become Israel; that is, he now is possessing simultaneously qualities of both Jacob and Esau, while Esau remains only Esau. And Esau therefore retreats.

Esau was inclined even earlier to leave the Holy Land, because he lived in Seir (32:4). But his relocation to there is now final. Jacob's arrival only reinforces this desire in Esau. In parallel with Jacob becoming Israel, Esau becomes Edom – he receives a name that is, as already noted, associated with *adam*, "man." Esau becomes the "universal man," the primary focal point for the development of a "universal" civilization, which in the future will derive its spirituality from Israel.

43.2. The Kings of Edom and the Kings of Israel (36:31)

לא וְאֵ֙לֶּה֙ הַמְּלָכִ֔ים אֲשֶׁ֥ר מָלְכ֖וּ בְּאֶ֣רֶץ אֱד֑וֹם לִפְנֵ֥י מְלָךְ־
מֶ֖לֶךְ לִבְנֵ֥י יִשְׂרָאֵֽל:

[31] These are the kings who reigned in the land of Edom before any king reigned over the Israelites.

This verse is not merely telling us a fact of chronology, but is stressing an essential point. The Jews are by no means the leaders in matters of public administration. Quite the contrary, preeminence in organizational and state matters remains with Esau, and the Jews must learn this from him.

43.3. The Descendants of Esau and the Birth of Amalek (36:12)

יב וְתִמְנַע ׀ הָיְתָה פִילֶגֶשׁ לֶאֱלִיפַז בֶּן־עֵשָׂו וַתֵּלֶד לֶאֱלִיפַז
אֶת־עֲמָלֵק אֵלֶּה בְּנֵי עָדָה אֵשֶׁת עֵשָׂו:

[12] Timna was a concubine of Esau's son Eliphaz; she bore Amalek to Eliphaz. Those were the descendants of Esau's wife Adah.

[12] Timna was a concubine of Esau's son Eliphaz: The Midrash notes that this verse is difficult to reconcile with Timna's origins as a Horite princess (as follows from verses 20-22). How then did Timna suffer such a diminution of status, to become just a lowly concubine to Esau's son Eliphaz?

The Midrash explains this as follows. Timna understood that the Jews were a nation with a brilliant future ahead. She therefore approached Abraham, requesting that she undergo *giyur* (conversion); that is, she wanted to be accepted as a Jew. But Abraham declined her request, regarding her motives as excessively "practical." Abraham believed that Timna was not interested in serving the Almighty, and only wished to improve her worldly status.

So Timna then approached Isaac, but he too sent her away. Nor would Jacob accept her. Timna then said: "Let me be a concubine in Abraham's family, and not a queen among the nations of the world." So she went and became a concubine to Eliphaz, Esau's son, and bore him Amalek, who later oppressed Israel.

Timna harbored a grudge toward Abraham, Isaac, and Jacob for not accepting her, and Amalek, the son that she bore to Eliphaz, inherited her indignation. But Amalek learned hostility toward Jacob from his father Eliphaz as well. From this combination of indignation and hostility the Amalekites emerged, who were so imbued with hatred toward Israel that they could not be reconciled even to its very existence.

Thus, the Midrash believes that the birth of Amalek was the result of excessively stringent requirements in matters of *giyur*. And this is an important lesson that we, too, must learn from the story.

At the same time, we should not consider the birth of Amalek as simply the result of a random mistake. His appearance was an historical necessity. From the moment that Abraham undertook his monumental work, there was a feeling that something momentous was taking place, and many individuals among the surrounding nations wanted to cast their lot with the Chosen People.

But in some cases, when that aspiration cannot find a positive outlet, it finds a negative one, and thus was Amalek born. Therefore, the very existence of Amalek in the world is a constitutive, essential aspect of Israeli identity. After all, there will always be people and nations who want to be Israel and are frustrated that they cannot become him. This will always be the primary cause of anti-Semitism.

The conflict of Israel vs. Amalek is essential for advancing the world toward the era of Messianic light, which will enable all of mankind to finally achieve a level of accession to Israel and its Torah.

* * *

Before the Torah proceeds (beginning with the next chapter) to give a detailed account of the main line, the story of

Jacob's family, it offers, in its typical fashion in such cases, a brief description of what is now the side line: the descendants of Esau.

We can say that at this juncture, with Jacob's transformation to *Israel*, and Esau to *Edom* – the Torah's depiction of the life of the Patriarchs is now complete. Jacob-Israel himself lives on, but the Torah's further narrative will relate, primarily, to the lives of his children.

Weekly Portion
Vayeshev

Chapter 44

Conflicts Within Jacob's Family

44.1. The Four Final Portions of Genesis

The four final weekly portions of the book of Genesis tell the story of Jacob's children. A recurring theme in these portions is the alternating rises and falls of Judah and Joseph.

The sons of Jacob as individuals:
(9) Vayeshev (37:1-40:23)
  1. Judah's fall, and his inability to cope with the task of leading the Jewish people.
(10) Mikketz (41:1-44:17)
  2. The exaltation of Joseph in Egypt.

The sons of Jacob as the ancestors of the tribes:
(11) Vayigash (44:18-47:27)
  1. Joseph's fall before his brothers.
(12) Vayechi (47:28-50:26)
  2. The rise of Judah as the foundation of the future Jewish kingdom.

The narrative revolves around the two most prominent Jewish leaders, Joseph and Judah, whose relationship determines the dynamics of all of Jewish life. Joseph and Judah are the origin and the foundation of their two respective Messianic characters, the Messiah of the House of Joseph and the Messiah of the House of Judah. Those two are operative throughout all Jewish history, and even up to the present day. An analysis of their relationship is essential for understanding biblical history, and the modern State of Israel.

44.2. Joseph and the Yesod Attribute in the Structure of the Jewish People

Joseph is the only one of Jacob's twelve sons who also figures as one of the seven key personalities who shaped the soul of the Jewish nation, and whose corresponding seven attributes are personified in the *Sefirot* tree. Joseph's *Sefirah* is *Yesod*, "foundation."

(See the illustration at §5.6, "The *Sefirot* tree.")

The triangle formed by *Chesed*, *Gevurah*, and *Tiferet* (Abraham, Isaac and Jacob, respectively) represents the level of human emotions and aspirations. And the triangle of *Netzach*, *Hod*, and *Yesod* (Moshe, Aaron and Joseph, respectively) located just below it represents the level of actual practice, and correlation with reality.

Yesod collects and concentrates the light that has passed through the right, left, and center lines of the *Sefirot* tree. However, *Yesod* is only the preparation for realization of Divine goals, which happens at the stage of *Malchut*, corresponding to King David, of the house of Judah.

Yesod, Joseph's attribute, is a product of *Tiferet*, the attribute of Jacob. The story of Joseph and his brothers begins by emphasizing this connection: "This, then, is the line of Jacob: Joseph" (37: 2). But Joseph brings this quality down to the level of practice, and correlation with reality.

Jacob as *Tiferet* represents a balance between the attribute of *Chesed*, as personified by Abraham (the desire to give), and *Gevurah*, as personified by Isaac (the desire to hold). Joseph, *Yesod*, is the projection of this equilibrium to a lower level of practical activity, i.e., correctly assessing one's immediate situation. If *Tiferet* is an understanding of the theoretically correct proportions of giving vs. holding – "the good and right" thing to do – then *Yesod* is the correct assessment of practical options: What can possibly be done to correct a situation.

Along the central line of the *Sefirot* tree are those categories that strike a balance between right extroversion, which seeks to give, and left introversion, which seeks to hold. As we move from top to bottom on the tree, the attributes become more "practical." The level of *Da'at* (knowledge) is a deep understanding of someone or something assimilating it into oneself. The level of *Tiferet* is one's sense of what is needed by another person or thing. And *Yesod* is an assessment of just how that can be accomplished. Finally, the level of *Malchut* is the action itself.

Joseph, in a sense, stands between the Patriarchs, the founders of the Jewish people, and their descendants, the nation itself. Two tribes will descend from Joseph, and not just one, as with all the other brothers. Since the founders of those tribes are Joseph's sons, Manasseh and Ephraim, Joseph has the status of a partial Patriarch. Thus, he occupies an intermediate position between his father and his brothers (notwithstanding that chronologically he is the youngest among them). And this is a constant source of conflict within the family.

Joseph's true passion in life is correcting the world around him. He seeks to intervene in every situation that comes to his attention. All in all this works out for him quite well, because Joseph is extraordinarily successful in everything he undertakes.

Wherever Joseph happens to find himself, he quickly becomes the boss, or even the chief executive. In his father's house he is distinguished by a multi-colored tunic, a gift from his father, and he orders his brothers around, teaching them proper behavior. Suddenly a slave, he immediately becomes the steward in the house of Potiphar (39:4). In prison, he is appointed to the post of prison warden (39:21). And when he leaves the prison, he becomes the second in command over all of Egypt. In the end, he manages to reform his brothers as well. All this is thanks to his ability to rule the world around him and achieve a practical result. "The Lord lent success to everything he undertook" (39:3).

We are told that Joseph was remarkably handsome, and that he was meticulous about his appearance (39:6). In European literature he is even called "Joseph the Beautiful." But in Jewish tradition he has received instead a different moniker: "Joseph the Righteous." Of all Biblical characters, Joseph alone is endowed with that title.

We read in the book of Proverbs (10:25), "*Tzaddik yesod olam*," "The righteous is an everlasting foundation," which in a more literal translation means "The righteous is the foundation of the world." Jewish tradition understands this verse to be saying that a righteous person is one who follows the path of righteousness in the real world, while in constant confrontation with its problems. Judaism idealizes not hermetic righteousness, which avoids society in order to escape worldly problems, but righteousness of action, that is, proper behavior in the civilized, workaday world.

Accordingly, the Kabbalah associates the category of *Yesod* with righteousness. Thus, *Yesod* is the correct assessment of a situation that leads to proper action in the world around us. And this is Joseph's attribute.

Joseph was sold into slavery as a matter of supreme justice, because he misused the powers granted to him. In an effort to correct his brothers' behavior, he says things that devalue their dignity and are personally offensive. As a result, he is sent to Egypt, and then thrown into prison. But all this is for Joseph a "higher education," the process of refining his *Yesod* attribute, and a lesson in how to accurately assess the world around him.

Having sunk to the lowest of the low, incarcerated in an Egyptian prison, Joseph correctly formulates his *Yesod* attribute. Whereupon he is liberated, successfully governs all of Egypt, and even acquires the inner fortitude he needs to correct his brothers.

Joseph's dreams, in which his parents and his brothers are all bowing to him, are providential – he truly has the potential to become king. But in his view of the world there is an important flaw, namely, he absolutizes his regal status, which seems to him the Jewish ideal.

Later, however, toward the end of Genesis, it turns out that Joseph was wrong. His kingdom is only temporary, and the scepter must subsequently pass to the house of Judah (meaning that the attribute of *Malchut*, Kingdom, corresponds not to Joseph, but to King David, of the tribe of Judah). The kingdom of Joseph is thus only the initial stage of development of the greater Jewish kingdom – although this initial stage can be realized only through him.

Joseph has yet another important characteristic that is necessary for properly implementing the *Yesod* attribute, for the correction of the world. Joseph is the *ba'al hachalomot*

(37:19), the "master of dreams." Complementing his impressive pragmatic talents, he also has a dream, a vision, and a higher aspiration. Joseph's dream of sheaves of corn presents this vision to us in the form of a prosperous agricultural economy striving to feed humanity, for the common good of all. The lesson we are meant to learn from this is that a correct assessment of the surrounding world cannot be built solely on a cold analysis of the facts and on bare calculations, but must necessarily include a dream – a higher idea and a loftier goal.

The dreamers of the world are the only true realists.

44.3. The Messiah-Kings of the House of Joseph and the House of Judah

Earlier in this commentary we discussed the two ancestral lines of the Jewish people, which descend from the two wives of Jacob-Israel – Rachel and Leah, respectively.

(See this relationship presented in tabular form at §36.13. "Jacob and Israel as the Two Lines of the Jewish People.")

Rachel's son Joseph and Leah's son Judah represent the two central lines of Jewish history. Two Messianic directions descend from them: *Mashiach ben Yosef* and *Mashiach ben Yehudah* (hereinafter referred to as *Mashiach ben David*). Viewed this way, the last four portions of the book of Genesis present the dynamics of four different approaches. Joseph and Judah first appear as independent personalities, and then gradually develop in their Messianic directions.

We have already discussed (§34.8) that one of the aspects of the work of the Jewish people in the world is to carry out *tikkun*, "correcting the world," gathering the sparks that have scattered due to *shevirat keilim*, the "shattering of vessels," after which the *kelippot*, "shells," were seized.

The process of collecting sparks happens in several stages. First, the shell that hides the Divine sparks must be penetrated. Next, we need to connect to the spark, and "seize" it. And finally, the sparks must be brought together by weaving them into a single network, a "vessel" capable of containing them and receiving the Divine light. Thus, a connection between the Almighty and the human race is created.

The various segments of the Jewish people perform different functions within this process. Throughout his entire life, Joseph demonstrated remarkable skill at managing the material world, a faculty that even today is an important Jewish trait, as seen, for example, in Jewish managers, financiers, engineers, and scientists. The king from Joseph's line (*Mashiach ben Yosef*), who organizes Jewish life in the fields of economics, security, and all aspects of material well-being, is the king responsible for addressing "earthly needs." This is an important stage, but the process is then still far from complete. After Joseph's descendants have prepared the material foundation, the descendants of Judah will arrive on the scene to propitiously continue the work.

The kingdom of Joseph is only a preliminary stage. It creates conditions that are conducive to penetrating the *kelippah* (shell), and facilitates connecting to the spark. But merely revealing the sparks is not enough; they must also be joined into a unified whole. The Kingdom of Joseph therefore only opens a path for the Kingdom of Judah, who is charged with the task of promoting the idea of human dialogue with God, and transmitting the Divine light to mankind.

The Kingdom of Joseph leads, but it only allows the Jews to exist, and to create a political state, which Judah and David must then imbue with inner vitality.

When in ancient times, after the era of the Judges, the

Jewish people were ready to create a state, their first nationalist king was Shaul (Saul) of the tribe of Benjamin (i.e., from the house of Joseph). Only after that did the kingdom pass to the dynasty of David, who was of the tribe of Judah.

In the future too, *Mashiach ben Joseph* must arrive first, preparing the external political framework, and working to penetrate the "shell," to give access to the "sparks." *Mashiach ben David* will then follow, bringing the Divine light to the world and combining those sparks into a unified system of Holy Vessels.

Chapter 45

Joseph: The Inexperience of Youth

45.1. The Structure of the Vayeshev Portion

Judah's fall happens in the *Vayeshev* portion. It consists of three separate stories.

(1) *The sale of Joseph.* The brothers, suspecting Joseph of intending to expel them from the family, want to kill him outright, but Judah urges that Joseph be sold instead, and the brothers obey.

(2) *Judah's separation from his brothers.* His children, and the story of Tamar, which causes Judah to repent.

(3) *Joseph begins his stay in Egypt.* (This happens in parallel with the preceding.) Joseph's life in Potiphar's house, the incident with Potiphar's wife, Joseph's imprisonment, and his interpretation of the dreams of Pharaoh's two courtiers.

45.2. Life in Canaan and Jacob's Premature Aspirations (37:1)

א וַיֵּשֶׁב יַעֲקֹב בְּאֶרֶץ מְגוּרֵי אָבִיו בְּאֶרֶץ כְּנָעַן׃

[1] Now Jacob was settled in the land where his father had sojourned, the land of Canaan.

[1] Now Jacob was settled in the land where his father had sojourned: The Midrash notes that this verse, which uses two similar terms, *vayeshev*, and *megurei*, contrasts Jacob's circumstances with those of his ancestors. *Vayeshev*, "settled," refers to a permanent abode, but *megurei*, "sojourned," implies only a temporary residence. In other words, Jacob settled permanently where his ancestors had resided only temporarily. Abraham and Isaac felt insecure in their new land, much like strangers. But Jacob decides that everything now is different, that he can live a much more secure existence than they did.

The difference between the two expressions reflects Jacob's aspirations, which we might even call Messianic. He identifies the redemption that God had promised with his own return to the Land.

The first period of Jewish history is defined by the Covenant Between the Parts (Gen. 15:9 ff.). God told Abraham that his descendants would be in exile for four hundred years, and that those years would span four generations (15:13-16). But these are not the same thing. The four hundred years mentioned there are obviously not meant as an exact figure, but only a symbolic, typological number.

We encounter the typology of the number four, and multiples thereof, not infrequently. We see it, for example, in the expression "and the land had rest forty years" (Judges 3:11, 5:31, 8:28). The number four is associated, essentially, with historical periods, and accordingly, the four hundred years of slavery as predicted to Abraham means not an exact number of calendar years, but a period of servitude that would span four different eras.

As Jacob sees it, these four eras – four generational transitions ("And they shall return here in the fourth generation" [15:16]) – have already occurred. The first generation is Abraham, the second is Isaac, the third is Jacob himself, and the fourth is Jacob's own children. Jacob therefore believes that his return with his children to the Land of Israel means that the birth of the nation and the end of exile have been achieved. Indeed, Abraham's prophetic vision referred to a nation descended from Abraham, and, in Jacob's view, he and his children could already be considered a nation.

We have already noted (§13.8. "Babylon and Egypt") that the birth of the Jewish nation happened in two stages – first with Jacob's family's flight from Laban's house, and later at the Exodus from Egypt. Jacob correctly sensed the completion of the first stage, and he therefore believed that the creation of the Jewish nation too was now complete, that all their ordeals were already in the past, and that the *geulah* (redemption) – the era of the Return of the Exiles and the revelation of the Messianic light had arrived. (All of the above are events associated with the Jews' free and independent existence in the Land of Israel.)

But as it later turned out, Jacob had experienced only the first *geulah*, the "return of the Patriarchs," which had yet to be followed by the second stage, the exile and subsequent return of their descendants. Jacob, however, had no knowledge of that.

The departure of Jacob's family from Babylon represented the birth of the Jewish nation at the level of "exodus from the father," and the Exodus from Egypt was their birth at the level of "exodus from the mother." In other words, the "father" of the Jewish people is Babylon and their "mother" is Egypt. In order to achieve the unification of all mankind, the Jewish people must unite those two main branches of the river that issued from Eden (2:10-14).

45.3. Joseph as the Cause of the Crisis (37:2)

ב אֵלֶּה | תֹּלְדוֹת יַעֲקֹב יוֹסֵף בֶּן־שְׁבַע־עֶשְׂרֵה ...

[2] This, then, is the line of Jacob: At seventeen years of age, Joseph ...

[2] This, then, is the line of Jacob: ... Joseph: These words serve as an introduction to the entire subsequent story of Joseph's conflict with his brothers. The literal translation is "This is the offspring (*toldot*) of Jacob: Joseph ..." that is, the verse is divided not by a period, but by a colon. Jacob's primary offspring is Joseph, whom Jacob wants to consider his firstborn. After all, Rachel was the wife whom Jacob had originally intended to marry, and Joseph was Rachel's first child. But it is also Joseph who will prevent Jacob from finding tranquility in the secure possession of his own Land.

After completing the first stage of his exile – a long interval during which he had to undergo strenuous ordeals and find working solutions to vexing problems with Esau and Laban – Jacob had found peace. But after eleven years of tranquil life in his own Land (Joseph, who was six years old when they left Laban, is now seventeen), Jacob let down his guard and made the mistake of underestimating the complexity of the goings on in his own family. As the Midrash explains, Jacob was quite sure that even more peaceful times were approaching – the Messianic era. But his son Joseph challenged that assumption. Joseph, unable to reconcile himself to the imperfection of this world, could not be content with Jacob's isolated achievements. Joseph needed to correct the world for all of mankind.

Even after you have achieved marked success, it is important to understand that that is but one stage along life's path. Remaining vigilant is critical if you want to be prepared for further changes.

45.4. The Inexperience of Youth (37:2)

ג ... יוֹסֵף בֶּן־שְׁבַע־עֶשְׂרֵה שָׁנָה הָיָה רֹעֶה אֶת־אֶחָיו
בַּצֹּאן וְהוּא נַעַר ...

[2] ... At seventeen years of age, Joseph tended the flocks with his brothers, as a helper ...

[2] Tended the flocks with his brothers: The Hebrew particle *et* can mean, as translated here, "with," or it can indicate the accusative case, introducing the object of the action. Thus, one can understand the passage in two different ways: "Joseph was herding (the sheep) with his brothers," or "Joseph was herding his brothers (among the sheep)." That is, he was trying to reeducate them.

The Midrash relates that Joseph, the youngest among the brothers, approached them with advice on how they should graze their father's sheep. And because his advice proved exactly right, the brothers hated him for that even more.

As a helper: The literal translation is not "helper," but "lad." But do we need to be told that, after just reading that Joseph at the time was seventeen years old, the prime age of adolescence? We must therefore understand the passage as revealing a certain characteristic of Joseph's behavior, and not just his age. Joseph, behaving like a youth, failed to perceive that his advice was downright painful to his brothers. Due to his inexperience, Joseph could not properly realize his potential for correcting the world around him. Joseph is a righteous man, who wishes everyone only the absolute best. But he is still incapable of behaving properly.

Like all the Patriarchs, who personify their *Sefirah* attributes, the *Yesod* attribute in Joseph undergoes faceting throughout his lifetime, being constantly improved. Joseph has uncommon potential for correcting the world around him, but he must first undergo a rigorous educational process in order to learn how to use that potential correctly. In that process, "Joseph as individual" becomes *Mashiach ben Yosef.*

45.5. Countering the Dominance of Leah's Sons (37:2)

ב ... אֶת־בְּנֵי בִלְהָה וְאֶת־בְּנֵי זִלְפָּה נְשֵׁי אָבִיו וַיָּבֵא יוֹסֵף אֶת־דִּבָּתָם רָעָה אֶל־אֲבִיהֶם:

[2] ... to the sons of his father's wives Bilhah and Zilpah. And Joseph brought bad reports of them to their father.

[2] Of his father's wives: The Torah stresses that Bilhah and Zilpah are Jacob's wives, not his maidservants. The Midrash on this occasion notes that Leah's four eldest sons (Reuben, Simeon, Levi, and Judah) had established a strict hierarchy, considering themselves the leaders both in age and status. Joseph, seeking equity, made it a point to consort with the sons of Bilhah and Zilpah, as if to emphasize that they were his father's wives, and not just maidservants.

And Joseph brought bad reports of them to their father: Because Joseph complains to his father about Leah's sons' arrogance, the older brothers consider him a direct threat to the family hierarchy they have established.

However, it later becomes clear that the system of relations under which the sons of Leah dominate will persist among the Jewish people for many centuries to come. When after the Exodus from Egypt the Jews wander through the desert, this hierarchy will still find expression in the manner that the tribes are grouped into camps (Num. 2:1 ff.). Only much later, after each tribe has received its inheritance in the Land of Israel, will unification of the tribes into one nation become possible.

Joseph prematurely wishes to dismantle the hierarchy established by Leah's sons, because he considers it fundamentally unfair. He fails to understand, however, that the current hierarchical structure of the future nation is the correct one. Joseph's inept actions therefore result in his being expelled and sold into slavery.

Chapter 46

Joseph's Conflict
With His Brothers

46.1. The Familial and Nationalist Approaches in Contrast (37:3)

ג וְיִשְׂרָאֵל אָהַב אֶת־יוֹסֵף מִכָּל־בָּנָיו כִּי־בֶן־זְקֻנִים הוּא
לוֹ ...

[3] Now Israel loved Joseph best of all his sons, for he was the child of his old age ...

[3] Now Israel loved Joseph best: This third verse contrasts with the second: "This is the offspring (*toldot*) of Jacob: Joseph." The change of name from Jacob to Israel reveals one of the causes of this situation. If *Jacob* considers Joseph his primary offspring, this is normal, because Jacob, on a personal level, is realized in Joseph himself. But as *Israel*, he is no longer just a family, but a nation, and the family hierarchy should no longer be based on paternal feelings, but on the principles of building that future nation. Jacob-Israel's awareness of this change will come to him at the end of his life, as expressed in his blessings to his children immediately before his death.

The two previous weekly portions, *Vayetze* and *Vayishlach*, were concerned with Jacob's correction as an individual, whereas this portion, *Vayeshev*, until the end of the book of Genesis, tells of Israel's correction as a nation.

Had Jacob been able, openly and clearly, to allocate a place in the national hierarchy to each of his sons, they would have then been convinced that Joseph posed no danger to them, and that no one was going to expel them from the family. But Jacob was not able to do this, and the conflict escalated into enmity.

The child of his old age: The expression *ben zekunim*, "child of old age," usually refers to the youngest child in the family. But in this case, the youngest son is Benjamin, not Joseph. The reason for this shift of designation is not only Benjamin's extreme youth (if Joseph was seventeen years old, then Benjamin must have been only about ten), but also the particular wisdom that Joseph possessed. *Zaken*, "old," in Hebrew can refer to either age or wisdom. Thus, *ben zekunim* here can be translated as either "son of old age" or "wise son."

Because Joseph and his father have similar perceptions of the world, Jacob understands Joseph well. But he makes the same mistake that Abraham and Isaac did. He sees his continuation in the son who is most comprehensible to him. (Jacob understands Joseph's wisdom, because *Yesod* extends *Tiferet*.) This error on Jacob's part will be corrected only at the very end of the events in the book of Genesis.

46.2. Joseph's "Ornamented Tunic" (37:3-4)

ג ... וְעָשָׂה לוֹ כְּתֹנֶת פַּסִּים: ד וַיִּרְאוּ אֶחָיו כִּי־אֹתוֹ
אָהַב אֲבִיהֶם מִכָּל־אֶחָיו וַיִּשְׂנְאוּ אֹתוֹ וְלֹא יָכְלוּ דַּבְּרוֹ
לְשָׁלֹם:

[3] ... and he had made him an ornamented tunic.
[4] And when his brothers saw that their father loved him more than any of his brothers, they hated him so that they could not speak a friendly word to him.

[3] An ornamented tunic: Literally, "a striped shirt." Stripes of different colors joined into a single shirt symbolize the unification of diverse aspects, the unity of a versatile people. But it was also a symbol of Joseph's power over all these colors.

Expanding on this story, the Midrash says that it was a long-sleeved shirt, indicating that Joseph, unlike all the other brothers, was not expected to engage in manual labor. "He studied Torah at home with his father." (That is, he received spiritual knowledge from Jacob's family heritage.) Now and again Joseph would go out to his brothers and explain to them how to live correctly. "Father and I learned such and such. Do you behave accordingly or do you not?" It is easy to see why the brothers did not take kindly to such talk.

By rights, that shirt should have belonged not to Joseph, but to Benjamin, because Benjamin would become the mainstay of the family. It was thus not by chance that the brothers later saw fit to strip Joseph of that shirt. Saul, the first of the kings of Israel, who will unite all the tribes, will descend from Benjamin. Moreover, the future Temple will be built in Benjamin's territory.

And according to Tradition, the flag of the tribe of Benjamin, like jasper, the gem that it resembled, was striped and multi-colored.

For Jacob to dress Joseph in this shirt was fundamentally wrong. Thus, it could not but arouse indignation among the brothers.

[4] They hated him so that they could not speak a friendly word to him: The Midrash sees this as evidence of the brothers' honesty. Deeply offended by their father and by Joseph, they did not dissemble, or attempt to give a false impression that everything was just fine.

46.3. Joseph's Dreams (37:5-10)

ה וַיַּחֲלֹם יוֹסֵף חֲלוֹם וַיַּגֵּד לְאֶחָיו וַיּוֹסִפוּ עוֹד שְׂנֹא אֹתוֹ: ו וַיֹּאמֶר אֲלֵיהֶם שִׁמְעוּ־נָא הַחֲלוֹם הַזֶּה אֲשֶׁר חָלָמְתִּי: ז וְהִנֵּה אֲנַחְנוּ מְאַלְּמִים אֲלֻמִּים בְּתוֹךְ הַשָּׂדֶה וְהִנֵּה קָמָה אֲלֻמָּתִי וְגַם־נִצָּבָה וְהִנֵּה תְסֻבֶּינָה אֲלֻמֹּתֵיכֶם וַתִּשְׁתַּחֲוֶיןָ לַאֲלֻמָּתִי: ח וַיֹּאמְרוּ לוֹ אֶחָיו הֲמָלֹךְ תִּמְלֹךְ עָלֵינוּ אִם־מָשׁוֹל תִּמְשֹׁל בָּנוּ וַיּוֹסִפוּ עוֹד שְׂנֹא אֹתוֹ עַל־חֲלֹמֹתָיו וְעַל־דְּבָרָיו: ט וַיַּחֲלֹם עוֹד חֲלוֹם אַחֵר וַיְסַפֵּר אֹתוֹ לְאֶחָיו וַיֹּאמֶר הִנֵּה חָלַמְתִּי חֲלוֹם עוֹד וְהִנֵּה הַשֶּׁמֶשׁ וְהַיָּרֵחַ וְאַחַד עָשָׂר כּוֹכָבִים מִשְׁתַּחֲוִים לִי: י וַיְסַפֵּר אֶל־אָבִיו וְאֶל־אֶחָיו וַיִּגְעַר־בּוֹ אָבִיו וַיֹּאמֶר לוֹ מָה הַחֲלוֹם הַזֶּה אֲשֶׁר חָלָמְתָּ הֲבוֹא נָבוֹא אֲנִי וְאִמְּךָ וְאַחֶיךָ לְהִשְׁתַּחֲו ֹת לְךָ אָרְצָה:

[5] Once Joseph had a dream which he told to his brothers; and they hated him even more.

[6] He said to them, "Hear this dream which I have dreamed:
[7] There we were binding sheaves in the field, when suddenly my sheaf stood up and remained upright; then your sheaves gathered around and bowed low to my sheaf."
[8] His brothers answered, "Do you mean to reign over us? Do you mean to rule over us?" And they hated him even more for his talk about his dreams.
[9] He dreamed another dream and told it to his brothers, saying, "Look, I have had another dream: And this time, the sun, the moon, and eleven stars were bowing down to me."
[10] And when he told it to his father and brothers, his father berated him. "What," he said to him, "is this dream you have dreamed? Are we to come, I and your mother and your brothers, and bow low to you to the ground?

[7] There we were binding sheaves in the field: This is yet another source of the brothers' hatred. In Joseph's dream they are all binding sheaves, i.e., engaged in agriculture. But the brothers are by no means farmers – they are sheep and cattle breeders.

We have already explained the conflict between herders and farmers. Agriculture is much more profitable than cattle breeding, and produces significantly more food. But it enslaves the farmer. The brothers want to be free, and so they are outraged by Joseph's agricultural dreams.

(As also noted earlier, the Jewish people were eventually able to practice farming without compromising their essential freedom. But how they were able to achieve that is revealed only in subsequent books of the Torah.)

Joseph yearns to repair the world and to feed its inhabitants. He therefore dreams of sheaves of corn. Nor is it any accident that Joseph is ultimately sold to Egypt, which, on the one hand, is "the land of slavery," but on the other, is also the breadbasket of the ancient world – just the place for Joseph to fulfill his mission. We can even say that Joseph from the very beginning subconsciously yearned to live in Egypt, because only from there was it possible for him to provide sustenance to the entire surrounding world.

Joseph arrived in the Land of Israel around the age of seven, having already spent his most innocent childhood years in Paddan-aram, Laban's land. And that is why he is now so favorably disposed to other countries, to going "abroad," which he sees through the prism of his positive, carefree childhood. But Joseph's brothers were already twelve to fifteen years old when they left Paddan-aram, and well understand that their family had only narrowly and miraculously avoided perishing altogether. Therefore, unlike Joseph, they value life in their Land and are loath to the idea of losing it.

[8] And they hated him even more for his talk about his dreams: They hated him for his dreaming itself – that he dreams, and they do not. And they hated him for telling over his dreams to them, which to them showed that he laid conscious claims to a unique mission and a dominant role in the family.

[8] Do you mean to reign over us? Do you mean to rule over us?: The Hebrew synonyms *maloch* ("reign") and *mashol* ("rule") are significantly different. To reign means to govern with the consent of the governed and in harmony with them, but to rule means to impose one's will by force, with no regard for the wishes of those being ruled. In Joseph's dreams we indeed see his desire to reign, but we do not detect any hint of wanting to wield power. The brothers impute that to him on their own, for they incorrectly gauge Joseph's motives, which leads them to tangle with him.

[9] He dreamed another dream and told it to his brothers: The Torah does not report the brothers' reaction to his second dream, because this time around they refuse to even respond.

[10] And when he told it to his father and brothers: After the brothers' reject him, Joseph chooses the moment when the brothers are together with their father, and he retells his dream to all of them together. Joseph so yearns for his brothers to acknowledge his royal status, despite their resistance. And his pretensions now include reigning not only over all his brothers, but even over Jacob himself.

46.4. Joseph's Brothers' Fears, and Jacob's Position

But in fact, the brothers' fears are by no means baseless. Before we blame the brothers, we must try to understand them.

Dreams play a huge role in Joseph's life. The brothers will later call Joseph a dreamer, "the master of dreams." No one else in the Torah is called that. On the lips of his brothers it is just a contemptuous nickname, but in fact it is Joseph's great virtue that he is a dreamer who wants to realize his grand ideas.

Basically, Joseph's ideas were not all that bad, but at that time they contravened the entire established system of family life. Joseph's realist brothers therefore perceived him as a cocky dreamer-fanatic who endangered their very existence, while trying to force them to transition from livestock breeding to farming (which, besides being to them highly unpleasant work, in their minds also reeked of enslavement, making it a spiritually depraved occupation). Still worse, he wanted to lead them back into exile, to Egypt.

But the brothers have yet one more reason to fear Joseph. Their whole family history leads them to perceive his actions as challenging their existence within the family, and in a sense, even threatening their lives. In the history of Abraham's family it has already happened more than once that one son (usually the youngest) inherited everything, while the others were summarily excluded and expelled.

Isaac received Abraham's entire spiritual heritage, plus the Land of Israel, while Ishmael, Hagar's son, was forced out. And only one generation later, Jacob received Isaac's spiritual and material blessings, while Esau went off to Mount Seir. Thus, Joseph's brothers had reason to fear that the same thing would happen to them, Jacob's sons. They feared that the formation of the chosen people was still a work in progress; thus, their father's favoritism toward Joseph seemed anything but harmless to them. They began to suspect that Jacob intended to transfer his entire inheritance to Joseph, and to remove all the rest of them far from himself.

Had Joseph, at very least, paid less attention to his father's favoritism, had he not shown his brothers that he too considered himself special, then their fears would have been less serious. But seeing that Joseph held himself above all the rest, and even informed on them to their father, the brothers suspected Joseph of plotting evil against them, and wanting to push them out of the family. Thus, when it seemed to them that their worst (albeit, as *we* know, erroneous) suspicions had been confirmed, they dealt a preemptive strike, condemning Joseph to death.

Of course, all this does not in the least justify the brothers' actions. But we must nonetheless do our best to understand them. The brothers acted not out of envy or anger. They were just sadly mistaken.

In order to avoid an open conflict, Jacob does not explain to the brothers their mistake; he only quenches the outward manifestation of the quarrel. In response to Joseph's story about his dream, Jacob says, "Are we to come, I and your mother and your brothers, and bow low to you?" He emphasizes the inconsistencies in Joseph's dream. Rachel is dead; how can she possibly come and bow low to Joseph?

But Jacob's tactic was misguided. Instead of trying, together with Joseph and all the brothers, to decipher the meaning of Joseph's dreams, Jacob reprimands him, thereby giving the brothers reason to believe that from that moment Joseph had ceased to be Jacob's "favorite," and that perhaps even Jacob now agrees that his presumptuous son must be removed from the family. The brothers now have a sense that ridding themselves of Joseph would not be too alarming a thought even for Jacob himself, since he has now shown that he is ready for that, and, subconsciously, perhaps even actually wants it.

Thus, Jacob's reproach to Joseph in the presence of all hardly corrected the situation, and perhaps even served indirectly as one of the causes of Joseph's being sold into slavery.

46.5. The Outcome of a Dream Follows Its Interpretation

Joseph, the "master of dreams," not only has dreams of

his own, but also deciphers the dreams of others (first Pharaoh's courtiers, and then Pharaoh himself), a skill that elevates him to the apex of power in Egypt. Jewish tradition says that "the outcome of a dream will follow its interpretation." (That is, the outcome of a dream retold will accord with the interpretation proposed for it by the listeners.) In this case, for example, Joseph in the end becomes king over his brothers because the brothers interpreted his dreams in just that way.

Dreams (and their predictions) often come true simply because people believe in them and try to prevent them from coming true. A prediction is realized only for those who believe in it. Faith in a dream causes it to become substantiated in reality, sometimes even against the actual wishes of the believer.

Among the notable examples of this in non-Jewish culture, we recall the Greek tale of Oedipus. According to a prediction, he had to kill his father and marry his mother. His father, disturbed by the prophecy, sends him away, and because Oedipus grew up not knowing his parents, everything ultimately happens just as predicted. Had his parents ignored the prophecy and let Oedipus remain in the family, those events would quite likely never have happened. Similarly, in *The Song of the Wise Oleg*, the horse kills Oleg only because he, fearing the prediction of "death by a horse," has sent the horse away.

Since, as we have said, "the outcome of a dream will follow its interpretation" – and, specifically, the interpretation given to it by the people to whom it is told – Jewish tradition teaches that when someone tells us of their dream, we should immediately suggest only a favorable interpretation. This is an important element of how we demonstrate love for our fellow human beings and improve the world.

But if, on the other hand, upon hearing a dream the listener responds with a negative interpretation, an offensive attitude, or even actual imprecations, we must not think that we should respond with some form of extreme action in order to avert the danger. We must refuse to believe that interpretation, and then nothing at all will come of it.

Joseph shared his dreams with his brothers for the express purpose of learning what interpretations they would suggest. If only the brothers had interpreted Joseph's dreams differently than they did, history could have taken a vastly different turn. We must never forget that the difficult situations we encounter in life are the tasks assigned to us by the Almighty. And that by solving such problems, we are improving ourselves, our families, our nation, and the world at large.

46.6. Joseph's Economic Messianism

Joseph does not yearn for power over his brothers (which is what they fear). He only wants to strengthen his family and help it be successful – economically first, then spiritually. He therefore understands his dreams differently from how his father and brothers understand them. From his brothers' point of view these dreams reflect Joseph's personal aspirations, but as he sees them, they speak of a path that is important not only for him and his family, but for the entire surrounding world.

Joseph's brothers believe that when he dreams of them bowing to him, it means that he longs to rule over them. That is, since during the day Joseph dreams of becoming king, his dreams at night are along the very same lines. But in fact, Joseph yearns to save humanity, especially in the economic sphere. And therefore, unlike the brothers who see their life centering around the Land of Israel, he sees that center abroad, in Egypt.

The brothers are herdsmen. This suits them, and they do not want anything else. But Joseph believes that rather than breeding cattle they should be farmers, a far more productive occupation than cattle breeding. And he is convinced that only farming can save humanity. The sun, moon, and stars that bow to Joseph represent the submission of heavenly bodies, and, in a practical sense, of all natural phenomena, to the will of man, such that an agricultural people can then exploit them for their needs.

According to Joseph, enabling mankind to achieve material prosperity should be the task of the Jewish people.

Joseph is not completely wrong in entertaining this view. For example, if we evaluate the contribution of the Jewish people to the growth of the material well-being of mankind in the twentieth century, we can see that the results they achieved are highly significant.

However, it would be a mistake to believe that this is the primary Jewish contribution to civilization. The purpose of the kingdom of Joseph is only to prepare a platform for the reign of Judah. But that said, Judah must also appreciate Joseph, and understand that economic prosperity is neither antithetical to a higher idea nor a hindrance to it, but, on the contrary, it is the sound material basis for the realization of that idea.

Joseph's desire to engage in farming represents his pretensions to leadership among the brothers in the domain of economic, day-to-day life, in which, by virtue of their seniority, they deem themselves more experienced and knowledgeable. But Joseph believes that his family should be engaged in cultivating the land; in other words, he expects his brothers to heed his opinion, even if this means disregarding their own experience. They must "bow" to him in this. Joseph's self-confidence is the source of the brothers' indignation.

Moreover, when Joseph dreams first of the sun, and then of the moon and stars, the brothers see in those symbols a transition from day to night. Night always means *galut*, exile. And yet Joseph genuinely believes that his entire family should relocate to a foreign country in order to feed not only themselves, but all peoples near and far. When Joseph sees the sun, moon, and stars all at the same time, to him this represents the simultaneity of day and night; that is, the equality of the Land of Israel and all foreign lands. Thus, to Joseph it is irrelevant from which place he will influence humanity, and he is prepared to do so even from exile. But the brothers completely disagree with Joseph on this point.

46.7. Jacob Understands That Joseph is Right (37:11)

יא וַיְקַנְאוּ־בוֹ אֶחָיו וְאָבִיו שָׁמַר אֶת־הַדָּבָר׃

[11] So his brothers were wrought up at him, and his father kept the matter in mind.

[11] His father kept the matter in mind: Deep down, Jacob believes in the veracity of Joseph's dreams, even if it is clear to him that not everything in them can be true.

(We should note that any inconsistencies in Joseph's dreams are not necessarily fundamental. For example, it could be assumed that instead of Rachel, who is already deceased, the "moon" that bows to Joseph is her maidservant Bilhah.)

We can therefore suggest a different interpretation for this verse, namely, that Jacob's reprimand was generally intended only to appease Joseph's brothers, while Jacob himself sensed the prophetic meaning of the dream, and remembered it.

46.8. Joseph Yearns for Brotherhood, but He Carries It Too Far (37:12-17)

יב וַיֵּלְכוּ אֶחָיו לִרְעוֹת אֶת־צֹאן אֲבִיהֶם בִּשְׁכֶם: יג וַיֹּאמֶר יִשְׂרָאֵל אֶל־יוֹסֵף הֲלוֹא אַחֶיךָ רֹעִים בִּשְׁכֶם לְכָה וְאֶשְׁלָחֲךָ אֲלֵיהֶם וַיֹּאמֶר לוֹ הִנֵּנִי: יד וַיֹּאמֶר לוֹ לֶךְ־נָא רְאֵה אֶת־שְׁלוֹם אַחֶיךָ וְאֶת־שְׁלוֹם הַצֹּאן וַהֲשִׁבֵנִי דָּבָר וַיִּשְׁלָחֵהוּ מֵעֵמֶק חֶבְרוֹן וַיָּבֹא שְׁכֶמָה: טו וַיִּמְצָאֵהוּ אִישׁ וְהִנֵּה תֹעֶה בַּשָּׂדֶה וַיִּשְׁאָלֵהוּ הָאִישׁ לֵאמֹר מַה־תְּבַקֵּשׁ: טז וַיֹּאמֶר אֶת־אַחַי אָנֹכִי מְבַקֵּשׁ הַגִּידָה־נָּא לִי אֵיפֹה הֵם רֹעִים: יז וַיֹּאמֶר הָאִישׁ נָסְעוּ מִזֶּה כִּי שָׁמַעְתִּי אֹמְרִים נֵלְכָה דֹּתָיְנָה וַיֵּלֶךְ יוֹסֵף אַחַר אֶחָיו וַיִּמְצָאֵם בְּדֹתָן:

[12] One time, when his brothers had gone to pasture their father's flock at Shechem,
[13] Israel said to Joseph, "Your brothers are pasturing at Shechem. Come, I will send you to them." He answered, "I am ready."
[14] And he said to him, "Go and see how your brothers are and how the flocks are faring, and bring me back word." So he sent him from the valley of Hebron. When he reached Shechem,
[15] a man came upon him wandering in the fields. The man asked him, "What are you looking for?"

*[16] He answered, "I am looking for my brothers.
Could you tell me where they are pasturing?"
[17] The man said, "They have gone from here, for
I heard them say: Let us go to Dothan." So Joseph
followed his brothers and found them at Dothan.*

**[12] One time, when his brothers had gone to pasture
their father's flock at Shechem:** Shechem is the place
where Jacob's family first bought land, and where later, after
the incident of Dinah, the city territory itself became, to
some extent, their possession ("spoils of war"). The brothers
therefore go to graze their flocks even at such a distance, in
order to assert their ownership of the area. The locals still
remember the brothers and fear them. In Shechem and its
environs the brothers can be considered regional overlords.

His brothers had gone to pasture their father's flock:
Whenever the Torah uses this kind of expression, it is meant
to symbolize leadership.

**So he sent him from the valley of Hebron. When he
reached Shechem ...:** Hebron and Shechem are contrasted
here. Jacob lives in Hebron, but the brothers have gone to
Shechem to graze their father's sheep. The two places are
rather far apart, not less than a two-day journey.

Perhaps a split is now brewing in the family. Since the
brothers cannot denigrate Joseph by arguing with their
father, they just move away from him. The departure to
Shechem is thus not merely a relocation to neighboring
pastureland for economic reasons. Rather, it is something
akin to the future confrontation of the northern and southern tribes of Israel, the disintegration of Solomon's empire

into the northern and southern kingdoms having centers in Shechem and Hebron.

[13] Israel said to Joseph: Israel, not Jacob. Here the Patriarch acts in the national interest, rather than his own personal interest, and he is thus Israel.

Your brothers are pasturing at Shechem: That is, they are realizing their leadership there. Because Jacob-Israel himself has failed to establish a proper hierarchy in the family – which was his duty, actually – he hopes that his children can figure it out on their own and make peace among themselves.

But it turns out that in this kind of situation, establishing a hierarchy "from below" can happen only through a direct confrontation.

I am ready: These words always indicate both assent and willingness. Joseph does not suspect that the brothers are capable of acting improperly, and he therefore, like his father, fails to assess the situation correctly.

[17] The man said, "They have gone from here, for I heard them say: Let us go to Dothan." So Joseph followed his brothers and found them at Dothan: The purity and nobility of Joseph's character are evident here. He so earnestly and righteously yearns to restore fraternal relations, that in search of his brothers he follows the angel's directions even further, to Dothan (which lies northwest of Shechem).

Jacob had asked Joseph only to find his brothers in Shechem, but Joseph goes well beyond his father's instructions. And the direct result is that the brothers seize Joseph and sell him into slavery.

In our efforts to restore positive relations with our

brothers from whom we have been separated (and restoring fraternal relations is surely a matter of utmost importance!), we must be willing to meet them halfway. But even when making concessions we should not exceed the boundaries established by Jewish tradition (here, the boundaries that Jacob had indicated to Joseph).

Another essential point is that identifying those boundaries is not straightforward, for it depends on the specifics of each individual situation. But that is a separate, complex topic beyond the scope of this discussion.

Chapter 47

The Sale of Joseph

47.1. Reuben Rescues Joseph from Certain Death (37: 18-22)

יח וַיִּרְאוּ אֹתוֹ מֵרָחֹק וּבְטֶרֶם יִקְרַב אֲלֵיהֶם וַיִּתְנַכְּלוּ
אֹתוֹ לַהֲמִיתוֹ: יט וַיֹּאמְרוּ אִישׁ אֶל־אָחִיו הִנֵּה בַּעַל
הַחֲלֹמוֹת הַלָּזֶה בָּא: כ וְעַתָּה | לְכוּ וְנַהַרְגֵהוּ וְנַשְׁלִכֵהוּ
בְּאַחַד הַבֹּרוֹת וְאָמַרְנוּ חַיָּה רָעָה אֲכָלָתְהוּ וְנִרְאֶה מַה־
יִּהְיוּ חֲלֹמֹתָיו: כא וַיִּשְׁמַע רְאוּבֵן וַיַּצִּלֵהוּ מִיָּדָם וַיֹּאמֶר
לֹא נַכֶּנּוּ נָפֶשׁ: כב וַיֹּאמֶר אֲלֵהֶם | רְאוּבֵן אַל־תִּשְׁפְּכוּ־
דָם הַשְׁלִיכוּ אֹתוֹ אֶל־הַבּוֹר הַזֶּה אֲשֶׁר בַּמִּדְבָּר וְיָד אַל־
תִּשְׁלְחוּ־בוֹ לְמַעַן הַצִּיל אֹתוֹ מִיָּדָם לַהֲשִׁיבוֹ אֶל־אָבִיו:

*[18] They saw him from afar, and before he came
close to them they conspired to kill him.
[19] They said to one another, "Here comes that
dreamer!
[20] Come now, let us kill him and throw him
into one of the pits; and we can say, 'A savage
beast devoured him.' We shall see what comes
of his dreams!"
[21] But when Reuben heard it, he tried to save*

him from them. He said, "Let us not take his life."
[22] And Reuben went on, "Shed no blood! Cast
him into that pit out in the wilderness, but do
not touch him yourselves" – intending to save
him from them and restore him to his father.

[19] They said to one another, "...let us kill him": The literal translation is "One man said to the other." The Midrash understands this as referring to Simeon and Levi, and believes that they were the primary instigators to killing Joseph. (Reuben planned to return Joseph to his father, and Judah suggested selling him. The youngest of Leah's own sons, and the sons of Bilhah and Zilpah all the more, felt no particular animosity toward Joseph. The Midrash thus concludes that the plan to murder Joseph originated with Simeon and Levi.)

"Here comes that dreamer!": The mere fact that Joseph has dreams, that he has a vision of a better world, sets him apart from them.

[21] But when Reuben heard it .... He said...: Reuben, the eldest, feels responsible for his younger brother. Here again we see Reuben's "simple humanity."

And Reuben heard, and said: We shall not deprive him of his life! And Reuben said to them: Don't shed blood: Reuben addresses his brothers twice, because they refused to hear him the first time.

[22] Cast him into that pit out in the wilderness, but do not touch him yourselves: When the brothers reject his first proposal, Reuben must compromise. "Well, let's not kill Joseph right away. We'll just throw him into the pit, and then we will talk further."

Intending to save him from them and restore him to his father: Reuben is not hoping to reconcile Joseph with his brothers (it is not in his power to accomplish that). But he wants, at very least, to restore Joseph to his father; that is, to restore the prior state of affairs, where the brothers are on their own, and Rachel's two sons are with Jacob, but everyone is alive. Reuben wants to keep the atrocities to a minimum.

47.2. Selling Joseph as a Means of Reeducating Him (37:23-27)

כג וַיְהִי כַּאֲשֶׁר־בָּא יוֹסֵף אֶל־אֶחָיו וַיַּפְשִׁיטוּ אֶת־יוֹסֵף
אֶת־כֻּתָּנְתּוֹ אֶת־כְּתֹנֶת הַפַּסִּים אֲשֶׁר עָלָיו: כד וַיִּקָּחֻהוּ
וַיַּשְׁלִכוּ אֹתוֹ הַבֹּרָה וְהַבּוֹר רֵק אֵין בּוֹ מָיִם: כה וַיֵּשְׁבוּ
לֶאֱכָל־לֶחֶם וַיִּשְׂאוּ עֵינֵיהֶם וַיִּרְאוּ וְהִנֵּה אֹרְחַת
יִשְׁמְעֵאלִים בָּאָה מִגִּלְעָד וּגְמַלֵּיהֶם נֹשְׂאִים נְכֹאת וּצְרִי
וָלֹט הוֹלְכִים לְהוֹרִיד מִצְרָיְמָה: כו וַיֹּאמֶר יְהוּדָה אֶל־
אֶחָיו מַה־בֶּצַע כִּי נַהֲרֹג אֶת־אָחִינוּ וְכִסִּינוּ אֶת־דָּמוֹ: כז
לְכוּ וְנִמְכְּרֶנּוּ לַיִּשְׁמְעֵאלִים וְיָדֵנוּ אַל־תְּהִי־בוֹ כִּי־אָחִינוּ
בְשָׂרֵנוּ הוּא וַיִּשְׁמְעוּ אֶחָיו:

[23] When Joseph came up to his brothers, they stripped Joseph of his tunic, the ornamented tunic that he was wearing,
[24] and took him and cast him into the pit. The pit was empty; there was no water in it.
[25] Then they sat down to a meal. Looking up,

they saw a caravan of Ishmaelites coming from
Gilead, their camels bearing gum, balm, and
ladanum to be taken to Egypt.
[26] Then Judah said to his brothers, "What do
we gain by killing our brother and covering up
his blood?
[27] Come, let us sell him to the Ishmaelites, but
let us not do away with him ourselves. After all,
he is our brother, our own flesh." His brothers
agreed.

[23] They stripped Joseph of his tunic: As already discussed,
the symbolically multi-colored shirt was originally intended
not for Joseph, but for his brother Benjamin, the younger of
Rachel's two sons. Benjamin was a versatile personality of
diverse accomplishments, including a gift for effecting unification. But Joseph expropriated that role unto himself.

[24] The pit was empty; there was no water in it: This is
clearly redundant. The Midrash therefore explains: There
was no water in that pit, but there were snakes and scorpions living there. Which we can understand also in a figura-
tive sense: Where the life-affirming *aqua pura* of the Torah
is lacking, snakes and scorpions are sure to soon appear.

[25] Then they sat down to a meal: This detail should be
understood not only in its simple, everyday sense, for it carries a weightier message. The point emphasized here is that
only "*then* they sat down to a meal." The brothers had not
yet eaten that day, because, according to Jewish law, judges
adjudicating a capital case are forbidden to eat until a ver-
dict is rendered.

The brothers considered their deliberations and actions nothing less than Joseph's trial and sentencing. Because Joseph had threatened their very existence in the family, the brothers tried and sentenced him.

Looking up, they saw a caravan: With that out of the way, they saw fit to "look up," i.e., to shift their gaze from Joseph and the ongoing family problems to a wider view of the world around them. They saw a caravan, and their position changed.

Their camels bearing gum, balm, and ladanum: The Midrash adds: Because Joseph's descent to Egypt was an historical necessity, God, in order to assure Joseph a pleasant journey, expressly sent him a caravan carrying balsam and other aromatic spices, rather than unpleasant goods of some kind, although surely there were also many such caravans traveling the roads.

To be taken to Egypt: Literally, "On their way to bring down to Egypt." (That is, on their way to bring *Joseph* down to Egypt.) Joseph was sold into slavery in Egypt not because his brothers randomly noticed a caravan that just happened to be passing by. That caravan was passing at just that moment on its way to Egypt not by chance, but as part of the Divine Plan that required Joseph to be its passenger.

As already discussed, we can trace Joseph's connection with Egypt – the breadbasket of the Mediterranean – back to his first dream of the sheaves. Because Joseph, an "economic messianist," considers it the primary task of the Jewish people to materially improve the world, his descent to Egypt is inevitable.

[26] Then Judah said to his brothers: It is Judah who decides Joseph's fate, and at this moment their confrontation begins. Moreover, the story here is about Joseph's fall, his descent into Egypt, but in fact, it is Judah who falls (morally), even if – at the external level, at least – Judah seems to be reinforcing his status as the leader among the brothers.

What do we gain by killing our brother and covering up his blood?: Literally, "'What profit [do we gain] if we slay our brother and conceal his blood?" Judah's words to the effect that there is more profit in selling Joseph than in killing him are not entirely clear. What "profit" can one speak of here?

The explanation is as follows. The brothers fear not only Joseph himself, but the ideas that he is advancing. Joseph is so keen on his economic messianism that he is even prepared to go into exile for it. But the brothers know from personal experience that life in a foreign land will only end badly, because it is not possible there to wield the necessary influence. Abraham could not influence Nimrod, nor could their father Jacob change Laban's world. From the brother's point of view, then, Joseph's ideology is extremely dangerous.

As already noted, Joseph has no issues with living in a foreign country, and one of the reasons for this, perhaps, is that when Jacob and his family fled from Laban, Joseph was only about six years old. His brothers, who were then much older, remember how unpleasant and dangerous the situation was – and how they barely escaped with their lives.

But six-year-old Joseph had no comprehension of any of those dangers. He now cherishes the memories of his childhood in Paddan-aram (Babylon), and especially the image of his mother Rachel, who died almost immediately upon their return to the Land of Israel. Joseph therefore sees nothing wrong with taking up permanent residence in a foreign land.

It should be noted that Joseph will later encourage his whole family to emigrate from Canaan to Egypt, rather than having them remain in Canaan and supporting them there. Only at the very end of his life, in the process of abandoning his own long-standing fixation on Egypt – that is, as he advances to the position of *Mashiach ben Yosef* – do we read: "So Joseph made the sons of Israel swear, saying, "When God has taken notice of you, you shall carry up my bones from here" (i.e., from Egypt [50:25]).

Thus, the threat that the brothers are feeling is coming not from Joseph himself, but, overwhelmingly, from the ideas that he chooses to advance. The brothers therefore conclude that even if they kill Joseph, the problem will by no means be resolved, and Joseph's ideas will yet endure, for there will be someone else in the family who will promote them. In order to eradicate Joseph's ideas, they will have change Joseph himself, so that he will himself abandon them.

With just that in mind, Judah was able to persuade his brothers that Joseph should be sold to Egypt specifically. As if saying to them, "Well, just let him go, so he can realize his dreams there." And to his little brother: "Knock yourself out, Joseph! Egypt is just the right place for you to conduct your experiments. After personally experiencing their tangible results, maybe then you will finally mend your misguided ways."

Only at the end of his life is Joseph indeed convinced that his extraordinarily successful *galut* (Diaspora-oriented) self-realization, his exceptional ability to fully actualize his ideas, has ultimately yielded no long-term results. When he understands that his ideas were erroneous, and feels remorse for having devoted his whole life to implementing them, then by expressing his solemn request, "You shall carry up my bones from here," he has finally found his correction.

Joseph, in his role of second-in-command to Pharaoh, brought enlightenment to Egypt and rescued it from hunger. And in recognition of those accomplishments Egypt calmly and promptly forgot all about him. In this sense, Joseph ultimately experienced defeat. He could not, as he had hoped, feed all of humanity for all time to come, nor was he able to disseminate monotheism. And he failed even to gain the respect of the Egyptians for his people. But it was this overarching defeat that allowed Joseph to develop and advance. And his brothers, in order to afford Joseph that opportunity (but also to protect themselves from his ideas), had him carted off to Egypt.

Of course, we do not wish to suggest that these considerations actually figured into the brothers' plan. But this was indeed their plan at a subconscious level. The brothers (or Providence, through them) were prepared to give Joseph the opportunity to implement his plan, and to understand where it would lead, because that understanding was important for the further development of the Jewish nation. In a sense, the sale of Joseph was his only opportunity for re-education. On a conscious level, the brothers want to rid themselves of Joseph because he is a source of danger to them. But subconsciously they wish to give him the opportunity to be realized, and for life itself to become his teacher.

At the same time, it is important to emphasize that neither the Providential nature of Joseph's sale, nor the brothers' genuine fear of losing their status in the family, can absolve them in any way of their guilt or responsibility. Moreover, the sale of Joseph, which they intended as the means to eliminating the danger he poses to them, becomes instead the cause of their misfortunes.

There is an important lesson here for the Jewish people.

When conflicts arise among them, as is bound to happen, neither side should ever demonize the other, nor deem it appropriate to do battle with other Jews by any means. On the contrary – in spite of their differences, all Jews remain brothers. And that is the lesson that Joseph's brothers will finally have learned when at the end of their lives they are once again united with Joseph.

47.3. Who Sold Joseph into Slavery to Egypt? (37:28-36)

כח וַיַּעַבְרוּ אֲנָשִׁים מִדְיָנִים סֹחֲרִים וַיִּמְשְׁכוּ וַיַּעֲלוּ
אֶת־יוֹסֵף מִן־הַבּוֹר וַיִּמְכְּרוּ אֶת־יוֹסֵף לַיִּשְׁמְעֵאלִים
בְּעֶשְׂרִים כָּסֶף וַיָּבִיאוּ אֶת־יוֹסֵף מִצְרָיְמָה: כט וַיָּשָׁב
רְאוּבֵן אֶל־הַבּוֹר וְהִנֵּה אֵין־יוֹסֵף בַּבּוֹר וַיִּקְרַע אֶת־
בְּגָדָיו: ל וַיָּשָׁב אֶל־אֶחָיו וַיֹּאמַר הַיֶּלֶד אֵינֶנּוּ וַאֲנִי אָנָה
אֲנִי־בָא: לא וַיִּקְחוּ אֶת־כְּתֹנֶת יוֹסֵף וַיִּשְׁחֲטוּ שְׂעִיר
עִזִּים וַיִּטְבְּלוּ אֶת־הַכֻּתֹּנֶת בַּדָּם: לב וַיְשַׁלְּחוּ אֶת־כְּתֹנֶת
הַפַּסִּים וַיָּבִיאוּ אֶל־אֲבִיהֶם וַיֹּאמְרוּ זֹאת מָצָאנוּ הַכֶּר־
נָא הַכְּתֹנֶת בִּנְךָ הִוא אִם־לֹא: לג וַיַּכִּירָהּ וַיֹּאמֶר כְּתֹנֶת
בְּנִי חַיָּה רָעָה אֲכָלָתְהוּ טָרֹף טֹרַף יוֹסֵף: לד וַיִּקְרַע
יַעֲקֹב שִׂמְלֹתָיו וַיָּשֶׂם שַׂק בְּמָתְנָיו וַיִּתְאַבֵּל עַל־בְּנוֹ
יָמִים רַבִּים: לה וַיָּקֻמוּ כָל־בָּנָיו וְכָל־בְּנֹתָיו לְנַחֲמוֹ
וַיְמָאֵן לְהִתְנַחֵם וַיֹּאמֶר כִּי־אֵרֵד אֶל־בְּנִי אָבֵל שְׁאֹלָה
וַיֵּבְךְּ אֹתוֹ אָבִיו: לו וְהַמְּדָנִים מָכְרוּ אֹתוֹ אֶל־מִצְרָיִם
לְפוֹטִיפַר סְרִיס פַּרְעֹה שַׂר הַטַּבָּחִים:

[28] When Midianite traders passed by, they pulled Joseph up out of the pit. They sold Joseph for twenty pieces of silver to the Ishmaelites, who brought Joseph to Egypt.
[29] When Reuben returned to the pit and saw

that Joseph was not in the pit, he rent his clothes.
[30] Returning to his brothers, he said, "The boy is gone! Now, what am I to do?"
[31] Then they took Joseph's tunic, slaughtered a kid, and dipped the tunic in the blood.
[32] They had the ornamented tunic taken to their father, and they said, "We found this. Please examine it; is it your son's tunic or not?"
[33] He recognized it, and said, "My son's tunic! A savage beast devoured him! Joseph was torn by a beast!"
[34] Jacob rent his clothes, put sackcloth on his loins, and observed mourning for his son many days.
[35] All his sons and daughters sought to comfort him; but he refused to be comforted, saying, "No, I will go down mourning to my son in Sheol." Thus his father bewailed him.
[36] The Midianites, meanwhile, sold him in Egypt to Potiphar, a courtier of Pharaoh and his chief steward.

[28] They pulled Joseph up out of the pit. They sold Joseph ... to the Ishmaelites: In the original Hebrew text: "Midianite traders passed by, they pulled, they raised Joseph from the pit, they sold Joseph ... and they brough Joseph to Egypt." The Torah does not reveal who actually sold Joseph to Egypt. The brothers had planned it, but the Midianites pulled Joseph from the pit and sold him to the Ishmaelites, who then brought him to Egypt.

[29] When Reuben returned to the pit and saw that Joseph

was not in the pit, he rent his clothes: When Reuben sees that Joseph is not in the pit, he runs to the brothers with his question, to which they offer no response. Thus, the text gives us to understand that even the brothers themselves do not know Joseph's fate. (This may be the reason that later, in Egypt, it never occurs to the brothers that the man they are dealing with is Joseph.)

The brothers, because it was their decision to sell Joseph, are still held accountable, and cannot be absolved of their guilt. Although they did not personally sell Joseph, the Torah constructs the story so as to have us believe that it was the brothers who contracted the sale.

[35] But he refused to be comforted: These words are interpreted to mean that at some level, at least, Jacob felt reasonably convinced that Joseph had not actually perished. When a person dies, the anguish of his loved ones who mourn for him will sooner or later subside or dull. But because Joseph was in reality still alive, Jacob could not be consoled.

[36] Sold him in Egypt to Potiphar, a courtier of Pharaoh: Joseph finds himself not in any ordinary Egyptian house, but on the estate of a courtier to Pharaoh. This marks the beginning of Joseph's future career in Egypt.

Chapter 48

Judah and Tamar

48.1. Diminishing Judah's Status (38:1)

א וַיְהִי בָּעֵת הַהִוא וַיֵּרֶד יְהוּדָה מֵאֵת אֶחָיו וַיֵּט עַד־
אִישׁ עֲדֻלָּמִי וּשְׁמוֹ חִירָה:

[1] About that time Judah left his brothers and camped near a certain Adullamite whose name was Hirah.

The story of Joseph is interrupted by the incident of Judah and Tamar.

[1] Judah left his brothers: Literally, "Judah descended from his brothers," which refers not only to geographical distance, but to a decline in Judah's social status. In their situation of family tension, coupled with Jacob's intense mourning, the brothers had no desire to communicate with Judah, at whose urging Joseph had been sold. Thus, Judah's authority and status among them was critically shaken.

This *Vayeshev* portion tells of Judah's fall, his "descent."

The story of how "Joseph was taken down to Egypt" (39:1), for which Judah is to blame, is pre-empted by the story of how Judah himself "descends" from his former status. Joseph is "taken down" to Egypt by force, but Judah "descends" as the result of his own actions.

And camped near a certain Adullamite whose name was Hirah: The Midrash identifies this name with Hiram, king of Tyre, Heb. *Tzor* (located in what is today Lebanon; see 1 Kings 5:15). Thus "Hirah" and "Hiram" are understood here as titles of the kings of Phoenicia, just as all the kings of Egypt bear the title "Pharaoh," and all Philistines kings are "Abimelech."

(Needless to say, the Midrash does not mean that this Hirah is literally the very same Hiram who lived a thousand years later and collaborated with Solomon. Rather, by identifying the historical figure of whom the Torah speaks here with a much later one, the Midrash is emphasizing Israel's enduring influence on Phoenicia, its northern neighbor.)

Phoenicia, in modern-day Lebanon, Israel's closest neighbor to the north, exerts its influence on both Judah and Joseph, but in entirely different ways.

Judah, in the person of his descendant, King Solomon, asks the Phoenician king to assist in building the Temple, in order to promote monotheism among humanity, and Hiram actively obliges him. But in the Northern Kingdom, Joseph's descendants face the opposite situation. Jezebel, the daughter of the King of Phoenicia, becomes the wife of King Ahab of the Northern Kingdom, bringing with her the idols and worshippers of Baal (1 Kings 16:31). In communicating with Phoenicia, Judah brings positive advancement to the world, while Joseph's descendants are a negative influence. Phoenicia is a source of enormous power, but how this power will be directed depends on what Israel is doing and who their leader is.

If Israel is represented by the line of Judah, in which spirituality dominates as the central criterion, then its connection with Phoenicia does not interfere. Quite the contrary, Phoenicia's preeminence in the material realm helps Judah build the Temple. But Joseph's house, which is already deeply enmeshed in all things material, and for whom higher values take no priority over worldly values, is morally enslaved by its connection with Phoenicia.

The House of Judah represents the special connection of the Jewish state with God, and as such has the potential to redirect the forces of the world around it for good, while the House of Joseph, representing the material and ordinary – albeit Jewish – state, exhibits no such potential.

The modern State of Israel is built on Joseph's principles, i.e., to "just be no worse than all the others." It can successfully exist on par with other countries, but it does not have the potential to correct humanity and influence it. Israel will have that ability only after it adopts the principles of Judah, thus becoming a unique, Biblical state.

Judah's relationship with the Phoenicians could thus be positive, overall. Judah, unlike Joseph, is not interested in leaving the Land of Israel. He wants to integrate with the local population, which in his opinion includes numerous upright individuals living in the same Land, and not only by chance.

The problem is, however, that by choosing to build this connection, Judah distances himself from his brothers. And any schism within the Jewish people always leads to spiritual descent.

Thus, Judah's fall, which began with the sale of Joseph, continues with his moving away from his brothers and focusing his attention on relations with the local Canaanite population.

48.2. Judah's Sons and Their Marriages to Tamar (38:2-11)

ב וַיַּרְא־שָׁם יְהוּדָה בַּת־אִישׁ כְּנַעֲנִי וּשְׁמוֹ שׁוּעַ וַיִּקָּחֶהָ
וַיָּבֹא אֵלֶיהָ: ג וַתַּהַר וַתֵּלֶד בֵּן וַיִּקְרָא אֶת־שְׁמוֹ עֵר: ד
וַתַּהַר עוֹד וַתֵּלֶד בֵּן וַתִּקְרָא אֶת־שְׁמוֹ אוֹנָן: ה וַתֹּסֶף עוֹד
וַתֵּלֶד בֵּן וַתִּקְרָא אֶת־שְׁמוֹ שֵׁלָה וְהָיָה בִכְזִיב בְּלִדְתָּהּ
אֹתוֹ: ו וַיִּקַּח יְהוּדָה אִשָּׁה לְעֵר בְּכוֹרוֹ וּשְׁמָהּ תָּמָר: ז
וַיְהִי עֵר בְּכוֹר יְהוּדָה רַע בְּעֵינֵי יי וַיְמִתֵהוּ יי: ח וַיֹּאמֶר
יְהוּדָה לְאוֹנָן בֹּא אֶל־אֵשֶׁת אָחִיךָ וְיַבֵּם אֹתָהּ וְהָקֵם
זֶרַע לְאָחִיךָ: ט וַיֵּדַע אוֹנָן כִּי לֹא לוֹ יִהְיֶה הַזָּרַע וְהָיָה
אִם־בָּא אֶל־אֵשֶׁת אָחִיו וְשִׁחֵת אַרְצָה לְבִלְתִּי נְתָן־זֶרַע
לְאָחִיו: י וַיֵּרַע בְּעֵינֵי יי אֲשֶׁר עָשָׂה וַיָּמֶת גַּם־אֹתוֹ: יא
וַיֹּאמֶר יְהוּדָה לְתָמָר כַּלָּתוֹ שְׁבִי אַלְמָנָה בֵית־אָבִיךְ עַד־
יִגְדַּל שֵׁלָה בְנִי כִּי אָמַר פֶּן־יָמוּת גַּם־הוּא כְּאֶחָיו וַתֵּלֶךְ
תָּמָר וַתֵּשֶׁב בֵּית אָבִיהָ:

[2] There Judah saw the daughter of a certain Canaanite whose name was Shua, and he married her and cohabited with her.

[3] She conceived and bore a son, and he named him Er.

[4] She conceived again and bore a son, and named him Onan.

[5] Once again she bore a son, and named him Shelah; he was at Chezib when she bore him.

[6] Judah got a wife for Er his first-born; her name was Tamar.

[7] But Er, Judah's first-born, was displeasing to the Lord, and the Lord took his life.

[8] Then Judah said to Onan, "Join with your brother's wife and do your duty by her as a brother-in-law, and provide offspring for your brother."

[9] But Onan, knowing that the seed would not count as his, let it go to waste whenever he joined with his brother's wife, so as not to provide offspring for his brother.

[10] What he did was displeasing to the Lord, and He took his life also.

[11] Then Judah said to his daughter-in-law Tamar, "Stay as a widow in your father's house until my son Shelah grows up" – for he thought, "He too might die like his brothers." So Tamar went to live in her father's house.

[2] There Judah saw the daughter of a certain Canaanite whose name was Shua, and he married her and cohabited with her: Judah marries a Canaanite woman, in direct violation of the family tradition. It had always been a family principle even from the time of Abraham that one must not enter into a marriage with the Canaanites. Rather, a man must choose a wife from among the *ivrim* (Hebrews). But Judah believes that the birth of the Jewish nation is now already complete, and that it is now acceptable to assimilate Canaanite elements within himself. Moreover, it is noteworthy that Jacob too seems to agree, since he does not object to Judah's marriage.

The respective merits and failings of Joseph and Judah are mutually complementary. Joseph is guided by the idea, quite correct as far it goes, that one must begin to act through correction of the material. But he mistakenly believes that such action is possible from *galut* (exile), that is, from a foreign country. Judah, on the contrary, is quite right in maintaining that spiritual values are primary, but his mistake is believing that one can properly act without considering the nation's overall circumstances.

Judah, confident that the Jewish nation is already fully formed, believes that it is now permissible to marry a Canaanite, because the Jewish nation is now a complete, organic entity, and can assimilate Canaanite elements into itself with impunity. But, in fact, that organic, national identity must have Joseph's concepts as their foundation, which always take reality into account. Therefore, by selling Joseph – and, as a result, parting company with his brothers – Judah loses support for his spiritual strength.

[5] He was at Chezib when she bore him: The name of the place, "Keziv," seems neither informative nor essential to the story itself. (And, in fact, this place is mentioned nowhere else in the Torah.) The Midrash therefore associates it with *achzavah*, "disappointment," the result that came of Judah's attempt to build a family by marrying into the Canaanites.

Both Joseph and Judah are doomed to see their personal plans end in failure. Only then will each of them find his correction, to become *Mashiach ben Yosef* and *Mashiach ben David*, respectively.

[6] Her name was Tamar: Judah's first wife remains anonymous (only the name of her father, Shua, is revealed), and this is because she is not an important personality in her own right. Judah marries her not for her own merits, but only because he wishes to integrate with the local residents.

As for Tamar, on the other hand, we do know her name, but not her genealogy, since this too was unimportant to Judah. The Midrash states that Tamar was a descendant of Melchizedek ("King Melchizedek of Salem ... a priest of God Most High," 14:18). Tamar was thus a descendant of Noah's son Shem, and related to the *ivrim* (Hebrews), while the Canaanite peoples are descendants of Shem's brother Ham.

[8] Then Judah said to Onan, "Join with your brother's wife and do your duty by her as a brother-in-law": Judah orders Onan to enter into a levirate marriage with the widow of his childless brother.

The concept of levirate marriage (*yibbum*) requires that when a man dies childless, his widow will remain "part of the family." Rather than leaving to go her separate way, one of the surviving brothers is expected to marry her in order to perpetuate the lineage of the deceased.

But Judah's plan fails, and ultimately he must himself fulfill the family's levirate obligation. (Later, after the giving of the Torah, the practice was restricted only to brothers of the deceased, but in those days the custom was to allow other relatives as well to perform levirate marriage.)

[9] Let it go to waste whenever he joined with his brother's wife: In European languages, the term "onanism," derived from Onan's behavior here, over time came to refer to masturbation. But Onan's actual offense described in the Torah here was *coitus interruptus*.

[10] And He took his life also: The Midrash understands the addition of the words "his life also" to mean that the cause (not disclosed in the text) of Er's premature death was the same. He too "displeased" God by not wanting children, and not letting Tamar conceive.

[11] "Stay as a widow in your father's house until my son Shelah grows up" - for he thought, "He too might die like his brothers": Judah does not understand why his sons are dying. There is a huge psychological gap between Judah and his children – between the generation that came to the Land of Israel as adults, and the new generation that has grown up there. Judah does not understand what is happening to his sons, and why. He begins to regard Tamar as a "dangerous woman" who brings death to any man who marries her. (Does she somehow exert a physically noxious influence on her husbands?) Quite naturally, Judah is afraid to allow his third son to marry Tamar.

48.3. Tamar Demonstrates Her Resolve (38:12-18)

יב וַיִּרְבּוּ הַיָּמִים וַתָּמָת בַּת־שׁוּעַ אֵשֶׁת־יְהוּדָה וַיִּנָּחֶם יְהוּדָה וַיַּעַל עַל־גֹּזְזֵי צֹאנוֹ הוּא וְחִירָה רֵעֵהוּ הָעֲדֻלָּמִי תִּמְנָתָה: יג וַיֻּגַּד לְתָמָר לֵאמֹר הִנֵּה חָמִיךְ עֹלֶה תִמְנָתָה לָגֹז צֹאנוֹ: יד וַתָּסַר בִּגְדֵי אַלְמְנוּתָהּ מֵעָלֶיהָ וַתְּכַס בַּצָּעִיף וַתִּתְעַלָּף וַתֵּשֶׁב בְּפֶתַח עֵינַיִם אֲשֶׁר עַל־דֶּרֶךְ תִּמְנָתָה כִּי רָאֲתָה כִּי־גָדַל שֵׁלָה וְהִוא לֹא־נִתְּנָה לוֹ לְאִשָּׁה: טו וַיִּרְאֶהָ יְהוּדָה וַיַּחְשְׁבֶהָ לְזוֹנָה כִּי כִסְּתָה פָּנֶיהָ: טז וַיֵּט אֵלֶיהָ אֶל־הַדֶּרֶךְ וַיֹּאמֶר הָבָה־נָּא אָבוֹא אֵלַיִךְ כִּי לֹא יָדַע כִּי כַלָּתוֹ הִוא וַתֹּאמֶר מַה־תִּתֶּן־לִי כִּי תָבוֹא אֵלָי: יז וַיֹּאמֶר אָנֹכִי אֲשַׁלַּח גְּדִי־עִזִּים מִן־הַצֹּאן וַתֹּאמֶר אִם־תִּתֵּן עֵרָבוֹן עַד שָׁלְחֶךָ: יח וַיֹּאמֶר מָה הָעֵרָבוֹן אֲשֶׁר אֶתֶּן־לָךְ וַתֹּאמֶר חֹתָמְךָ וּפְתִילֶךָ וּמַטְּךָ אֲשֶׁר בְּיָדֶךָ וַיִּתֶּן־לָהּ וַיָּבֹא אֵלֶיהָ וַתַּהַר לוֹ:

[12] A long time afterward, Shua's daughter, the wife of Judah, died. When his period of mourning was over, Judah went up to Timnah to his sheepshearers, together with his friend Hirah the Adullamite.
[13] And Tamar was told, "Your father-in-law is coming up to Timnah for the sheepshearing."
[14] So she took off her widow's garb, covered her face with a veil, and, wrapping herself up,

*sat down at the entrance to Enaim, which is
on the road to Timnah; for she saw that Shelah
was grown up, yet she had not been given to
him as wife.*

*[15] When Judah saw her, he took her for a harlot;
for she had covered her face.*

*[16] So he turned aside to her by the road and
said, "Here, let me sleep with you" – for he did not
know that she was his daughter-in-law. "What,"
she asked, "will you pay for sleeping with me?"*

*[17] He replied, "I will send a kid from my flock."
But she said, "You must leave a pledge until you
have sent it."*

*[18] And he said, "What pledge shall I give you?"
She replied, "Your seal and cord, and the staff
which you carry." So he gave them to her and
slept with her, and she conceived by him.*

**[12] When his period of mourning was over, Judah went
up to Timnah to his sheepshearers:** The verb describing Judah's action in this verse, "went up," and his action
at the beginning of the story, "Judah descended from his
brothers" (38:1, literal translation), are opposites. With the
death of Shua's daughter, Judah's attempt to mingle with
the Canaanites has ended in failure. His two sons have died
by this time, and the third too has a troubled marriage. But
even so, Judah, in contrast to his initial descent, is now gradually beginning to rise. This trend is still not outwardly visible, but a man's "descent" or "ascent" is directly related to
the kind of woman he marries, and it is in this that Judah's
situation has now changed.

[13] And Tamar was told, "Your father-in-law is coming up to Timnah for the sheepshearing": Recognizing that she will not be given to Shelah as a wife, Tamar observes what is happening in Judah's house. She knows that his wife has died, that the mourning period has ended, and that Judah has gone to shear the sheep. In those days, sheep shearing had the character of a country fair – a celebration where they would eat, drink, and woo.

[14] So she took off her widow's garb, covered her face with a veil, and, wrapping herself up, sat down at the entrance to Enaim, which is on the road to Timnah: Having learned that Judah is in the market for a new wife, Tamar now wishes to take advantage of the situation in order to bear him children. For her uncommon courage and her commitment to a higher goal (bearing Judah a child and restoring him to the status of a leader), and for her willingness to overstep the bounds of decency, even to the point of risking her own life, Tamar's reward is that the Messiah himself will descend from her.

Covered her face with a veil, and, wrapping herself up: The cultural mores of the time required a harlot to conceal her face. Prostitution was allowed, but was nonetheless considered shameful.

[18] And he said, "What pledge shall I give you?" She replied, "Your seal and cord, and the staff which you carry." So he gave them to her: Tamar's demand for a pledge seems unreasonably excessive. How could Judah have agreed to give her his seal, his cord, and his staff – every item in his possession attesting to his noble status?

We understand that Judah's consent demonstrates his (perhaps subconscious) desire to renounce his status, forfeit his mission as leader, and revert to being just an ordinary citizen. All of that began with his departure from his brothers and his marriage to a Canaanite woman, but here it is expressed in his willingness to leave his staff and seal with a harlot as a pledge. Judah agrees to give Tamar all the visible signs of his absolute authority, as if he is doing so at her request, while he himself wants only to renounce everything that they represent. Later we will see that only Tamar can rescue Judah from a terminal fall.

48.4. Zonah, the Ordinary Harlot, and Kedeshah, the Temple Harlot (38:19-21)

יט וַתָּקָם וַתֵּלֶךְ וַתָּסַר צְעִיפָהּ מֵעָלֶיהָ וַתִּלְבַּשׁ בִּגְדֵי
אַלְמְנוּתָהּ: כ וַיִּשְׁלַח יְהוּדָה אֶת־גְּדִי הָעִזִּים בְּיַד רֵעֵהוּ
הָעֲדֻלָּמִי לָקַחַת הָעֵרָבוֹן מִיַּד הָאִשָּׁה וְלֹא מְצָאָהּ: כא
וַיִּשְׁאַל אֶת־אַנְשֵׁי מְקֹמָהּ לֵאמֹר אַיֵּה הַקְּדֵשָׁה הִוא
בָעֵינַיִם עַל־הַדָּרֶךְ וַיֹּאמְרוּ לֹא־הָיְתָה בָזֶה קְדֵשָׁה:

[19] Then she went on her way. She took off her veil and again put on her widow's garb.
[20] Judah sent the kid by his friend the Adullamite, to redeem the pledge from the woman; but he could not find her.
[21] He inquired of the people of that town, "Where is the cult prostitute, the one at Enaim, by the road?" But they said, "There has been no prostitute here."

[21] He inquired of the people of that town, "Where is the cult prostitute, the one at Enaim, by the road?": Above

(v. 15), *zonah* is the word used to denote a harlot, but here the word is *kedeshah*. The word *zonah* is used today to refer to a woman of loose morals and behavior. It comes from the same Hebrew root as the word *mazon*, "food that sustains" – something that a person innately desires. The word emphasizes instinctive passion, a biological desire like hunger.

The word *kedeshah* derives from the root *K-D-SH*, whence also *kadosh*, "holy, consecrated," but here in the sense of consecration to debauchery specifically. The term *kedeshah* refers not only to sexual passions, but, rather, to pagan temple prostitution – sex in the name of satisfying the needs of the universe, as associated with the personalization of natural forces that is typical of paganism.

Temple prostitution was a highly developed practice in ancient Canaan. In the shrines of Astarte, for example, it was even a religious norm. Sexual relations with the priestess of Astarte symbolized the earth being fertilized by rain. Such practices are highly seductive, both emotionally and spiritually, and it is not by chance that among the pagans they became an important element of worship. And that is precisely why the Torah absolutely forbids it to the Jews (Deut. 23:18).

Tamar is here called *kedeshah* precisely because she yearned to make contact with Judah – and did so – for a higher purpose, and not merely for the sake of momentary pleasure or profit. At first Judah "took her for a *zonah*" (38:15), but as it turned out he was mistaken, for Tamar was playing the role of *kedeshah*.

Judah tried to make good on his debt, not personally, but through "his friend the Adullamite." But he failed at that attempt. Judah could not avoid meeting personally with Tamar and taking personal responsibility for his act.

But they said, "There has been no prostitute here": The inhabitants of the place answered, "There has been no *kedeshah* here," i.e., temple prostitution is not practiced in these parts.

Tamar's motives were not ordinary and "provincial" – simply to bear a child and create family ties – but ethereal and universal: to elevate Judah, and to produce from him the ancestral line of the Messiah.

48.5. Tamar's Objective is to Exalt Judah (38:22-26)

כב וַיָּשָׁב אֶל־יְהוּדָה וַיֹּאמֶר לֹא מְצָאתִיהָ וְגַם אַנְשֵׁי הַמָּקוֹם אָמְרוּ לֹא־הָיְתָה בָזֶה קְדֵשָׁה: כג וַיֹּאמֶר יְהוּדָה תִּקַּח־לָהּ פֶּן נִהְיֶה לָבוּז הִנֵּה שָׁלַחְתִּי הַגְּדִי הַזֶּה וְאַתָּה לֹא מְצָאתָהּ: כד וַיְהִי ׀ כְּמִשְׁלֹשׁ חֳדָשִׁים וַיֻּגַּד לִיהוּדָה לֵאמֹר זָנְתָה תָּמָר כַּלָּתֶךָ וְגַם הִנֵּה הָרָה לִזְנוּנִים וַיֹּאמֶר יְהוּדָה הוֹצִיאוּהָ וְתִשָּׂרֵף: כה הִוא מוּצֵאת וְהִיא שָׁלְחָה אֶל־חָמִיהָ לֵאמֹר לְאִישׁ אֲשֶׁר־אֵלֶּה לּוֹ אָנֹכִי הָרָה וַתֹּאמֶר הַכֶּר־נָא לְמִי הַחֹתֶמֶת וְהַפְּתִילִים וְהַמַּטֶּה הָאֵלֶּה: כו וַיַּכֵּר יְהוּדָה וַיֹּאמֶר צָדְקָה מִמֶּנִּי כִּי־עַל־כֵּן לֹא־נְתַתִּיהָ לְשֵׁלָה בְנִי וְלֹא־יָסַף עוֹד לְדַעְתָּהּ:

[22] So he returned to Judah and said, "I could not find her; moreover, the townspeople said: There has been no prostitute here."
[23] Judah said, "Let her keep them, lest we become a laughingstock. I did send her this kid, but you did not find her."
[24] About three months later, Judah was told, "Your daughter-in-law Tamar has played the harlot; in fact, she is with child by harlotry."

"Bring her out," said Judah, "and let her be burned."

[25] As she was being brought out, she sent this message to her father-in-law, "I am with child by the man to whom these belong." And she added, "Examine these: whose seal and cord and staff are these?"

[26] Judah recognized them, and said, "She is more in the right than I, inasmuch as I did not give her to my son Shelah." And he was not intimate with her again.

[23] Judah said, "Let her keep them, lest we become a laughing-stock": Judah cares about his image in the eyes of others, but he seems indifferent to the fate of those symbols of power that he left with Tamar as a pledge.

[24] Judah was told, "Your daughter-in-law Tamar has played the harlot": Tamar has no husband, but she is considered legally married: she is "inside" the family (see §47.2 on v. 39:12) because of her connection to Judah through the obligation of *yibbum*, levirate marriage. She is therefore expected to wait for Judah's next son, and to marry him.

In fact, she is with child by harlotry." "Bring her out," said Judah, "and let her be burned": When it comes to light that she is pregnant, the only possible conclusion is that she is guilty of fornication. Legally speaking, and for those times, Judah's decision to exact the death penalty seems quite correct.

[25] As she was being brought out, she sent this message to her father-in-law, "I am with child by the man to

whom these belong": Why did Tamar wait until the very last moment to go public with the truth about Judah? Why did she see fit to escalate the conflict, rather than producing all the evidence much earlier? Had she done so during the discovery phase of her trial, couldn't all these complications have been averted from the very beginning?

[26] Judah recognized them, and said, "She is more in the right than I": Tamar deliberately puts Judah in a very uncomfortable position. He must voluntarily and publicly come clean, acknowledging his guilt, and intervening in the wheels of justice after they have already been set in motion. But Judah does exactly that. He publicly admits his mistake.

Tamar's primary goal is not to save her own skin, but to elevate Judah by restoring his innate leadership qualities. Although Judah has "descended" of late, Tamar is fully cognizant of his greatness and his potential. And in the end, Tamar is successful at achieving her goal.

Tamar brings the situation to a head by forcing Judah to exert arduous efforts that lead to a spiritual breakthrough. And as things turn out, Tamar was not at all mistaken in her intuitive understanding of Judah's personality.

What would any ordinary leader have done in Judah's place? Upon learning that Tamar was pregnant with his child, he would not have demanded her execution, but would have spared no effort to hush up the case under false pretenses of judicial compassion.

But Judah does nothing of the kind. He publicly admits that he has been with that woman, and that he has mismanaged his family. Judah's great merit is in this act, which elevates him to a precipitously higher plane. Judah is capable of repenting and improving, and it is this quality that is the source of his spiritual leadership.

Tamar's goal, then, in presenting back to Judah the items of his pledge, was not her own salvation, but Judah's correction, to restore him to the level of the task he was destined to accomplish.

King David, a descendant of Judah, will experience a similar situation with Bath-sheba. And although no one in that case will spring a trap for David, he too will be forced to publicly admit having committed an unworthy act.

And he was not intimate with her again: The original Hebrew can be translated in either of two opposite senses: "He thenceforth was not intimate with her," or "He thenceforth did not cease being intimate with her."

Combining these two meanings, we can say that Judah became at this moment an entirely new person. The former Judah was not intimate with Tamar again. But the new Judah did not cease being intimate with her.

48.6. The Birth of Perez and Zerah (38:27-30)

כז וַיְהִי בְּעֵת לִדְתָּהּ וְהִנֵּה תְאוֹמִים בְּבִטְנָהּ: כח וַיְהִי בְלִדְתָּהּ וַיִּתֶּן־יָד וַתִּקַּח הַמְיַלֶּדֶת וַתִּקְשֹׁר עַל־יָדוֹ שָׁנִי לֵאמֹר זֶה יָצָא רִאשֹׁנָה: כט וַיְהִי | כְּמֵשִׁיב יָדוֹ וְהִנֵּה יָצָא אָחִיו וַתֹּאמֶר מַה־פָּרַצְתָּ עָלֶיךָ פָּרֶץ וַיִּקְרָא שְׁמוֹ פָּרֶץ: ל וְאַחַר יָצָא אָחִיו אֲשֶׁר עַל־יָדוֹ הַשָּׁנִי וַיִּקְרָא שְׁמוֹ זָרַח:

[27] When the time came for her to give birth, there were twins in her womb!
[28] While she was in labor, one of them put out his hand, and the midwife tied a crimson thread on that hand, to signify: This one came out first.
[29] But just then he drew back his hand, and

out came his brother; and she said, "What a
breach you have made for yourself!" So he was
named Perez.
[30] Afterward his brother came out, on whose hand
was the crimson thread; he was named Zerah.

[27] There were twins in her womb!: Tamar bears Judah two sons, Perez ("breach") and Zerah (dawn, "bright red, crimson horizon"). We can assume that Judah, in performing levirate marriage, is restoring the names of Er and Onan, and Tamar therefore gives birth to twins, to replace, as it were, Judah's two sons who themselves died childless. But actually, Perez and Zerah more clearly exhibit features of Jacob and Esau.

[28] One of them put out his hand, and the midwife tied a crimson thread on that hand, to signify: This one came out first: Zerah, with the crimson thread, is directly associated with Esau, Edom, which also means "red."

[29] And she said, "What a breach you have made for yourself!" So he was named Perez: Perez, breaching past Zerah and ahead of him, corresponds to Jacob, who eventually surpassed Esau.

Perez and Zerah will later become the two main lines of the tribe of Judah, but Shelah, although he is older than them, will be mentioned only incidentally. Moreover, the line of David and of the Messiah is the line of Perez. The Sabbath hymn *"Lecha Dodi"* explicitly refers to the Messiah as "the Son of Perez." Rabbi A. I. Kook explains in this connection that the Messiah breaches walls and breaks down barriers. Thus, the Messiah is the descendant of Perez, and not of the more ordinary – albeit radiant – Zerah.

Chapter 49

Joseph Serves Potiphar

49.1. Joseph's Success as a Sign of Divine Beneficence (39:1-6)

א וְיוֹסֵף הוּרַד מִצְרָיְמָה וַיִּקְנֵהוּ פּוֹטִיפַר סְרִיס פַּרְעֹה שַׂר הַטַּבָּחִים אִישׁ מִצְרִי מִיַּד הַיִּשְׁמְעֵאלִים אֲשֶׁר הוֹרִדֻהוּ שָׁמָּה: ב וַיְהִי יי אֶת־יוֹסֵף וַיְהִי אִישׁ מַצְלִיחַ וַיְהִי בְּבֵית אֲדֹנָיו הַמִּצְרִי: ג וַיַּרְא אֲדֹנָיו כִּי יי אִתּוֹ וְכֹל אֲשֶׁר־הוּא עֹשֶׂה יי מַצְלִיחַ בְּיָדוֹ: ד וַיִּמְצָא יוֹסֵף חֵן בְּעֵינָיו וַיְשָׁרֶת אֹתוֹ וַיַּפְקִדֵהוּ עַל־בֵּיתוֹ וְכָל־יֶשׁ־לוֹ נָתַן בְּיָדוֹ: ה וַיְהִי מֵאָז הִפְקִיד אֹתוֹ בְּבֵיתוֹ וְעַל כָּל־אֲשֶׁר יֶשׁ־לוֹ וַיְבָרֶךְ יי אֶת־בֵּית הַמִּצְרִי בִּגְלַל יוֹסֵף וַיְהִי בִּרְכַּת יי בְּכָל־אֲשֶׁר יֶשׁ־לוֹ בַּבַּיִת וּבַשָּׂדֶה: ו וַיַּעֲזֹב כָּל־אֲשֶׁר־לוֹ בְּיַד־יוֹסֵף וְלֹא־יָדַע אִתּוֹ מְאוּמָה כִּי אִם־הַלֶּחֶם אֲשֶׁר־הוּא אוֹכֵל וַיְהִי יוֹסֵף יְפֵה־תֹאַר וִיפֵה מַרְאֶה:

[1] When Joseph was taken down to Egypt, a certain Egyptian, Potiphar, a courtier of Pharaoh and his chief steward, bought him from the Ishmaelites who had brought him there.
[2] The Lord was with Joseph, and he was a

successful man; and he stayed in the house of his Egyptian master.

[3] And when his master saw that the Lord was with him and that the Lord lent success to everything he undertook,

[4] he took a liking to Joseph. He made him his personal attendant and put him in charge of his household, placing in his hands all that he owned.

[5] And from the time that the Egyptian put him in charge of his household and of all that he owned, the Lord blessed his house for Joseph's sake, so that the blessing of the Lord was upon everything that he owned, in the house and outside.

[6] He left all that he had in Joseph's hands and, with him there, he paid attention to nothing save the food that he ate. Now Joseph was well built and handsome.

After the story of Judah, the Torah returns to the parallel story of Joseph, contrasting them.

[1] When Joseph was taken down to Egypt, a certain Egyptian, Potiphar, a courtier of Pharaoh [2] … Joseph … was a successful man; and he stayed in the house of his Egyptian master: To Joseph's good fortune, his new master is an Egyptian nobleman. Moreover, Joseph is assigned to work at home, and not in the field, where Joseph would have had more difficulty demonstrating his unique talents.

[3] And when his master saw that the Lord was with him

and that the Lord lent success to everything he undertook: Joseph's material success is a direct result of Divine support, blessing, and attention. And since Joseph always declares this openly, his master too comes to believe that it is God who "lent success to everything Joseph undertook." Joseph promotes the idea of Divine Providence everywhere around him. Material as well as spiritual success are evident in everything he does.

[5] And from the time that the Egyptian put him in charge of his household and of all that he owned, the Lord blessed his house for Joseph's sake: Joseph – the *ish matzliach*, "successful man" – later came to symbolize the righteous individual to whom God grants economic success. It is a well-known sociological principle that if a society's religious ideology positively associates Divine support with economic success, that society will develop much more successfully than one which idealizes poverty. In Jewish tradition, the image of Joseph represents this idea most clearly.

[6] Now Joseph was well built and handsome: Based on these words, European culture gave Joseph the title "Joseph the beautiful." But in Jewish tradition, as we noted earlier, he is called "Joseph the Righteous."

Beauty is Joseph's inherited attribute, which was passed to him through Rachel (29:19), and this aspect is particularly important for him. As we have already noted, beauty represents the idea of power over everything material, an idea that characterizes Joseph in all areas of his life.

The Midrash understands the words "well built and handsome" as indicating that Joseph had now begun to preen. Joseph does not consider it a problem that he is in exile, far from his father and the Land of Israel, and he decides that, having achieved success and now occupying a responsible position, he must appear at all times stately and elegant. This misunderstanding soon leads Joseph to a predicament in the person of Potiphar's wife, which lands him in prison. All this is meant to make Joseph understand that he has not yet by far achieved a normal life.

49.2. Joseph and Potiphar's Wife (39:7-12)

זַ וַיְהִ֗י אַחַר֙ הַדְּבָרִ֣ים הָאֵ֔לֶּה וַתִּשָּׂ֧א אֵֽשֶׁת־אֲדֹנָ֛יו אֶת־
עֵינֶ֖יהָ אֶל־יוֹסֵ֑ף וַתֹּ֖אמֶר שִׁכְבָ֥ה עִמִּֽי: ח וַיְמָאֵ֓ן ׀ וַיֹּ֨אמֶר֙
אֶל־אֵ֣שֶׁת אֲדֹנָ֔יו הֵ֣ן אֲדֹנִ֔י לֹא־יָדַ֥ע אִתִּ֖י מַה־בַּבָּ֑יִת וְכֹ֥ל
אֲשֶׁר־יֶשׁ־ל֖וֹ נָתַ֥ן בְּיָדִֽי: ט אֵינֶ֨נּוּ גָד֜וֹל בַּבַּ֣יִת הַזֶּה֮ מִמֶּ֒נִּי֒
וְלֹֽא־חָשַׂ֤ךְ מִמֶּ֨נִּי֙ מְא֔וּמָה כִּ֥י אִם־אוֹתָ֖ךְ בַּאֲשֶׁ֣ר אַתְּ־
אִשְׁתּ֑וֹ וְאֵ֞יךְ אֶֽעֱשֶׂ֤ה הָֽרָעָה֙ הַגְּדֹלָ֣ה הַזֹּ֔את וְחָטָ֖אתִי
לֵֽאלֹהִֽים: י וַיְהִ֕י כְּדַבְּרָ֥הּ אֶל־יוֹסֵ֖ף י֣וֹם ׀ י֑וֹם וְלֹא־שָׁמַ֥ע
אֵלֶ֛יהָ לִשְׁכַּ֥ב אֶצְלָ֖הּ לִהְי֥וֹת עִמָּֽהּ: יא וַיְהִי֙ כְּהַיּ֣וֹם הַזֶּ֔ה
וַיָּבֹ֥א הַבַּ֖יְתָה לַעֲשׂ֣וֹת מְלַאכְתּ֑וֹ וְאֵ֨ין אִ֜ישׁ מֵאַנְשֵׁ֥י הַבַּ֛יִת
שָׁ֖ם בַּבָּֽיִת: יב וַתִּתְפְּשֵׂ֧הוּ בְּבִגְד֛וֹ לֵאמֹ֖ר שִׁכְבָ֣ה עִמִּ֑י וַיַּעֲזֹ֤ב
בִּגְד֙וֹ בְּיָדָ֔הּ וַיָּ֖נָס וַיֵּצֵ֥א הַחֽוּצָה:

[7] After a time, his master's wife cast her eyes upon Joseph and said, "Lie with me."
[8] But he refused. He said to his master's wife, "Look, with me here, my master gives no thought to anything in this house, and all that he owns he has placed in my hands.
[9] He wields no more authority in this house than I, and he has withheld nothing from me except yourself, since you are his wife. How then could I do this most wicked thing, and sin before God?"

[10] And much as she coaxed Joseph day after day, he did not yield to her request to lie beside her, to be with her.
[11] One such day, he came into the house to do his work. None of the household being there inside,
[12] she caught hold of him by his garment and said, "Lie with me!" But he left his garment in her hand and got away and fled outside.

[7] After a time, his master's wife cast her eyes upon Joseph and said, "Lie with me": The story of Joseph and Potiphar's wife echoes motifs of the previous story of Judah and his wives, contrasting with it and revealing another aspect of the differences between Joseph and Judah.

Potiphar's wife is the symbol of Egyptian femininity. She sees the life force embodied in the seed of Israel, and wants to claim it for herself. This is a constant test that awaits the Jew in *galut*, in exile.

[9] How then could I do this most wicked thing, and sin before God?": We see in Joseph's resistance that his ethical arguments have a religious foundation. Jewish monotheism includes not only the idea of the One God, but also the belief that this God demands of human beings to behave morally. This kind of ethical monotheism became the foundation of the further spiritual development of mankind.

[11] One such day: According to the Midrash, that day happened to be an Egyptian holiday. Everyone had gone off to attend the celebration, and no one was home.

He came into the house to do his work: If everyone has gone off to celebrate, why is Joseph working? The Midrash mentions two possibilities. Perhaps he really did have actual work to perform that day. Or, he had in fact decided to surrender to Potiphar's wife's advances, and "to do his work" refers to a tryst to which they had formerly agreed. If so, the Midrash believes that Joseph changed his mind and ran off only at the very last moment, after the image of his father Jacob suddenly appeared before him. Ultimately, then, according to this Midrash, Joseph resisted Potiphar's wife's advances not merely based on religious considerations, but because of his strong sense of family and national identity.

For Joseph, and materially motivated righteous individuals like him, the main danger is the threat of physical assimilation among other nations. It is important for him to remain a Jew, and he therefore stops precisely before the danger of a mixed union and the birth of descendants from it.

But for Judah this is not a problem, because he believes that his unique Jewish spirituality is so strong that he can successfully assimilate into himself any foreign influence.

[12] But he left his garment in her hand and got away and fled outside: We notice two points in the incident of Joseph and Potiphar's wife. First, the role of Joseph's garment, which receives special emphasis in the story. And second, the word *hachutzah*, "outward, outside," repeated four times in reference to Joseph's fleeing from Potiphar's wife (v. 12, 13, 15, and 18).

(It is interesting that this word, *hachutzah*, appears in the Torah in only two places: Here, and in the context of *yibbum*, levirate marriage (Deut. 25:5). There, however, the word refers to something that the Torah is saying should not be allowed to happen, i.e., for the widow of the childless man to marry "outside" her late husband's family. (Rather, she should remain *within* the family by marrying one of her late husband's brothers.) In this point we notice a commonality with the story of Judah and Tamar.)

But as concerns Joseph and Potiphar's wife, the repetition of *hachutzah* no less than four times clearly indicates that fleeing "outward, outside" is for Joseph an especially important concept in the general sense. Joseph "flees outside" not merely to escape harassment by Potiphar's wife, but because it is his overall tendency to strive constantly "outward." And again, also important for Joseph is the matter of his garment, which the brothers once stripped from him, and now Potiphar's wife does the same.

Joseph is a "man of the world." he wants to free himself from the narrow confines of the Land of Israel, from the traditional occupation of cattle breeding, and from a life of narrowly nationalist substance within the family clan. Joseph is attracted to the larger world, to the monumental Egyptian civilization, and to a highly developed agriculture. Given this lifestyle, clothing is a matter of particular significance and importance. His clothing must command respect from the outside world, or no one will want to have any dealings with him.

When the world with which Joseph interacts (his brothers, and Potiphar's wife) divest him of his clothing, this is meant to demonstrate to Joseph the fallacies and superficiality of his worldview. But Joseph is not yet ready to learn that lesson. He will feel the deficiencies of clothing only toward the end of his life, when he calls on the Children of Israel to fulfill his last wish: "Carry up my bones from here" (50:25)

49.3. Potiphar Throws Joseph into Prison (39:13-23)

יג וַיְהִי כִּרְאוֹתָהּ כִּי־עָזַב בִּגְדוֹ בְּיָדָהּ וַיָּנָס הַחוּצָה: יד

וַתִּקְרָא לְאַנְשֵׁי בֵיתָהּ וַתֹּאמֶר לָהֶם לֵאמֹר רְאוּ הֵבִיא
לָנוּ אִישׁ עִבְרִי לְצַחֶק בָּנוּ בָּא אֵלַי לִשְׁכַּב עִמִּי וָאֶקְרָא
בְּקוֹל גָּדוֹל: **טו** וַיְהִי כְשָׁמְעוֹ כִּי־הֲרִימֹתִי קוֹלִי וָאֶקְרָא
וַיַּעֲזֹב בִּגְדוֹ אֶצְלִי וַיָּנָס וַיֵּצֵא הַחוּצָה: **טז** וַתַּנַּח בִּגְדוֹ
אֶצְלָהּ עַד־בּוֹא אֲדֹנָיו אֶל־בֵּיתוֹ: **יז** וַתְּדַבֵּר אֵלָיו כַּדְּבָרִים
הָאֵלֶּה לֵאמֹר בָּא־אֵלַי הָעֶבֶד הָעִבְרִי אֲשֶׁר־הֵבֵאתָ לָּנוּ
לְצַחֶק בִּי: **יח** וַיְהִי כַּהֲרִימִי קוֹלִי וָאֶקְרָא וַיַּעֲזֹב בִּגְדוֹ
אֶצְלִי וַיָּנָס הַחוּצָה: **יט** וַיְהִי כִשְׁמֹעַ אֲדֹנָיו אֶת־דִּבְרֵי
אִשְׁתּוֹ אֲשֶׁר דִּבְּרָה אֵלָיו לֵאמֹר כַּדְּבָרִים הָאֵלֶּה עָשָׂה
לִי עַבְדֶּךָ וַיִּחַר אַפּוֹ: **כ** וַיִּקַּח אֲדֹנֵי יוֹסֵף אֹתוֹ וַיִּתְּנֵהוּ
אֶל־בֵּית הַסֹּהַר מְקוֹם אֲשֶׁר־אסורי (אֲסִירֵי) הַמֶּלֶךְ
אֲסוּרִים וַיְהִי־שָׁם בְּבֵית הַסֹּהַר: **כא** וַיְהִי יי אֶת־יוֹסֵף
וַיֵּט אֵלָיו חָסֶד וַיִּתֵּן חִנּוֹ בְּעֵינֵי שַׂר בֵּית־הַסֹּהַר: **כב**
וַיִּתֵּן שַׂר בֵּית־הַסֹּהַר בְּיַד־יוֹסֵף אֵת כָּל־הָאֲסִירִם אֲשֶׁר
בְּבֵית הַסֹּהַר וְאֵת כָּל־אֲשֶׁר עֹשִׂים שָׁם הוּא הָיָה עֹשֶׂה:
כג אֵין | שַׂר בֵּית־הַסֹּהַר רֹאֶה אֶת־כָּל־מְאוּמָה בְּיָדוֹ
בַּאֲשֶׁר יי אִתּוֹ וַאֲשֶׁר־הוּא עֹשֶׂה יי מַצְלִיחַ:

*[13] When she saw that he had left it in her hand
and had fled outside,
[14] she called out to her servants and said to
them, "Look, he had to bring us a Hebrew to
dally with us! This one came to lie with me; but
I screamed loud.
[15] And when he heard me screaming at the top
of my voice, he left his garment with me and got
away and fled outside."
[16] She kept his garment beside her, until his
master came home.
[17] Then she told him the same story, saying,
"The Hebrew slave whom you brought into our
house came to me to dally with me;
[18] but when I screamed at the top of my voice,*

he left his garment with me and fled outside."

[19] When his master heard the story that his wife told him, namely, "Thus and so your slave did to me," he was furious.

[20] So Joseph's master had him put in prison, where the king's prisoners were confined. But even while he was there in prison,

[21] the Lord was with Joseph: He extended kindness to him and disposed the chief jailer favorably toward him.

[22] The chief jailer put in Joseph's charge all the prisoners who were in that prison, and he was the one to carry out everything that was done there.

[23] The chief jailer did not supervise anything that was in Joseph's charge, because the Lord was with him, and whatever he did the Lord made successful.

[14] She called out to her servants and said to them: For her husband to believe her, Potiphar's wife must first win over public opinion. For this she turns to her domestic servants.

Look, he had to bring us a Hebrew to dally with us! ... [17] The Hebrew slave whom you brought into our house came to me to dally with me: Potiphar's wife presents the incident differently to her servants and to her husband.

She tells the servants that "he" (by which she means Potiphar) "had to bring us a Hebrew to dally with us!" That is, *all* of us, as if to say that she considers the servants her equals – which she does in order to garner greater support.

But to her husband she says that "the Hebrew slave" came

(that is, of his own accord) "to dally with *me*." In other words, he is threatening the integrity of their family.

[19] When his master heard the story that his wife told him, namely, "Thus and so your slave did to me," he was furious: Initially Potiphar offers almost no response to his wife's words. She therefore continues in her further attempts to provoke his anger, adding, "Thus and so your slave did to me." The Midrash explains that she said all of this to Potiphar during their intimate relations (hence, "*Thus and so your slave did to me*").

[20] So Joseph's master had him put in prison, where the king's prisoners were confined: It seems that Potiphar, even in the fit of anger skillfully aroused by his wife, did not really believe her, otherwise he would simply have had Joseph executed. But Joseph, despite the gravity of the accusations, only ends up in prison. And not just an ordinary prison, but a privileged, "special prison" for dignitaries, under Potiphar's personal jurisdiction. Later we will see (40:3-4) that Potiphar remained Joseph's master and maintained contact with him – because he understood Joseph's uncommon aptitude and importance.

[23] The chief jailer did not supervise anything that was in Joseph's charge, because the Lord was with him, and whatever he did the Lord made successful: This verse parallels verse 39:6: "[Potiphar] paid attention to nothing save the food that [Joseph] ate." Wherever Joseph goes, he becomes a steward, but not a master: there is always a higher authority over him.

Joseph had been the *de facto* commander over his brothers in Jacob's house. He then managed the Potiphar estate, then the prison, and, finally, he became second-in-command to Pharaoh over all of Egypt – because it was obvious to all that "the Lord lent success to everything he undertook." Jewish resourcefulness for transforming and managing the material world is immense. But we must remember that all that makes sense only when it is not an end in itself, but a foundation for promoting higher values.

Joseph himself, having enormous potential to correct the world, failed his tests twice. The first time was with his father. The situation ends in defeat: Joseph is sold and sent to Egypt. And Joseph's second failure is in Potiphar's house, where events also end in his defeat, and he is sent to prison.

Joseph is not just a great man, but a righteous man, except that he is too focused on himself. First, he delights in his dreams (that is, his universal aspiration: he yearns to reform the world). Then he preens, reveling in his own beauty and his ability to manage Potiphar's house. But he still neither feels nor understands that the purpose of all his efforts and accomplishments in this world is only to lay a foundation for the future – the kingdom of Judah.

Joseph had to experience slavery, prison, power over Egypt, and disappointment in the consequences of all his social experiments, so that he could declare at the very end of his life: "God intended it for good, so as to bring about the present result – the survival of many people." (50:20). This is his correction – his transition from Joseph to *Mashiach ben Yosef*.

49.4. Two Aspects of Jewish Chosenness: Segulah and Bechirah

As already noted, the incident of Joseph and the wife of

Potiphar in the Torah immediately follows the incident of Judah and Tamar. This prompts us to attempt a comparison of the two stories.

In the situation with Potiphar's wife, Joseph does not succumb to temptation, nor does he commit any offense. Judah, however, does commit an offense with Tamar, but he later corrects himself. Joseph belongs to the category of the completely righteous, but Judah is in the category of reformed sinners. Joseph's life centers around correcting the world materially, while the central focus of Judah's life is correcting the world spiritually.

The potentials of Joseph and Judah are developed as the categories of *Mashiach ben Yosef*, the nationalist-secular Messianic aspect, and *Mashiach ben Yehudah* (hereinafter *Mashiach ben David*), the nationalist-religious Messianic aspect. Their relationship corresponds to two complementary aspects of Jewish chosenness, *Segulah*, "chosenness by nature," and *Bechirah*, "chosenness by personal decision." *Bechirah* means free choice to follow the Jewish Doctrine, while *Segulah* is that part of the Jewish soul that under any and all conditions leaves a Jew a Jew: *Segulah* is indestructible. It is not conditional on any particular actions, and does not depend on keeping the commandments.

The Jewishness of non-religious Jews is *Segulah*, while for religious Jews it is *Segulah* and *Bechirah* in combination. In the minds of religious Jews, *Bechirah* outstrips *Segulah*. To them, Jewish behavior and conduct always take first place. But a non-religious Jew will remind us that "once you are born a Jew, you forever remain a Jew." In other words, to him the emphasis is on *Segulah*.

For Joseph and *Mashiach ben Yosef*, for nationalist-secular Jewry, *Segulah* is the highest ideal. Later, when the brothers appear before Joseph in Egypt, they mistake him for an

Egyptian. His appearance and behavior are just like those of everyone else in pagan Egypt. Nonetheless, no matter how he behaves and no matter how he dresses, he remains a Jew. The worst thing for him is physical assimilation – marriage with a non-Jew – because the result will be that his children will no longer be like him.

Joseph can lose his *Segulah* through personal assimilation, and in the event of such a fall, there is virtually no possibility of a straightforward return. His non-Jewish children can again become Jews only by following a religious trajectory. This impossibility of return greatly hinders Joseph and plays an important role in the piety of his actions.

But in Judah we have a completely different type of chosenness. For him, *Segulah* is only the foundation, the basis for the further development of *Bechirah*, "chosenness by personal decision." To Judah, the path of *Teshuvah*, repentance, is therefore always open.

Tamar was able to check Judah's fall, thus giving him the opportunity to begin his correction. Having repented, he first returns to his place as leader, but he then proceeds to a yet higher level, thereby advancing the line of the Messiah.

We have previously discussed in some detail that the Messiah can arise only from an entangled, problematic, dysfunctional situation, which is the reason that one of the names of the Messiah is "son of the fall." If *Teshuvah*, repentance, occurs after the fall, it not only retroactively corrects the crime, but raises a person even higher than he was before his misconduct. Repentance retrospectively renders the fall "useful" in a sense – directed toward goodness. Thus, repentance reveals those sparks of the Divine light that are contained even in a previously committed sin, and which the thoroughly righteous could have never revealed.

Since Judah can repent, his fall is not critically irrevocable, as it would be for Joseph. On the contrary, through repentance and reconstruction he paves the way for the Messiah.

49.5. Pharaoh's Cupbearer and the Baker in Prison (40:1-5)

א וַיְהִי אַחַר הַדְּבָרִים הָאֵלֶּה חָטְאוּ מַשְׁקֵה מֶלֶךְ־
מִצְרַיִם וְהָאֹפֶה לַאֲדֹנֵיהֶם לְמֶלֶךְ מִצְרָיִם׃ ב וַיִּקְצֹף
פַּרְעֹה עַל שְׁנֵי סָרִיסָיו עַל שַׂר הַמַּשְׁקִים וְעַל שַׂר
הָאוֹפִים׃ ג וַיִּתֵּן אֹתָם בְּמִשְׁמַר בֵּית שַׂר הַטַּבָּחִים אֶל־
בֵּית הַסֹּהַר מְקוֹם אֲשֶׁר יוֹסֵף אָסוּר שָׁם׃ ד וַיִּפְקֹד שַׂר
הַטַּבָּחִים אֶת־יוֹסֵף אִתָּם וַיְשָׁרֶת אֹתָם וַיִּהְיוּ יָמִים
בְּמִשְׁמָר׃ ה וַיַּחַלְמוּ חֲלוֹם שְׁנֵיהֶם אִישׁ חֲלֹמוֹ בְּלַיְלָה
אֶחָד אִישׁ כְּפִתְרוֹן חֲלֹמוֹ הַמַּשְׁקֶה וְהָאֹפֶה אֲשֶׁר לְמֶלֶךְ
מִצְרַיִם אֲשֶׁר אֲסוּרִים בְּבֵית הַסֹּהַר׃

[1] Some time later, the cupbearer and the baker of the king of Egypt gave offense to their lord the king of Egypt.
[2] Pharaoh was angry with his two courtiers, the chief cupbearer and the chief baker,
[3] and put them in custody, in the house of the chief steward, in the same prison house where Joseph was confined.
[4] The chief steward assigned Joseph to them, and he attended them. When they had been in custody for some time,
[5] both of them – the cupbearer and the baker of the king of Egypt, who were confined in the prison – dreamed in the same night, each his own dream and each dream with its own meaning.

There is an important stylistic difference between verses 1 and 5 of this passage, on the one hand, and verses 2, 7, 9, and 11, on the other. In the first group of verses, the protagonists of this story are "the cupbearer, the baker, and the king of Egypt," but in the second group they are "the chief of the butlers, the chief of the bakers, and Pharaoh."

Rabbi Mordechai Breuer, a leading Torah scholar of our time, has pioneered the concept of *bechinot* – the various Divine aspects of a situation that intersect one another in a single passage of the Torah. Rabbi Breuer explains that the differences of phrasing mentioned in the previous paragraph are a continuation of the ambiguity in the sale of Joseph that we have already noted: Who actually sold Joseph – the Midianites, or Joseph's brothers?

This difference corresponds to the two levels of Divine control that are operative in this story. On the one hand, the brothers commit a sin and are punished and corrected. (It is then the brothers who cast Joseph into the pit, and God raises him from there. And Potiphar who throws Joseph into prison, and again God raises him from there.)

But on the other hand, it is a Divine necessity that Joseph (and the Jewish people) will go down to Egypt. Joseph descends gradually. He is in captivity with the Midianites, becomes a slave to Potiphar, serves in prison, and, finally, is confined to a pit (v. 15). And all this because Joseph's re-education (and likewise that of the Jewish people after him) made it necessary for him to descend to Egypt's lowest depths before he could rise again to reach its heights.

However, due to the technical (Hebrew) complexities of this analysis, we will not investigate the topic here in any detail.

49.6. Joseph Deciphers the Dreams of Pharaoh's Courtiers (40:6-23)

‫ו וַיָּבֹא אֲלֵיהֶם יוֹסֵף בַּבֹּקֶר וַיַּרְא אֹתָם וְהִנָּם זֹעֲפִים:‬
‫ז וַיִּשְׁאַל אֶת־סְרִיסֵי פַרְעֹה אֲשֶׁר אִתּוֹ בְמִשְׁמַר בֵּית‬
‫אֲדֹנָיו לֵאמֹר מַדּוּעַ פְּנֵיכֶם רָעִים הַיּוֹם: ח וַיֹּאמְרוּ אֵלָיו‬
‫חֲלוֹם חָלַמְנוּ וּפֹתֵר אֵין אֹתוֹ וַיֹּאמֶר אֲלֵהֶם יוֹסֵף הֲלוֹא‬
‫לֵאלֹהִים פִּתְרֹנִים סַפְּרוּ־נָא לִי: ט וַיְסַפֵּר שַׂר־הַמַּשְׁקִים‬
‫אֶת־חֲלֹמוֹ לְיוֹסֵף וַיֹּאמֶר לוֹ בַּחֲלוֹמִי וְהִנֵּה־גֶפֶן לְפָנָי: י‬
‫וּבַגֶּפֶן שְׁלֹשָׁה שָׂרִיגִם וְהִוא כְפֹרַחַת עָלְתָה נִצָּהּ הִבְשִׁילוּ‬
‫אַשְׁכְּלֹתֶיהָ עֲנָבִים: יא וְכוֹס פַּרְעֹה בְּיָדִי וָאֶקַּח אֶת־‬
‫הָעֲנָבִים וָאֶשְׂחַט אֹתָם אֶל־כּוֹס פַּרְעֹה וָאֶתֵּן אֶת־הַכּוֹס‬
‫עַל־כַּף פַּרְעֹה: יב וַיֹּאמֶר לוֹ יוֹסֵף זֶה פִּתְרֹנוֹ שְׁלֹשֶׁת‬
‫הַשָּׂרִגִים שְׁלֹשֶׁת יָמִים הֵם: יג בְּעוֹד | שְׁלֹשֶׁת יָמִים יִשָּׂא‬
‫פַרְעֹה אֶת־רֹאשֶׁךָ וַהֲשִׁיבְךָ עַל־כַּנֶּךָ וְנָתַתָּ כוֹס־פַּרְעֹה‬
‫בְּיָדוֹ כַּמִּשְׁפָּט הָרִאשׁוֹן אֲשֶׁר הָיִיתָ מַשְׁקֵהוּ: יד כִּי אִם־‬
‫זְכַרְתַּנִי אִתְּךָ כַּאֲשֶׁר יִיטַב לָךְ וְעָשִׂיתָ־נָּא עִמָּדִי חָסֶד‬
‫וְהִזְכַּרְתַּנִי אֶל־פַּרְעֹה וְהוֹצֵאתַנִי מִן־הַבַּיִת הַזֶּה: טו כִּי־‬
‫גֻנֹּב גֻּנַּבְתִּי מֵאֶרֶץ הָעִבְרִים וְגַם־פֹּה לֹא־עָשִׂיתִי מְאוּמָה‬
‫כִּי־שָׂמוּ אֹתִי בַּבּוֹר: טז וַיַּרְא שַׂר־הָאֹפִים כִּי טוֹב פָּתָר‬
‫וַיֹּאמֶר אֶל־יוֹסֵף אַף־אֲנִי בַּחֲלוֹמִי וְהִנֵּה שְׁלֹשָׁה סַלֵּי‬
‫חֹרִי עַל־רֹאשִׁי: יז וּבַסַּל הָעֶלְיוֹן מִכֹּל מַאֲכַל פַּרְעֹה‬
‫מַעֲשֵׂה אֹפֶה וְהָעוֹף אֹכֵל אֹתָם מִן־הַסַּל מֵעַל רֹאשִׁי:‬
‫יח וַיַּעַן יוֹסֵף וַיֹּאמֶר זֶה פִּתְרֹנוֹ שְׁלֹשֶׁת הַסַּלִּים שְׁלֹשֶׁת‬
‫יָמִים הֵם: יט בְּעוֹד | שְׁלֹשֶׁת יָמִים יִשָּׂא פַרְעֹה אֶת־‬
‫רֹאשְׁךָ מֵעָלֶיךָ וְתָלָה אוֹתְךָ עַל־עֵץ וְאָכַל הָעוֹף אֶת־‬
‫בְּשָׂרְךָ מֵעָלֶיךָ: כ וַיְהִי | בַּיּוֹם הַשְּׁלִישִׁי יוֹם הֻלֶּדֶת‬
‫אֶת־פַּרְעֹה וַיַּעַשׂ מִשְׁתֶּה לְכָל־עֲבָדָיו וַיִּשָּׂא אֶת־רֹאשׁ |‬
‫שַׂר הַמַּשְׁקִים וְאֶת־רֹאשׁ שַׂר הָאֹפִים בְּתוֹךְ עֲבָדָיו: כא‬
‫וַיָּשֶׁב אֶת־שַׂר הַמַּשְׁקִים עַל־מַשְׁקֵהוּ וַיִּתֵּן הַכּוֹס עַל־‬
‫כַּף פַּרְעֹה: כב וְאֵת שַׂר הָאֹפִים תָּלָה כַּאֲשֶׁר פָּתַר לָהֶם‬
‫יוֹסֵף: כג וְלֹא־זָכַר שַׂר־הַמַּשְׁקִים אֶת־יוֹסֵף וַיִּשְׁכָּחֵהוּ:‬

[6] When Joseph came to them in the morning, he saw that they were distraught.

[7] He asked Pharaoh's courtiers, who were with him in custody in his master's house, saying, "Why do you appear downcast today?"

[8] And they said to him, "We had dreams, and there is no one to interpret them." So Joseph said to them, "Surely God can interpret! Tell me [your dreams]."

[9] Then the chief cupbearer told his dream to Joseph. He said to him, "In my dream, there was a vine in front of me.

[10] On the vine were three branches. It had barely budded, when out came its blossoms and its clusters ripened into grapes.

[11] Pharaoh's cup was in my hand, and I took the grapes, pressed them into Pharaoh's cup, and placed the cup in Pharaoh's hand."

[12] Joseph said to him, "This is its interpretation: The three branches are three days.

[13] In three days Pharaoh will pardon you and restore you to your post; you will place Pharaoh's cup in his hand, as was your custom formerly when you were his cupbearer.

[14] But think of me when all is well with you again, and do me the kindness of mentioning me to Pharaoh, so as to free me from this place.

[15] For in truth, I was kidnapped from the land of the Hebrews; nor have I done anything here that they should have put me in the dungeon."

[16] When the chief baker saw how favorably he had interpreted, he said to Joseph, "In my dream, similarly, there were three openwork baskets on my head.

[17] In the uppermost basket were all kinds of food for Pharaoh that a baker prepares; and the birds were eating it out of the basket above my head."
[18] Joseph answered, "This is its interpretation: The three baskets are three days.
[19] In three days Pharaoh will lift off your head and impale you upon a pole; and the birds will pick off your flesh."
[20] On the third day – his birthday – Pharaoh made a banquet for all his officials, and he singled out his chief cupbearer and his chief baker from among his officials.
[21] He restored the chief cupbearer to his cupbearing, and he placed the cup in Pharaoh's hand;
[22] but the chief baker he impaled – just as Joseph had interpreted to them.
[23] Yet the chief cupbearer did not think of Joseph; he forgot him.

[6] That they were distraught: They sense the bizarre nature of their dreams rather intensely. In Egypt, such dreams were not a common occurrence.

[8] And they said to him, "We had dreams, and there is no one to interpret them": A series of prophetic dreams in the Torah began with Joseph's dreams. (Things have a way of beginning with the Jews.) Joseph then "infects" the courtiers of Pharaoh imprisoned with him to have dreams of their own, after which the chief cupbearer, after gaining his freedom, "infects" even Pharaoh himself with that same inclination to dream.

[8] So Joseph said to them, "Surely God can interpret!: Joseph loses no time in emphasizing to Pharaoh's courtiers that the interpretation of dreams comes from God. But in these dreams themselves there are important details which highlight the differences between the cupbearer and the baker.

[11] Pharaoh's cup was in my hand, and I took the grapes, pressed them into Pharaoh's cup, and placed the cup in Pharaoh's hand": The cupbearer dreamed that he was squeezing grapes and serving Pharaoh the juice. That is, he is properly executing his duties in every respect.

[16] In my dream, similarly, there were three openwork baskets on my head. [17] In the uppermost basket were all kinds of food for Pharaoh that a baker prepares; and the birds were eating it out of the basket above my head: The baker, however, dreams of his own passivity, and also sees birds pecking bread from the basket atop his head.

Birds will not normally peck bread from a basket that is resting on the head of a living person. In other words, while the cupbearer dreams that he is alive and well and doing useful work, the baker is, essentially, already inert and defunct. Joseph interprets their respective dreams for them accordingly.

Joseph can see the obvious symbolism that appears in dreams. All this seems strange to the Egyptians, because Egypt is not a country of dreams, but a country of order, where there is no place for such things, because the ability to decipher dreams is not rooted in their culture.

Prophetic dreams were not a component of Egyptian civilization. The Egyptian mentality was enslaved by the constancy and immutability of the natural cycle. Therefore, when Pharaoh later has a dream that predicts a change of reality, none of the Egyptians can interpret it.

[14] But think of me when all is well with you again, and do me the kindness of mentioning me to Pharaoh: Although Joseph has no connection whatsoever with Pharaoh, he asks the cupbearer to mention him to Pharaoh. It was Potiphar, not Pharaoh, who first acquired Joseph and then ejected him. But because Joseph, in order to implement his program of remaking Egypt, needs to assume a position that only Pharaoh himself can appoint him to, he considers the opportunity just now arisen as a signal that Divine assistance will be soon forthcoming.

[15] For in truth, I was kidnapped from the land of the Hebrews": These words of Joseph demonstrate that the land of Canaan belonged to the *ivrim*, Hebrews, the descendants of Eber, even before the Canaanites arrived there.

[23] Yet the chief cupbearer did not think of Joseph; he forgot him: Literally, "Yet the chief cupbearer did not remember Joseph, and forgot him." Not only did the chief of the cupbearers not "remember Joseph" before Pharaoh, he even – in his own mind – forgot Joseph. This lesson should have once again demonstrated to Joseph the futility of the hopes he had placed in Egypt. But Joseph is not yet ready to learn any such a lesson.

Weekly Portion
Mikketz

Chapter 50

The Exaltation of Joseph

50.1. Joseph and Judah in the Weekly Portions of Mikketz and Vayigash

The *Mikketz* portion begins with Joseph leaving prison and being exalted over Egypt. And it ends with Joseph at the pinnacle of his ascent, the reunion of Joseph and his brothers, and their repentance. But from the moment that Judah begins to defend Benjamin, Joseph is spiraling downward, which will be the topic of the next weekly portion, *Vayigash*.

Throughout all of Jewish history, Joseph and Judah are usually out of phase. But it is not an actual requirement that this must always be so. On the contrary, the Messianic process is characterized by the simultaneous strengthening of both forces, Joseph and Judah. However, to achieve joint advancement they must learn to interact creatively, which is one of the primary tasks of a well-organized Jewish life.

50.2. Pharaoh's Dream (41:1-16)

א וַיְהִי מִקֵּץ שְׁנָתַיִם יָמִים וּפַרְעֹה חֹלֵם וְהִנֵּה עֹמֵד

עַל־הַיְאֹר: **ב** וְהִנֵּה מִן־הַיְאֹר עֹלֹת שֶׁבַע פָּרוֹת יְפוֹת
מַרְאֶה וּבְרִיאֹת בָּשָׂר וַתִּרְעֶינָה בָּאָחוּ: **ג** וְהִנֵּה שֶׁבַע
פָּרוֹת אֲחֵרוֹת עֹלוֹת אַחֲרֵיהֶן מִן־הַיְאֹר רָעוֹת מַרְאֶה
וְדַקּוֹת בָּשָׂר וַתַּעֲמֹדְנָה אֵצֶל הַפָּרוֹת עַל־שְׂפַת הַיְאֹר: **ד**
וַתֹּאכַלְנָה הַפָּרוֹת רָעוֹת הַמַּרְאֶה וְדַקֹּת הַבָּשָׂר אֵת שֶׁבַע
הַפָּרוֹת יְפֹת הַמַּרְאֶה וְהַבְּרִיאֹת וַיִּיקַץ פַּרְעֹה: **ה** וַיִּישָׁן
וַיַּחֲלֹם שֵׁנִית וְהִנֵּה | שֶׁבַע שִׁבֳּלִים עֹלוֹת בְּקָנֶה אֶחָד
בְּרִיאוֹת וְטֹבוֹת: **ו** וְהִנֵּה שֶׁבַע שִׁבֳּלִים דַּקּוֹת וּשְׁדוּפֹת
קָדִים צֹמְחוֹת אַחֲרֵיהֶן: **ז** וַתִּבְלַעְנָה הַשִּׁבֳּלִים הַדַּקּוֹת
אֵת שֶׁבַע הַשִּׁבֳּלִים הַבְּרִיאוֹת וְהַמְּלֵאוֹת וַיִּיקַץ פַּרְעֹה
וְהִנֵּה חֲלוֹם: **ח** וַיְהִי בַבֹּקֶר וַתִּפָּעֶם רוּחוֹ וַיִּשְׁלַח וַיִּקְרָא
אֶת־כָּל־חַרְטֻמֵּי מִצְרַיִם וְאֶת־כָּל־חֲכָמֶיהָ וַיְסַפֵּר פַּרְעֹה
לָהֶם אֶת־חֲלֹמוֹ וְאֵין־פּוֹתֵר אוֹתָם לְפַרְעֹה: **ט** וַיְדַבֵּר
שַׂר הַמַּשְׁקִים אֶת־פַּרְעֹה לֵאמֹר אֶת־חֲטָאַי אֲנִי מַזְכִּיר
הַיּוֹם: **י** פַּרְעֹה קָצַף עַל־עֲבָדָיו וַיִּתֵּן אֹתִי בְּמִשְׁמַר בֵּית
שַׂר הַטַּבָּחִים אֹתִי וְאֵת שַׂר הָאֹפִים: **יא** וַנַּחַלְמָה חֲלוֹם
בְּלַיְלָה אֶחָד אֲנִי וָהוּא אִישׁ כְּפִתְרוֹן חֲלֹמוֹ חָלָמְנוּ:
יב וְשָׁם אִתָּנוּ נַעַר עִבְרִי עֶבֶד לְשַׂר הַטַּבָּחִים וַנְּסַפֶּר־לוֹ
וַיִּפְתָּר־לָנוּ אֶת־חֲלֹמֹתֵינוּ אִישׁ כַּחֲלֹמוֹ פָּתָר: **יג** וַיְהִי
כַּאֲשֶׁר פָּתַר־לָנוּ כֵּן הָיָה אֹתִי הֵשִׁיב עַל־כַּנִּי וְאֹתוֹ תָלָה:
יד וַיִּשְׁלַח פַּרְעֹה וַיִּקְרָא אֶת־יוֹסֵף וַיְרִיצֻהוּ מִן־הַבּוֹר
וַיְגַלַּח וַיְחַלֵּף שִׂמְלֹתָיו וַיָּבֹא אֶל־פַּרְעֹה: **טו** וַיֹּאמֶר
פַּרְעֹה אֶל־יוֹסֵף חֲלוֹם חָלַמְתִּי וּפֹתֵר אֵין אֹתוֹ וַאֲנִי
שָׁמַעְתִּי עָלֶיךָ לֵאמֹר תִּשְׁמַע חֲלוֹם לִפְתֹּר אֹתוֹ: **טז** וַיַּעַן
יוֹסֵף אֶת־פַּרְעֹה לֵאמֹר בִּלְעָדָי אֱלֹהִים יַעֲנֶה אֶת־שְׁלוֹם
פַּרְעֹה:

*[1] After two years' time, Pharaoh dreamed that
he was standing by the Nile,
[2] when out of the Nile there came up seven
cows, handsome and sturdy, and they grazed
in the reed grass.
[3] But presently, seven other cows came up from*

the Nile close behind them, ugly and gaunt, and stood beside the cows on the bank of the Nile;
[4] and the ugly gaunt cows ate up the seven handsome sturdy cows. And Pharaoh awoke.
[5] He fell asleep and dreamed a second time: Seven ears of grain, solid and healthy, grew on a single stalk.
[6] But close behind them sprouted seven ears, thin and scorched by the east wind.
[7] And the thin ears swallowed up the seven solid and full ears. Then Pharaoh awoke: it was a dream!
[8] Next morning, his spirit was agitated, and he sent for all the magicians of Egypt, and all its wise men; and Pharaoh told them his dreams, but none could interpret them for Pharaoh.
[9] The chief cupbearer then spoke up and said to Pharaoh, "I must make mention today of my offenses.
[10] Once Pharaoh was angry with his servants, and placed me in custody in the house of the chief steward, together with the chief baker.
[11] We had dreams the same night, he and I, each of us a dream with a meaning of its own.
[12] A Hebrew youth was there with us, a servant of the chief steward; and when we told him our dreams, he interpreted them for us, telling each of the meaning of his dream.
[13] And as he interpreted for us, so it came to pass: I was restored to my post, and the other was impaled."
[14] Thereupon Pharaoh sent for Joseph, and he was rushed from the dungeon. He had his hair

*cut and changed his clothes, and he appeared
before Pharaoh.*
*[15] And Pharaoh said to Joseph, "I have had a
dream, but no one can interpret it. Now I have
heard it said of you that for you to hear a dream
is to tell its meaning."*
*[16] Joseph answered Pharaoh, saying, "Not I!
God will see to Pharaoh's welfare."*

[1] After two years' time: The Midrash adds that because Joseph
put too much trust in the chief of the cupbearers and his assistance, God delayed his release from prison for another two years.

[7] It was a dream!: "Dream," in the singular. Pharaoh sensed
that these were two dreams about essentially the same thing.

[8] Pharaoh told them his dreams: Here too the Hebrew
text has *chalomo*, "his dream," in the singular.

But none could interpret them for Pharaoh: "Them" is
now in the plural. Although Pharaoh had suggested to his
magicians that it was but one dream, they interpreted it as
two different dreams, which is why Pharaoh could not accept
what they were proposing.

The Midrash adds that the magicians could not interpret
Pharaoh's dreams as relevant to Egypt as a whole, and interpreted them instead as pertaining only to Pharaoh personally: "You will beget seven children, and you will be bereft
of seven children." Although the magicians were willing to
allow that much could happen to Pharaoh as an individual,
they were sure as a matter of principle that no changes could
befall Egypt and the Nile.

[14] He was rushed from the dungeon. He had his hair cut and changed his clothes, and he appeared before Pharaoh: Joseph, a prisoner languishing in a pit, is the very dregs of Egypt, unshaved and unkempt. The Torah here stresses the enormous gap between Joseph's status and that of Pharaoh, who resided in the palace just upstairs.

[16] Not I! God will see to Pharaoh's welfare: Joseph emphasizes from the outset that the interpretation of dreams comes not from him, but from God, and that his role is only to explicate to Pharaoh the Divine response.

50.3. Joseph Interprets Pharaoh's Dream (41:17-37)

יז וַיְדַבֵּר פַּרְעֹה אֶל־יוֹסֵף בַּחֲלֹמִי הִנְנִי עֹמֵד עַל־שְׂפַת הַיְאֹר: **יח** וְהִנֵּה מִן־הַיְאֹר עֹלֹת שֶׁבַע פָּרוֹת בְּרִיאוֹת בָּשָׂר וִיפֹת תֹּאַר וַתִּרְעֶינָה בָּאָחוּ: **יט** וְהִנֵּה שֶׁבַע־פָּרוֹת אֲחֵרוֹת עֹלוֹת אַחֲרֵיהֶן דַּלּוֹת וְרָעוֹת תֹּאַר מְאֹד וְרַקּוֹת בָּשָׂר לֹא־רָאִיתִי כָהֵנָּה בְּכָל־אֶרֶץ מִצְרַיִם לָרֹעַ: **כ** וַתֹּאכַלְנָה הַפָּרוֹת הָרַקּוֹת וְהָרָעוֹת אֵת שֶׁבַע הַפָּרוֹת הָרִאשֹׁנוֹת הַבְּרִיאֹת: **כא** וַתָּבֹאנָה אֶל־קִרְבֶּנָה וְלֹא נוֹדַע כִּי־בָאוּ אֶל־קִרְבֶּנָה וּמַרְאֵיהֶן רַע כַּאֲשֶׁר בַּתְּחִלָּה וָאִיקָץ: **כב** וָאֵרֶא בַּחֲלֹמִי וְהִנֵּה ׀ שֶׁבַע שִׁבֳּלִים עֹלֹת בְּקָנֶה אֶחָד מְלֵאֹת וְטֹבוֹת: **כג** וְהִנֵּה שֶׁבַע שִׁבֳּלִים צְנֻמוֹת דַּקּוֹת שְׁדֻפוֹת קָדִים צֹמְחוֹת אַחֲרֵיהֶם: **כד** וַתִּבְלַעְןָ הַשִּׁבֳּלִים הַדַּקֹּת אֵת שֶׁבַע הַשִּׁבֳּלִים הַטֹּבוֹת וָאֹמַר אֶל־הַחַרְטֻמִּים וְאֵין מַגִּיד לִי: **כה** וַיֹּאמֶר יוֹסֵף אֶל־פַּרְעֹה חֲלוֹם פַּרְעֹה אֶחָד הוּא אֵת אֲשֶׁר הָאֱלֹהִים עֹשֶׂה הִגִּיד לְפַרְעֹה: **כו** שֶׁבַע פָּרֹת הַטֹּבֹת שֶׁבַע שָׁנִים הֵנָּה וְשֶׁבַע הַשִּׁבֳּלִים הַטֹּבֹת שֶׁבַע שָׁנִים הֵנָּה חֲלוֹם אֶחָד הוּא: **כז** וְשֶׁבַע הַפָּרוֹת הָרַקּוֹת וְהָרָעֹת הָעֹלֹת אַחֲרֵיהֶן שֶׁבַע שָׁנִים הֵנָּה וְשֶׁבַע הַשִּׁבֳּלִים הָרֵקוֹת שְׁדֻפוֹת הַקָּדִים

יִהְיוּ שֶׁבַע שְׁנֵי רָעָב: **כח** הוּא הַדָּבָר אֲשֶׁר דִּבַּרְתִּי אֶל־
פַּרְעֹה אֲשֶׁר הָאֱלֹהִים עֹשֶׂה הֶרְאָה אֶת־פַּרְעֹה: **כט** הִנֵּה
שֶׁבַע שָׁנִים בָּאוֹת שָׂבָע גָּדוֹל בְּכָל־אֶרֶץ מִצְרָיִם: **ל** וְקָמוּ
שֶׁבַע שְׁנֵי רָעָב אַחֲרֵיהֶן וְנִשְׁכַּח כָּל־הַשָּׂבָע בְּאֶרֶץ מִצְרַיִם
וְכִלָּה הָרָעָב אֶת־הָאָרֶץ: **לא** וְלֹא־יִוָּדַע הַשָּׂבָע בָּאָרֶץ
מִפְּנֵי הָרָעָב הַהוּא אַחֲרֵי־כֵן כִּי־כָבֵד הוּא מְאֹד: **לב**
וְעַל הִשָּׁנוֹת הַחֲלוֹם אֶל־פַּרְעֹה פַּעֲמָיִם כִּי־נָכוֹן הַדָּבָר
מֵעִם הָאֱלֹהִים וּמְמַהֵר הָאֱלֹהִים לַעֲשֹׂתוֹ: **לג** וְעַתָּה
יֵרֶא פַרְעֹה אִישׁ נָבוֹן וְחָכָם וִישִׁיתֵהוּ עַל־אֶרֶץ מִצְרָיִם:
לד יַעֲשֶׂה פַרְעֹה וְיַפְקֵד פְּקִדִים עַל־הָאָרֶץ וְחִמֵּשׁ אֶת־
אֶרֶץ מִצְרַיִם בְּשֶׁבַע שְׁנֵי הַשָּׂבָע: **לה** וְיִקְבְּצוּ אֶת־כָּל־
אֹכֶל הַשָּׁנִים הַטֹּבוֹת הַבָּאֹת הָאֵלֶּה וְיִצְבְּרוּ־בָר תַּחַת
יַד־פַּרְעֹה אֹכֶל בֶּעָרִים וְשָׁמָרוּ: **לו** וְהָיָה הָאֹכֶל לְפִקָּדוֹן
לָאָרֶץ לְשֶׁבַע שְׁנֵי הָרָעָב אֲשֶׁר תִּהְיֶיןָ בְּאֶרֶץ מִצְרָיִם
וְלֹא־תִכָּרֵת הָאָרֶץ בָּרָעָב: **לז** וַיִּיטַב הַדָּבָר בְּעֵינֵי פַרְעֹה
וּבְעֵינֵי כָּל־עֲבָדָיו:

[17] Then Pharaoh said to Joseph, "In my dream, I was standing on the bank of the Nile,

[18] when out of the Nile came up seven sturdy and well-formed cows and grazed in the reed grass.

[19] Presently there followed them seven other cows, scrawny, ill-formed, and emaciated – never had I seen their likes for ugliness in all the land of Egypt!

[20] And the seven lean and ugly cows ate up the first seven cows, the sturdy ones;

[21] but when they had consumed them, one could not tell that they had consumed them, for they looked just as bad as before. And I awoke.

[22] In my other dream, I saw seven ears of grain, full and healthy, growing on a single stalk;

[23] but right behind them sprouted seven ears, shriveled, thin, and scorched by the east wind.

[24] And the thin ears swallowed the seven healthy ears. I have told my magicians, but none has an explanation for me."

[25] And Joseph said to Pharaoh, "Pharaoh's dreams are one and the same: God has told Pharaoh what He is about to do.

[26] The seven healthy cows are seven years, and the seven healthy ears are seven years; it is the same dream.

[27] The seven lean and ugly cows that followed are seven years, as are also the seven empty ears scorched by the east wind; they are seven years of famine.

[28] It is just as I have told Pharaoh: God has revealed to Pharaoh what He is about to do.

[29] Immediately ahead are seven years of great abundance in all the land of Egypt.

[30] After them will come seven years of famine, and all the abundance in the land of Egypt will be forgotten. As the land is ravaged by famine,

[31] no trace of the abundance will be left in the land because of the famine thereafter, for it will be very severe.

[32] As for Pharaoh having had the same dream twice, it means that the matter has been determined by God, and that God will soon carry it out.

[33] "Accordingly, let Pharaoh find a man of discernment and wisdom, and set him over the land of Egypt.

[34] And let Pharaoh take steps to appoint

overseers over the land, and organize the land
of Egypt in the seven years of plenty.
[35] Let all the food of these good years that
are coming be gathered, and let the grain be
collected under Pharaoh's authority as food to
be stored in the cities.
[36] Let that food be a reserve for the land for the
seven years of famine which will come upon the
land of Egypt, so that the land may not perish
in the famine."
[37] The plan pleased Pharaoh and all his
courtiers.

[15] And Pharaoh said to Joseph, "I have had a dream":
Unlike the Torah's description of the dream itself and the
subsequent retelling of it to the magicians (41:7-8), here Pharaoh does not express his feeling that they were two dreams
about the same thing.

**[25] And Joseph said to Pharaoh, "Pharaoh's dreams are
one and the same":** Joseph himself understands that the
two dreams are in fact just one.

Three points distinguish Joseph's interpretation of Pharaoh's dream:

**As for Pharaoh having had the same dream twice, it
means that the matter has been determined by God,
and that God will soon carry it out:** Joseph interprets both
parts of the dream as a single whole, explaining the repetition of the dream as emphasizing that it will happen soon,
and without fail.

God has revealed to Pharaoh what He is about to do: Joseph interprets the dream as pertaining to the Egyptian state, which accords with Pharaoh's inner sense of what the dream means.

Accordingly, let Pharaoh find ...: Joseph not only speaks of the impending danger, but proposes an action plan for averting it, although no one has asked him to do so. Despite the enormous disparity of status between himself and Pharaoh, Joseph does not hesitate to offer his unsolicited advice. This is a classic example of Jewish chutzpah – impudence.

50.4. Egyptian Stability and the Disturbing Influence of Dreams

Why can't the Egyptian magicians solve the riddle of Pharaoh's dream? First there is food (cows, corn), and then there is no food. Isn't Joseph's interpretation completely obvious? But we have already explained the reason that the magicians are unable to see it. From the Egyptian point of view, changes in Egypt's way of life are impossible. The Nile overflows its banks every year, providing the country with food, and this is a law of nature. Therefore, there never was nor could there ever be in Egypt anything like a famine.

From the Torah's accounts of the lives of both Abraham and Isaac (12:10, 26:1), we see that when there is famine in Canaan, Egypt always has food.

In the magicians' conception, the whole of Egypt derives its stability, constancy, and integrity from the Nile River, which reliably irrigates the country and forever provides food.

Stability is just the flip side of stagnation. But Egypt

cannot imagine itself without it. Jewish tradition calls Egypt "the land of slavery," because all its inhabitants are slaves – even Pharaoh himself is a slave to the River. Therefore, the Egyptians are not disposed to having prophetic dreams. For what is a dream, after all? It is a novelty, an ideal, a desire to achieve something impossible by breaking loose from the natural state of affairs and events. Dreams represent aspirations, the freedom to search for – and the possibility of attaining – outcomes that have not yet been considered. And who brings them to Egypt (and gradually infects with those dreams various Egyptian dignitaries, and even Pharaoh himself)? It is that restless Jew, Joseph, to whom dreams speak of change, and a call to action.

The Nile, a paragon of constancy and a decisive factor in driving Egyptian civilization, is preeminent there. In his dream, Pharaoh sees himself "standing by the Nile" (v. 1) – literally, "above the river." But in retelling his dream to Joseph, Pharaoh cannot bring himself to say the words "above the River," and says instead that in his dream he is "standing on the bank of the Nile" (41:17). Pharaoh cannot imagine man being above nature, for he is enslaved to it, like all the rest of Egyptian civilization. If in a dream Pharaoh sees himself standing above the River, this must mean that the river is not absolute, that its superior status has been undermined. In his own mind Pharaoh is afraid to admit to any such possibility, and therefore, when retelling the dream he introduces into his wording a subtle change.

50.5. Joseph is Appointed Governor of Egypt (41:38-44)

לח וַיֹּאמֶר פַּרְעֹה אֶל־עֲבָדָיו הֲנִמְצָא כָזֶה אִישׁ אֲשֶׁר רוּחַ

אֱלֹהִים בּוֹ: **לט** וַיֹּאמֶר פַּרְעֹה אֶל־יוֹסֵף אַחֲרֵי הוֹדִיעַ
אֱלֹהִים אוֹתְךָ אֶת־כָּל־זֹאת אֵין־נָבוֹן וְחָכָם כָּמוֹךָ: **מ**
אַתָּה תִּהְיֶה עַל־בֵּיתִי וְעַל־פִּיךָ יִשַּׁק כָּל־עַמִּי רַק הַכִּסֵּא
אֶגְדַּל מִמֶּךָּ: **מא** וַיֹּאמֶר פַּרְעֹה אֶל־יוֹסֵף רְאֵה נָתַתִּי אֹתְךָ
עַל כָּל־אֶרֶץ מִצְרָיִם: **מב** וַיָּסַר פַּרְעֹה אֶת־טַבַּעְתּוֹ מֵעַל
יָדוֹ וַיִּתֵּן אֹתָהּ עַל־יַד יוֹסֵף וַיַּלְבֵּשׁ אֹתוֹ בִּגְדֵי־שֵׁשׁ וַיָּשֶׂם
רְבִד הַזָּהָב עַל־צַוָּארוֹ: **מג** וַיַּרְכֵּב אֹתוֹ בְּמִרְכֶּבֶת הַמִּשְׁנֶה
אֲשֶׁר־לוֹ וַיִּקְרְאוּ לְפָנָיו אַבְרֵךְ וְנָתוֹן אֹתוֹ עַל כָּל־אֶרֶץ
מִצְרָיִם: **מד** וַיֹּאמֶר פַּרְעֹה אֶל־יוֹסֵף אֲנִי פַרְעֹה וּבִלְעָדֶיךָ
לֹא־יָרִים אִישׁ אֶת־יָדוֹ וְאֶת־רַגְלוֹ בְּכָל־אֶרֶץ מִצְרָיִם:

[38] And Pharaoh said to his courtiers, "Could
we find another like him, a man in whom is the
spirit of God?"
[39] So Pharaoh said to Joseph, "Since God has
made all this known to you, there is none so
discerning and wise as you.
[40] You shall be in charge of my court, and by
your command shall all my people be directed;
only with respect to the throne shall I be superior
to you."
[41] Pharaoh further said to Joseph, "See, I put
you in charge of all the land of Egypt."
[42] And removing his signet ring from his hand,
Pharaoh put it on Joseph's hand; and he had
him dressed in robes of fine linen, and put a gold
chain about his neck.
[43] He had him ride in the chariot of his second-
in-command, and they cried before him,
"Abrek!" Thus he placed him over all the land
of Egypt.
[44] Pharaoh said to Joseph, "I am Pharaoh; yet
without you, no one shall lift up hand or foot in

all the land of Egypt."

[39] So Pharaoh said to Joseph, "Since God has made all this known to you, there is none so discerning and wise as you: Because Joseph stresses that dreams and their interpretation come only from God, Pharaoh accepts his proposal.

[42] And removing his signet ring from his hand, Pharaoh put it on Joseph's hand; and he had him dressed in robes of fine linen, and put a gold chain about his neck: A ring and a chain with the royal insignia are symbols of power, and the right to issue decrees.

[43] Thus he placed him over all the land of Egypt: Pharaoh shows extraordinary facility for making radical and highly responsible decisions. Apparently, Pharaoh's dream made a strong impression on him – including, perhaps, those details of the dream that he did not retell even to Joseph (e.g., that he was standing "above" the River).

Joseph astonished Pharaoh not only by deciphering his dreams, but by demonstrating a profound understanding of Egypt's economic situation. Moreover, here was a man (Joseph) who, upon learning about the famine that was imminent, was neither flustered nor perturbed, but immediately suggested a detailed plan of action (notwithstanding that Joseph had only just heard the dream from Pharaoh and had had no time to ponder it and devise a plan).

Pharaoh is of course also struck by Joseph's colossal impudence. Taking it upon himself to offer unsolicited advice to Pharaoh himself was very risky, but Pharaoh senses that Joseph's plan provinces security in a situation of very real danger. And it is Pharaoh's contention that since Joseph was able to propose such a plan, then he will be able to implement it as well.

Joseph demonstrates his willingness to change the world. Pharaoh is careful care to maintain his supreme power, and transfers to Joseph only the functions of economic management. But as will become apparent from the subsequent narrative, even the most complete and intensive management of the economy alone is not enough to effect positive change in the world, although the idea of "changing the world by feeding everyone" will continue to attract and seduce the Jewish followers of Joseph for several millennia, right up to this day.

50.6. Joseph Marries Asenath, Daughter of Poti-Phera (41:45)

מה וַיִּקְרָא פַרְעֹה שֵׁם־יוֹסֵף צָפְנַת פַּעְנֵחַ וַיִּתֶּן־לוֹ אֶת־
אָסְנַת בַּת־פּוֹטִי פֶרַע כֹּהֵן אֹן לְאִשָּׁה וַיֵּצֵא יוֹסֵף עַל־
אֶרֶץ מִצְרָיִם:

[45] Pharaoh then gave Joseph the name Zaphenath-paneah; and he gave him for a wife Asenath daughter of Poti-phera, priest of On. Thus Joseph emerged in charge of the land of Egypt. –

[45] **Zaphenath-paneah:** Literally "revealer of the hidden," i.e. able to decipher that which is encoded.

And he gave him for a wife Asenath daughter of Poti-phera, priest of On: Because the priests wield immense power in Egypt and are its very soul, Joseph wants to come to a meeting of the minds with them, to effectively become one of them. He therefore takes a wife from the priestly class. But despite all his efforts, Joseph fails to change Egypt at its root.

Asenath daughter of Poti-phera: The name "Poti-phera" is rather similar to the name "Potiphar." In fact, the Midrash believes that they are one and the same person, and that Joseph's master was exalted (promoted from chief of the security to priest) because Joseph himself was exalted.

Thus, in the opinion of the Midrash, Potiphar's wife's intuition was quite correct. She sensed that through Joseph something new and important was about to happen in Egypt, and that Joseph had to achieve consanguinity with Egypt in some sense. But she was mistaken in thinking that all that was meant to happen through her (for ultimately it did happen, but only through her daughter Asenath). Thus, although she had arrived at an important and valid conclusion, Potiphar's wife proposed an immoral path for its implementation.

The lesson for us here is that if our comprehension of God's ways leads to unworthy actions, then our comprehension must be faulty. Our sense of morality and justice should intuitively keep us from making mistakes in judgment when we search for religious truths.

The Midrash adds, however, that Asenath was Potiphar's daughter by adoption only; she was actually Dinah's daughter from Dinah's rape by Shechem. (The name Asenath is usually interpreted as derived from *ason*, "accident, misfortune," in this case meaning rape.) According to the Midrash, Asenath, who as a daughter of Shechem was denigrated in the family, abandoned them and landed in Egypt, and was then subsequently adopted by the Potiphar family.

This midrash should not be taken literally, of course. Its intent is simply to connect the marriage of Joseph and the daughter of a priest of Egypt to the incident of Joseph and Potiphar's wife, and also to the story of Dinah and Shechem. We noted earlier that the tragedy of Dinah in Shechem was the outcome of Jacob's failed attempt to "unite with the finest exemplars of the non-Jewish world." According to Jacob's plan, a thirteenth tribe of Israel was to be annexed to the Jewish people through Dinah, and that tribe would serve as a bridge between the Jews and the nations of the world. But all that failed to come to fruition, because Shechem raped Dinah, instead of marrying her in the normal way.

Joseph is now trying to rectify that situation by establishing the necessary ties with the gentile world. In a certain sense, we can imagine that Ephraim, Joseph's younger son, would become that thirteenth tribe. The Prophet Hosea (7:8) says: "Ephraim is mixed among the nations." That is, through him the nations of the world will create their connection with the Jews.

Note that Joseph's Tomb, *Kever Yosef*, is located in Shechem, the same place where the rape of Dinah occurred. This underscores Joseph's intention to channel his idea of joining the non-Jewish clan to the Jewish people in a more proper direction.

50.7. Joseph Reaps a Harvest, and Begets Children (41:46-52)

מו וְיוֹסֵף בֶּן־שְׁלֹשִׁים שָׁנָה בְּעָמְדוֹ לִפְנֵי פַּרְעֹה מֶלֶךְ־מִצְרָיִם וַיֵּצֵא יוֹסֵף מִלִּפְנֵי פַרְעֹה וַיַּעֲבֹר בְּכָל־אֶרֶץ מִצְרָיִם: **מז** וַתַּעַשׂ הָאָרֶץ בְּשֶׁבַע שְׁנֵי הַשָּׂבָע לִקְמָצִים:

מח וַיִּקְבֹּץ אֶת־כָּל־אֹכֶל | שֶׁבַע שָׁנִים אֲשֶׁר הָיוּ בְּאֶרֶץ מִצְרַיִם וַיִּתֶּן־אֹכֶל בֶּעָרִים אֹכֶל שְׂדֵה־הָעִיר אֲשֶׁר סְבִיבֹתֶיהָ נָתַן בְּתוֹכָהּ: מט וַיִּצְבֹּר יוֹסֵף בָּר כְּחוֹל הַיָּם הַרְבֵּה מְאֹד עַד כִּי־חָדַל לִסְפֹּר כִּי־אֵין מִסְפָּר: נ וּלְיוֹסֵף יֻלַּד שְׁנֵי בָנִים בְּטֶרֶם תָּבוֹא שְׁנַת הָרָעָב אֲשֶׁר יָלְדָה־לּוֹ אָסְנַת בַּת־פּוֹטִי פֶרַע כֹּהֵן אוֹן: נא וַיִּקְרָא יוֹסֵף אֶת־ שֵׁם הַבְּכוֹר מְנַשֶּׁה כִּי־נַשַּׁנִי אֱלֹהִים אֶת־כָּל־עֲמָלִי וְאֵת כָּל־בֵּית אָבִי: נב וְאֵת שֵׁם הַשֵּׁנִי קָרָא אֶפְרָיִם כִּי־הִפְרַנִי אֱלֹהִים בְּאֶרֶץ עָנְיִי:

[46] Joseph was thirty years old when he entered the service of Pharaoh king of Egypt. – Leaving Pharaoh's presence, Joseph traveled through all the land of Egypt.

[47] During the seven years of plenty, the land produced in abundance.

[48] And he gathered all the grain of the seven years that the land of Egypt was enjoying, and stored the grain in the cities; he put in each city the grain of the fields around it.

[49] So Joseph collected produce in very large quantity, like the sands of the sea, until he ceased to measure it, for it could not be measured.

[50] Before the years of famine came, Joseph became the father of two sons, whom Asenath daughter of Poti-phera, priest of On, bore to him.

[51] Joseph named the first-born Manasseh, meaning, "God has made me forget completely my hardship and my parental home."

[52] And the second he named Ephraim, meaning, "God has made me fertile in the land of my affliction."

[46] Joseph was thirty years old when he entered the service of Pharaoh king of Egypt: The chronology of Joseph's biography is as follows. At seventeen he was sold into slavery (37:2 ff.). He then spent a year with Potiphar, and at eighteen years of age he was thrown in prison. Joseph languished in prison for ten more years until he deciphered the dreams of Pharaoh's cupbearer and baker. And now, "after two years' time" (41:1), Joseph is thirty years old.

[47] During the seven years of plenty, the land produced in abundance. [48] And he gathered all the grain of the seven years that the land of Egypt was enjoying: It seems that a very plentiful harvest allowed Joseph to collect "*all* the grain," that is, far more than that fifth of the crop (41:34, alternate translation) of which he had originally spoken to Pharaoh.

He put in each city the grain of the fields around it: The Midrash believes that creating a warehouse near each place where grain grew facilitated the preservation of that grain, and sees in this concept evidence of Joseph's exceptional managerial abilities.

[49] So Joseph collected produce in very large quantity, like the sands of the sea: Besides having almost unlimited power, Joseph was given vast material resources for implementing an ongoing program of radical economic reorganization in Egypt.

[50] Before the years of famine came, Joseph became the father of two sons: Joseph's sons are born against this backdrop of abundance, and he perceives this as a significant aspect of his success.

[51] Manasseh, meaning, "God has made me forget completely my hardship and my parental home." [52] ... Ephraim, meaning, "God has made me fertile in the land of my affliction": In these names we see Joseph's desire to distance himself psychologically from his entire past. A very similar propensity is often observed among the Jews of the *galut* (Diaspora) at the height of their success.

The name Manasseh is formed from the root "N-Sh-H" "to relegate to oblivion," "to forget." By giving his son this name Joseph seems to proclaim, "How wonderful it is that I have been able to abandon my father's house and put all that behind me." In this way, he shows his deep resentment towards the abandoned family – for he says, "God has made me forget completely my hardship and my parental home," and not just "God has made me forget completely the hardship of my parental home."

Joseph calls the second son Ephraim, from "P-R-H," "to be fruitful," because "God has made me fertile in the land of my affliction." That is, "I left my father and my family, and although I experienced suffering along the way, in my life I am now totally successful, productive, and fulfilled."

50.8. Why Did Joseph Not Make Contact with His Father?

And yet, why does Joseph not make contact with his family, and inform his father of his whereabouts? Is it because of a feeling of resentment, perhaps? At first, while he was a slave or languishing in prison, Joseph might have been unable to do that. But he later ruled Egypt for seven whole years. Why did Joseph during all this time not bother to send his father a message to say that he was alive and well?

There are two different answers to this question. The first, suggested by Nachmanides, is that Joseph all this time remembered his dreams, and understood that his sudden promotion to power in Egypt could not be accidental. Joseph was therefore certain that the rest of his dreams would also come true, and that the brothers would eventually arrive. But he felt that there was no need to say anything in advance. Upon the brothers' arrival, he would undertake to reeducate them.

Indeed, as we shall see in due course, had Joseph notified his family that he was alive, he could not have had the same influence on his brothers as he ultimately did. Nachmanides believes that Joseph sought his brothers' remorse and correction, and their subsequent participation in the Egyptian reorganization. In order to accomplish that, he had to reveal himself only when he did, and no sooner.

But an alternate answer suggests that Joseph had no interest in communicating with his father, and he really did intend to break his connection with his family, because he considered even his father complicit in the brothers' actions. Joseph was at that time just a naive seventeen-year-old lad. Didn't his father understand that sending Joseph to his brothers was a bad idea? Or perhaps his father was even a willing participant in the conspiracy against him?

According to this view, reeducating his brothers was not a part of Joseph's plan at all; he only wanted to wrest Benjamin away from them, for fear that the the brothers would try to destroy Benjamin too. The underlying premise of this approach is that Joseph, who had forgotten the dreams of his youth, was not expecting his brothers to arrive in Egypt at all, and remembered the dreams only when the brothers did actually arrive in Egypt (42:9). Given that, Joseph's meeting with the brothers contributed not only to their correction, but to Joseph's as well.

We need not consider these two approaches mutually exclusive. It is possible that the second motive was Joseph's state of mind at a conscious level, while the first motive was present only subconsciously.

50.9. Famine in Egypt, and How Joseph Addresses It (41:53-57)

נג וַתִּכְלֶינָה שֶׁבַע שְׁנֵי הַשָּׂבָע אֲשֶׁר הָיָה בְּאֶרֶץ מִצְרָיִם: **נד** וַתְּחִלֶּינָה שֶׁבַע שְׁנֵי הָרָעָב לָבוֹא כַּאֲשֶׁר אָמַר יוֹסֵף וַיְהִי רָעָב בְּכָל־הָאֲרָצוֹת וּבְכָל־אֶרֶץ מִצְרַיִם הָיָה לָחֶם: **נה** וַתִּרְעַב כָּל־אֶרֶץ מִצְרַיִם וַיִּצְעַק הָעָם אֶל־פַּרְעֹה לַלָּחֶם וַיֹּאמֶר פַּרְעֹה לְכָל־מִצְרַיִם לְכוּ אֶל־יוֹסֵף אֲשֶׁר־יֹאמַר לָכֶם תַּעֲשׂוּ: **נו** וְהָרָעָב הָיָה עַל כָּל־פְּנֵי הָאָרֶץ וַיִּפְתַּח יוֹסֵף אֶת־כָּל־אֲשֶׁר בָּהֶם וַיִּשְׁבֹּר לְמִצְרַיִם וַיֶּחֱזַק הָרָעָב בְּאֶרֶץ מִצְרָיִם: **נז** וְכָל־הָאָרֶץ בָּאוּ מִצְרַיְמָה לִשְׁבֹּר אֶל־יוֹסֵף כִּי־חָזַק הָרָעָב בְּכָל־הָאָרֶץ:

[53] The seven years of abundance that the land of Egypt enjoyed came to an end,
[54] and the seven years of famine set in, just as Joseph had foretold. There was famine in all lands, but throughout the land of Egypt there was bread.
[55] And when all the land of Egypt felt the hunger, the people cried out to Pharaoh for bread; and Pharaoh said to all the Egyptians, "Go to Joseph; whatever he tells you, you shall do." –
[56] Accordingly, when the famine became severe in the land of Egypt, Joseph laid open all that was

within, and rationed out grain to the Egyptians.
The famine, however, spread over the whole
world.
[57] So all the world came to Joseph in Egypt
to procure rations, for the famine had become
severe throughout the world.

[54] There was famine in all lands, but throughout the land of Egypt there was bread: Reading the text superficially, we have before us a simple story about how the Egyptians were saved from starvation. The Midrash, however, sees in this narrative a second, deeper layer: Joseph's attempt to turn the Egyptians into a chosen people.

[55] Pharaoh said to all the Egyptians, "Go to Joseph; whatever he tells you, you shall do": The Midrash adds that in addition to selling bread, Joseph ordered the Egyptians who came to him to be circumcised. But they would not agree and returned to Pharaoh, who asked them, "If you do not want to obey Joseph, then why did you not prepare food supplies of your own, since you knew that there would be a famine?" To this the Egyptians replied that they had in fact stockpiled foodstuffs, but everything they had prepared had by now decayed. Pharaoh then ordered them to abide by Joseph's instructions.

The meaning of this Midrash (which of course we need not understand literally) is that Joseph's intent was to turn the Egyptians into a chosen people by having them undergo circumcision, which is the sign of chosenness, the covenant of Abraham.

[56] Joseph laid open all that was within, and rationed out grain to the Egyptians. The famine, however, spread over

the whole world: The Midrash interprets the words "Joseph laid open all that was within" as referring to the Egyptians themselves. Joseph wants to uncover something hidden within their souls, to reveal to them the meaning of their own spiritual aspirations. By leveraging the fact that he is saving the Egyptians from hunger, Joseph wants to force them to accept the concept of chosenness and to acknowledge their mission. It then becomes clear that what immediately follows, "The famine, however, spread over all the land") refers not only to famine in the literal sense, but to the spiritual hunger that has swept Egypt. When a person discovers spiritual food that he has never tried before, his hunger for it intensifies. And this is what happened in Egypt.

[57] So all the world came to Joseph in Egypt to procure rations: It seems that at this stage Joseph had achieved tremendous success in both economic and spiritual spheres.

Of course, all this is only a midrash. But the picture it paints demonstrates a situation that is very common among the Jews of the Diaspora, who come to regard the country where they are living as a new "light to the nations of the world." In the mid-19th century Rabbi Samson Raphael Hirsch saw Germany in just that light, as did the Jewish Communists of Soviet Russia in the 1920's.

The idea that Jews do not need to build their own separate national state at all recapitulates the approach adopted by Abraham, who, after marrying Hagar, resolved that through his close connection with Egypt he would influence the world. Even today we often hear certain American Jews saying that their ability to influence the world from the United States is far greater than any Jewish influence from Israel – by which they mean to say that all Jews should try to move to America, rather than wasting their energy building up tiny

Israel. Only when that kind of position crashes and burns (which is exactly what Joseph himself experienced in the end), will its supporters gradually begin to see the fallacy and futility of their approach, and will adopt instead the principle of *Mashiach ben Yosef*, whose essence is likewise material success – but only in the Land of Israel and with the Land of Israel.

Chapter 51

Joseph Induces His Brothers
to Repent

51.1. Joseph's Brothers Arrive in Egypt (42:1-9)

א וַיַּרְא יַעֲקֹב כִּי יֶשׁ־שֶׁבֶר בְּמִצְרָיִם וַיֹּאמֶר יַעֲקֹב
לְבָנָיו לָמָּה תִּתְרָאוּ: ב וַיֹּאמֶר הִנֵּה שָׁמַעְתִּי כִּי יֶשׁ־
שֶׁבֶר בְּמִצְרָיִם רְדוּ־שָׁמָּה וְשִׁבְרוּ־לָנוּ מִשָּׁם וְנִחְיֶה וְלֹא
נָמוּת: ג וַיֵּרְדוּ אֲחֵי־יוֹסֵף עֲשָׂרָה לִשְׁבֹּר בָּר מִמִּצְרָיִם:
ד וְאֶת־בִּנְיָמִין אֲחִי יוֹסֵף לֹא־שָׁלַח יַעֲקֹב אֶת־אֶחָיו
כִּי אָמַר פֶּן־יִקְרָאֶנּוּ אָסוֹן: ה וַיָּבֹאוּ בְּנֵי יִשְׂרָאֵל לִשְׁבֹּר
בְּתוֹךְ הַבָּאִים כִּי־הָיָה הָרָעָב בְּאֶרֶץ כְּנָעַן: ו וְיוֹסֵף הוּא
הַשַּׁלִּיט עַל־הָאָרֶץ הוּא הַמַּשְׁבִּיר לְכָל־עַם הָאָרֶץ וַיָּבֹאוּ
אֲחֵי יוֹסֵף וַיִּשְׁתַּחֲווּ־לוֹ אַפַּיִם אָרְצָה: ז וַיַּרְא יוֹסֵף אֶת־
אֶחָיו וַיַּכִּרֵם וַיִּתְנַכֵּר אֲלֵיהֶם וַיְדַבֵּר אִתָּם קָשׁוֹת וַיֹּאמֶר
אֲלֵהֶם מֵאַיִן בָּאתֶם וַיֹּאמְרוּ מֵאֶרֶץ כְּנַעַן לִשְׁבָּר־אֹכֶל:
ח וַיַּכֵּר יוֹסֵף אֶת־אֶחָיו וְהֵם לֹא הִכִּרֻהוּ: ט וַיִּזְכֹּר יוֹסֵף
אֵת הַחֲלֹמוֹת אֲשֶׁר חָלַם לָהֶם ...

*[1] When Jacob saw that there were food rations
to be had in Egypt, he said to his sons, "Why do
you keep looking at one another?*

[2] Now I hear," he went on, "that there are rations to be had in Egypt. Go down and procure rations for us there, that we may live and not die."

[3] So ten of Joseph's brothers went down to get grain rations in Egypt;

[4] for Jacob did not send Joseph's brother Benjamin with his brothers, since he feared that he might meet with disaster.

[5] Thus the sons of Israel were among those who came to procure rations, for the famine extended to the land of Canaan.

[6] Now Joseph was the vizier of the land; it was he who dispensed rations to all the people of the land. And Joseph's brothers came and bowed low to him, with their faces to the ground.

[7] When Joseph saw his brothers, he recognized them; but he acted like a stranger toward them and spoke harshly to them. He asked them, "Where do you come from?" And they said, "From the land of Canaan, to procure food."

[8] For though Joseph recognized his brothers, they did not recognize him.

[9] Recalling the dreams that he had dreamed about them ...

[1] Jacob saw that there were food rations to be had in Egypt: The Torah here uses not one of the more usual terms, *lechem* ("bread") or *ochel* ("food"), but the rather rare word *shever*, which means not only "rations," but also "shattering, breaking." Jacob sees that something is breaking in Egypt – a crisis is taking place. But any crisis is also a potential for advancement, and it is only natural that Jacob and his family would be involved in it.

[3] So ten of Joseph's brothers went down to get grain rations in Egypt: Jacob's sons have come down to Egypt as "Joseph brothers" specifically, an indication of their openness to repentance and correction.

[7] When Joseph saw his brothers, he recognized them ... [8] ... Joseph recognized his brothers: Verses 7 and 8 seem to say the same thing twice, which should be understood as emphasizing an especial kind of recognition. Joseph not only recognized them, but actively acknowledged them by treating them as brothers. And that is why he embarks immediately on implementing his plan for their reeducation.

[9] Recalling the dreams that he had dreamed about them: We have already mentioned earlier the two points of view on Joseph's behavior. Did he wish to forget about his family completely, and he therefore forgot about his dreams too, or was he just waiting for his brothers to arrive, so he could undertake correcting them? In the latter case, Joseph's "recalling the dreams that he had dreamed" does not mean that he had already forgotten them, but only that those dreams now dictated to him the necessary plan of action.

A person who has a dream need not attempt on his own to bring about its realization. And therefore, we should not imagine that Joseph's goal in behaving as he did was the realization of his dreams. More likely, because Joseph sensed that his dreams were a Divine suggestion to him as to how he could achieve the correction of his brothers, he constructed a plan of action based on those dreams.

In his original dream Joseph had seen eleven brothers

bowing to him, but now only ten stand before him. One brother (Benjamin) is missing. And this means that as the first order of the day Joseph must demand that all eleven brothers return to him together. But Joseph, as already noted, might also be worried about Benjamin's fate: Have the brothers perhaps now abused Benjamin too, Rachel's younger son and Joseph's little brother?

Even if Joseph had at some point wanted to forget his father's house and his brothers, he can no longer afford to do so. His anxiety about Benjamin forces him to keep the conversation going. Thus, Benjamin represents the point at which Joseph's plan (if he wished to forget about his family) breaks down. Joseph cannot separate from his father's house and live apart in Egypt while his younger brother still remains with Leah's sons. It is Benjamin who inextricably links Joseph with his brothers, and it is he who therefore later becomes the subject of Joseph's conflict with Judah.

Benjamin is the "up-and-coming generation," the future, and the leaders are therefore always vying to influence him, each one trying to win over Benjamin to his side. The Torah emphasizes (44:30) that Jacob's soul – i.e., the nation as a whole – is inextricably linked with the soul of Benjamin, which means that where Benjamin goes, the entire Jewish nation goes too.

Benjamin is the only one of Jacob's sons born in the Land of Israel. The struggle for him is a struggle for the Land of Israel itself and the future of the nation within it. It is no coincidence that after the split of the Kingdom of Israel into the Northern and Southern Kingdoms, after Benjamin had gone with Judah the other ten northern tribes disappeared completely, and all later Jewish history became the history of Judah.

Because Joseph cannot abandon Benjamin, he is forced

to remember his dreams and focus on them, in order to discover a means of correcting his brothers.

51.2. "You Have Come to See the Land in Its Nakedness." (42:9-12)

ט ... וַיֹּאמֶר אֲלֵהֶם מְרַגְּלִים אַתֶּם לִרְאוֹת אֶת־עֶרְוַת
הָאָרֶץ בָּאתֶם: י וַיֹּאמְרוּ אֵלָיו לֹא אֲדֹנִי וַעֲבָדֶיךָ בָּאוּ
לִשְׁבָּר־אֹכֶל: יא כֻּלָּנוּ בְּנֵי אִישׁ־אֶחָד נָחְנוּ כֵּנִים אֲנַחְנוּ
לֹא־הָיוּ עֲבָדֶיךָ מְרַגְּלִים: יב וַיֹּאמֶר אֲלֵהֶם לֹא כִּי־עֶרְוַת
הָאָרֶץ בָּאתֶם לִרְאוֹת:

[9] ... Joseph said to them, "You are spies, you have come to see the land in its nakedness."
[10] But they said to him, "No, my lord! Truly, your servants have come to procure food.
[11] We are all of us sons of the same man; we are honest men; your servants have never been spies!"
[12] And he said to them, "No, you have come to see the land in its nakedness!"

[9] ... Joseph said to them, "You are spies, you have come to see the land in its nakedness": The Midrash believes that apart from the immediate sense (i.e., it is an excuse to detain the brothers on charges of intent to reveal the military vulnerabilities of the land), this talk of "nakedness" also carries within it a hidden prophetic subtext. It is the brothers' destiny to see Egypt as the "mother" who will give birth to the future Jewish people. Thus, the word *ervah*, "nudity" – evoking the thought of sexual nudity – is used here.

We spoke earlier of the idea that the Jewish people can be seen as a pan-national personality, whose birth and life are patterned after human birth and the various other phases and events of life that humans experience as individuals.

In this manner, Jacob's departure with his family from Babylon, and their later arrival in Egypt, are the nation's "conception" (in which Babylon is the father of the Jewish people, and Egypt is their mother).

The nation then grows and takes form under Egyptian slavery, "inside" the Egyptian national organism. This symbolizes pregnancy.

Then come the Ten Plagues, which are the labor pains. The water breaks (a portion of the sea splits) and the Jewish people are born just as they are leaving Egypt.

The child grows up and is sent to school – on Mount Sinai, to receive the Torah.

He comes of age and marries his beloved bride, the Land of Israel. (The marriage is realized in the form of a Jewish state in the Holy Land.)

And from this marriage the Messiah is born, the king of the Jewish state, who carries the Messianic light for the benefit of all mankind.

Thus, the hinting in the Torah text here to Egypt's female sexual nudity is hardly accidental. When Joseph's words are understood in this sense, their meaning is completely different. Joseph makes a prophetic proclamation to his brothers that resettling the entire family in Egypt will render Egypt fertile, such that the brothers have really come to "see the land in its nakedness," because the time has come for "conception," which will in turn pave the way for "birth," i.e., the Exodus.

Even Joseph himself is of course not aware that his words convey this meaning. But unconsciously imprisoned within

Joseph is *Mashiach ben Yosef*, who, besides seeing current events in their immediate context, sees also their Messianic implications, and it is from him that this subtext emanates.

51.3. Joseph Releases the Brothers but Demands That They Bring Benjamin (42:13-28)

יג וַיֹּאמְרוּ שְׁנֵים עָשָׂר עֲבָדֶיךָ אַחִים | אֲנַחְנוּ בְּנֵי אִישׁ־אֶחָד בְּאֶרֶץ כְּנָעַן וְהִנֵּה הַקָּטֹן אֶת־אָבִינוּ הַיּוֹם וְהָאֶחָד אֵינֶנּוּ: **יד** וַיֹּאמֶר אֲלֵהֶם יוֹסֵף הוּא אֲשֶׁר דִּבַּרְתִּי אֲלֵכֶם לֵאמֹר מְרַגְּלִים אַתֶּם: **טו** בְּזֹאת תִּבָּחֵנוּ חֵי פַרְעֹה אִם־תֵּצְאוּ מִזֶּה כִּי אִם־בְּבוֹא אֲחִיכֶם הַקָּטֹן הֵנָּה: **טז** שִׁלְחוּ מִכֶּם אֶחָד וְיִקַּח אֶת־אֲחִיכֶם וְאַתֶּם הֵאָסְרוּ וְיִבָּחֲנוּ דִּבְרֵיכֶם הַאֱמֶת אִתְּכֶם וְאִם־לֹא חֵי פַרְעֹה כִּי מְרַגְּלִים אַתֶּם: **יז** וַיֶּאֱסֹף אֹתָם אֶל־מִשְׁמָר שְׁלֹשֶׁת יָמִים: **יח** וַיֹּאמֶר אֲלֵהֶם יוֹסֵף בַּיּוֹם הַשְּׁלִישִׁי זֹאת עֲשׂוּ וִחְיוּ אֶת־הָאֱלֹהִים אֲנִי יָרֵא: **יט** אִם־כֵּנִים אַתֶּם אֲחִיכֶם אֶחָד יֵאָסֵר בְּבֵית מִשְׁמַרְכֶם וְאַתֶּם לְכוּ הָבִיאוּ שֶׁבֶר רַעֲבוֹן בָּתֵּיכֶם: **כ** וְאֶת־אֲחִיכֶם הַקָּטֹן תָּבִיאוּ אֵלַי וְיֵאָמְנוּ דִבְרֵיכֶם וְלֹא תָמוּתוּ וַיַּעֲשׂוּ־כֵן: **כא** וַיֹּאמְרוּ אִישׁ אֶל־אָחִיו אֲבָל אֲשֵׁמִים | אֲנַחְנוּ עַל־אָחִינוּ אֲשֶׁר רָאִינוּ צָרַת נַפְשׁוֹ בְּהִתְחַנְנוֹ אֵלֵינוּ וְלֹא שָׁמָעְנוּ עַל־כֵּן בָּאָה אֵלֵינוּ הַצָּרָה הַזֹּאת: **כב** וַיַּעַן רְאוּבֵן אֹתָם לֵאמֹר הֲלוֹא אָמַרְתִּי אֲלֵיכֶם | לֵאמֹר אַל־תֶּחֶטְאוּ בַיֶּלֶד וְלֹא שְׁמַעְתֶּם וְגַם־דָּמוֹ הִנֵּה נִדְרָשׁ: **כג** וְהֵם לֹא יָדְעוּ כִּי שֹׁמֵעַ יוֹסֵף כִּי הַמֵּלִיץ בֵּינֹתָם: **כד** וַיִּסֹּב מֵעֲלֵיהֶם וַיֵּבְךְּ וַיָּשָׁב אֲלֵהֶם וַיְדַבֵּר אֲלֵהֶם וַיִּקַּח מֵאִתָּם אֶת־שִׁמְעוֹן וַיֶּאֱסֹר אֹתוֹ לְעֵינֵיהֶם: **כה** וַיְצַו יוֹסֵף וַיְמַלְאוּ אֶת־כְּלֵיהֶם בָּר וּלְהָשִׁיב כַּסְפֵּיהֶם אִישׁ אֶל־שַׂקּוֹ וְלָתֵת לָהֶם צֵדָה לַדָּרֶךְ וַיַּעַשׂ לָהֶם כֵּן: **כו** וַיִּשְׂאוּ אֶת־שִׁבְרָם עַל־חֲמֹרֵיהֶם וַיֵּלְכוּ מִשָּׁם: **כז** וַיִּפְתַּח הָאֶחָד אֶת־שַׂקּוֹ לָתֵת מִסְפּוֹא לַחֲמֹרוֹ בַּמָּלוֹן וַיַּרְא אֶת־כַּסְפּוֹ וְהִנֵּה־הוּא בְּפִי אַמְתַּחְתּוֹ: **כח**

וַיֹּאמֶר אֶל־אֶחָיו הוּשַׁב כַּסְפִּי וְגַם הִנֵּה בְאַמְתַּחְתִּי
וַיֵּצֵא לִבָּם וַיֶּחֶרְדוּ אִישׁ אֶל־אָחִיו לֵאמֹר מַה־זֹּאת עָשָׂה
אֱלֹהִים לָנוּ:

[13] And they replied, "We your servants were twelve brothers, sons of a certain man in the land of Canaan; the youngest, however, is now with our father, and one is no more."

[14] But Joseph said to them, "It is just as I have told you: You are spies!

[15] By this you shall be put to the test: unless your youngest brother comes here, by Pharaoh, you shall not depart from this place!

[16] Let one of you go and bring your brother, while the rest of you remain confined, that your words may be put to the test whether there is truth in you. Else, by Pharaoh, you are nothing but spies!"

[17] And he confined them in the guardhouse for three days.

[18] On the third day Joseph said to them, "Do this and you shall live, for I am a God-fearing man.

[19] If you are honest men, let one of you brothers be held in your place of detention, while the rest of you go and take home rations for your starving households;

[20] but you must bring me your youngest brother, that your words may be verified and that you may not die." And they did accordingly.

[21] They said to one another, "Alas, we are being punished on account of our brother, because we looked on at his anguish, yet paid no heed as he

pleaded with us. That is why this distress has come upon us."

[22] Then Reuben spoke up and said to them, "Did I not tell you, 'Do no wrong to the boy'? But you paid no heed. Now comes the reckoning for his blood."

[23] They did not know that Joseph understood, for there was an interpreter between him and them.

[24] He turned away from them and wept. But he came back to them and spoke to them; and he took Simeon from among them and had him bound before their eyes.

[25] Then Joseph gave orders to fill their bags with grain, return each one's money to his sack, and give them provisions for the journey; and this was done for them.

[26] So they loaded their asses with the rations and departed from there.

[27] As one of them was opening his sack to give feed to his donkey at the night encampment, he saw his money right there at the mouth of his bag.

[28] And he said to his brothers, "My money has been returned! It is here in my bag!" Their hearts sank; and, trembling, they turned to one another, saying, "What is this that God has done to us?"

[16] By Pharaoh, you are nothing but spies!": Joseph first puts the brothers under arrest, and swearing upon Pharaoh's life, he accuses them of espionage.

[18] On the third day Joseph said to them, "Do this and you shall live, for I am a God-fearing man: After three days Joseph changes his point of view, declaring, "I am a God-fearing man," and releases all but one of the brothers, on the condition that they will bring the youngest brother with them on their next trip.

With this change of position, Joseph, as part of his brothers' reeducation, wants to show them that one's attitude towards others is very dependent on what he considers life's central value to be.

If the primary value is, as in the Egyptian system, Egypt's security (hence, "by Pharaoh," i.e., "I swear by the life of Pharaoh"), then to Joseph, who is responsible for the security of the Egyptian state, no one is above suspicion. And since there are grounds to fear that the brothers are indeed spies, the most prudent course of action is to proactively arrest them.

But if, on the other hand, one's value system is based on fear of God, presumption of innocence is of paramount importance: all persons are considered innocent until proven guilty.

Thus, in the first instance, when addressing his brothers Joseph formulates the "presumption of guilt" and the accusation: "Unless your youngest brother comes here, by Pharaoh, you shall not depart from this place!" But in the second instance, it is about his intention to confirm his brothers' innocence: "If you are honest men, let one of you brothers..."

This lesson that Joseph wants to communicate to his brothers is a reflection of their own wrongful attitude toward Joseph. The brothers had an actual basis for suspecting that Joseph was trying to become their father's sole heir by expelling them from the family. But what should guide them more cogently in deciding which course of action to take? The fact that there are suspicions, and Joseph therefore needs to be killed or sold? Or the fact that, despite any suspicions, there is always a presumption of innocence, and they must therefore undertake no hostile action until Joseph's guilt is proven?

[21] They said to one another, "Alas, we are being punished on account of our brother": Joseph's lesson to the brothers has the desired effect, and immediately after hearing him say, "I am a God-fearing man" they confess their guilt. This recognition becomes the beginning of their repentance.

That is why this distress has come upon us: The brothers are coming to understand that their misfortune is a consequence of having sold Joseph.

[23] They did not know that Joseph understood, for there was an interpreter between him and them: According to Tradition, this interpreter was Manasseh, Joseph's eldest son.

[24] He turned away from them and wept: Joseph's tears demonstrate how difficult it is for him to play the role he has taken upon himself. Because Joseph loves his brothers, he is motivated strictly by his desire to correct them, in order to restore family unity.

And he took Simeon from among them: As previously mentioned, the Midrash believes that it was Simon (together with Levi) who first proposed that Joseph be killed.

And had him bound before their eyes: The words "before their eyes" seem superfluous. The Midrash therefore believes that Joseph's intent in detaining Simon was only, through the arrest, to intensify the total effect of his message in the eyes of the brothers. After their departure, Simon will be immediately freed.

[25] Then Joseph gave orders to fill their bags with grain, return each one's money to his sack: Joseph puts money in the brothers' bags as a lesson for them to respect the presumption of innocence even in a situation where there is much circumstantial evidence arguing in favor of a person's guilt. On the way home the brothers find their money in their bags, forcing them once again to relive their feelings of guilt over how they had treated Joseph.

[28] Their hearts sank; and, trembling, they turned to one another, saying, "What is this that God has done to us?": The brothers' anguish helps them to understand that what is happening to them is the will of Higher Providence, and not merely a simple chain of coincidences.

Jewish tradition distinguishes four stages of *teshuvah*, the process of repentance, namely: Acknowledging one's mistakes (the brothers have already done this); experiencing the emotional turmoil of being wrong (this is happening now, at the moment that the brothers find the money in their bags); correcting the actual consequences of one's wrongful actions; and avoiding any similar misconduct in the future (the brothers will undergo this final stage of repentance at a later time). Thus, Joseph leads his brothers through each successive stage of *teshuvah* in order that their repentance will be complete and enduring.

51.4. The Brothers Return to Their Father in Canaan (42:29-38)

כט וַיָּבֹאוּ אֶל־יַעֲקֹב אֲבִיהֶם אַרְצָה כְּנָעַן וַיַּגִּידוּ לוֹ אֵת
כָּל־הַקֹּרֹת אֹתָם לֵאמֹר: ל דִּבֶּר הָאִישׁ אֲדֹנֵי הָאָרֶץ אִתָּנוּ
קָשׁוֹת וַיִּתֵּן אֹתָנוּ כִּמְרַגְּלִים אֶת־הָאָרֶץ: לא וַנֹּאמֶר

אֵלָיו כֵּנִים אֲנָחְנוּ לֹא הָיִינוּ מְרַגְּלִים: **לב** שְׁנֵים־עָשָׂר
אֲנַחְנוּ אַחִים בְּנֵי אָבִינוּ הָאֶחָד אֵינֶנּוּ וְהַקָּטֹן הַיּוֹם
אֶת־אָבִינוּ בְּאֶרֶץ כְּנָעַן: **לג** וַיֹּאמֶר אֵלֵינוּ הָאִישׁ אֲדֹנֵי
הָאָרֶץ בְּזֹאת אֵדַע כִּי כֵנִים אַתֶּם אֲחִיכֶם הָאֶחָד הַנִּיחוּ
אִתִּי וְאֶת־רַעֲבוֹן בָּתֵּיכֶם קְחוּ וָלֵכוּ: **לד** וְהָבִיאוּ אֶת־
אֲחִיכֶם הַקָּטֹן אֵלַי וְאֵדְעָה כִּי לֹא מְרַגְּלִים אַתֶּם כִּי
כֵנִים אַתֶּם אֶת־אֲחִיכֶם אֶתֵּן לָכֶם וְאֶת־הָאָרֶץ תִּסְחָרוּ:
לה וַיְהִי הֵם מְרִיקִים שַׂקֵּיהֶם וְהִנֵּה־אִישׁ צְרוֹר־כַּסְפּוֹ
בְּשַׂקּוֹ וַיִּרְאוּ אֶת־צְרֹרוֹת כַּסְפֵּיהֶם הֵמָּה וַאֲבִיהֶם
וַיִּירָאוּ: **לו** וַיֹּאמֶר אֲלֵהֶם יַעֲקֹב אֲבִיהֶם אֹתִי שִׁכַּלְתֶּם
יוֹסֵף אֵינֶנּוּ וְשִׁמְעוֹן אֵינֶנּוּ וְאֶת־בִּנְיָמִן תִּקָּחוּ עָלַי הָיוּ
כֻלָּנָה: **לז** וַיֹּאמֶר רְאוּבֵן אֶל־אָבִיו לֵאמֹר אֶת־שְׁנֵי בָנַי
תָּמִית אִם־לֹא אֲבִיאֶנּוּ אֵלֶיךָ תְּנָה אֹתוֹ עַל־יָדִי וַאֲנִי
אֲשִׁיבֶנּוּ אֵלֶיךָ: **לח** וַיֹּאמֶר לֹא־יֵרֵד בְּנִי עִמָּכֶם כִּי־אָחִיו
מֵת וְהוּא לְבַדּוֹ נִשְׁאָר וּקְרָאָהוּ אָסוֹן בַּדֶּרֶךְ אֲשֶׁר תֵּלְכוּ־
בָהּ וְהוֹרַדְתֶּם אֶת־שֵׂיבָתִי בְּיָגוֹן שְׁאוֹלָה:

[29] *When they came to their father Jacob in
the land of Canaan, they told him all that had
befallen them, saying,*
[30] *"The man who is lord of the land spoke harshly
to us and accused us of spying on the land.*
[31] *We said to him, 'We are honest men; we have
never been spies!*
[32] *There were twelve of us brothers, sons by
the same father; but one is no more, and the
youngest is now with our father in the land of
Canaan.'*
[33] *But the man who is lord of the land said
to us, 'By this I shall know that you are honest
men: leave one of your brothers with me, and
take something for your starving households
and be off.*

[34] And bring your youngest brother to me, that I may know that you are not spies but honest men. I will then restore your brother to you, and you shall be free to move about in the land.'"

[35] As they were emptying their sacks, there, in each one's sack, was his money-bag! When they and their father saw their money-bags, they were dismayed.

[36] Their father Jacob said to them, "It is always me that you bereave: Joseph is no more and Simeon is no more, and now you would take away Benjamin. These things always happen to me!"

[37] Then Reuben said to his father, "You may kill my two sons if I do not bring him back to you. Put him in my care, and I will return him to you."

[38] But he said, "My son must not go down with you, for his brother is dead and he alone is left. If he meets with disaster on the journey you are taking, you will send my white head down to Sheol in grief."

[30] The man who is lord of the land spoke harshly to us and accused us of spying on the land: In retelling the events, the brothers do not report their initial arrest, and they also change certain other details, choosing to emphasize the possibility of positive developments in the future.

[35] When they and their father saw their money-bags, they were dismayed: What can Jacob be thinking? All the brothers have returned but one. In their bags they have bread, but their money is untouched. Conclusion: they have sold Simon.

After avoiding suspicion for having in fact sold Joseph, the brothers are now suspected of a sale that never happened, and of which they are completely innocent.

[36] It is always me that you bereave: Joseph is no more and Simeon is no more, and now you would take away Benjamin: Jacob does not accuse his sons outright of selling Simon, but he seems to entertain the thought, which only reinforces his reluctance to send Benjamin with them the next time around. If they had no qualms about selling Simon, what would prevent them from selling Benjamin too? Thus, after finding their money restored to their bags the brothers are now in a much more difficult position with respect to their father.

[37] Then Reuben said to his father, "You may kill my two sons if I do not bring him back to you": The Midrash emphasizes that Reuben's proposal that he kill Jacob's own grandchildren seems completely preposterous. Reuben is human to the core. He is motivated always by the best of intentions, and he wants to do well for everyone. But because he is not able to see himself from the outside, he is constantly engaged in stupidities and absurdities.

[38] But he said, "My son must not go down with you, for his brother is dead and he alone is left": Jacob does not even bother to address Reuben's proposal. He just stresses Benjamin's special status among the brothers, which only further complicates their decision-making.

51.5. Judah's Leadership Begins (43:1-14)

א וְהָרָעָב כָּבֵד בָּאָרֶץ: ב וַיְהִי כַּאֲשֶׁר כִּלּוּ לֶאֱכֹל אֶת־הַשֶּׁבֶר אֲשֶׁר הֵבִיאוּ מִמִּצְרָיִם וַיֹּאמֶר אֲלֵיהֶם אֲבִיהֶם

שֻׁבוּ שִׁבְרוּ־לָנוּ מְעַט־אֹכֶל: **ג** וַיֹּאמֶר אֵלָיו יְהוּדָה
לֵאמֹר הָעֵד הֵעִד בָּנוּ הָאִישׁ לֵאמֹר לֹא־תִרְאוּ פָנַי בִּלְתִּי
אֲחִיכֶם אִתְּכֶם: **ד** אִם־יֶשְׁךָ מְשַׁלֵּחַ אֶת־אָחִינוּ אִתָּנוּ
נֵרְדָה וְנִשְׁבְּרָה לְךָ אֹכֶל: **ה** וְאִם־אֵינְךָ מְשַׁלֵּחַ לֹא נֵרֵד
כִּי־הָאִישׁ אָמַר אֵלֵינוּ לֹא־תִרְאוּ פָנַי בִּלְתִּי אֲחִיכֶם
אִתְּכֶם: **ו** וַיֹּאמֶר יִשְׂרָאֵל לָמָה הֲרֵעֹתֶם לִי לְהַגִּיד לָאִישׁ
הַעוֹד לָכֶם אָח: **ז** וַיֹּאמְרוּ שָׁאוֹל שָׁאַל־הָאִישׁ לָנוּ
וּלְמוֹלַדְתֵּנוּ לֵאמֹר הַעוֹד אֲבִיכֶם חַי הֲיֵשׁ לָכֶם אָח וַנַּגֶּד־
לוֹ עַל־פִּי הַדְּבָרִים הָאֵלֶּה הֲיָדוֹעַ נֵדַע כִּי יֹאמַר הוֹרִידוּ
אֶת־אֲחִיכֶם: **ח** וַיֹּאמֶר יְהוּדָה אֶל־יִשְׂרָאֵל אָבִיו שִׁלְחָה
הַנַּעַר אִתִּי וְנָקוּמָה וְנֵלֵכָה וְנִחְיֶה וְלֹא נָמוּת גַּם־אֲנַחְנוּ
גַם־אַתָּה גַּם־טַפֵּנוּ: **ט** אָנֹכִי אֶעֶרְבֶנּוּ מִיָּדִי תְּבַקְשֶׁנּוּ
אִם־לֹא הֲבִיאֹתִיו אֵלֶיךָ וְהִצַּגְתִּיו לְפָנֶיךָ וְחָטָאתִי לְךָ
כָּל־הַיָּמִים: **י** כִּי לוּלֵא הִתְמַהְמָהְנוּ כִּי־עַתָּה שַׁבְנוּ זֶה
פַעֲמָיִם: **יא** וַיֹּאמֶר אֲלֵהֶם יִשְׂרָאֵל אֲבִיהֶם אִם־כֵּן |
אֵפוֹא זֹאת עֲשׂוּ קְחוּ מִזִּמְרַת הָאָרֶץ בִּכְלֵיכֶם וְהוֹרִידוּ
לָאִישׁ מִנְחָה מְעַט צֳרִי וּמְעַט דְּבַשׁ נְכֹאת וָלֹט בָּטְנִים
וּשְׁקֵדִים: **יב** וְכֶסֶף מִשְׁנֶה קְחוּ בְיֶדְכֶם וְאֶת־הַכֶּסֶף
הַמּוּשָׁב בְּפִי אַמְתְּחֹתֵיכֶם תָּשִׁיבוּ בְיֶדְכֶם אוּלַי מִשְׁגֶּה
הוּא: **יג** וְאֶת־אֲחִיכֶם קָחוּ וְקוּמוּ שׁוּבוּ אֶל־הָאִישׁ: **יד**
וְאֵל שַׁדַּי יִתֵּן לָכֶם רַחֲמִים לִפְנֵי הָאִישׁ וְשִׁלַּח לָכֶם אֶת־
אֲחִיכֶם אַחֵר וְאֶת־בִּנְיָמִין וַאֲנִי כַּאֲשֶׁר שָׁכֹלְתִּי שָׁכָלְתִּי:

[1] *But the famine in the land was severe.*
[2] *And when they had eaten up the rations
which they had brought from Egypt, their father
said to them, "Go again and procure some food
for us."*
[3] *But Judah said to him, "The man warned us,
'Do not let me see your faces unless your brother
is with you.'*
[4] *If you will let our brother go with us, we will
go down and procure food for you;*

[5] but if you will not let him go, we will not go down, for the man said to us, 'Do not let me see your faces unless your brother is with you.'"

[6] And Israel said, "Why did you serve me so ill as to tell the man that you had another brother?"

[7] They replied, "But the man kept asking about us and our family, saying, 'Is your father still living? Have you another brother?' And we answered him accordingly. How were we to know that he would say, 'Bring your brother here'?"

[8] Then Judah said to his father Israel, "Send the boy in my care, and let us be on our way, that we may live and not die – you and we and our children.

[9] I myself will be surety for him; you may hold me responsible: if I do not bring him back to you and set him before you, I shall stand guilty before you forever.

[10] For we could have been there and back twice if we had not dawdled."

[11] Then their father Israel said to them, "If it must be so, do this: take some of the choice products of the land in your baggage, and carry them down as a gift for the man – some balm and some honey, gum, ladanum, pistachio nuts, and almonds.

[12] And take with you double the money, carrying back with you the money that was replaced in the mouths of your bags; perhaps it was a mistake.

[13] Take your brother too; and go back at once to the man.

[14] And may El Shaddai dispose the man to mercy toward you, that he may release to you your other brother, as well as Benjamin. As for me, if I am to be bereaved, I shall be bereaved."

[2] Their father said to them, "Go again and procure some food for us": After Jacob rejects Reuben's proposal the brothers fall silent, preferring to wait until the moment when Jacob himself will again raise the issue.

[3] The man warned us, 'Do not let me see your faces unless your brother is with you.'... [5] for the man said to us, 'Do not let me see your faces unless your brother is with you.'": For additional emphasis, Judah states his position and then repeats it a second time, that returning to Egypt without Benjamin is unthinkable. He wants to make sure that Jacob understands how futile that would be.

[7] They replied, "But the man kept asking about us and our family, saying, 'Is your father still living? Have you another brother?'": The story as the brothers tell it here is different from how it actually happened. After Joseph had accused them of spying they themselves volunteered that one brother was missing (42:13).

Their having sold Joseph has always remained a sore spot for them, because they are living, as it were, a perpetual lie. So, when Joseph too accuses them of lying (that is, of being spies), their instinctive response, as if to justify themselves, is to begin talking about their missing brother.

But of course they cannot speak candidly about all that to their father, and so they recount the events differently from what actually occurred.

[8] Then Judah said to his father Israel: At a critical juncture Judah assumes personal responsibility for Benjamin, and from that moment his leadership in the family is restored.

[8] Then Judah said to his father Israel, "Send the boy in my care, and let us be on our way, that we may live and not die – you and we and our children": Although Judah offers Jacob no material guarantees, his words evince a deep sense of mutual responsibility, and this is what Jacob finds most persuasive (apart from the problem of acute hunger, which Judah mentions as well).

[13] Take your brother too; and go back at once to the man: Joseph's actions have put the brothers in a situation where they must answer for each other. Without unity they cannot possibly solve the problem.

[14] As for me, if I am to be bereaved, I shall be bereaved: Literally, "As for me, if I am to remain childless, so shall I be childless." Jacob's two sons from Rachel, Joseph and Benjamin, are so important to him, that without them he feels that he has no children at all. But Leah's sons understand why Jacob is saying this, and they do not take offense. At this moment, precisely in a situation of calamity, the idea of *kelal yisrael*, the mutual responsibility of all Jews, is born.

51.6. The Brothers in Joseph's House (43:15-44:2)

טו וַיִּקְחוּ הָאֲנָשִׁים אֶת־הַמִּנְחָה הַזֹּאת וּמִשְׁנֶה־כֶּסֶף
לָקְחוּ בְיָדָם וְאֶת־בִּנְיָמִן וַיָּקֻמוּ וַיֵּרְדוּ מִצְרַיִם וַיַּעַמְדוּ
לִפְנֵי יוֹסֵף: **טז** וַיַּרְא יוֹסֵף אִתָּם אֶת־בִּנְיָמִין וַיֹּאמֶר
לַאֲשֶׁר עַל־בֵּיתוֹ הָבֵא אֶת־הָאֲנָשִׁים הַבָּיְתָה וּטְבֹחַ

טֶבַח וְהָכֵן כִּי אִתִּי יֹאכְלוּ הָאֲנָשִׁים בַּצׇּהֳרָיִם: **יז** וַיַּעַשׂ הָאִישׁ כַּאֲשֶׁר אָמַר יוֹסֵף וַיָּבֵא הָאִישׁ אֶת־הָאֲנָשִׁים בֵּיתָה יוֹסֵף: **יח** וַיִּירְאוּ הָאֲנָשִׁים כִּי הוּבְאוּ בֵּית יוֹסֵף וַיֹּאמְרוּ עַל־דְּבַר הַכֶּסֶף הַשָּׁב בְּאַמְתְּחֹתֵינוּ בַּתְּחִלָּה אֲנַחְנוּ מוּבָאִים לְהִתְגֹּלֵל עָלֵינוּ וּלְהִתְנַפֵּל עָלֵינוּ וְלָקַחַת אֹתָנוּ לַעֲבָדִים וְאֶת־חֲמֹרֵינוּ: **יט** וַיִּגְּשׁוּ אֶל־ הָאִישׁ אֲשֶׁר עַל־בֵּית יוֹסֵף וַיְדַבְּרוּ אֵלָיו פֶּתַח הַבָּיִת: **כ** וַיֹּאמְרוּ בִּי אֲדֹנִי יָרֹד יָרַדְנוּ בַּתְּחִלָּה לִשְׁבׇּר־אֹכֶל: **כא** וַיְהִי כִּי־בָאנוּ אֶל־הַמָּלוֹן וַנִּפְתְּחָה אֶת־אַמְתְּחֹתֵינוּ וְהִנֵּה כֶסֶף־אִישׁ בְּפִי אַמְתַּחְתּוֹ כַּסְפֵּנוּ בְּמִשְׁקָלוֹ וַנָּשֶׁב אֹתוֹ בְּיָדֵנוּ: **כב** וְכֶסֶף אַחֵר הוֹרַדְנוּ בְיָדֵנוּ לִשְׁבׇּר־אֹכֶל לֹא יָדַעְנוּ מִי־שָׂם כַּסְפֵּנוּ בְּאַמְתְּחֹתֵינוּ: **כג** וַיֹּאמֶר שָׁלוֹם לָכֶם אַל־תִּירָאוּ אֱלֹהֵיכֶם וֵאלֹהֵי אֲבִיכֶם נָתַן לָכֶם מַטְמוֹן בְּאַמְתְּחֹתֵיכֶם כַּסְפְּכֶם בָּא אֵלָי וַיּוֹצֵא אֲלֵהֶם אֶת־שִׁמְעוֹן: **כד** וַיָּבֵא הָאִישׁ אֶת־הָאֲנָשִׁים בֵּיתָה יוֹסֵף וַיִּתֶּן־מַיִם וַיִּרְחֲצוּ רַגְלֵיהֶם וַיִּתֵּן מִסְפּוֹא לַחֲמֹרֵיהֶם: **כה** וַיָּכִינוּ אֶת־הַמִּנְחָה עַד־בּוֹא יוֹסֵף בַּצׇּהֳרָיִם כִּי שָׁמְעוּ כִּי־שָׁם יֹאכְלוּ לָחֶם: **כו** וַיָּבֹא יוֹסֵף הַבַּיְתָה וַיָּבִיאוּ לוֹ אֶת־הַמִּנְחָה אֲשֶׁר־בְּיָדָם הַבָּיְתָה וַיִּשְׁתַּחֲווּ־לוֹ אָרְצָה: **כז** וַיִּשְׁאַל לָהֶם לְשָׁלוֹם וַיֹּאמֶר הֲשָׁלוֹם אֲבִיכֶם הַזָּקֵן אֲשֶׁר אֲמַרְתֶּם הַעוֹדֶנּוּ חָי: **כח** וַיֹּאמְרוּ שָׁלוֹם לְעַבְדְּךָ לְאָבִינוּ עוֹדֶנּוּ חָי וַיִּקְּדוּ וישתחו (וַיִּשְׁתַּחֲווּ): **כט** וַיִּשָּׂא עֵינָיו וַיַּרְא אֶת־בִּנְיָמִין אָחִיו בֶּן־אִמּוֹ וַיֹּאמֶר הֲזֶה אֲחִיכֶם הַקָּטֹן אֲשֶׁר אֲמַרְתֶּם אֵלָי וַיֹּאמַר אֱלֹהִים יׇחְנְךָ בְּנִי: **ל** וַיְמַהֵר יוֹסֵף כִּי־נִכְמְרוּ רַחֲמָיו אֶל־אָחִיו וַיְבַקֵּשׁ לִבְכּוֹת וַיָּבֹא הַחַדְרָה וַיֵּבְךְּ שָׁמָּה: **לא** וַיִּרְחַץ פָּנָיו וַיֵּצֵא וַיִּתְאַפַּק וַיֹּאמֶר שִׂימוּ לָחֶם: **לב** וַיָּשִׂימוּ לוֹ לְבַדּוֹ וְלָהֶם לְבַדָּם וְלַמִּצְרִים הָאֹכְלִים אִתּוֹ לְבַדָּם כִּי לֹא יוּכְלוּן הַמִּצְרִים לֶאֱכֹל אֶת־הָעִבְרִים לֶחֶם כִּי־תוֹעֵבָה הִוא לְמִצְרָיִם: **לג** וַיֵּשְׁבוּ לְפָנָיו הַבְּכֹר כִּבְכֹרָתוֹ וְהַצָּעִיר כִּצְעִרָתוֹ וַיִּתְמְהוּ הָאֲנָשִׁים אִישׁ אֶל־רֵעֵהוּ: **לד** וַיִּשָּׂא מַשְׂאֹת מֵאֵת פָּנָיו אֲלֵהֶם וַתֵּרֶב מַשְׂאַת בִּנְיָמִן מִמַּשְׂאֹת כֻּלָּם חָמֵשׁ יָדוֹת וַיִּשְׁתּוּ וַיִּשְׁכְּרוּ עִמּוֹ:

אָ וַיְצַו אֶת־אֲשֶׁר עַל־בֵּיתוֹ לֵאמֹר מַלֵּא אֶת־אַמְתְּחֹת הָאֲנָשִׁים אֹכֶל כַּאֲשֶׁר יוּכְלוּן שְׂאֵת וְשִׂים כֶּסֶף־אִישׁ בְּפִי אַמְתַּחְתּוֹ: בּ וְאֶת־גְּבִיעִי גְּבִיעַ הַכֶּסֶף תָּשִׂים בְּפִי אַמְתַּחַת הַקָּטֹן וְאֵת כֶּסֶף שִׁבְרוֹ וַיַּעַשׂ כִּדְבַר יוֹסֵף אֲשֶׁר דִּבֵּר:

[15] So the men took that gift, and they took with them double the money, as well as Benjamin. They made their way down to Egypt, where they presented themselves to Joseph.

[16] When Joseph saw Benjamin with them, he said to his house steward, "Take the men into the house; slaughter and prepare an animal, for the men will dine with me at noon."

[17] The man did as Joseph said, and he brought the men into Joseph's house.

[18] But the men were frightened at being brought into Joseph's house. "It must be," they thought, "because of the money replaced in our bags the first time that we have been brought inside, as a pretext to attack us and seize us as slaves, with our pack animals."

[19] So they went up to Joseph's house steward and spoke to him at the entrance of the house.

[20] "If you please, my lord," they said, "we came down once before to procure food.

[21] But when we arrived at the night encampment and opened our bags, there was each one's money in the mouth of his bag, our money in full. So we have brought it back with us.

[22] And we have brought down with us other money to procure food. We do not know who put the money in our bags."

[23] He replied, "All is well with you; do not be afraid. Your God, the God of your father, must have put treasure in your bags for you. I got your payment." And he brought out Simeon to them.

[24] Then the man brought the men into Joseph's house; he gave them water to bathe their feet, and he provided feed for their asses.

[25] They laid out their gifts to await Joseph's arrival at noon, for they had heard that they were to dine there.

[26] When Joseph came home, they presented to him the gifts that they had brought with them into the house, bowing low before him to the ground.

[27] He greeted them, and he said, "How is your aged father of whom you spoke? Is he still in good health?"

[28] They replied, "It is well with your servant our father; he is still in good health." And they bowed and made obeisance.

[29] Looking about, he saw his brother Benjamin, his mother's son, and asked, "Is this your youngest brother of whom you spoke to me?" And he went on, "May God be gracious to you, my boy."

[30] With that, Joseph hurried out, for he was overcome with feeling toward his brother and was on the verge of tears; he went into a room and wept there.

[31] Then he washed his face, reappeared, and – now in control of himself – gave the order, "Serve the meal."

[32] They served him by himself, and them by

themselves, and the Egyptians who ate with him by themselves; for the Egyptians could not dine with the Hebrews, since that would be abhorrent to the Egyptians.

[33] As they were seated by his direction, from the oldest in the order of his seniority to the youngest in the order of his youth, the men looked at one another in astonishment.

[34] Portions were served them from his table; but Benjamin's portion was several times that of anyone else. And they drank their fill with him.

(44:1) Then he instructed his house steward as follows, "Fill the men's bags with food, as much as they can carry, and put each one's money in the mouth of his bag.

[2] Put my silver goblet in the mouth of the bag of the youngest one, together with his money for the rations." And he did as Joseph told him.

[16] Take the men into the house: This was highly unusual. No other customer was ever invited to Joseph's residence.

[23] He replied, "All is well with you; do not be afraid. Your God, the God of your father, must have put treasure in your bags for you": Joseph had planned everything in advance and given appropriate instructions to his steward, who here demonstrates sympathy for the brothers and speaks of God as the guiding force behind everything that is happening.

[28] It is well with your servant our father: The words "your servant, our father" are repeated here five times. According to the Midrash, since Joseph heard these words ten times (five times directly, and five times through the interpreter), but he never objected, his life was shortened by ten years. Joseph therefore lived only one hundred ten years, and not one hundred twenty, the assumed minimum for a righteous individual.

[30] He went into a room and wept there: Joseph's tears once again demonstrate that the role he has taken upon himself is a very difficult one.

[32] For the Egyptians could not dine with the Hebrews, since that would be abhorrent to the Egyptians: We see once again that the *ivrim* (Hebrews) are a recognized ethnonym that includes not only the family of Abraham. And we see too that the brothers know, for it is common knowledge, that Joseph is a Hebrew and not an Egyptian. How could the brothers not be be aware of the story of Joseph's astonishing exaltation in Egypt, given that all of Egypt has heard of it. And when Joseph, like his brothers, is served food separately from the Egyptians, and at the same time, "portions were served them from his table," his Hebrew essence is openly revealed.

We note in passing: It is clear from here that even when a Hebrew herdsman becomes second-in-command to Pharaoh in Egypt, the Egyptian farmers still shun him. Although Joseph is Egypt's savior, he remains a stranger to the locals. In fact, the gap between Egyptians and Hebrews is still so great that the Egyptians will not deign to eat with them. The brothers however make no connection between these events and their lost brother. Because they remember their conflict with Joseph as a family matter exclusively, it never occurs to them to promote it to the public plane.

[33] As they were seated by his direction, from the oldest in the order of his seniority to the youngest in the order of his youth, the men looked at one another in astonishment: Rather than "they were seated by his direction," the literal translation is simply "they sat," which would normally be understood to mean that it was the brothers themselves who took up those positions. But what, then, was the reason for their astonishment? The Midrash therefore explains that it was Joseph who had them seated in order of seniority, and the brothers were astounded at how Joseph could have had such knowledge.

[34] But Benjamin's portion was several times that of anyone else: We have already discussed the four stages of *teshuvah* (repentance), the last of which must always be to avoid repeating the same mistake when one finds himself again in the same (or similar) situation. Therefore, Joseph, after leading his brothers through the initial stages of *teshuvah*, now models for them the process of "selling one's brother" (as we shall presently explain), so that they can adequately prove themselves, and thus complete the process of their correction.

For staging this situation of "selling the brother," first Joseph needs Benjamin, who, like him, is Rachel's son – the "younger Joseph" as it were – whom Leah's sons were inclined from the start to dislike and consider a competitor. Secondly, Joseph needs to treat Benjamin as the favorite, just as Joseph himself was once his father's favorite. Benjamin therefore now receives the very best dishes, and his share is "several times" greater (v. 34; literally, "five times") than that of all the rest.

[2] Put my silver goblet in the mouth of the bag of the

youngest one: Finally, Joseph portrays Benjamin as a criminal who has stolen the goblet, just as Joseph himself was once a criminal in the eyes of his brothers. After all, people don't sell their "good" brothers. Joseph therefore needs to model the situation as the sale of a "bad" brother – the son of a different mother, an upstart and a thief. When, after all this, Judah stands up for Benjamin, it becomes clear that the brothers have indeed repented.

Had he revealed himself to them any earlier, Joseph would have gained influence over his brothers, but he could not have prompted them to repent. A king has full discretion to inflict on his subjects any physical act of his own choosing, but he has no power over their inner selves. Joseph must therefore restrain himself with all his might, in order to continue his game, and to see it through to its logical conclusion – which in the end he will not be able to do in any case.

51.7. Joseph's Goblet is Found in Benjamin's Bag (44:1-17)

א וַיְצַו אֶת־אֲשֶׁר עַל־בֵּיתוֹ לֵאמֹר מַלֵּא אֶת־אַמְתְּחֹת הָאֲנָשִׁים אֹכֶל כַּאֲשֶׁר יוּכְלוּן שְׂאֵת וְשִׂים כֶּסֶף־אִישׁ בְּפִי אַמְתַּחְתּוֹ: ב וְאֶת־גְּבִיעִי גְּבִיעַ הַכֶּסֶף תָּשִׂים בְּפִי אַמְתַּחַת הַקָּטֹן וְאֵת כֶּסֶף שִׁבְרוֹ וַיַּעַשׂ כִּדְבַר יוֹסֵף אֲשֶׁר דִּבֵּר: ג הַבֹּקֶר אוֹר וְהָאֲנָשִׁים שֻׁלְּחוּ הֵמָּה וַחֲמֹרֵיהֶם: ד הֵם יָצְאוּ אֶת־הָעִיר לֹא הִרְחִיקוּ וְיוֹסֵף אָמַר לַאֲשֶׁר עַל־בֵּיתוֹ קוּם רְדֹף אַחֲרֵי הָאֲנָשִׁים וְהִשַּׂגְתָּם וְאָמַרְתָּ אֲלֵהֶם לָמָּה שִׁלַּמְתֶּם רָעָה תַּחַת טוֹבָה: ה הֲלוֹא זֶה אֲשֶׁר יִשְׁתֶּה אֲדֹנִי בּוֹ וְהוּא נַחֵשׁ יְנַחֵשׁ בּוֹ הֲרֵעֹתֶם אֲשֶׁר עֲשִׂיתֶם: ו וַיַּשִּׂגֵם וַיְדַבֵּר אֲלֵהֶם אֶת־הַדְּבָרִים הָאֵלֶּה: ז וַיֹּאמְרוּ אֵלָיו לָמָּה יְדַבֵּר אֲדֹנִי כַּדְּבָרִים הָאֵלֶּה חָלִילָה לַעֲבָדֶיךָ מֵעֲשׂוֹת כַּדָּבָר הַזֶּה: ח הֵן כֶּסֶף אֲשֶׁר מָצָאנוּ בְּפִי

אַמְתְּחֹתֵינוּ הֱשִׁיבֹנוּ אֵלֶיךָ מֵאֶרֶץ כְּנָעַן וְאֵיךְ נִגְנֹב מִבֵּית אֲדֹנֶיךָ כֶּסֶף אוֹ זָהָב: **ט** אֲשֶׁר יִמָּצֵא אִתּוֹ מֵעֲבָדֶיךָ וָמֵת וְגַם־אֲנַחְנוּ נִהְיֶה לַאדֹנִי לַעֲבָדִים: **י** וַיֹּאמֶר גַּם־עַתָּה כְדִבְרֵיכֶם כֶּן־הוּא אֲשֶׁר יִמָּצֵא אִתּוֹ יִהְיֶה־לִּי עָבֶד וְאַתֶּם תִּהְיוּ נְקִיִּם: **יא** וַיְמַהֲרוּ וַיּוֹרִדוּ אִישׁ אֶת־אַמְתַּחְתּוֹ אָרְצָה וַיִּפְתְּחוּ אִישׁ אַמְתַּחְתּוֹ: **יב** וַיְחַפֵּשׂ בַּגָּדוֹל הֵחֵל וּבַקָּטֹן כִּלָּה וַיִּמָּצֵא הַגָּבִיעַ בְּאַמְתַּחַת בִּנְיָמִן: **יג** וַיִּקְרְעוּ שִׂמְלֹתָם וַיַּעֲמֹס אִישׁ עַל־חֲמֹרוֹ וַיָּשֻׁבוּ הָעִירָה: **יד** וַיָּבֹא יְהוּדָה וְאֶחָיו בֵּיתָה יוֹסֵף וְהוּא עוֹדֶנּוּ שָׁם וַיִּפְּלוּ לְפָנָיו אָרְצָה: **טו** וַיֹּאמֶר לָהֶם יוֹסֵף מָה־הַמַּעֲשֶׂה הַזֶּה אֲשֶׁר עֲשִׂיתֶם הֲלוֹא יְדַעְתֶּם כִּי־נַחֵשׁ יְנַחֵשׁ אִישׁ אֲשֶׁר כָּמֹנִי: **טז** וַיֹּאמֶר יְהוּדָה מַה־נֹּאמַר לַאדֹנִי מַה־נְּדַבֵּר וּמַה־נִּצְטַדָּק הָאֱלֹהִים מָצָא אֶת־עֲוֹן עֲבָדֶיךָ הִנֶּנּוּ עֲבָדִים לַאדֹנִי גַּם־אֲנַחְנוּ גַּם אֲשֶׁר־נִמְצָא הַגָּבִיעַ בְּיָדוֹ: **יז** וַיֹּאמֶר חָלִילָה לִּי מֵעֲשׂוֹת זֹאת הָאִישׁ אֲשֶׁר נִמְצָא הַגָּבִיעַ בְּיָדוֹ הוּא יִהְיֶה־לִּי עָבֶד וְאַתֶּם עֲלוּ לְשָׁלוֹם אֶל־אֲבִיכֶם:

[1] *Then he instructed his house steward as follows, "Fill the men's bags with food, as much as they can carry, and put each one's money in the mouth of his bag.*
[2] *Put my silver goblet in the mouth of the bag of the youngest one, together with his money for the rations." And he did as Joseph told him.*
[3] *With the first light of morning, the men were sent off with their pack animals.*
[4] *They had just left the city and had not gone far, when Joseph said to his steward, "Up, go after the men! And when you overtake them, say to them, 'Why did you repay good with evil?*
[5] *It is the very one from which my master drinks and which he uses for divination. It was a wicked thing for you to do!'"*

[6] He overtook them and spoke those words to them.

[7] And they said to him, "Why does my lord say such things? Far be it from your servants to do anything of the kind!

[8] Here we brought back to you from the land of Canaan the money that we found in the mouths of our bags. How then could we have stolen any silver or gold from your master's house!

[9] Whichever of your servants it is found with shall die; the rest of us, moreover, shall become slaves to my lord."

[10] He replied, "Although what you are proposing is right, only the one with whom it is found shall be my slave; but the rest of you shall go free."

[11] So each one hastened to lower his bag to the ground, and each one opened his bag.

[12] He searched, beginning with the oldest and ending with the youngest; and the goblet turned up in Benjamin's bag.

[13] At this they rent their clothes. Each reloaded his pack animal, and they returned to the city.

[14] When Judah and his brothers reentered the house of Joseph, who was still there, they threw themselves on the ground before him.

[15] Joseph said to them, "What is this deed that you have done? Do you not know that a man like me practices divination?"

[16] Judah replied, "What can we say to my lord? How can we plead, how can we prove our innocence? God has uncovered the crime of your servants. Here we are, then, slaves of my lord, the

rest of us as much as he in whose possession the goblet was found."

[17] But he replied, "Far be it from me to act thus! Only he in whose possession the goblet was found shall be my slave; the rest of you go back in peace to your father."

[1] And put each one's money in the mouth of his bag: Joseph once again returns to his brothers their money, as an indication that the theft of the goblet is staged, and also that they should not expect that their money alone will be enough to clear them of all charges.

[2] Put my silver goblet in the mouth of the bag of the youngest one: The goblet is a valuable article in its own right, but it is also an instrument of divination and intuition. Joseph is intimating to his brothers that they must focus their intuition to the greatest extent possible, in order to arrive at the correct decision.

[9] Whichever of your servants it is found with shall die; the rest of us, moreover, shall become slaves to my lord: The brothers are convinced beyond all doubt of their own innocence (which is itself unreasonable, given that silver has already appeared once before in their sacks). Thus, they do not hesitate in the slightest to condemn the thief, whoever he might be, to death, under the full severity of the law, and also to condemn themselves to bondage. Self-confidence is always a bad adviser.

[10] Only the one with whom it is found shall be my slave; but the rest of you shall go free: Joseph's steward proposes a much more lenient punishment than the one the brothers had proposed.

[12] He searched, beginning with the oldest: He does it this way in order to avoid any suspicion that he had prior knowledge of whose sack held the goblet.

[14] When Judah and his brothers reentered the house of Joseph: Judah goes first, having vouched personally for Benjamin.

[16] God has uncovered the crime of your servants: Judah says "servants" in the plural, because he understands that what is happening is the work of Divine Justice repaying them for their earlier sin, and that the punishment should therefore pertain to all the brothers equally.

[17] Only he in whose possession the goblet was found shall be my slave; the rest of you go back in peace to your father: Joseph puts them in a situation of facing a difficult choice. The can "sell out" Benjamin and return home, or they can stand up for him.

Joseph's objective is not to subject his brothers to an ordeal, but to reeducate them.

Weekly Portion
Vayigash

Chapter 52

Joseph Reveals Himself to His Brothers

52.1. Joseph's Fall

Weekly portion *Vayigash* is the story of Joseph's fall.

Judah, as we shall see, stood up for Benjamin and did not "sell out" his brother. Thus, it would seem, the fourth and final stage of repentance has been accomplished ("when you find yourself again in the same situation, do not repeat your past mistakes") and Joseph's plan too could now be considered achieved.

However, Judah's act is not yet the final correction. Joseph had a further plan to correct his brothers – a plan that he could not, however, successfully implement.

As Joseph is unable to complete the correction of the brothers, he transports the whole family to Egypt, and also makes every effort to rebuild Egypt, believing that it will bring the country prosperity, but at the same time he decisively turns its inhabitants into slaves of Pharaoh.

This entire undertaking was wrong from the get-go. But it had to be traversed, and its incorrectness eventually recognized, so that the transformation from Joseph to *Mashiach ben Yosef* could occur.

52.2. Judah Stands Up for Benjamin (44:18-34)

יח וַיִּגַּשׁ אֵלָיו יְהוּדָה וַיֹּאמֶר בִּי אֲדֹנִי יְדַבֶּר־נָא עַבְדְּךָ
דָבָר בְּאָזְנֵי אֲדֹנִי וְאַל־יִחַר אַפְּךָ בְּעַבְדֶּךָ כִּי כָמוֹךָ
כְּפַרְעֹה: **יט** אֲדֹנִי שָׁאַל אֶת־עֲבָדָיו לֵאמֹר הֲיֵשׁ־לָכֶם
אָב אוֹ־אָח: **כ** וַנֹּאמֶר אֶל־אֲדֹנִי יֶשׁ־לָנוּ אָב זָקֵן וְיֶלֶד
זְקֻנִים קָטָן וְאָחִיו מֵת וַיִּוָּתֵר הוּא לְבַדּוֹ לְאִמּוֹ וְאָבִיו
אֲהֵבוֹ: **כא** וַתֹּאמֶר אֶל־עֲבָדֶיךָ הוֹרִדֻהוּ אֵלָי וְאָשִׂימָה
עֵינִי עָלָיו: **כב** וַנֹּאמֶר אֶל־אֲדֹנִי לֹא־יוּכַל הַנַּעַר לַעֲזֹב
אֶת־אָבִיו וְעָזַב אֶת־אָבִיו וָמֵת: **כג** וַתֹּאמֶר אֶל־עֲבָדֶיךָ
אִם־לֹא יֵרֵד אֲחִיכֶם הַקָּטֹן אִתְּכֶם לֹא תֹסִפוּן לִרְאוֹת
פָּנָי: **כד** וַיְהִי כִּי עָלִינוּ אֶל־עַבְדְּךָ אָבִי וַנַּגֶּד־לוֹ אֵת דִּבְרֵי
אֲדֹנִי: **כה** וַיֹּאמֶר אָבִינוּ שֻׁבוּ שִׁבְרוּ־לָנוּ מְעַט־אֹכֶל:
כו וַנֹּאמֶר לֹא נוּכַל לָרֶדֶת אִם־יֵשׁ אָחִינוּ הַקָּטֹן אִתָּנוּ
וְיָרַדְנוּ כִּי־לֹא נוּכַל לִרְאוֹת פְּנֵי הָאִישׁ וְאָחִינוּ הַקָּטֹן
אֵינֶנּוּ אִתָּנוּ: **כז** וַיֹּאמֶר עַבְדְּךָ אָבִי אֵלֵינוּ אַתֶּם יְדַעְתֶּם
כִּי שְׁנַיִם יָלְדָה־לִּי אִשְׁתִּי: **כח** וַיֵּצֵא הָאֶחָד מֵאִתִּי וָאֹמַר
אַךְ טָרֹף טֹרָף וְלֹא רְאִיתִיו עַד־הֵנָּה: **כט** וּלְקַחְתֶּם גַּם־
אֶת־זֶה מֵעִם פָּנַי וְקָרָהוּ אָסוֹן וְהוֹרַדְתֶּם אֶת־שֵׂיבָתִי
בְּרָעָה שְׁאֹלָה: **ל** וְעַתָּה כְּבֹאִי אֶל־עַבְדְּךָ אָבִי וְהַנַּעַר
אֵינֶנּוּ אִתָּנוּ וְנַפְשׁוֹ קְשׁוּרָה בְנַפְשׁוֹ: **לא** וְהָיָה כִּרְאוֹתוֹ
כִּי־אֵין הַנַּעַר וָמֵת וְהוֹרִידוּ עֲבָדֶיךָ אֶת־שֵׂיבַת עַבְדְּךָ
אָבִינוּ בְּיָגוֹן שְׁאֹלָה: **לב** כִּי עַבְדְּךָ עָרַב אֶת־הַנַּעַר מֵעִם
אָבִי לֵאמֹר אִם־לֹא אֲבִיאֶנּוּ אֵלֶיךָ וְחָטָאתִי לְאָבִי כָּל־
הַיָּמִים: **לג** וְעַתָּה יֵשֶׁב־נָא עַבְדְּךָ תַּחַת הַנַּעַר עֶבֶד לַאדֹנִי
וְהַנַּעַר יַעַל עִם־אֶחָיו: **לד** כִּי־אֵיךְ אֶעֱלֶה אֶל־אָבִי
וְהַנַּעַר אֵינֶנּוּ אִתִּי פֶּן אֶרְאֶה בָרָע אֲשֶׁר יִמְצָא אֶת־אָבִי:

[18] Then Judah went up to him and said, "Please,

my lord, let your servant appeal to my lord, and do not be impatient with your servant, you who are the equal of Pharaoh.

[19] My lord asked his servants, 'Have you a father or another brother?'

[20] We told my lord, 'We have an old father, and there is a child of his old age, the youngest; his full brother is dead, so that he alone is left of his mother, and his father dotes on him.'

[21] Then you said to your servants, 'Bring him down to me, that I may set eyes on him.'

[22] We said to my lord, 'The boy cannot leave his father; if he were to leave him, his father would die.'

[23] But you said to your servants, 'Unless your youngest brother comes down with you, do not let me see your faces.'

[24] When we came back to your servant my father, we reported my lord's words to him.

[25] "Later our father said, 'Go back and procure some food for us.'

[26] We answered, 'We cannot go down; only if our youngest brother is with us can we go down, for we may not show our faces to the man unless our youngest brother is with us.'

[27] Your servant my father said to us, 'As you know, my wife bore me two sons.

[28] But one is gone from me, and I said: Alas, he was torn by a beast! And I have not seen him since.

[29] If you take this one from me, too, and he meets with disaster, you will send my white head down to Sheol in sorrow.'

*[30] "Now, if I come to your servant my father
and the boy is not with us – since his own life is
so bound up with his –*
*[31] when he sees that the boy is not with us, he
will die, and your servants will send the white
head of your servant our father down to Sheol
in grief.*
*[32] Now your servant has pledged himself for
the boy to my father, saying, 'If I do not bring
him back to you, I shall stand guilty before my
father forever.'*
*[33] Therefore, please let your servant remain as
a slave to my lord instead of the boy, and let the
boy go back with his brothers.*
*[34] For how can I go back to my father unless
the boy is with me? Let me not be witness to the
woe that would overtake my father!"*

[18] You who are the equal of Pharaoh: When Judah com-
pares Joseph to Pharaoh, we can understand this in either
a positive or negative sense (referring either to Joseph's
greatness, or to unworthy behavior on his part, respectively).

[19] My lord asked his servants: Judah's recapitulation of
that earlier conversation is not entirely accurate.

**[22] We said to my lord, 'The boy cannot leave his father;
if he were to leave him, his father would die.' [23] But
you said to your servants, 'Unless your youngest brother
comes down with you, do not let me see your faces':** Without mentioning the charges of espionage, Judah focuses his
attention only on Benjamin, on his special connection with

Jacob, and on the Egyptian governor's unfathomable request to lay eyes on Benjamin.

[27] As you know, my wife bore me two sons: Although it is surely extraordinarily difficult for Judah, a son of Leah, to utter such words, Judah adopts his father's position here, saying that Jacob's true wife was Rachel.

With these words, however, the whole situation begins to change. Until now Joseph thought that Leah's sons were trying to displace Rachel's sons (or to even be rid of them completely). But Joseph now realizes that he was wrong.

[28] But one is gone from me, and I said: Alas, he was torn by a beast! And I have not seen him since: Until now Joseph could not understand what actually happened in the family that led to his being sold into Egypt. Only now he knows for the first time that his father did not betray him at all.

[32] Now your servant has pledged himself for the boy to my father: When Joseph learns of the guarantee that Judah has given for Benjamin's safe return, this completely changes how he views the existing relationship between the sons of Leah and of Rachel.

[34] Let me not be witness to the woe that would overtake my father: Judah not only makes a very dramatic and emotional speech; he reveals the situation in their family. Now Joseph knows that the brothers accept Jacob's statement that (as he put it) he has only two sons from his wife. And Joseph sees in their humility true greatness.

Joseph now learns how important he is to Jacob ("As you know, my wife bore me two sons"). And that Judah has vouched for his brother Benjamin, the "younger Joseph."

Joseph now realizes that his entire former understanding of the situation was distorted, and that his previous views were erroneous.

52.3. "Joseph Could No Longer Control Himself" (45:1)

א וְלֹא־יָכֹל יוֹסֵף לְהִתְאַפֵּק לְכֹל הַנִּצָּבִים עָלָיו וַיִּקְרָא
הוֹצִיאוּ כָל־אִישׁ מֵעָלָי וְלֹא־עָמַד אִישׁ אִתּוֹ בְּהִתְוַדַּע
יוֹסֵף אֶל־אֶחָיו:

[1] Joseph could no longer control himself before all his attendants, and he cried out, "Have everyone withdraw from me!" So there was no one else about when Joseph made himself known to his brothers.

[1] Joseph could no longer control himself ... Joseph made himself known to his brothers: Because Judah has agreed to give primacy to the sons of Rachel, Joseph, who had previously misunderstood the whole situation, can now no longer see conflict between the sons of Rachel and the sons of Leah. He therefore cannot continue his plan and, unable to withstand his own internal stress, he reveals himself to his brothers.

Besides liberating Benjamin, Judah has also brought Joseph to the point where he cannot restrain himself and confesses everything. The brothers' ordeal has ended, but Joseph cannot complete his plan. In the future, this will turn out to be yet a much more serious problem, in more ways than one.

When the Torah says that "Joseph could no longer control

himself," the implication is that he in fact wanted to control himself, but could not. He had not been planning to reveal himself to his brothers so soon, which can only mean that Joseph at that moment had not yet fully implemented his plan, that he was still planning something else. But what could that be, given that (as it would seem) the brothers had already completed the process of their repentance?

As already discussed, the brothers have by now undergone all the stages of their *teshuvah*, repentance. They have admitted acting improperly, and have suffered genuine anxiety for their sin of selling Joseph. And, finally, they have now not sold out or abandoned Benjamin, the "younger Joseph," Rachel's son, the official favorite who had received special gifts, but who, at the same time, is the criminal who stole the goblet (as they have been led to believe, at least). It would seem that Joseph's job of correcting his brothers is done. What else, then, could he be planning, and why?

The essence of the problem is that the brothers, as Joseph sees it, had committed not just one, but two related and consecutive sins that demanded correction. They have indeed atoned for their sin of selling Joseph (or casting him into the pit). But that was their second sin, while their first sin still remains, namely, their refusal to recognize Joseph as king. From Joseph's point of view, this sin is no less serious than the other, and Joseph was therefore planning to correct it with additional actions, but he could not realize his plan.

We have noted above that Joseph chose to act on his dreams not because a person should properly strive to realize his dreams (Judaism itself imposes no such obligation on any person), but because in those dreams he saw God prompting him with the proper strategy for correcting his brothers.

Josephs first dream is realized when the brothers arrive in

Egypt the second (not the first) time, because only then are they all together to a man, and Joseph manages to bring the brothers to complete repentance for their sin of selling him into slavery. But now, Joseph would have been planning the implementation of his second dream, in order to correct his brothers' second sin – rejecting his royal status.

Apparently, Joseph was now intending to detain Benjamin, and to demand that his father Jacob come himself to Egypt, with his wives and children, to fetch Benjamin. Had Joseph made that demand, the brothers would have had no choice but to return home for their father, and to bring the entire family back to Egypt to stand before Joseph.

That would have been the realization of the second dream – the sun, moon, and stars worshipping Joseph. Had Joseph waited to reveal himself to his family at that moment, the effect would have been so powerful that the brothers, in all likelihood, could not have doubted that it was all happening according to the Divine will, and they would have acknowledged the legitimacy and necessity of Joseph's kingship in its material and also spiritual aspects.

But Joseph was unable to realize this plan. And although the brothers seem to reconcile with Joseph and recognize his supremacy on a practical level, no such recognition occurs on the level of spiritual values, and the divide between them is not bridged. At later stages of Jewish history this will result in remoteness of relations between the tribes of Joseph and Judah, the Northern and Southern kingdoms. They will live separately, and their relations will not always be amicable.

It is very difficult for Joseph and Judah to acknowledge each other's spiritual importance. We can compare this to the situation in Israel today, where the non-religious Zionists and the ultra-Orthodox *Haredim* each find it difficult to acknowledge that the opposite side has important values that their own direction lacks. Indeed, in our time, these "Joseph-like" and "Judah-like" camps do not kill (nor do they usually sell) each other, but mutual respect is very lacking. The ultra-Orthodox *Haredim* (an extreme form of Judah) regard the Israeli statehood created by the people of Joseph as only a technical foundation, but they do not recognize its spiritual value. And the extreme supporters of Joseph, on the other hand (whose ideology is to build a state solely in its material aspects), see no importance in religious tradition.

But until all these aspects find their correction, such that not only material-political but also spiritual recognition is mutually granted, the Messianic process cannot advance. Thus, the work that Joseph was not able to complete in Egypt remains for us to complete in the course of Jewish history.

52.4. Joseph Reveals Himself to His Brothers (45:2-3)

ב וַיִּתֵּן אֶת־קֹלוֹ בִּבְכִי וַיִּשְׁמְעוּ מִצְרַיִם וַיִּשְׁמַע בֵּית
פַּרְעֹה: ג וַיֹּאמֶר יוֹסֵף אֶל־אֶחָיו אֲנִי יוֹסֵף הַעוֹד אָבִי
חָי וְלֹא־יָכְלוּ אֶחָיו לַעֲנוֹת אֹתוֹ כִּי נִבְהֲלוּ מִפָּנָיו:

[2] His sobs were so loud that the Egyptians could hear, and so the news reached Pharaoh's palace.
[3] Joseph said to his brothers, "I am Joseph. Is my father still well?" But his brothers could not answer him, so dumfounded were they on account of him.

[3] Is my father still well?: Literally, "Does my father still live?" It would seem that this is a rhetorical question, because Joseph has already received the answer. But the actual meaning of Joseph's question is different. The emphasis is on "my": Does Jacob continue to live and manage the family as "Joseph's father," or is he completely subordinated to Leah's sons and their rules? Is there a place in the family not only for shallow, paternalistical care of Rachel's sons, but to incorporate their spiritual living space as well?

So dumfounded were they on account of him: But the brothers have no answer for Joseph on this question, which is yet another indicator that their education is still not complete.

52.5. Joseph Summons His Family to Egypt (45:4-15)

ד וַיֹּאמֶר יוֹסֵף אֶל־אֶחָיו גְּשׁוּ־נָא אֵלַי וַיִּגָּשׁוּ וַיֹּאמֶר אֲנִי יוֹסֵף אֲחִיכֶם אֲשֶׁר־מְכַרְתֶּם אֹתִי מִצְרָיְמָה: ה וְעַתָּה | אַל־תֵּעָצְבוּ וְאַל־יִחַר בְּעֵינֵיכֶם כִּי־מְכַרְתֶּם אֹתִי הֵנָּה כִּי לְמִחְיָה שְׁלָחַנִי אֱלֹהִים לִפְנֵיכֶם: ו כִּי־זֶה שְׁנָתַיִם הָרָעָב בְּקֶרֶב הָאָרֶץ וְעוֹד חָמֵשׁ שָׁנִים אֲשֶׁר אֵין־חָרִישׁ וְקָצִיר: ז וַיִּשְׁלָחֵנִי אֱלֹהִים לִפְנֵיכֶם לָשׂוּם לָכֶם שְׁאֵרִית בָּאָרֶץ וּלְהַחֲיוֹת לָכֶם לִפְלֵיטָה גְּדֹלָה: ח וְעַתָּה לֹא־אַתֶּם שְׁלַחְתֶּם אֹתִי הֵנָּה כִּי הָאֱלֹהִים וַיְשִׂימֵנִי לְאָב לְפַרְעֹה וּלְאָדוֹן לְכָל־בֵּיתוֹ וּמֹשֵׁל בְּכָל־אֶרֶץ מִצְרָיִם: ט מַהֲרוּ וַעֲלוּ אֶל־אָבִי וַאֲמַרְתֶּם אֵלָיו כֹּה אָמַר בִּנְךָ יוֹסֵף שָׂמַנִי אֱלֹהִים לְאָדוֹן לְכָל־מִצְרָיִם רְדָה אֵלַי אַל־תַּעֲמֹד: י וְיָשַׁבְתָּ בְאֶרֶץ־גֹּשֶׁן וְהָיִיתָ קָרוֹב אֵלַי אַתָּה וּבָנֶיךָ וּבְנֵי בָנֶיךָ וְצֹאנְךָ וּבְקָרְךָ וְכָל־אֲשֶׁר־לָךְ: יא וְכִלְכַּלְתִּי אֹתְךָ שָׁם כִּי־עוֹד חָמֵשׁ שָׁנִים רָעָב פֶּן־תִּוָּרֵשׁ אַתָּה וּבֵיתְךָ וְכָל־אֲשֶׁר־לָךְ: יב וְהִנֵּה עֵינֵיכֶם רֹאוֹת וְעֵינֵי אָחִי בִנְיָמִין כִּי־

פִי הַמְדַבֵּר אֲלֵיכֶם: **יג** וְהִגַּדְתֶּם לְאָבִי אֶת־כָּל־כְּבוֹדִי
בְּמִצְרַיִם וְאֵת כָּל־אֲשֶׁר רְאִיתֶם וּמִהַרְתֶּם וְהוֹרַדְתֶּם
אֶת־אָבִי הֵנָּה: **יד** וַיִּפֹּל עַל־צַוְּארֵי בִנְיָמִן־אָחִיו וַיֵּבְךְּ
וּבִנְיָמִן בָּכָה עַל־צַוָּארָיו: **טו** וַיְנַשֵּׁק לְכָל־אֶחָיו וַיֵּבְךְּ
עֲלֵהֶם וְאַחֲרֵי כֵן דִּבְּרוּ אֶחָיו אִתּוֹ:

[4] Then Joseph said to his brothers, "Come
forward to me." And when they came forward,
he said, "I am your brother Joseph, he whom you
sold into Egypt.

[5] Now, do not be distressed or reproach
yourselves because you sold me hither; it was
to save life that God sent me ahead of you.

[6] It is now two years that there has been famine
in the land, and there are still five years to come
in which there shall be no yield from tilling.

[7] God has sent me ahead of you to ensure your
survival on earth, and to save your lives in an
extraordinary deliverance.

[8] So, it was not you who sent me here, but God;
and He has made me a father to Pharaoh, lord
of all his household, and ruler over the whole
land of Egypt.

[9] "Now, hurry back to my father and say to
him: Thus says your son Joseph, 'God has made
me lord of all Egypt; come down to me without
delay.

[10] You will dwell in the region of Goshen, where
you will be near me – you and your children and
your grandchildren, your flocks and herds, and
all that is yours.

[11] There I will provide for you – for there are
yet five years of famine to come – that you and

your household and all that is yours may not suffer want.'

[12] You can see for yourselves, and my brother Benjamin for himself, that it is indeed I who am speaking to you.

[13] And you must tell my father everything about my high station in Egypt and all that you have seen; and bring my father here with all speed."

[14] With that he embraced his brother Benjamin around the neck and wept, and Benjamin wept on his neck.

[15] He kissed all his brothers and wept upon them; only then were his brothers able to talk to him.

[4] I am your brother Joseph: Joseph feels great satisfaction for having reunited the family. He loves his brothers and wishes them well. But there are important shortcomings in his approach, and in his plans for the family's future development.

[5] It was to save life that God sent me ahead of you: Joseph sees himself as God's emissary, and feels that everything that happens to him is a part of the Divine plan.

[8] So, it was not you who sent me here, but God; and He has made me a father to Pharaoh, lord of all his household, and ruler over the whole land of Egypt: Joseph has never experienced disappointment in Egypt. Moreover, he considers himself in some sense even superior to Pharaoh himself. Pharaoh, in his view, is only Egypt's titular head, while he, Joseph, is the true ruler ("a father to Pharaoh").

[10] You will dwell in the region of Goshen ... that you and your household and all that is yours may not suffer want: Motivated by concern for his family, Joseph tells the brothers to take their father and move to Egypt. Now Joseph could certainly leave his family in Canaan and supply them with bread there. Compared to the innumerable reserves of grain that he has collected in Egypt, the needs of a small family are rather insignificant. Recall that Joseph answered to no one, as demonstrated by his returning the brothers' money to their bags.

[13] And you must tell my father everything about my high station in Egypt: Most likely, the highly dubious plan that Joseph offers his father and brothers is based on ideological rather than economic considerations. He has not abandoned his plans for restructuring Egypt, and for this he needs allies and assistants. Moreover, we clearly see a certain vanity in Joseph's words. All of this is a sign of Joseph's fall.

[14] With that he embraced his brother Benjamin around the neck and wept: The word "neck" appears here in an unusual form, *tzaverei*; which means, literally, "necks." Why is the plural used here?

The Midrash sees here an allusion to the two Temples, which would be located in Jerusalem, Benjamin's territory. (In the Song of Songs [7:5] the Temple is likewise compared to the human neck). Says the Midrash: "Joseph weeps on Benjamin's 'necks' for the destruction of not just one but two Temples that will be located in the territory of Benjamin."

The meaning of this midrash is that Joseph cried not merely because he was emotionally overwhelmed by this reunion with his beloved brother, but because he knows he has not completed his work, and he understands what the future result of that will be. Joseph could not fully realize his plan to truly and fully unite the brothers, to get Judah to acknowledge the importance of Joseph's kingdom, and to imbue the spirit of Judaism with a proper understanding of the spiritual value that resides within the material. These failings, in the end, became the cause of the destruction of both the first and second Temples.

Chapter 53

Jacob's Family Descends
to Egypt

53.1. Pharaoh Invites Jacob's Family to Egypt (45:16-24)

טז וְהַקֹּל נִשְׁמַע בֵּית פַּרְעֹה לֵאמֹר בָּאוּ אֲחֵי יוֹסֵף וַיִּיטַב
בְּעֵינֵי פַרְעֹה וּבְעֵינֵי עֲבָדָיו: **יז** וַיֹּאמֶר פַּרְעֹה אֶל־יוֹסֵף
אֱמֹר אֶל־אַחֶיךָ זֹאת עֲשׂוּ טַעֲנוּ אֶת־בְּעִירְכֶם וּלְכוּ־
בֹאוּ אַרְצָה כְּנָעַן: **יח** וּקְחוּ אֶת־אֲבִיכֶם וְאֶת־בָּתֵּיכֶם
וּבֹאוּ אֵלָי וְאֶתְּנָה לָכֶם אֶת־טוּב אֶרֶץ מִצְרַיִם וְאִכְלוּ
אֶת־חֵלֶב הָאָרֶץ: **יט** וְאַתָּה צֻוֵּיתָה זֹאת עֲשׂוּ קְחוּ־לָכֶם
מֵאֶרֶץ מִצְרַיִם עֲגָלוֹת לְטַפְּכֶם וְלִנְשֵׁיכֶם וּנְשָׂאתֶם אֶת־
אֲבִיכֶם וּבָאתֶם: **כ** וְעֵינְכֶם אַל־תָּחֹס עַל־כְּלֵיכֶם כִּי־טוּב
כָּל־אֶרֶץ מִצְרַיִם לָכֶם הוּא: **כא** וַיַּעֲשׂוּ־כֵן בְּנֵי יִשְׂרָאֵל
וַיִּתֵּן לָהֶם יוֹסֵף עֲגָלוֹת עַל־פִּי פַרְעֹה וַיִּתֵּן לָהֶם צֵדָה
לַדָּרֶךְ: **כב** לְכֻלָּם נָתַן לָאִישׁ חֲלִפוֹת שְׂמָלֹת וּלְבִנְיָמִן
נָתַן שְׁלֹשׁ מֵאוֹת כֶּסֶף וְחָמֵשׁ חֲלִפֹת שְׂמָלֹת: **כג** וּלְאָבִיו
שָׁלַח כְּזֹאת עֲשָׂרָה חֲמֹרִים נֹשְׂאִים מִטּוּב מִצְרָיִם וְעֶשֶׂר
אֲתֹנֹת נֹשְׂאֹת בָּר וָלֶחֶם וּמָזוֹן לְאָבִיו לַדָּרֶךְ: **כד** וַיְשַׁלַּח
אֶת־אֶחָיו וַיֵּלֵכוּ וַיֹּאמֶר אֲלֵהֶם אַל־תִּרְגְּזוּ בַּדָּרֶךְ:

[16] The news reached Pharaoh's palace:

"Joseph's brothers have come." Pharaoh and his courtiers were pleased.

[17] And Pharaoh said to Joseph, "Say to your brothers, 'Do as follows: load up your beasts and go at once to the land of Canaan.

[18] Take your father and your households and come to me; I will give you the best of the land of Egypt and you shall live off the fat of the land.'

[19] And you are bidden [to add], 'Do as follows: take from the land of Egypt wagons for your children and your wives, and bring your father here.

[20] And never mind your belongings, for the best of all the land of Egypt shall be yours.'"

[21] The sons of Israel did so; Joseph gave them wagons as Pharaoh had commanded, and he supplied them with provisions for the journey.

[22] To each of them, moreover, he gave a change of clothing; but to Benjamin he gave three hundred pieces of silver and several changes of clothing.

[23] And to his father he sent the following: ten he-asses laden with the best things of Egypt, and ten she-asses laden with grain, bread, and provisions for his father on the journey.

[24] As he sent his brothers off on their way, he told them, "Do not be quarrelsome on the way."

[16] Pharaoh and his courtiers were pleased: Joseph's former status as a slave in the house of Potiphar was well known to all. Although Joseph himself insisted that he was born a free man, and that he had been sold illegally, this was in no way actually confirmed, and the Egyptians could therefore have always assumed that it was all a mere fabrication. But now that he can show Egypt his father and brothers, Joseph's freeborn status is proven, an important development both for Joseph himself and for Pharaoh's court.

[18] Take your father and your households and come to me; I will give you the best of the land of Egypt: Pharaoh might have believed that if just one Hebrew could save Egypt from starvation and enrich the country, then the entire Jacob family would bring Egypt fabulous prosperity.

We should note that sensible rulers often decide to invite Jews to their country with the goal of promoting the welfare of their state. This has been repeated many times throughout Jewish history.

[21] Joseph gave them wagons as Pharaoh had commanded: Wagons were issued in Egypt only with Pharaoh's sanction, because they were considered a "strategic mode of transportation."

[22] To each of them, moreover, he gave a change of clothing; but to Benjamin he gave three hundred pieces of silver and several changes of clothing: Joseph wants the brothers to finally rise to a level where they no longer experience envy if one of them receives more than all the others.

[24] He told them, "Do not be quarrelsome on the way": That is, refrain from quarreling about who was innocent and who was guilty in selling Joseph, because the main thing is to move forward rather than concentrating on the past. While it is crucial that we understand the meaning of past events, we must also accept that because multiple interpretations for those events always exist, there is no point in quibbling, let alone feuding, over which is the correct interpretation. The main thing is to move on.

53.2. Jacob Goes Down to Egypt (45:25-46:7)

כה וַיַּעֲלוּ מִמִּצְרָיִם וַיָּבֹאוּ אֶרֶץ כְּנַעַן אֶל־יַעֲקֹב אֲבִיהֶם: כו וַיַּגִּדוּ לוֹ לֵאמֹר עוֹד יוֹסֵף חַי וְכִי־הוּא מֹשֵׁל בְּכָל־אֶרֶץ מִצְרָיִם וַיָּפָג לִבּוֹ כִּי לֹא־הֶאֱמִין לָהֶם: כז וַיְדַבְּרוּ אֵלָיו אֵת כָּל־דִּבְרֵי יוֹסֵף אֲשֶׁר דִּבֶּר אֲלֵהֶם וַיַּרְא אֶת־הָעֲגָלוֹת אֲשֶׁר־שָׁלַח יוֹסֵף לָשֵׂאת אֹתוֹ וַתְּחִי רוּחַ יַעֲקֹב אֲבִיהֶם: כח וַיֹּאמֶר יִשְׂרָאֵל רַב עוֹד־יוֹסֵף בְּנִי חָי אֵלְכָה וְאֶרְאֶנּוּ בְּטֶרֶם אָמוּת:

א וַיִּסַּע יִשְׂרָאֵל וְכָל־אֲשֶׁר־לוֹ וַיָּבֹא בְּאֵרָה שָּׁבַע וַיִּזְבַּח זְבָחִים לֵאלֹהֵי אָבִיו יִצְחָק: ב וַיֹּאמֶר אֱלֹהִים | לְיִשְׂרָאֵל בְּמַרְאֹת הַלַּיְלָה וַיֹּאמֶר יַעֲקֹב | יַעֲקֹב וַיֹּאמֶר הִנֵּנִי: ג וַיֹּאמֶר אָנֹכִי הָאֵל אֱלֹהֵי אָבִיךָ אַל־תִּירָא מֵרְדָה מִצְרַיְמָה כִּי־לְגוֹי גָּדוֹל אֲשִׂימְךָ שָׁם: ד אָנֹכִי אֵרֵד עִמְּךָ מִצְרַיְמָה וְאָנֹכִי אַעַלְךָ גַם־עָלֹה וְיוֹסֵף יָשִׁית יָדוֹ עַל־עֵינֶיךָ: ה וַיָּקָם יַעֲקֹב מִבְּאֵר שָׁבַע וַיִּשְׂאוּ בְנֵי־יִשְׂרָאֵל אֶת־יַעֲקֹב אֲבִיהֶם וְאֶת־טַפָּם וְאֶת־נְשֵׁיהֶם בָּעֲגָלוֹת אֲשֶׁר־שָׁלַח פַּרְעֹה לָשֵׂאת אֹתוֹ: ו וַיִּקְחוּ אֶת־מִקְנֵיהֶם וְאֶת־רְכוּשָׁם אֲשֶׁר רָכְשׁוּ בְּאֶרֶץ כְּנַעַן וַיָּבֹאוּ מִצְרָיְמָה יַעֲקֹב וְכָל־זַרְעוֹ אִתּוֹ: ז בָּנָיו וּבְנֵי בָנָיו אִתּוֹ בְּנֹתָיו וּבְנוֹת בָּנָיו וְכָל־זַרְעוֹ הֵבִיא אִתּוֹ מִצְרָיְמָה:

[25] They went up from Egypt and came to their father Jacob in the land of Canaan.
[26] And they told him, "Joseph is still alive; yes, he is ruler over the whole land of Egypt." His

heart went numb, for he did not believe them.

[27] But when they recounted all that Joseph had said to them, and when he saw the wagons that Joseph had sent to transport him, the spirit of their father Jacob revived.

[28] "Enough!" said Israel. "My son Joseph is still alive! I must go and see him before I die."

(46:1) So Israel set out with all that was his, and he came to Beer-sheba, where he offered sacrifices to the God of his father Isaac.

[2] God called to Israel in a vision by night: "Jacob! Jacob!" He answered, "Here."

[3] And He said, "I am God, the God of your father. Fear not to go down to Egypt, for I will make you there into a great nation.

[4] I Myself will go down with you to Egypt, and I Myself will also bring you back; and Joseph's hand shall close your eyes."

[5] So Jacob set out from Beer-sheba. The sons of Israel put their father Jacob and their children and their wives in the wagons that Pharaoh had sent to transport him;

[6] and they took along their livestock and the wealth that they had amassed in the land of Canaan. Thus Jacob and all his offspring with him came to Egypt:

[7] he brought with him to Egypt his sons and grandsons, his daughters and granddaughters – all his offspring.

[26] His heart went numb, for he did not believe them:
It is not easy for Jacob to believe the joyful news, but he

quickly accepts it as true. Subconsciously, he has always felt that Joseph was alive.

The Midrash asks: But wasn't Jacob a prophet? Why then did he not know with certainty that Joseph was still alive? The answer given by the Midrash is that Jacob was in mourning for Joseph, and mourning suppresses prophecy.

[27] The spirit of their father Jacob revived. [28] Said Israel. "My son Joseph is still alive! I must go and see him": Once *Jacob* knows that Joseph is alive, he again becomes *Israel*. His full-fledged "national" character is reborn.

[46:1] So Israel set out with all that was his, and he came to Beer-sheba: Because Beer-sheba is on the border to the Land of Israel, it is there that Jacob asks God's permission to go again into exile.

He offered sacrifices to the God of his father Isaac: Isaac was ordered to remain in Israel throughout his entire life (26:3). "The God of Isaac" is that aspect of Divinity that prohibits leaving the Land of Israel.

[2] God called to Israel in a vision by night: Night and night visions are a symbol of exile.

God called to Israel ... "Jacob! Jacob!": Since this is now about going into the Exile, Israel again becomes Jacob.

When so many years before Jacob returned to the Land of Israel, God changed his name to "Israel." And now, as he leaves it again, he is losing his national character and becoming again just a family, Jacob. "Israel" is the Jews' identity in their own country, the state of *gadlut* (greatness) maximally realized. Jacob, on the other hand, is that deficient degree of Jewish self-realization that prevails when the people are in exile, in its state of *katnut*, "smallness."

But we should not assume that this condition is unambiguously negative. The ability to return to the *katnut* state from time to time allows the Jewish nation to remain eternal. The state of *gadlut*, greatness, cannot be consistently maintained. There are periods when it is necessary to return to the condition of Jacob in order to wait out difficult times. With this understanding, "Jacob" represents the period of Israel's "hibernation," but also the guarantee of its eternity.

As already noted, Jacob's name change to "Israel" was different from Abraham's name change from "Abram." In the latter case, the name "Abram" was completely abolished, replaced by "Abraham." But when God gave Jacob the name "Israel," the new name was only an addition to the name "Jacob," which was neither abolished nor replaced.

With these two names of their third Patriarch, the Almighty gives the Jewish people two legitimate modes of existence: to exist as Jacob, or as Israel. The choice depends on the era. In some periods, the Jews exist as an independent nation in their own land, as did the Patriarch Israel. But in other periods they exist more in the manner of Jacob – a family and a religious community that needs merely to survive in exile.

However, even when the Jews are in exile, they retain the memory of their existence as an independent people, and the knowledge that they must eventually return to their previous, self-sufficient state. Therefore, even in foreign lands they remain an independent people, although this is not always visible. It sometimes seems that they are only a religious community or an ethnic group there.

[6] They took along their livestock and the wealth that they had amassed in the land of Canaan. Thus Jacob and

all his offspring with him came to Egypt: The Torah is emphasizing that the Jacob family went down to Egypt *in toto*, and in all aspects: children, grandchildren, wives, and property. All aspects of life had to descend into Egypt in order to be completely rebuilt there, and only then to leave Egypt as an entirely new entity.

[5] The sons of Israel put their father Jacob ... in the wagons: The opposition here is striking: *Jacob*, but the sons of *Israel*. As they now go into exile they are the "sons of Israel," raised in their own land.

53.3. "These Are the Names of the Israelites Who Came to Egypt" (46:8-27)

ח וְאֵלֶּה שְׁמוֹת בְּנֵי־יִשְׂרָאֵל הַבָּאִים מִצְרַיְמָה יַעֲקֹב וּבָנָיו בְּכֹר יַעֲקֹב רְאוּבֵן: ט וּבְנֵי רְאוּבֵן חֲנוֹךְ וּפַלּוּא וְחֶצְרֹן וְכַרְמִי: י וּבְנֵי שִׁמְעוֹן יְמוּאֵל וְיָמִין וְאֹהַד וְיָכִין וְצֹחַר וְשָׁאוּל בֶּן־הַכְּנַעֲנִית: יא וּבְנֵי לֵוִי גֵּרְשׁוֹן קְהָת וּמְרָרִי: יב וּבְנֵי יְהוּדָה עֵר וְאוֹנָן וְשֵׁלָה וָפֶרֶץ וָזָרַח וַיָּמָת עֵר וְאוֹנָן בְּאֶרֶץ כְּנַעַן וַיִּהְיוּ בְנֵי־פֶרֶץ חֶצְרֹן וְחָמוּל: יג וּבְנֵי יִשָּׂשכָר תּוֹלָע וּפֻוָּה וְיוֹב וְשִׁמְרֹן: יד וּבְנֵי זְבֻלוּן סֶרֶד וְאֵלוֹן וְיַחְלְאֵל: טו אֵלֶּה | בְּנֵי לֵאָה אֲשֶׁר יָלְדָה לְיַעֲקֹב בְּפַדַּן אֲרָם וְאֵת דִּינָה בִתּוֹ כָּל־נֶפֶשׁ בָּנָיו וּבְנוֹתָיו שְׁלֹשִׁים וְשָׁלֹשׁ: טז וּבְנֵי גָד צִפְיוֹן וְחַגִּי שׁוּנִי וְאֶצְבֹּן עֵרִי וַאֲרוֹדִי וְאַרְאֵלִי: יז וּבְנֵי אָשֵׁר יִמְנָה וְיִשְׁוָה וְיִשְׁוִי וּבְרִיעָה וְשֶׂרַח אֲחֹתָם וּבְנֵי בְרִיעָה חֶבֶר וּמַלְכִּיאֵל: יח אֵלֶּה בְּנֵי זִלְפָּה אֲשֶׁר־נָתַן לָבָן לְלֵאָה בִתּוֹ וַתֵּלֶד אֶת־אֵלֶּה לְיַעֲקֹב שֵׁשׁ עֶשְׂרֵה נָפֶשׁ: יט בְּנֵי רָחֵל אֵשֶׁת יַעֲקֹב יוֹסֵף וּבִנְיָמִן: כ וַיִּוָּלֵד לְיוֹסֵף בְּאֶרֶץ מִצְרַיִם אֲשֶׁר יָלְדָה־לּוֹ אָסְנַת בַּת־פּוֹטִי פֶרַע כֹּהֵן אֹן אֶת־מְנַשֶּׁה וְאֶת־אֶפְרָיִם: כא וּבְנֵי בִנְיָמִן בֶּלַע וָבֶכֶר וְאַשְׁבֵּל גֵּרָא וְנַעֲמָן

אֲחִי וָרֹאשׁ מֻפִּים וְחֻפִּים וָאָרְדְּ: **כב** אֵלֶּה בְּנֵי רָחֵל אֲשֶׁר
יֻלַּד לְיַעֲקֹב כָּל־נֶפֶשׁ אַרְבָּעָה עָשָׂר: **כג** וּבְנֵי־דָן חֻשִׁים:
כד וּבְנֵי נַפְתָּלִי יַחְצְאֵל וְגוּנִי וְיֵצֶר וְשִׁלֵּם: **כה** אֵלֶּה בְּנֵי
בִלְהָה אֲשֶׁר־נָתַן לָבָן לְרָחֵל בִּתּוֹ וַתֵּלֶד אֶת־אֵלֶּה לְיַעֲקֹב
כָּל־נֶפֶשׁ שִׁבְעָה: **כו** כָּל־הַנֶּפֶשׁ הַבָּאָה לְיַעֲקֹב מִצְרַיְמָה
יֹצְאֵי יְרֵכוֹ מִלְּבַד נְשֵׁי בְנֵי־יַעֲקֹב כָּל־נֶפֶשׁ שִׁשִּׁים וָשֵׁשׁ:
כז וּבְנֵי יוֹסֵף אֲשֶׁר־יֻלַּד־לוֹ בְמִצְרַיִם נֶפֶשׁ שְׁנָיִם כָּל־
הַנֶּפֶשׁ לְבֵית־יַעֲקֹב הַבָּאָה מִצְרַיְמָה שִׁבְעִים:

[8] These are the names of the Israelites, Jacob
and his descendants, who came to Egypt. Jacob's
first-born Reuben;

[9] Reuben's sons: Enoch, Pallu, Hezron, and
Carmi.

[10] Simeon's sons: Jemuel, Jamin, Ohad, Jachin,
Zohar, and Saul the son of a Canaanite woman.

[11] Levi's sons: Gershon, Kohath, and Merari.

[12] Judah's sons: Er, Onan, Shelah, Perez, and
Zerah – but Er and Onan had died in the land
of Canaan; and Perez's sons were Hezron and
Hamul.

[13] Issachar's sons: Tola, Puvah, Iob, and
Shimron.

[14] Zebulun's sons: Sered, Elon, and Jahleel.

[15] Those were the sons whom Leah bore
to Jacob in Paddan-aram, in addition to his
daughter Dinah. Persons in all, male and female:
33.

[16] Gad's sons: Ziphion, Haggi, Shuni, Ezbon,
Eri, Arodi, and Areli.

[17] Asher's sons: Imnah, Ishvah, Ishvi, and
Beriah, and their sister Serah. Beriah's sons:
Heber and Malchiel.

[18] These were the descendants of Zilpah, whom Laban had given to his daughter Leah. These she bore to Jacob – 16 persons.

[19] The sons of Jacob's wife Rachel were Joseph and Benjamin.

[20] To Joseph were born in the land of Egypt Manasseh and Ephraim, whom Asenath daughter of Poti-phera priest of On bore to him.

[21] Benjamin's sons: Bela, Becher, Ashbel, Gera, Naaman, Ehi, Rosh, Muppim, Huppim, and Ard.

[22] These were the descendants of Rachel who were born to Jacob – 14 persons in all.

[23] Dan's son: Hushim.

[24] Naphtali's sons: Jahzeel, Guni, Jezer, and Shillem.

[25] These were the descendants of Bilhah, whom Laban had given to his daughter Rachel. These she bore to Jacob – 7 persons in all.

[26] All the persons belonging to Jacob who came to Egypt – his own issue, aside from the wives of Jacob's sons – all these persons numbered 66.

[27] And Joseph's sons who were born to him in Egypt were two in number. Thus the total of Jacob's household who came to Egypt was seventy persons.

[8] These are the names of the Israelites, Jacob and his descendants, who came to Egypt: The Midrash says that even the names themselves, and not only the people bearing those names, came down to Egypt. We noted previously that in Hebrew the name of an object is more than just a name – it is an indicator of the goal and purpose of the person or object so named. In a certain sense, then, the very goals of the Israelites and the purpose of their existence are now descending into Egypt.

[27] The total of Jacob's household who came to Egypt was seventy persons: The Torah notes very precisely the number of Jacob's descendants from each branch of the family, and then gives the grand total as well, by which we are given to understand that these numbers arose not randomly or by chance.

The number 70 is understood in Jewish tradition as representing the original seventy nations of the world as enumerated in the tenth chapter of Genesis. Israel is itself a microcosm – the root of humanity. Because the task of the Jewish people is to emit Divine light to all the peoples of the world, the Jewish nation must contain the seeds of the souls of all the nations of the world. (This connection is emphasized in Deuteronomy 32:8: "When the Most High gave nations their homes and set the divisions of man, He fixed the boundaries of peoples in relation to Israel's numbers.")

Arrival of Jacob's family to Egypt, which makes possible the birth of the Jewish people in the future, carries universal import for the future correction of the entire world. In order for that universal potential to be realized, the essence of each of these seventy nations of the world must undergo a "ripening" process in Egypt.

53.4. Jacob Sends Judah Ahead to Joseph (46:28)

כח וְאֶת־יְהוּדָה שָׁלַח לְפָנָיו אֶל־יוֹסֵף לְהוֹרֹת לְפָנָיו
גֹּשְׁנָה וַיָּבֹאוּ אַרְצָה גֹּשֶׁן:

[28] He had sent Judah ahead of him to Joseph, to point the way before him to Goshen. So when they came to the region of Goshen,

[28] He had sent Judah ahead of him to Joseph, to point the way before him to Goshen: This verse, and the fact that Jacob "sent Judah ahead of him," seem incidental to the story at best, and not significant enough to require mention. The Midrash therefore understands the word "*lehorot*" (here translated as "to point the way") somewhat differently, with a meaning of instructing or teaching. (It is the very same root as that of the word "Torah.") The Midrash thus reads this verse as "He had sent Judah ahead of him, to build *yeshivot* – institutions of Torah learning – in Egypt" (whose purpose was to enable the nation to survive in exile).

Of course, this Midrash cannot be taken literally, especially since it is impossible to create a *yeshivah* where there are still no Jews. The meaning of the Midrash is actually different. For the period of the exile, Jacob puts Judah in charge of the Jewish nation; that is, he puts Judah above Joseph. Moreover, Jacob sends Judah not just to Egypt generally, but to Joseph specifically. In other words, Judah must teach the Torah also to Joseph.

Joseph and Judah will both change in the course of history, each under the other's influence. By standing up for Benjamin, Judah taught Joseph an important lesson. And Joseph likewise, in leading his brothers to repentance, had a significant influence on Judah. Under this mutual influence each acquires a new essence – which is to say, new entities are born from them: *Mashiach ben Yosef* and *Mashiach ben David*.

53.5. Jacob is Reunited with Joseph (46:29-30)

כט וַיֶּאְסֹר יוֹסֵף מֶרְכַּבְתּוֹ וַיַּעַל לִקְרַאת־יִשְׂרָאֵל אָבִיו
גֹּשְׁנָה וַיֵּרָא אֵלָיו וַיִּפֹּל עַל־צַוָּארָיו וַיֵּבְךְּ עַל־צַוָּארָיו
עוֹד: ל וַיֹּאמֶר יִשְׂרָאֵל אֶל־יוֹסֵף אָמוּתָה הַפָּעַם אַחֲרֵי
רְאוֹתִי אֶת־פָּנֶיךָ כִּי עוֹדְךָ חָי:

*[29] Joseph ordered his chariot and went to
Goshen to meet his father Israel; he presented
himself to him and, embracing him around the
neck, he wept on his neck a good while.*
*[30] Then Israel said to Joseph, "Now I can die,
having seen for myself that you are still alive."*

[29] Joseph ordered his chariot: This fact *per se* seems to
be an unimportant and unnecessary detail. But the concept
of "chariot" is connected with an idea of utmost importance
in Jewish mysticism, first encountered as the *Merkavah*, the
chariot on which the Almighty is seated in the famous vision
of the prophet Ezekiel (Ezek. 1).

In the human world, the terms "chariot" used in this sense
refers to a person through whom, in a given situation, the
Divine influence is manifested, on whom the *Shechinah*, the
Divine presence, rests. Until now, the Patriarchs were the
chariots, but now the chariot is Joseph. Jacob sees that the
Shechinah rests on Joseph, and that God reveals Himself to
the world through him.

He presented himself to him: *Vayera elav* – The Torah uses
this curious expression also in the story of Abraham (18:1):
"The Lord appeared to him by the terebinths of Mamre." The
word "appear" as used in the Torah generally means revealing

something that is hidden; thus, the term is appropriate when used with reference to God. When God appears to man, the Divine is revealed and the world is renewed. In this instance, then, we can understand the words "He presented himself to him" as indicating that God reveals himself to the world – and to Jacob's family – through Joseph.

[30] Then Israel said to Joseph, "Now I can die": He means that at this moment Israel is actually dying, and again becoming Jacob.

Having seen for myself: Literally, "having seen your face." Jacob used the same turn of phrase earlier, in his meeting with Esau ("for to see your face is like seeing the face of God"; 33:10). We noted there that this expression is always associated either with a revelation by God, or when a person meets with a powerful ruler, to indicate that he is regarded as a deity ("I shall not see your face again," says Moses to Pharaoh [Exod. 10:28]). Upon arriving in Egypt, Israel's national existence ceases, and is replaced by "Jacob," a family-communal, religious existence.

That you are still alive: Jacob reveres Joseph, for Joseph is still alive. But when Joseph dies, the material life of the Diaspora dies, and Joseph's power is transformed into *Mashiach ben Yosef*. His return to the Land then begins, and when that return is finally complete, Israel is resurrected again.

The outcome of Jacob and Joseph's reunion is as follows. Jacob acknowledges Joseph's plan as a Divine process and agrees to obey his instructions. At this moment, Joseph's second dream comes true, but only to certain extent, not completely. The brothers, after all, are not participating in the conversation. The Torah makes no mention of them here, because, even if physically present, they are spiritually distant. They feel nothing of what Jacob feels before Joseph, and the reunion has no effect on them.

53.6. Joseph's Brothers Have an Audience with Pharaoh (46:31-47:6)

לא וַיֹּאמֶר יוֹסֵף אֶל־אֶחָיו וְאֶל־בֵּית אָבִיו אֶעֱלֶה וְאַגִּידָה לְפַרְעֹה וְאֹמְרָה אֵלָיו אַחַי וּבֵית־אָבִי אֲשֶׁר בְּאֶרֶץ־כְּנַעַן בָּאוּ אֵלָי: **לב** וְהָאֲנָשִׁים רֹעֵי צֹאן כִּי־אַנְשֵׁי מִקְנֶה הָיוּ וְצֹאנָם וּבְקָרָם וְכָל־אֲשֶׁר לָהֶם הֵבִיאוּ: **לג** וְהָיָה כִּי־יִקְרָא לָכֶם פַּרְעֹה וְאָמַר מַה־מַּעֲשֵׂיכֶם: **לד** וַאֲמַרְתֶּם אַנְשֵׁי מִקְנֶה הָיוּ עֲבָדֶיךָ מִנְּעוּרֵינוּ וְעַד־עַתָּה גַּם־אֲנַחְנוּ גַּם־אֲבֹתֵינוּ בַּעֲבוּר תֵּשְׁבוּ בְּאֶרֶץ גֹּשֶׁן כִּי־תוֹעֲבַת מִצְרַיִם כָּל־רֹעֵה צֹאן:

א וַיָּבֹא יוֹסֵף וַיַּגֵּד לְפַרְעֹה וַיֹּאמֶר אָבִי וְאַחַי וְצֹאנָם וּבְקָרָם וְכָל־אֲשֶׁר לָהֶם בָּאוּ מֵאֶרֶץ כְּנָעַן וְהִנָּם בְּאֶרֶץ גֹּשֶׁן: **ב** וּמִקְצֵה אֶחָיו לָקַח חֲמִשָּׁה אֲנָשִׁים וַיַּצִּגֵם לִפְנֵי פַרְעֹה: **ג** וַיֹּאמֶר פַּרְעֹה אֶל־אֶחָיו מַה־מַּעֲשֵׂיכֶם וַיֹּאמְרוּ אֶל־פַּרְעֹה רֹעֵה צֹאן עֲבָדֶיךָ גַּם־אֲנַחְנוּ גַּם־אֲבוֹתֵינוּ: **ד** וַיֹּאמְרוּ אֶל־פַּרְעֹה לָגוּר בָּאָרֶץ בָּאנוּ כִּי־אֵין מִרְעֶה לַצֹּאן אֲשֶׁר לַעֲבָדֶיךָ כִּי־כָבֵד הָרָעָב בְּאֶרֶץ כְּנָעַן וְעַתָּה יֵשְׁבוּ־נָא עֲבָדֶיךָ בְּאֶרֶץ גֹּשֶׁן: **ה** וַיֹּאמֶר פַּרְעֹה אֶל־יוֹסֵף לֵאמֹר אָבִיךָ וְאַחֶיךָ בָּאוּ אֵלֶיךָ: **ו** אֶרֶץ מִצְרַיִם לְפָנֶיךָ הִוא בְּמֵיטַב הָאָרֶץ הוֹשֵׁב אֶת־אָבִיךָ וְאֶת־אַחֶיךָ יֵשְׁבוּ בְּאֶרֶץ גֹּשֶׁן וְאִם־יָדַעְתָּ וְיֶשׁ־בָּם אַנְשֵׁי־חַיִל וְשַׂמְתָּם שָׂרֵי מִקְנֶה עַל־אֲשֶׁר־לִי:

[31] Then Joseph said to his brothers and to his father's household, "I will go up and tell the news

to Pharaoh, and say to him, 'My brothers and my father's household, who were in the land of Canaan, have come to me.

[32] The men are shepherds; they have always been breeders of livestock, and they have brought with them their flocks and herds and all that is theirs.'

[33] So when Pharaoh summons you and asks, 'What is your occupation?'

[34] you shall answer, 'Your servants have been breeders of livestock from the start until now, both we and our fathers' - so that you may stay in the region of Goshen. For all shepherds are abhorrent to Egyptians.'"

[47:1] Then Joseph came and reported to Pharaoh, saying, "My father and my brothers, with their flocks and herds and all that is theirs, have come from the land of Canaan and are now in the region of Goshen."

[2] And selecting a few of his brothers, he presented them to Pharaoh.

[3] Pharaoh said to his brothers, "What is your occupation?" They answered Pharaoh, "We your servants are shepherds, as were also our fathers.

[4] We have come," they told Pharaoh, "to sojourn in this land, for there is no pasture for your servants' flocks, the famine being severe in the land of Canaan. Pray, then, let your servants stay in the region of Goshen."

[5] Then Pharaoh said to Joseph, "As regards your father and your brothers who have come to you,

[6] the land of Egypt is open before you: settle your father and your brothers in the best part of the land; let them stay in the region of Goshen.

*And if you know any capable men among them,
put them in charge of my livestock."*

[34] So that you may stay in the region of Goshen: Although Joseph brings the family to Egypt, he still settles them separately. For Joseph as a "secular nationalist," physical separation of the Jews and opposition to mixed marriages are important priorities. As he lacks Judah's spirituality, this is the only way that Joseph can preserve the Jewish people.

[47:2] And selecting a few of his brothers, he presented them to Pharaoh: Literally, "five of his brothers." Five is a sacred number to the Egyptians, but the Jews' sacred number is seven. Both of these numbers derive from the same general principle, but the respective approaches are different.

Five represents the four directions plus the center (the "I" and the four points). Seven is the six directions (including 'up' and 'down') and the center. The difference between the Egyptian and Jewish perceptions of the world around them is that for Jews, unlike the Egyptians, the top and bottom are also regarded as cardinal points.

A Jew's world is not only what he sees all around him – right, left, front and back – but also what is beneath his feet and in heaven above. What happened to us before birth and what will happen after death is all a part of the the unity that comprises the natural universe, not something otherworldly that is beyond our world. But for the Egyptians, what is above and below belongs only to the "higher" or "lower" realms, and has no application whatsoever to the natural world.

[4] We have come ... to sojourn in this land: *Lagur,* "to sojourn," means a temporary stay, which differs from what

Joseph's wants for his family (46:34), "so that you may stay in the region of Goshen," that is, to remain there permanently. Although the brothers are subordinated to Joseph, they see nothing permanent in their resettlement in Egypt, let alone anything of actual spiritual value.

[6] The land of Egypt is open before you: settle your father and your brothers in the best part of the land: Jewish cattle breeders are absolutely no cause for concern to Pharaoh, and he offers exceptionally conducive conditions for resettling them in Egypt.

Put them in charge of my livestock: We saw earlier (45:16) that Pharaoh was so pleased with Joseph's idea of bringing his whole family to Egypt, that he even ordered Joseph to quickly collect Jacob and all his children and grandchildren, and even to have them jettison their belongings as necessary, in order to arrive without delay.

Now we learn that Pharaoh himself has herds that require shepherds. But for the Egyptians this is a problem: "For all shepherds are abhorrent to Egyptians" (46:34). This suggests that the Pharaoh of Joseph's era, an owner of herds, was an atypical Pharaoh. He might not even have been an Egyptian by birth.

This Pharaoh might have been one of the Hyksos, or some other of the Semitic tribes that conquered Egypt during that period, which would explain why he felt out of his element in Egypt. Coming himself from a shepherding background, Pharaoh is truly pleased that shepherds were arriving in Egypt, although he prefers even so to settle them separately.

This hypothesis could also explain why Pharaoh so readily agrees to appoint Joseph as ruler over Egypt, and why mutual understanding arises immediately between Pharaoh and the

Jacob family. It also clarifies what we read at the beginning of Exodus (1:8): "A new king arose over Egypt who did not know Joseph." After the Hyksos were driven out of Egypt, the next Pharaohs were again true Egyptians.

The progression of world history, the succession of dynasties, and the hegemony of different nations and countries in turn might seem entirely unrelated to the Jews. But in fact, those instances in which we do see a Jewish connection demonstrate that all events are orchestrated by God for correcting and reeducating the Jewish people.

53.7. Jacob Blesses Pharaoh (47:7-10)

ז וַיָּבֵא יוֹסֵף אֶת־יַעֲקֹב אָבִיו וַיַּעֲמִדֵהוּ לִפְנֵי פַרְעֹה
וַיְבָרֶךְ יַעֲקֹב אֶת־פַּרְעֹה: ח וַיֹּאמֶר פַּרְעֹה אֶל־יַעֲקֹב
כַּמָּה יְמֵי שְׁנֵי חַיֶּיךָ: ט וַיֹּאמֶר יַעֲקֹב אֶל־פַּרְעֹה יְמֵי שְׁנֵי
מְגוּרַי שְׁלֹשִׁים וּמְאַת שָׁנָה מְעַט וְרָעִים הָיוּ יְמֵי שְׁנֵי חַיַּי
וְלֹא הִשִּׂיגוּ אֶת־יְמֵי שְׁנֵי חַיֵּי אֲבֹתַי בִּימֵי מְגוּרֵיהֶם: י
וַיְבָרֶךְ יַעֲקֹב אֶת־פַּרְעֹה וַיֵּצֵא מִלִּפְנֵי פַרְעֹה:

[7] Joseph then brought his father Jacob and presented him to Pharaoh; and Jacob greeted Pharaoh.

[8] Pharaoh asked Jacob, "How many are the years of your life?"

[9] And Jacob answered Pharaoh, "The years of my sojourn [on earth] are one hundred and thirty. Few and hard have been the years of my life, nor do they come up to the life spans of my fathers during their sojourns."

[10] Then Jacob bade Pharaoh farewell, and left Pharaoh's presence.

[8] Pharaoh asked Jacob, "How many are the years of your life?": Pharaoh, seeing a gray-haired old man standing before him, is interested to learn how old he is. Apparently, people in those times did not usually live to such an advanced age.

[9] Few and hard have been the years of my life, nor do they come up to the life spans of my fathers during their sojourns: The Midrash adds that since the Jews' elder patriarch Abraham had come to Egypt two hundred years earlier, Pharaoh wonders if this is still the same person. Jacob therefore explains that Abraham was one of his ancestors, and also notes that his own life has been far more turbulent than that of his ancestors. To wit: In his youth, he was in conflict with Esau and had to flee from him to Haran. Then, there was the deceit perpetrated by Laban, the acrimonious parting with him, and doing battle with an angel. On Jacob's return home he experienced a painful meeting with Esau, the rape of Dinah in Shechem, and the tragic death of his beloved wife Rachel. And finally, he grieved for twenty years over Joseph's assumed, violent death.

[10] Then Jacob bade Pharaoh farewell: Literally, "Jacob blessed Pharaoh, and took leave of Pharaoh." Because Pharaoh greatly values Joseph's abilities, he seems to regard Joseph's father Jacob as miracle worker. Pharaoh is therefore gratified at the close of their conversation to receive a blessing from Jacob.

This dialogue is also symbolically significant for Israel on the national level. Jacob (the Jewish Diaspora) gives Pharaoh his blessing (they enrich the lands in which they live). But Pharaoh (the given country of their residence) wonders just how old Jacob (the Jewish nation) is. The extreme antiquity of the Jewish people inspires dread in the much younger surrounding cultures. Moreover, the fear of the Jews that erupts in anti-Semitism is based in part on the spectacular ancientness of the Jewish people – the image of "the eternal Jew."

However, Jacob himself (Diaspora Jewry) does not feel how wonderful and successful the life of the Jewish people is, compared with all other peoples on earth. The Jewish community of the Diaspora continually and invariably asserts that "few and hard have been the years of my life." They feel that their life is a total disaster, especially against the historical background of their ancestors who lived autonomously in their own Land. Only in the Land of Israel can the Jewish people experience a normal and satisfying national life.

Chapter 54

Joseph's Egyptian Reforms

54.1. Joseph's Economic Revolution (47:11-21)

יא וַיּוֹשֵׁב יוֹסֵף אֶת־אָבִיו וְאֶת־אֶחָיו וַיִּתֵּן לָהֶם אֲחֻזָּה בְּאֶרֶץ מִצְרַיִם בְּמֵיטַב הָאָרֶץ בְּאֶרֶץ רַעְמְסֵס כַּאֲשֶׁר צִוָּה פַרְעֹה: יב וַיְכַלְכֵּל יוֹסֵף אֶת־אָבִיו וְאֶת־אֶחָיו וְאֵת כָּל־בֵּית אָבִיו לֶחֶם לְפִי הַטָּף: יג וְלֶחֶם אֵין בְּכָל־הָאָרֶץ כִּי־כָבֵד הָרָעָב מְאֹד וַתֵּלַהּ אֶרֶץ מִצְרַיִם וְאֶרֶץ כְּנַעַן מִפְּנֵי הָרָעָב: יד וַיְלַקֵּט יוֹסֵף אֶת־כָּל־הַכֶּסֶף הַנִּמְצָא בְאֶרֶץ־מִצְרַיִם וּבְאֶרֶץ כְּנַעַן בַּשֶּׁבֶר אֲשֶׁר־הֵם שֹׁבְרִים וַיָּבֵא יוֹסֵף אֶת־הַכֶּסֶף בֵּיתָה פַרְעֹה: טו וַיִּתֹּם הַכֶּסֶף מֵאֶרֶץ מִצְרַיִם וּמֵאֶרֶץ כְּנַעַן וַיָּבֹאוּ כָל־מִצְרַיִם אֶל־יוֹסֵף לֵאמֹר הָבָה־לָּנוּ לֶחֶם וְלָמָּה נָמוּת נֶגְדֶּךָ כִּי אָפֵס כָּסֶף: טז וַיֹּאמֶר יוֹסֵף הָבוּ מִקְנֵיכֶם וְאֶתְּנָה לָכֶם בְּמִקְנֵיכֶם אִם־אָפֵס כָּסֶף: יז וַיָּבִיאוּ אֶת־מִקְנֵיהֶם אֶל־יוֹסֵף וַיִּתֵּן לָהֶם יוֹסֵף לֶחֶם בַּסּוּסִים וּבְמִקְנֵה הַצֹּאן וּבְמִקְנֵה הַבָּקָר וּבַחֲמֹרִים וַיְנַהֲלֵם בַּלֶּחֶם בְּכָל־מִקְנֵהֶם בַּשָּׁנָה הַהִוא: יח וַתִּתֹּם הַשָּׁנָה הַהִוא וַיָּבֹאוּ אֵלָיו בַּשָּׁנָה הַשֵּׁנִית וַיֹּאמְרוּ לוֹ לֹא־נְכַחֵד מֵאֲדֹנִי כִּי אִם־תַּם הַכֶּסֶף וּמִקְנֵה הַבְּהֵמָה אֶל־אֲדֹנִי לֹא נִשְׁאַר לִפְנֵי אֲדֹנִי בִּלְתִּי אִם־גְּוִיָּתֵנוּ וְאַדְמָתֵנוּ: יט לָמָּה נָמוּת לְעֵינֶיךָ גַּם־אֲנַחְנוּ גַּם אַדְמָתֵנוּ קְנֵה־אֹתָנוּ וְאֶת־אַדְמָתֵנוּ בַּלָּחֶם

וְנִחְיֶה אֲנַחְנוּ וְאַדְמָתֵנוּ עֲבָדִים לְפַרְעֹה וְתֶן־זֶרַע וְנִחְיֶה
וְלֹא נָמוּת וְהָאֲדָמָה לֹא תֵשָׁם: כ וַיִּקֶן יוֹסֵף אֶת־כָּל־
אַדְמַת מִצְרַיִם לְפַרְעֹה כִּי־מָכְרוּ מִצְרַיִם אִישׁ שָׂדֵהוּ כִּי־
חָזַק עֲלֵהֶם הָרָעָב וַתְּהִי הָאָרֶץ לְפַרְעֹה: כא וְאֶת־הָעָם
הֶעֱבִיר אֹתוֹ לֶעָרִים מִקְצֵה גְבוּל־מִצְרַיִם וְעַד־קָצֵהוּ:

[11] So Joseph settled his father and his brothers, giving them holdings in the choicest part of the land of Egypt, in the region of Rameses, as Pharaoh had commanded.

[12] Joseph sustained his father, and his brothers, and all his father's household with bread, down to the little ones.

[13] Now there was no bread in all the world, for the famine was very severe; both the land of Egypt and the land of Canaan languished because of the famine.

[14] Joseph gathered in all the money that was to be found in the land of Egypt and in the land of Canaan, as payment for the rations that were being procured, and Joseph brought the money into Pharaoh's palace.

[15] And when the money gave out in the land of Egypt and in the land of Canaan, all the Egyptians came to Joseph and said, "Give us bread, lest we die before your very eyes; for the money is gone!"

[16] And Joseph said, "Bring your livestock, and I will sell to you against your livestock, if the money is gone.

[17] So they brought their livestock to Joseph, and Joseph gave them bread in exchange for the horses, for the stocks of sheep and cattle, and the

asses; thus he provided them with bread that year in exchange for all their livestock.

[18] And when that year was ended, they came to him the next year and said to him, "We cannot hide from my lord that, with all the money and animal stocks consigned to my lord, nothing is left at my lord's disposal save our persons and our farmland.

[19] Let us not perish before your eyes, both we and our land. Take us and our land in exchange for bread, and we with our land will be serfs to Pharaoh; provide the seed, that we may live and not die, and that the land may not become a waste."

[20] So Joseph gained possession of all the farm land of Egypt for Pharaoh, every Egyptian having sold his field because the famine was too much for them; thus the land passed over to Pharaoh.

[21] And he removed the population town by town, from one end of Egypt's border to the other.

[12] Joseph sustained his father, and his brothers, and all his father's household: The entire Jacob clan was regarded as Joseph's personal family – therefore, unlike other inhabitants of Egypt, they did not pay for bread and were permitted to keep their money and their herds. This privileged position, which the Egyptians initially accepted as the natural order of things, later became, apparently, one of the reasons for the Egyptians' hostile attitude towards Jews.

No matter how hard Joseph worked to ensure the survival of the Egyptians in difficult years, and to establish a normal life for both Egyptians and Jews in Egypt, he was unable to avert a conflict. Such conflicts are also a regular feature of Jewish life in exile.

[14] Joseph gathered in all the money that was to be found in the land of Egypt and in the land of Canaan, as payment for the rations that were being procured: Joseph senses that his own *raison dêtre* is to restructure Egyptian life. He strives to establish material conditions for the people that can save them from hunger, and to create a system that would also help prevent hunger in the future. As already noted, Joseph is the personification of Jewish "economic messianism."

And Yosef brought this silver into the house of Pharaoh: Joseph collected the grain in the manner of a "food tax" and sold it for silver, and soon all Egyptian silver was in Pharaoh's hands. All moneys had become the property of the state, and cash flow entirely ceased due to the country's universal lack of cash.

[16] And Joseph said, "Bring your livestock": We see that the Egyptians did have large animals useful for plowing – horses and donkeys – and small livestock as well. The target of their hate was only the professional herders of sheep.

[20] So Joseph gained possession of all the farm land of Egypt for Pharaoh: In this manner Joseph abolished all private property in Egypt, and from that moment the Egyptians lost their connection with the land, and also their personal freedom.

[21] And he removed the population town by town, from one end of Egypt's border to the other: All property now belonged to the state. In order to leave the people with fewer memories of their lost land, Joseph translocated them from one end of Egypt to the other, thus severing them from their roots, from their former life, and from their old attitudes, and rendering them psychologically "rootless."

So long as a person lives in his own house and next to his own field, even when they are no longer legally his, he retains a tribal memory, a sense of connection with the past. But now, when the famine continues, even this, the last stage of the reform (relocation and separation of the people from their roots) raises no objections.

As a result, the Egyptians have become a people deprived not only of their private property and any means of future production, but also their home and their motherland – simply put, their entire former culture. They are now totally dependent on Pharaoh, while their employer and "bread-winner" Joseph believes that, thanks to that dependence, he can actually begin to reeducate them. Thus, Joseph hopes to reform Egypt, believing that the people, deprived of their independence and living under conditions of forced equality, will change for the better.

With this modernization, Joseph dismantles Egypt's old economic structures and creates new ones – organized state socialism – having bought up the people's property for the state, and now apportioned to them allotments of land on behalf of the state. Joseph cannot appreciate human personal freedom, not even his own, because economic indicators are for him much more important.

Joseph underestimates the harm he is doing to himself, nor does he see how destructive this process is for Egypt, and what a blow the Jewish people will suffer in the process, as they become enslaved by it.

Joseph is well versed in the Egyptian economy, but has a

poor understanding of the Egyptian soul. This is the perennial problem of Jewish reformers in foreign lands, who always strive for the very best, and always fail to achieve their goal.

54.2. The Land of the Priests (47:22)

כב רַק אַדְמַת הַכֹּהֲנִים לֹא קָנָה כִּי חֹק לַכֹּהֲנִים מֵאֵת פַּרְעֹה וְאָכְלוּ אֶת־חֻקָּם אֲשֶׁר נָתַן לָהֶם פַּרְעֹה עַל־כֵּן לֹא מָכְרוּ אֶת־אַדְמָתָם:

[22] Only the land of the priests he did not take over, for the priests had an allotment from Pharaoh, and they lived off the allotment which Pharaoh had made to them; therefore they did not sell their land.

[22] For the priests had an allotment from Pharaoh: Because the priests received their share of bread directly from Pharaoh, they had no need during the years of famine to buy bread or to sell their land. Their power and authority thus remained unchanged. Joseph married into that class of society, hoping that through them he could influence Egypt, but he failed in the endeavor.

54.3. The Egyptians' Gratitude and Their Consent to Serfdom (47:23-26)

כג וַיֹּאמֶר יוֹסֵף אֶל־הָעָם הֵן קָנִיתִי אֶתְכֶם הַיּוֹם וְאֶת־אַדְמַתְכֶם לְפַרְעֹה הֵא־לָכֶם זֶרַע וּזְרַעְתֶּם אֶת־הָאֲדָמָה: **כד** וְהָיָה בַּתְּבוּאֹת וּנְתַתֶּם חֲמִישִׁית לְפַרְעֹה וְאַרְבַּע

הַיָּדֹת יִהְיֶה לָכֶם לְזֶרַע הַשָּׂדֶה וּלְאָכְלְכֶם וְלַאֲשֶׁר
בְּבָתֵּיכֶם וְלֶאֱכֹל לְטַפְּכֶם: **כה** וַיֹּאמְרוּ הֶחֱיִתָנוּ נִמְצָא־
חֵן בְּעֵינֵי אֲדֹנִי וְהָיִינוּ עֲבָדִים לְפַרְעֹה: **כו** וַיָּשֶׂם אֹתָהּ
יוֹסֵף לְחֹק עַד־הַיּוֹם הַזֶּה עַל־אַדְמַת מִצְרַיִם לְפַרְעֹה
לַחֹמֶשׁ רַק אַדְמַת הַכֹּהֲנִים לְבַדָּם לֹא הָיְתָה לְפַרְעֹה:

[23] Then Joseph said to the people, "Whereas I have this day acquired you and your land for Pharaoh, here is seed for you to sow the land.
[24] And when harvest comes, you shall give one-fifth to Pharaoh, and four-fifths shall be yours as seed for the fields and as food for you and those in your households, and as nourishment for your children."
[25] And they said, "You have saved our lives! We are grateful to my lord, and we shall be serfs to Pharaoh."
[26] And Joseph made it into a land law in Egypt, which is still valid, that a fifth should be Pharaoh's; only the land of the priests did not become Pharaoh's.

[23] Here is seed for you to sow the land: The people are now economically independent, and the state provides them with the tools of their labor.

[24] And when harvest comes, you shall give one-fifth to Pharaoh: The relatively high tax proposed by Joseph, twenty percent, was initially intended as a means of salvation from hunger, but is now becoming a permanent solution. The tax supports the economic power of the state, which now controls its citizens, but also bears responsibility for them. It seems to Joseph that this new political order will be a boon to the inhabitants of the state.

[25] And they said, "You have saved our lives! We are grateful to my lord, and we shall be serfs to Pharaoh: The Egyptians understand Joseph's merit in saving them from starvation, and they seem quite amenable to becoming slaves on a stable supply of basic necessities.

[26] And Joseph made it into a land law in Egypt, which is still valid: Joseph, originally called up to manage a crisis, now institutes permanent legislation for the future, exceeding the bounds of his authority, and thereby paving the way for his own downfall.

54.4. The Jews Put Down Roots in Egypt (47:27)

כז וַיֵּשֶׁב יִשְׂרָאֵל בְּאֶרֶץ מִצְרַיִם בְּאֶרֶץ גֹּשֶׁן וַיֵּאָחֲזוּ בָהּ
וַיִּפְרוּ וַיִּרְבּוּ מְאֹד:

[27] Thus Israel settled in the country of Egypt, in the region of Goshen; they acquired holdings in it, and were fertile and increased greatly.

(27) They acquired holdings in it: What was initially planned as a temporary stay became a permanent one. But at the same time, the Jews did not reeducate Egypt. On the contrary, Egypt devoured the Jews.

Weekly Portion
Vayechi

Chapter 55

Joseph Becomes the Fourth Patriarch

55.1. Joseph's Oath to Bury Jacob in the Cave of Machpelah (47:28-31)

כח וַיְחִי יַעֲקֹב בְּאֶרֶץ מִצְרַיִם שְׁבַע עֶשְׂרֵה שָׁנָה וַיְהִי
יְמֵי־יַעֲקֹב שְׁנֵי חַיָּיו שֶׁבַע שָׁנִים וְאַרְבָּעִים וּמְאַת שָׁנָה:
כט וַיִּקְרְבוּ יְמֵי־יִשְׂרָאֵל לָמוּת וַיִּקְרָא | לִבְנוֹ לְיוֹסֵף
וַיֹּאמֶר לוֹ אִם־נָא מָצָאתִי חֵן בְּעֵינֶיךָ שִׂים־נָא יָדְךָ
תַּחַת יְרֵכִי וְעָשִׂיתָ עִמָּדִי חֶסֶד וֶאֱמֶת אַל־נָא תִקְבְּרֵנִי
בְּמִצְרָיִם: **ל** וְשָׁכַבְתִּי עִם־אֲבֹתַי וּנְשָׂאתַנִי מִמִּצְרַיִם
וּקְבַרְתַּנִי בִּקְבֻרָתָם וַיֹּאמַר אָנֹכִי אֶעֱשֶׂה כִדְבָרֶךָ: **לא**
וַיֹּאמֶר הִשָּׁבְעָה לִי וַיִּשָּׁבַע לוֹ וַיִּשְׁתַּחוּ יִשְׂרָאֵל עַל־רֹאשׁ
הַמִּטָּה:

[28] Jacob lived seventeen years in the land of Egypt, so that the span of Jacob's life came to one hundred and forty-seven years.
[29] And when the time approached for Israel to die, he summoned his son Joseph and said to him, "Do me this favor, place your hand under

my thigh as a pledge of your steadfast loyalty:
please do not bury me in Egypt.
[30] When I lie down with my fathers, take me up
from Egypt and bury me in their burial-place."
He replied, "I will do as you have spoken."
[31] And he said, "Swear to me." And he swore to
him. Then Israel bowed at the head of the bed.

After the Torah's account of Joseph's fall, we move on to weekly portion *Vayechi*, which tells of the rise of Judah. The main themes in this portion are Jacob's blessings to his sons, Jacob's death and interment in the cave of Machpelah, and the inauguration of the structure of the future Jewish nation.

[28] Jacob lived seventeen years in the land of Egypt: During that interval the famine in Egypt had long since ended, and Joseph's exalted status in in the eyes of the Egyptians had begun to fade.

[29] And when the time approached for Israel to die: These words speak of a precipitous descent into exile, which will be completely and finally realized only after Joseph's own death.

[31] And he said, "Swear to me": Not satisfied with a mere promise from Joseph, Jacob demands of his son a solemn oath. The Midrash notes that an oath performs several functions. It provides assurance that the promise will be ultimately fulfilled. It gives the person who has taken the oath the moral strength he needs for that fulfillment. And finally, the oath can help overcome future obstacles in relation to third parties – in this case, for example, with Pharaoh, from whom Joseph will need to obtain permission to stage his father's funeral. Joseph will successfully persuade Pharaoh of that urgency with the words, "My father made me swear, saying, "I am about to die. Be sure to bury me in the grave which I made ready for myself in the land of Canaan" (50:5).

Then Israel bowed at the head of the bed: Here Jacob is again called "Israel," because he will be buried in his own Land. And he bows to Joseph, because by helping his father Israel, Joseph's status is elevated, making him worthy of that honor.

55.2. Ephraim and Manasseh Are Raised to the Status of Tribes (48:1-9)

א וַיְהִי אַחֲרֵי הַדְּבָרִים הָאֵלֶּה וַיֹּאמֶר לְיוֹסֵף הִנֵּה אָבִיךָ חֹלֶה וַיִּקַּח אֶת־שְׁנֵי בָנָיו עִמּוֹ אֶת־מְנַשֶּׁה וְאֶת־אֶפְרָיִם: ב וַיֻּגַּד לְיַעֲקֹב וַיֹּאמֶר הִנֵּה בִּנְךָ יוֹסֵף בָּא אֵלֶיךָ וַיִּתְחַזֵּק יִשְׂרָאֵל וַיֵּשֶׁב עַל־הַמִּטָּה: ג וַיֹּאמֶר יַעֲקֹב אֶל־יוֹסֵף אֵל שַׁדַּי נִרְאָה־אֵלַי בְּלוּז בְּאֶרֶץ כְּנָעַן וַיְבָרֶךְ אֹתִי: ד וַיֹּאמֶר אֵלַי הִנְנִי מַפְרְךָ וְהִרְבִּיתִךָ וּנְתַתִּיךָ לִקְהַל עַמִּים וְנָתַתִּי אֶת־הָאָרֶץ הַזֹּאת לְזַרְעֲךָ אַחֲרֶיךָ אֲחֻזַּת עוֹלָם: ה וְעַתָּה שְׁנֵי־בָנֶיךָ הַנּוֹלָדִים לְךָ בְּאֶרֶץ מִצְרַיִם עַד־בֹּאִי אֵלֶיךָ מִצְרַיְמָה לִי־הֵם אֶפְרַיִם וּמְנַשֶּׁה כִּרְאוּבֵן וְשִׁמְעוֹן יִהְיוּ־לִי: ו וּמוֹלַדְתְּךָ אֲשֶׁר־הוֹלַדְתָּ אַחֲרֵיהֶם לְךָ יִהְיוּ עַל שֵׁם אֲחֵיהֶם יִקָּרְאוּ בְּנַחֲלָתָם: ז וַאֲנִי | בְּבֹאִי מִפַּדָּן מֵתָה עָלַי רָחֵל בְּאֶרֶץ כְּנַעַן בַּדֶּרֶךְ בְּעוֹד כִּבְרַת־אֶרֶץ לָבֹא אֶפְרָתָה וָאֶקְבְּרֶהָ שָּׁם בְּדֶרֶךְ אֶפְרָת הִוא בֵּית לָחֶם: ח וַיַּרְא יִשְׂרָאֵל אֶת־בְּנֵי יוֹסֵף וַיֹּאמֶר מִי־אֵלֶּה: ט וַיֹּאמֶר יוֹסֵף אֶל־אָבִיו בָּנַי הֵם אֲשֶׁר־נָתַן־לִי אֱלֹהִים בָּזֶה וַיֹּאמַר קָחֶם־נָא אֵלַי וַאֲבָרֲכֵם:

[1] Some time afterward, Joseph was told, "Your

father is ill." So he took with him his two sons,
Manasseh and Ephraim.

[2] When Jacob was told, "Your son Joseph has
come to see you," Israel summoned his strength
and sat up in bed.

[3] And Jacob said to Joseph, "El Shaddai
appeared to me at Luz in the land of Canaan,
and He blessed me,

[4] and said to me, 'I will make you fertile
and numerous, making of you a community
of peoples; and I will assign this land to your
offspring to come for an everlasting possession.'

[5] Now, your two sons, who were born to you in
the land of Egypt before I came to you in Egypt,
shall be mine; Ephraim and Manasseh shall be
mine no less than Reuben and Simeon.

[6] But progeny born to you after them shall be
yours; they shall be recorded instead of their
brothers in their inheritance.

[7] I [do this because], when I was returning from
Paddan, Rachel died, to my sorrow, while I was
journeying in the land of Canaan, when still
some distance short of Ephrath; and I buried her
there on the road to Ephrath – now Bethlehem.

[8] Noticing Joseph's sons, Israel asked, "Who
are these?"

[9] And Joseph said to his father, "They are my
sons, whom God has given me here." "Bring them
up to me," he said, "that I may bless them."

[2] Israel summoned his strength and sat up in bed: With
his last ounce of strength, Jacob exerts himself to be Israel,

so that Ephraim and Manasseh will receive their blessing from Israel rather than from Jacob.

[3] El Shaddai appeared to me at Luz: In Luz (Bethel) Jacob had long ago received God's promise that he would return from exile in Haran back to his own Land, and that after that return he would receive God's special blessing (28:13 ff.).

[4] I will make you fertile and numerous, making of you a community of peoples; and I will assign this land to your offspring: Jacob connects his blessing of Ephraim and Manasseh with his possession of the Land and his return to it, thus disabusing them of Joseph's idea of putting down roots in Egypt.

[5] Now, your two sons, who were born to you in the land of Egypt before I came to you in Egypt, shall be mine: Ephraim and Manasseh, who were born in isolation from the rest of Jacob's family, must now be directly connected with Jacob, and they must at the same time be elevated to the status of tribes. Thus, in addition to his receiving a double share as befits a first-born (Deut. 21:17), Joseph's own status is raised to that of "semi-Patriarch."

We would note that Jewish tradition has preserved the burial places of the Patriarchs and their wives, and Joseph's as well, but we know nothing of where all the other sons of Jacob were buried. This too raises Joseph closer to the level of the Patriarchs.

[7] Rachel died, to my sorrow, while I was journeying in the land of Canaan: Jacob apparently feels guilty, and makes excuses for having buried Rachel by the side of the road, and not in the family tomb in the Cave of Machpelah.

Jacob to some extent compensates for this deficiency in Rachel's funereal honors by raising Ephraim and Manasseh, her grandchildren, to the status of full tribes.

[8] Noticing Joseph's sons, Israel asked, "Who are these?": Jacob is of course well acquainted with his grandchildren, and in fact has just mentioned them by name. Jacob's question "Who are these?" is similar to God's question to Adam, "Where are you?" (3:9). Israel is asking Joseph: "Well, what can you actually tell me about these children?"

[9] And Joseph said to his father, "They are my sons, whom God has given me here": Joseph responds with what he considers most significant: that his sons were born right there in Egypt. But then Jacob reverses the order of their seniority, thereby completely upsetting Joseph's worldview.

Ephraim and Manasseh were born during that period of Joseph's life when his understanding of the inner workings of his family and the relationships within it was deficient. Joseph's sons, originally isolated from the rest of the Jewish nation, are now being reunited with it, becoming a symbol of restoration. The blessing that Jacob gives Ephraim and Manasseh is therefore very specific, and its wording will later become fixed in tradition as the formula used on every occasion when Jewish parents formally bless their children.

55.3. Jacob Blesses Ephraim and Manasseh (48:10-20)

י וְעֵינֵי יִשְׂרָאֵל כָּבְדוּ מִזֹּקֶן לֹא יוּכַל לִרְאוֹת וַיַּגֵּשׁ אֹתָם
אֵלָיו וַיִּשַּׁק לָהֶם וַיְחַבֵּק לָהֶם: יא וַיֹּאמֶר יִשְׂרָאֵל
אֶל־יוֹסֵף רְאֹה פָנֶיךָ לֹא פִלָּלְתִּי וְהִנֵּה הֶרְאָה אֹתִי
אֱלֹהִים גַּם אֶת־זַרְעֶךָ: יב וַיּוֹצֵא יוֹסֵף אֹתָם מֵעִם בִּרְכָּיו

וַיִּשְׁתַּחוּ לְאַפָּיו אָרְצָה: **יג** וַיִּקַּח יוֹסֵף אֶת־שְׁנֵיהֶם אֶת־
אֶפְרַיִם בִּימִינוֹ מִשְּׂמֹאל יִשְׂרָאֵל וְאֶת־מְנַשֶּׁה בִשְׂמֹאלוֹ
מִימִין יִשְׂרָאֵל וַיַּגֵּשׁ אֵלָיו: **יד** וַיִּשְׁלַח יִשְׂרָאֵל אֶת־יְמִינוֹ
וַיָּשֶׁת עַל־רֹאשׁ אֶפְרַיִם וְהוּא הַצָּעִיר וְאֶת־שְׂמֹאלוֹ עַל־
רֹאשׁ מְנַשֶּׁה שִׂכֵּל אֶת־יָדָיו כִּי מְנַשֶּׁה הַבְּכוֹר: **טו** וַיְבָרֶךְ
אֶת־יוֹסֵף וַיֹּאמַר הָאֱלֹהִים אֲשֶׁר הִתְהַלְּכוּ אֲבֹתַי לְפָנָיו
אַבְרָהָם וְיִצְחָק הָאֱלֹהִים הָרֹעֶה אֹתִי מֵעוֹדִי עַד־הַיּוֹם
הַזֶּה: **טז** הַמַּלְאָךְ הַגֹּאֵל אֹתִי מִכָּל־רָע יְבָרֵךְ אֶת־
הַנְּעָרִים וְיִקָּרֵא בָהֶם שְׁמִי וְשֵׁם אֲבֹתַי אַבְרָהָם וְיִצְחָק
וְיִדְגּוּ לָרֹב בְּקֶרֶב הָאָרֶץ: **יז** וַיַּרְא יוֹסֵף כִּי־יָשִׁית אָבִיו
יַד־יְמִינוֹ עַל־רֹאשׁ אֶפְרַיִם וַיֵּרַע בְּעֵינָיו וַיִּתְמֹךְ יַד־
אָבִיו לְהָסִיר אֹתָהּ מֵעַל רֹאשׁ־אֶפְרַיִם עַל־רֹאשׁ מְנַשֶּׁה:
יח וַיֹּאמֶר יוֹסֵף אֶל־אָבִיו לֹא־כֵן אָבִי כִּי־זֶה הַבְּכֹר
שִׂים יְמִינְךָ עַל־רֹאשׁוֹ: **יט** וַיְמָאֵן אָבִיו וַיֹּאמֶר יָדַעְתִּי
בְנִי יָדַעְתִּי גַּם־הוּא יִהְיֶה־לְּעָם וְגַם־הוּא יִגְדָּל וְאוּלָם
אָחִיו הַקָּטֹן יִגְדַּל מִמֶּנּוּ וְזַרְעוֹ יִהְיֶה מְלֹא־הַגּוֹיִם: **כ**
וַיְבָרֲכֵם בַּיּוֹם הַהוּא לֵאמוֹר בְּךָ יְבָרֵךְ יִשְׂרָאֵל לֵאמֹר
יְשִׂמְךָ אֱלֹהִים כְּאֶפְרַיִם וְכִמְנַשֶּׁה וַיָּשֶׂם אֶת־אֶפְרַיִם
לִפְנֵי מְנַשֶּׁה:

[10] *Now Israel's eyes were dim with age; he
could not see. So [Joseph] brought them close
to him, and he kissed them and embraced them.*
[11] *And Israel said to Joseph, "I never expected
to see you again, and here God has let me see
your children as well."*
[12] *Joseph then removed them from his knees,
and bowed low with his face to the ground.*
[13] *Joseph took the two of them, Ephraim with
his right hand – to Israel's left – and Manasseh
with his left hand – to Israel's right – and brought
them close to him.*
[14] *But Israel stretched out his right hand and*

laid it on Ephraim's head, though he was the younger, and his left hand on Manasseh's head – thus crossing his hands – although Manasseh was the first-born.

[15] And he blessed Joseph, saying, "The God in whose ways my fathers Abraham and Isaac walked, The God who has been my shepherd from my birth to this day –

[16] The Angel who has redeemed me from all harm – Bless the lads. In them may my name be recalled, And the names of my fathers Abraham and Isaac, And may they be teeming multitudes upon the earth."

[17] When Joseph saw that his father was placing his right hand on Ephraim's head, he thought it wrong; so he took hold of his father's hand to move it from Ephraim's head to Manasseh's.

[18] "Not so, Father," Joseph said to his father, "for the other is the first-born; place your right hand on his head."

[19] But his father objected, saying, "I know, my son, I know. He too shall become a people, and he too shall be great. Yet his younger brother shall be greater than he, and his offspring shall be plentiful enough for nations."

[20] So he blessed them that day, saying, "By you shall Israel invoke blessings, saying: God make you like Ephraim and Manasseh." Thus he put Ephraim before Manasseh.

[10] Now Israel's eyes were dim with age: We have twice before encountered "weak eyes" in this book of Genesis, with reference to Isaac and to Leah. In both of those cases, the Midrash understands that weakness as inattention to the surrounding environment, and aspiring instead to a higher meaning. According to the Midrash, Isaac's eyes grew dim as he lay on the altar (22:9). No longer noticing anything close by to himself, Isaac saw only the things that stood well off in the distance. And Leah was likewise initially of a mind to neglect the temporal, striving only for the eternal.

Here too, Israel, having attained extreme old age, is gazing far into the distance, no longer focusing on the present, and thinking instead about more lofty matters than his immediate surroundings.

[11] And here God has let me see your children as well: The descendants here are especially important, because only through them can Joseph remake himself as *Mashiach ben Yosef.*

[14] But Israel stretched out his right hand: The blessings to Ephraim and Manasseh are given in the name of Israel, not Jacob, because those blessings will have to be realized after the Exodus, when the Jews are already in the Land of Israel.

Thus crossing his hands – although Manasseh was the first-born: The purpose of this reordering is to amend the idea that Joseph had originally invested in the names of his children. "Joseph named the first-born Manasseh, meaning, 'God has made me forget completely my hardship and my parental home.' And the second he named Ephraim, meaning, 'God has made me fertile in the land of my affliction'" (41:51-52). In other words, Joseph was saying that he owed his success to his having forgotten his father's house. It is this incorrect belief that Israel now wants to change.

Manasseh represents "oblivion of things past," which can be realized, however, in different ways. Joseph believed that being completely oblivious to the past is the key to future success. Israel is telling Joseph that, by adopting a proper outlook, partial oblivion becomes possible, but it must be the *result* of one's success, and not vice versa. When Manasseh is not a leader, when he only complements Ephraim, then his "oblivion" becomes not the driving force, but only a technical auxiliary, having the property of "forgetting only that which would be truly superfluous to remember." And even then that oblivion cannot facilitate success; it must happen only after one is already advancing toward success.

After receiving Israel's blessing, Manasseh's tribe reverses its orientation and becomes a symbol not of forgetting but of memory. Precisely because Manasseh knows what oblivion is, he also understands better than anyone else what memory is.

Centuries later, Manasseh will be the only tribe to receive its allotment of territory on both sides of the Jordan, thus joining the Transjordan with the Land of Canaan. When during the conquest of the Promised Land the tribes of Gad and Reuben remained on the east bank of the Jordan River, and the remaining tribes moved on to the west bank, only the tribe of Manasseh tribe was in half between both banks, thus serving as a unifying link that would prevent the Jewish nation from splintering apart.

[15] And he blessed Joseph: Only after correctly positioning his hands on Joseph's sons' heads does Israel then bless Joseph, thus conveying that the blessing of Joseph's children is also intended to correct him. Joseph cannot be blessed without the correct relative placement of Ephraim and Manasseh.

[18] "Not so, Father," Joseph said to his father: But Joseph, contrary to his father Jacob's expectations, continues to believe that his father blesses his children incorrectly. That is, Joseph continues to put Manasseh above Ephraim.

[19] But his father objected, saying, "I know, my son, I know": "I know" twofold: I know who is chronologically older, and I know that you are mistaken in your assessment of their potentials.

[20] By you shall Israel invoke blessings, saying: "God make you like Ephraim and Manasseh": The purpose of Jacob's blessing was mainly to raise Ephraim and Manasseh to the level of his own children, but also to change Joseph's views on his success as the result of his oblivion. To accomplish this, Jacob not only frames a special blessing for Ephraim and Manasseh, but adds, "By you shall Israel invoke blessings, saying...." That is, the people of Israel will repeat the wording of this blessing throughout all their generations.

55.4. Joseph Receives an Additional Portion (48:21-22)

כא וַיֹּאמֶר יִשְׂרָאֵל אֶל־יוֹסֵף הִנֵּה אָנֹכִי מֵת וְהָיָה
אֱלֹהִים עִמָּכֶם וְהֵשִׁיב אֶתְכֶם אֶל־אֶרֶץ אֲבֹתֵיכֶם: כב
וַאֲנִי נָתַתִּי לְךָ שְׁכֶם אַחַד עַל־אַחֶיךָ אֲשֶׁר לָקַחְתִּי מִיַּד
הָאֱמֹרִי בְּחַרְבִּי וּבְקַשְׁתִּי:

[21] Then Israel said to Joseph, "I am about to die; but God will be with you and bring you back to the land of your fathers.
[22] And now, I assign to you one portion more than to your brothers, which I wrested from the Amorites with my sword and bow."

[22] And now, I assign to you one portion more than to your brothers: "One portion more" in the Hebrew text is *shechem achad.* Joseph's additional portion can be understood either as "one plot of land," or as "one Shechem" (the city of Shechem).

Shechem, where Joseph's tomb will later be located, sits exactly on the border between the territories of Ephraim and Manasseh. Jacob gives Joseph the city of Shechem as an inheritance, rather than dividing it between Joseph's sons. Jacob's intent is that this joint possession will unite the two tribes.

Which I wrested from the Amorites with my sword and bow: The reference is not to Jacob himself, who purchased that plot of land (33:19), but to his sons, who took the city by force.

Shechem is located at the very center of the Land of Israel. Although Jerusalem is the spiritual capital of the Land of Israel, Shechem is its material capital and geographical center. And that is why Joseph's descendants, having Shechem as their foundation, will be able to realize their aspirations of material success.

However, we can also understand this verse somewhat differently – as a blessing for Joseph to succeed in military affairs. Says Jacob, "I hereby give you an advantage, the ability to wrest land from the Amorites with sword and bow." This is important because, upon *Mashiach ben Yosef's* return to the Land of Israel, military prowess will be indispensable to him.

In addition to Joseph's superlative managerial abilities, he is now blessed with military prowess, which he did not previously have.

Chapter 56

Jacob Blesses His Sons

56.1. The Purpose and Meaning of Jacob's Blessings (49:1-2)

א וַיִּקְרָא יַעֲקֹב אֶל־בָּנָיו וַיֹּאמֶר הֵאָסְפוּ וְאַגִּידָה לָכֶם
אֵת אֲשֶׁר־יִקְרָא אֶתְכֶם בְּאַחֲרִית הַיָּמִים: ב הִקָּבְצוּ
וְשִׁמְעוּ בְּנֵי יַעֲקֹב וְשִׁמְעוּ אֶל־יִשְׂרָאֵל אֲבִיכֶם:

[1] And Jacob called his sons and said, "Come together that I may tell you what is to befall you in days to come.
[2] Assemble and hearken, O sons of Jacob; hearken to Israel your father:

[2] Assemble and hearken, O sons of Jacob; hearken to Israel your father: The Jews in exile, the sons of *Jacob*, must hear and accept the words of *Israel*, for only upon returning to the Land will the blessings of the tribes be truly realized.

These blessings make it especially clear that although Joseph is still king, spiritual leadership continues to manifest more decisively in Judah.

[1] That I may tell you what is to befall you in days to come:
Literally, "in the end of days," an expressions that always indicates the end of an era. To Jacob, the "end of days" means the return to the Land of Israel, and the whole point of the blessings that follow is to elaborate on the merits to be evinced by each tribe in the course of its subsistence on its Land.

With these blessings Jacob wants to assign to each tribe its own individual function, in order that upon their return to the Land of Israel, disagreements among the tribes can be avoided. Since the main source of conflict among the brothers was the issue of who would receive the kingdom, Jacob in his blessings makes a point of emphasizing those aspects of each tribe's character that made it generally unsuitable to lead the Jewish people (i.e., makes them ineligible to become kings).

56.2. The Blessing of Reuben (49:3-4)

ג רְאוּבֵן בְּכֹרִי אַתָּה כֹּחִי וְרֵאשִׁית אוֹנִי יֶתֶר שְׂאֵת וְיֶתֶר
עָז׃ ד פַּחַז כַּמַּיִם אַל־תּוֹתַר כִּי עָלִיתָ מִשְׁכְּבֵי אָבִיךָ אָז
חִלַּלְתָּ יְצוּעִי עָלָה׃

[3] Reuben, you are my first-born, my might and first fruit of my vigor, exceeding in rank and exceeding in honor.
[4] Unstable as water, you shall excel no longer; for when you mounted your father's bed, you brought disgrace – my couch he mounted!

[3] Reuben, you are my first-born: Reuben, as the first-born, enjoys the greatest abundance of possibilities, but he is incapable of being prudent, judicious, or fair. Reuben lost the birthright by his own doing – he was impetuous. No government has a right to make hasty decisions or to act without forethought.

[4] You shall excel no longer; for when you mounted your father's bed, you brought disgrace: As already noted, Reuben's offense was by no means as serious as a straightforward reading of the Torah text suggests. Reuben was therefore not excluded from being counted among the Twelve Tribes. But he was divested of the rights of the firstborn.

You shall excel no longer: And what are those rights that Reuben would have received? The kingdom, the priesthood, and a double share in his father's inheritance. But because Reuben forfeited the birthright, those three elements were divided among the remainder of the Jewish people. The double inheritance went to Joseph (two tribes, Ephraim and Manasseh), the kingdom went to Judah, and the priesthood to Levi.

56.3. The Blessing of Simeon and Levi (49: 5-7)

ה שִׁמְעוֹן וְלֵוִי אַחִים כְּלֵי חָמָס מְכֵרֹתֵיהֶם: ו בְּסֹדָם אַל־תָּבֹא נַפְשִׁי בִּקְהָלָם אַל־תֵּחַד כְּבֹדִי כִּי בְאַפָּם הָרְגוּ אִישׁ וּבִרְצֹנָם עִקְּרוּ־שׁוֹר: ז אָרוּר אַפָּם כִּי עָז וְעֶבְרָתָם כִּי קָשָׁתָה אֲחַלְּקֵם בְּיַעֲקֹב וַאֲפִיצֵם בְּיִשְׂרָאֵל:

[5] Simeon and Levi are a pair; their weapons are tools of lawlessness.
[6] Let not my person be included in their council, let not my being be counted in their

assembly. For when angry they slay men, and
when pleased they maim oxen.
[7] Cursed be their anger so fierce, and their
wrath so relentless. I will divide them in Jacob,
scatter them in Israel.

[5] Simeon and Levi are a pair; their weapons are tools of lawlessness: It is not clear from the text exactly what Jacob means here – the murder of the inhabitants of Shechem, or selling Joseph. Either way, Jacob takes Simeon and Levi to task for their rash actions. They are expert swordsmen – a valuable skill in and of itself – but they are thoughtless in the application of their energies, and their actions are those of fanatics. It is true that every nation must have a certain number of fanatics, but fanaticism makes it impossible to control the state. Seeing every situation only from their own point of view, fanatics are incapable of considering any opinion but their own.

[7] I will divide them in Jacob, scatter them in Israel: The benefits that Simeon and Levi can bring the nation are realized only when they are separated and scattered among all the other tribes. The tribe of Simeon will receive its allotment of territory inside the territory of Judah, and Levi will be resettled across different cities within all the other tribes. Like salt and pepper, they are important for the well-being of the people, but only in limited quantities, and when dispersed among the rest of the tribes.

The tribe of Levi later found it correction and received the priesthood, but the tribe of Simeon, on the contrary, experienced a downfall, lost its identity, and was wholly absorbed by the tribe of Judah.

56.4. The Blessing of Judah (49:8-12)

ח יְהוּדָה אַתָּה יוֹדוּךָ אַחֶיךָ יָדְךָ בְּעֹרֶף אֹיְבֶיךָ יִשְׁתַּחֲווּ לְךָ
בְּנֵי אָבִיךָ: ט גּוּר אַרְיֵה יְהוּדָה מִטֶּרֶף בְּנִי עָלִיתָ כָּרַע רָבַץ
כְּאַרְיֵה וּכְלָבִיא מִי יְקִימֶנּוּ: י לֹא־יָסוּר שֵׁבֶט מִיהוּדָה
וּמְחֹקֵק מִבֵּין רַגְלָיו עַד כִּי־יָבֹא שִׁילֹה וְלוֹ יִקְּהַת עַמִּים: יא
אֹסְרִי לַגֶּפֶן עִירֹה וְלַשֹּׂרֵקָה בְּנִי אֲתֹנוֹ כִּבֵּס בַּיַּיִן לְבֻשׁוֹ וּבְדַם־
עֲנָבִים סוּתֹה: יב חַכְלִילִי עֵינַיִם מִיָּיִן וּלְבֶן־שִׁנַּיִם מֵחָלָב:

*[8] You, O Judah, your brothers shall praise;
your hand shall be on the nape of your foes;
your father's sons shall bow low to you.
[9] Judah is a lion's whelp; on prey, my son, have
you grown. He crouches, lies down like a lion, like
the king of beasts – who dare rouse him?
[10] The scepter shall not depart from Judah,
nor the ruler's staff from between his feet; so
that tribute shall come to him and the homage
of peoples be his.
[11] He tethers his ass to a vine, his ass's foal to a
choice vine; he washes his garment in wine, his
robe in blood of grapes.
[12] His eyes are darker than wine; his teeth are
whiter than milk.*

[8] You, O Judah, your brothers shall praise: Judah is here
immediately distinguished in that all the other brothers
consent to his reign. Without this, kingship is impossible.

Your hand shall be on the nape of your foes: Judah can
destroy his enemies, or just as easily – should he so choose
– let them live, but force them to submit to his will.

[9] Judah is a lion's whelp: The Midrash understands "lion's whelp" as expressing not a single idea (i.e., a young lion), but two opposite ones. Judah is advancing from *gur* to *aryeh*, from lion's whelp to lion. At first he is slight, but when he becomes great, no one can displace him. Judah has inner dynamics, the ability to improve and repent – a critical prerequisite for the ruler of a kingdom.

On prey, my son, have you grown: An alternate translation is "You have risen from (i.e., abandoned) your prey." Judah is able to restrain himself just in time and change his point of view. Judah's main virtue is not that he is thoroughly righteous, but that he can remediate his sins.

He crouches, lies down like a lion, like the king of beasts – who dare rouse him?: Judah is always prepared just to wait, which in the end gives his deeds a solid foundation.

[10] The scepter shall not depart from Judah, nor the ruler's staff from between his feet; so that tribute shall come to him: This phrase reads in the original Hebrew, "*ad ki yavo shiloh*," a somewhat ambiguous construction that might be understood as "until he (Judah) comes to Shiloh." Shiloh is a geographic district in Samaria. But this is historically incorrect, given that clearly the "scepter" remained with Judah (so as to "not depart" from him) *after* Shiloh especially, when, during the period of Judges, there was a Jewish religious center there. Thus it would be inaccurate to interpret this verse as limiting Judah's eminence to the period *preceding* Shiloh.

The Midrash therefore interprets these words as "until Shiloh himself comes" (i.e., the Messiah), the idea here being that Judah will rule without interruption until his descendant the Messiah arrives.

[12] His eyes are darker than wine; His teeth are whiter than milk: Judah's territory abounds with vineyards (from Jerusalem unto Hebron) and pastures (from Hebron toward the south). Wine, which is red, represents the quality of *Gevurah*, justice, while milk, white, is the quality of *Chesed*, kindness. The kingdom can stand firm only when justice and mercy are united.

Thus, Judah's brothers acknowledge his authority. Judah can pursue his policies calmly and confidently. Rather than attempting to suppress others, he tries always to improve himself. It is therefore only right that the kingdom should belong to him.

The other brothers cannot create a lasting kingdom, because each of them, unlike Judah, is too narrowly focused, immersed only in his own individual concerns, to the detriment of all other aspects of life. Because of that, none of them is fit to be a leader of the nation as a whole. This shortcoming is made evident in each of their blessings.

56.5. Zebulun's Blessing (49:13)

יג זְבוּלֻן לְחוֹף יַמִּים יִשְׁכֹּן וְהוּא לְחוֹף אֳנִיֹּת וְיַרְכָתוֹ עַל־צִידֹן:

[13] Zebulun shall dwell by the seashore; he shall be a haven for ships, and his flank shall rest on Sidon.

[13] Shall dwell by the seashore; he shall be a haven for ships: Zebulun's occupations are fishing and international trade.

And his flank shall rest on Sidon: Zebulun's territory stretches from Haifa, approximately, and almost to Sidon (the city of Saida in modern Lebanon), which belonged to the Phoenicians, who likewise had a strong connection to the sea.

Zebulun is at the opposite end of the spectrum from the extremes of Simeon and Levi (who tend to religious zealotry, and typically circulate only among their own people). Zebulun is a man of very broad outlook. His trade brings him in contact with other nations – with Sidon, for example. But all this means that he is outwardly directed, and for that reason would not make a good king. External associations cannot be allowed to interfere with state interests.

56.6. Issachar's Blessing (49:14-15)

יד יִשָּׂשכָר חֲמֹר גָּרֶם רֹבֵץ בֵּין הַמִּשְׁפְּתָיִם: טו וַיַּרְא
מְנֻחָה כִּי טוֹב וְאֶת־הָאָרֶץ כִּי נָעֵמָה וַיֵּט שִׁכְמוֹ לִסְבֹּל
וַיְהִי לְמַס־עֹבֵד:

[14] Issachar is a strong-boned ass, crouching among the sheepfolds.
[15] When he saw how good was security, and how pleasant was the country, he bent his shoulder to the burden, and became a toiling serf.

[14] Issachar is a strong-boned ass, crouching among the sheepfolds: Issachar's territory is the extraordinarily fertile Jezreel Valley (between the mountainous regions of Samaria and the Galilee). The Midrash, however, understands

Issachar's blessing not in the sense of agricultural work, but of intense Torah study. He is like an donkey that can be made to carry a very sizeable burden.

[15] He bent his shoulder to the burden, and became a toiling serf: Tradition adds that Issachar and Zebulun have a symbiotic relationship. By mutual agreement, Zebulun provides for their combined material needs, and Issachar studies Torah for both of them. Moreover, since Zebulun provides for Issachar, Zebulun is seen as fulfilling even his own commandment of Torah study through Issachar, and receives a commensurate Heavenly reward.

(In the literal sense, Issachar produces an abundant agricultural yield, which Zebulun then sells to international markets – an arrangement that brings prosperity to both.)

[15] When he saw how good was security, and how pleasant was the country: Issachar was not fit to be king because he loved the quiet life and had no interest in leadership. Labor and teaching are interesting to him, but power and management are not. He is therefore quite satisfied to occupy a subordinate position.

A person who makes Torah study his regular occupation will often become so enamored of the spiritual life that he comes to believe he has no need for political independence at all. He might even consider his independence a useless burden, from which he wants to be relieved by freeing himself of all political responsibility. This implies that rabbis cannot properly govern a state, because a king is expected to look after all aspects of national life, and not only its spiritual side.

56.7. Dan's Blessing (49:16-18)

טז דָּן יָדִין עַמּוֹ כְּאַחַד שִׁבְטֵי יִשְׂרָאֵל: יז יְהִי־דָן נָחָשׁ
עֲלֵי־דֶרֶךְ שְׁפִיפֹן עֲלֵי־אֹרַח הַנֹּשֵׁךְ עִקְּבֵי־סוּס וַיִּפֹּל רֹכְבוֹ
אָחוֹר: יח לִישׁוּעָתְךָ קִוִּיתִי יי:

*[16] Dan shall govern his people, as one of the
tribes of Israel.*
*[17] Dan shall be a serpent by the road, a viper
by the path, that bites the horse's heels so that
his rider is thrown backward.*
[18] I wait for Your deliverance, O Lord!

**[16] Dan shall govern his people, as one of the tribes of
Israel:** Dan mostly considers himself a loner, and not a part
of the national collective. That is, he does not see himself
as operating within the system.

The tribe of Dan is so disorganized that it will prove itself
incapable of managing its initial allotment of land (Gush Dan,
in the vicinity of today's Tel Aviv). And so the tribe will relocate itself to the north, at the feet of Mount Hermon (which
is why another locality there is also called "Dan"). Later, when
Scripture wishes to delineate the territorial boundaries of
Israel, it uses the expression "from Dan to Beersheba" (Jud.
20:1, 2 Sam. 3:20). "Dan" refers to the northernmost point
of Jewish settlement, and "Beersheba" to the southernmost.

Dan is Joseph's extreme expression, something that was
laid down immediately at Dan's birth, when Rachel gave
Jacob her servant Bilhah, whose firstborn was Dan. Thus, Dan
was born so as to anticipate the birth of Joseph to Rachel.
Thus, Dan is the precursor to Joseph. And if we are talking
about Joseph's unwillingness to be satisfied with the limits

of the Jewish question, which therefore orients him to the peoples of the world, then all this is manifested yet more compellingly in Dan.

The Midrash believes that at a certain point in Jewish history some part of the tribe of Dan abandoned the Land of Israel. Ethiopian Jews consider themselves descendants of the tribe of Dan. But, on the other hand, some historians associate Dan with the Denyen people, who were Greeks, and they consider Dan an immigrant tribe, whose members were originally not Jewish (having descended from the Denyen), and only later integrated into the Jewish people. Needless to say, from the traditional Jewish point of view this is simply not true, since Dan is not an immigrant tribe, but one of Jacob's sons. Nonetheless, the idea that Dan is connected with other nations of the world is not without some "spiritual basis."

[17] Dan shall be a serpent by the road, a viper by the path, that bites the horse's heels so that his rider is thrown backward: This tactic of surprise attack is characteristic of a partisan, not a soldier. A classic example of such a man from the tribe of Dan is Samson, who battles the Philistines not as the member of a regular army, but as a lone partisan. The tribe of Dan is anarchist in nature and refuses to submit to any other power. Dan, in a certain sense, is the opposite of Judah, who is always organized and whose methods are always systematic.

[18] I wait for Your deliverance, O Lord!: Jacob beseeches God that even such a troubled tribe as Dan should not be completely severed from the Jewish nation. Thus we see that the Jewish people consists of two opposite poles: the tribe of Judah, representing royalty and statehood, and the tribe of Dan, representing the other extreme – anarchy, which is always trying to exceed the limits of the system.

And yet, for constructing the Tabernacle the Torah later requires two engineer-architects: Bezalel son of Uri of the tribe of Judah, and Oholiab son of Ahisamach of the tribe of Dan as his assistant (Exodus 30: 1, 6). The nation is built from all twelve tribes together: from Judah who leads, and from Dan who brings up the rear (Num. 10:14, 25). Thus, for creating the Tabernacle we need a synthesis of these two completely opposite elements.

At the same time, "Dan shall govern (literally, 'judge') his people," which is meant in the sense of an anarchist uprising that endeavors to restore justice where the prevailing system has failed.

It is self-evident that Dan is not fit for the role of king.

56.8. Gad's Blessing (49:19)

יט גָּד גְּדוּד יְגוּדֶנּוּ וְהוּא יָגֻד עָקֵב:

[19] Gad shall be raided by raiders, but he shall raid at their heels.

[19] Gad shall be raided by raiders, but he shall raid at their heels: Gad's territory is the northern Gilad on the east bank of the Jordan. Gad is a professional military man, a systematic warrior, not a partisan. He is a general in the regular army, and when the time comes to conquer the Land, his troops will fight valiantly and effectively.

Gad is an ideal fighter, but it is clear that such a person cannot be a leader of the people, because he sees every situation only from a military perspective.

Gad shall be raided by raiders: That is, if he sees that it is tactically necessary to retreat, then, being a military man, he will retreat, since that will not prevent him from driving back the enemy later. But Gad underestimates the non-military aspect (civil, psychological, historical, and so on) of his actions and the potential harm of retreating. His understanding, therefore, never goes beyond local, momentary expediency, which is insufficient for proper leadership of a country.

Governing a state cannot be reduced to exclusively local objectives. It is a multifaceted endeavor that is much too important to be entrusted to the military.

56.9. Asher's Blessing (49:20)

כ מֵאָשֵׁר שְׁמֵנָה לַחְמוֹ וְהוּא יִתֵּן מַעֲדַנֵּי־מֶלֶךְ:

[20] Asher's bread shall be rich, and he shall yield royal dainties.

Asher's territory is the country's northern region. Asher specializes in producing high-quality goods, delivered "to the royal table," that is, for the benefit of the entire nation. He is an outstanding economist and business executive. But of course, this is not enough for governing a state.

56.10. Naftali's Blessing (49:21)

כא נַפְתָּלִי אַיָּלָה שְׁלֻחָה הַנֹּתֵן אִמְרֵי־שָׁפֶר:

[21] Naphtali is a hind let loose, which yields
lovely fawns.

Naftali's territory is the eastern Galilee. His priorities are
aesthetics and literature. These are essential values that give
coherence to our overall worldview, but they, too, are insufficient for ruling a nation.

Writers and artists are essential to national life, but they
cannot manage a state.

56.11. Joseph's Inner Conflict and the Blessing He Receives (49:22-26)

כב בֵּן פֹּרָת יוֹסֵף בֵּן פֹּרָת עֲלֵי־עָיִן בָּנוֹת צָעֲדָה עֲלֵי־
שׁוּר: כג וַיְמָרֲרֻהוּ וָרֹבּוּ וַיִּשְׂטְמֻהוּ בַּעֲלֵי חִצִּים: כד
וַתֵּשֶׁב בְּאֵיתָן קַשְׁתּוֹ וַיָּפֹזּוּ זְרֹעֵי יָדָיו מִידֵי אֲבִיר יַעֲקֹב
מִשָּׁם רֹעֶה אֶבֶן יִשְׂרָאֵל: כה מֵאֵל אָבִיךָ וְיַעְזְרֶךָּ וְאֵת
שַׁדַּי וִיבָרְכֶךָּ בִּרְכֹת שָׁמַיִם מֵעָל בִּרְכֹת תְּהוֹם רֹבֶצֶת
תָּחַת בִּרְכֹת שָׁדַיִם וָרָחַם: כו בִּרְכֹת אָבִיךָ גָּבְרוּ עַל־
בִּרְכֹת הוֹרַי עַד־תַּאֲוַת גִּבְעֹת עוֹלָם תִּהְיֶיןָ לְרֹאשׁ יוֹסֵף
וּלְקָדְקֹד נְזִיר אֶחָיו:

[22] Joseph is a wild ass, A wild ass by a spring –
wild colts on a hillside.
[23] Archers bitterly assailed him; they shot at
him and harried him.
[24] Yet his bow stayed taut, and his arms were
made firm by the hands of the Mighty One of
Jacob – there, the Shepherd, the Rock of Israel –
[25] The God of your father who helps you,
and Shaddai who blesses you With blessings of

heaven above, blessings of the deep that couches below, blessings of the breast and womb.
[26] The blessings of your father surpass the blessings of my ancestors, to the utmost bounds of the eternal hills. May they rest on the head of Joseph, on the brow of the elect of his brothers.

[23] Bitterly assailed him; they shot at him and harried him: The territory of Joseph, that is, of the tribes of Ephraim and Manasseh, is Samaria (from Bethel to the Jezreel Valley), and also includes the Bashan and the Golan in the Transjordan. Joseph is in many ways suited for the role of king. But despite his marked successes in all matters and his generally high spiritual level, he cannot be appointed king of Israel, because he is too conflicted. This is why he is unpopular and unloved, and his own brothers are at odds with him.

A person who arouses excessive discontent (talented and successful though he may be) cannot lead the nation or become a central figure within it. But a Jewish king must do exactly that. Joseph could successfully rule Egypt, because royal power is characterized there by isolation from the people. But Joseph could not be a leader in the Land of Israel, where power can be effective only when it has the nation's full support.

And therefore, when later in Jewish history a king must arise from Joseph's house, that king will be Saul, a descendant of Benjamin, but it cannot be Joseph himself.

[26] The blessings of your father surpass the blessings of my ancestors brothers: Joseph receives a special blessing that is even greater than that of Abraham and Isaac.

May they rest on the head of Joseph, on the brow of the elect of his: However, Joseph's success provokes a negative attitude from his brothers, which likewise only hinders Joseph's power.

56.12. Benjamin's Blessing (49:27)

כז בִּנְיָמִין זְאֵב יִטְרָף בַּבֹּקֶר יֹאכַל עַד וְלָעֶרֶב יְחַלֵּק
שָׁלָל:

[27] Benjamin is a ravenous wolf; in the morning he consumes the foe, and in the evening he divides the spoil."

Benjamin occupies territory that is at Israel's center, extending from Jerusalem to Bethel. The Temple in Jerusalem stands within that territory.

[27] Benjamin is a ravenous wolf: Benjamin is a remarkable individual, with fine family families, but he is too tough. The people who get in his way are in danger of being torn to shreds, and he doesn't know how to complete what he has begun. In the future, there will even be a situation where all the tribes will go to war against the tribe of Benjamin.

And yet, Benjamin serves as a unifying force. Judah and Joseph are united thanks to him. Without Benjamin the kingdom cannot stand, but even so he cannot successfully rule it. Saul, the first king of Israel, was from the tribe of Benjamin, but his dynasty could not achieve permanence on the throne.

In the morning he consumes the foe, and in the evening he divides the spoil: The Midrash understands this to mean that he is active in the morning and in the evening, but not in the middle of the day. That is, he wields influence only at the beginning and at the end of a process.

In the "morning," in the days of Saul, a kingdom is created, and in the "evening," the Babylonian captivity, when the kingdom is already in its twilight, Mordechai and Esther – also from the tribe of Benjamin – assert their presence. But in the middle of the "day," Benjamin has no staying power. He knows how to initiate an era, and also how to end it, but maintaining stability throughout the interval is simply not in his character.

56.13. The Unity of Jacob's Children, and His Dying Wish to Be Buried in Hebron (49:28-33)

כח כָּל־אֵלֶּה שִׁבְטֵי יִשְׂרָאֵל שְׁנֵים עָשָׂר וְזֹאת אֲשֶׁר־דִּבֶּר לָהֶם אֲבִיהֶם וַיְבָרֶךְ אוֹתָם אִישׁ אֲשֶׁר כְּבִרְכָתוֹ בֵּרַךְ אֹתָם: כט וַיְצַו אוֹתָם וַיֹּאמֶר אֲלֵהֶם אֲנִי נֶאֱסָף אֶל־עַמִּי קִבְרוּ אֹתִי אֶל־אֲבֹתָי אֶל־הַמְּעָרָה אֲשֶׁר בִּשְׂדֵה עֶפְרוֹן הַחִתִּי: ל בַּמְּעָרָה אֲשֶׁר בִּשְׂדֵה הַמַּכְפֵּלָה אֲשֶׁר עַל־פְּנֵי־מַמְרֵא בְּאֶרֶץ כְּנָעַן אֲשֶׁר קָנָה אַבְרָהָם אֶת־הַשָּׂדֶה מֵאֵת עֶפְרֹן הַחִתִּי לַאֲחֻזַּת־קָבֶר: לא שָׁמָּה קָבְרוּ אֶת־אַבְרָהָם וְאֵת שָׂרָה אִשְׁתּוֹ שָׁמָּה קָבְרוּ אֶת־יִצְחָק וְאֵת רִבְקָה אִשְׁתּוֹ וְשָׁמָּה קָבַרְתִּי אֶת־לֵאָה: לב מִקְנֵה הַשָּׂדֶה וְהַמְּעָרָה אֲשֶׁר־בּוֹ מֵאֵת בְּנֵי־חֵת: לג וַיְכַל יַעֲקֹב לְצַוֹּת אֶת־בָּנָיו וַיֶּאֱסֹף רַגְלָיו אֶל־הַמִּטָּה וַיִּגְוַע וַיֵּאָסֶף אֶל־עַמָּיו:

[28] All these were the tribes of Israel, twelve in number, and this is what their father said to

*them as he bade them farewell, addressing to
each a parting word appropriate to him.*

*[29] Then he instructed them, saying to them,
"I am about to be gathered to my kin. Bury me
with my fathers in the cave which is in the field
of Ephron the Hittite,*

*[30] the cave which is in the field of Machpelah,
facing Mamre, in the land of Canaan, the field
that Abraham bought from Ephron the Hittite
for a burial site –*

*[31] there Abraham and his wife Sarah were
buried; there Isaac and his wife Rebekah were
buried; and there I buried Leah –*

*[32] the field and the cave in it, bought from the
Hittites."*

*[33] When Jacob finished his instructions to his
sons, he drew his feet into the bed and, breathing
his last, he was gathered to his people.*

[28] All these were the tribes of Israel: All twelve tribes
together form one nation, and when all the tribes comprise
a single entity, even with all their individual shortcomings
they achieve a state of equilibrium and harmony.

The tribes of Israel, twelve in number: The tribes are
always twelve in number, although in some cases Ephraim
and Manasseh are counted as one tribe, and sometimes as
two. This compensates for a similar situation with the Levites, who are sometimes included in the number of tribes,
but sometimes not.

Take, for example, the breastplate of the High Priest which
featured twelve precious stones (Exod. 28:21). Ephraim and

Manasseh are jointly represented there by a single stone and as one tribe, the tribe of Joseph, because the Levites are also in that count of twelve stones, having their own stone that represents them in the breastplate.

But on the other hand, in dividing the Land of Israel into territories, the Levites are not included in the count of the tribes, because they do not receive a portion in the Land (Num. 18, v. 20, 24). Therefore, for the purpose of apportioning the land, Ephraim and Manasseh are considered two distinct tribes.

He bade them farewell: Literally, "he blessed them." The Torah wishes to emphasize that Jacob blessed all twelve of his sons, including Reuben, Simeon, and Levi, notwithstanding that his words to them were not what we would normally expect in a blessing.

The unity of the Jewish tribes is not achieved through homogeneity. On the contrary, because the tribes are so dissimilar, and, accordingly, there is so much variation in the blessings they receive, the Jewish people are a unique and complex system, which is precisely what makes them a dynamic and viable organism. Israel demonstrates the unity of the Creator not through like-minded uniformity, but through the harmony of their complementary differences.

[29] I am about to be gathered to my kin. Bury me with my fathers in the cave: Jacob has already exacted an oath from Joseph to bury him not in Egypt, but in the cave of Machpelah. But he repeats that instruction here so that Machpelah will become not merely Jacob's personal tomb, but a focus of national unity and a central meeting place for all the tribes.

As he approaches death, and as the Jewish exile begins, Jacob seeks to reinforce in the minds of the nation the idea that the Land of Israel (and Hebron in particular) is the center of Jewish life. With his decision to be buried in the cave of Machpelah, a source of considerable inconvenience for his sons, Jacob demonstrates that there is an address to which the Jews must always return. Jacob thus gives all his descendants to understand that their life in Egypt, in exile, is nothing more than a temporary episode.

The Cave of Machpelah binds the Jewish people to the Patriarchs. Through ownership of the burial grounds of their ancestors, the descendants never cease to feel their predecessors' vital influence. In later centuries, the memory of the Patriarchs will help the Jewish people to maintain contact with the Land of Israel, and in the twentieth century even to return to that land once more.

56.14. Jacob's Funeral (50:1–13)

א וַיִּפֹּל יוֹסֵף עַל־פְּנֵי אָבִיו וַיֵּבְךְּ עָלָיו וַיִּשַּׁק־לוֹ: ב וַיְצַו יוֹסֵף אֶת־עֲבָדָיו אֶת־הָרֹפְאִים לַחֲנֹט אֶת־אָבִיו וַיַּחַנְטוּ הָרֹפְאִים אֶת־יִשְׂרָאֵל: ג וַיִּמְלְאוּ־לוֹ אַרְבָּעִים יוֹם כִּי כֵּן יִמְלְאוּ יְמֵי הַחֲנֻטִים וַיִּבְכּוּ אֹתוֹ מִצְרַיִם שִׁבְעִים יוֹם: ד וַיַּעַבְרוּ יְמֵי בְכִיתוֹ וַיְדַבֵּר יוֹסֵף אֶל־בֵּית פַּרְעֹה לֵאמֹר אִם־נָא מָצָאתִי חֵן בְּעֵינֵיכֶם דַּבְּרוּ־נָא בְּאָזְנֵי פַרְעֹה לֵאמֹר: ה אָבִי הִשְׁבִּיעַנִי לֵאמֹר הִנֵּה אָנֹכִי מֵת בְּקִבְרִי אֲשֶׁר כָּרִיתִי לִי בְּאֶרֶץ כְּנַעַן שָׁמָּה תִּקְבְּרֵנִי וְעַתָּה אֶעֱלֶה־נָּא וְאֶקְבְּרָה אֶת־אָבִי וְאָשׁוּבָה: ו וַיֹּאמֶר פַּרְעֹה עֲלֵה וּקְבֹר אֶת־אָבִיךָ כַּאֲשֶׁר הִשְׁבִּיעֶךָ: ז וַיַּעַל יוֹסֵף לִקְבֹּר אֶת־אָבִיו וַיַּעֲלוּ אִתּוֹ כָּל־עַבְדֵי פַרְעֹה זִקְנֵי בֵיתוֹ וְכֹל זִקְנֵי אֶרֶץ־מִצְרָיִם: ח וְכֹל בֵּית יוֹסֵף וְאֶחָיו וּבֵית אָבִיו רַק טַפָּם וְצֹאנָם וּבְקָרָם עָזְבוּ בְּאֶרֶץ גֹּשֶׁן: ט וַיַּעַל עִמּוֹ גַּם־רֶכֶב גַּם־פָּרָשִׁים וַיְהִי הַמַּחֲנֶה כָּבֵד מְאֹד: י וַיָּבֹאוּ עַד־גֹּרֶן הָאָטָד אֲשֶׁר בְּעֵבֶר הַיַּרְדֵּן וַיִּסְפְּדוּ־שָׁם

מִסְפֵּד גָּדוֹל וְכָבֵד מְאֹד וַיַּעַשׂ לְאָבִיו אֵבֶל שִׁבְעַת יָמִים: **יא** וַיַּרְא יוֹשֵׁב הָאָרֶץ הַכְּנַעֲנִי אֶת־הָאֵבֶל בְּגֹרֶן הָאָטָד וַיֹּאמְרוּ אֵבֶל־כָּבֵד זֶה לְמִצְרָיִם עַל־כֵּן קָרָא שְׁמָהּ אָבֵל מִצְרַיִם אֲשֶׁר בְּעֵבֶר הַיַּרְדֵּן: **יב** וַיַּעֲשׂוּ בָנָיו לוֹ כֵּן כַּאֲשֶׁר צִוָּם: **יג** וַיִּשְׂאוּ אֹתוֹ בָנָיו אַרְצָה כְּנַעַן וַיִּקְבְּרוּ אֹתוֹ בִּמְעָרַת שְׂדֵה הַמַּכְפֵּלָה אֲשֶׁר קָנָה אַבְרָהָם אֶת־הַשָּׂדֶה לַאֲחֻזַּת־קֶבֶר מֵאֵת עֶפְרֹן הַחִתִּי עַל־פְּנֵי מַמְרֵא:

[1] Joseph flung himself upon his father's face and wept over him and kissed him.
[2] Then Joseph ordered the physicians in his service to embalm his father, and the physicians embalmed Israel.
[3] It required forty days, for such is the full period of embalming. The Egyptians bewailed him seventy days;
[4] and when the wailing period was over, Joseph spoke to Pharaoh's court, saying, "Do me this favor, and lay this appeal before Pharaoh:
[5] 'My father made me swear, saying, "I am about to die. Be sure to bury me in the grave which I made ready for myself in the land of Canaan." Now, therefore, let me go up and bury my father; then I shall return.'"
[6] And Pharaoh said, "Go up and bury your father, as he made you promise on oath."
[7] So Joseph went up to bury his father; and with him went up all the officials of Pharaoh, the senior members of his court, and all of Egypt's dignitaries,
[8] together with all of Joseph's household, his brothers, and his father's household; only their children, their flocks, and their herds were left in the region of Goshen.

[9] Chariots, too, and horsemen went up with him; it was a very large troop.

[10] When they came to Goren ha-Atad, which is beyond the Jordan, they held there a very great and solemn lamentation; and he observed a mourning period of seven days for his father.

[11] And when the Canaanite inhabitants of the land saw the mourning at Goren ha-Atad, they said, "This is a solemn mourning on the part of the Egyptians." That is why it was named Abel-mizraim, which is beyond the Jordan.

[12] Thus his sons did for him as he had instructed them.

[13] His sons carried him to the land of Canaan, and buried him in the cave of the field of Machpelah, the field near Mamre, which Abraham had bought for a burial site from Ephron the Hittite.

[3] The Egyptians bewailed him seventy days: They believed that Joseph's immediate family had brought blessings to their country. It seems that all the Egyptians, following Pharaoh's example, considered Jacob a miracle worker.

[4] Joseph spoke to Pharaoh's court, saying, "Do me this favor, and lay this appeal before Pharaoh": After everything we know of Joseph's prominence in Egypt, it is astonishing to learn that he cannot address Pharaoh directly in asking permission to bury his father in Canaan. As the memory of the great Egyptian famine has now apparently faded, Joseph's merits have also been forgotten, and his position in Pharaoh's court is greatly diminished from what it had previously been. Joseph was indispensable to the Egyptians in their hour of desperation. But now that the system he created for the new Egypt continues to function without his involvement, Joseph is again nothing more to them than an annoying foreigner.

[5] 'My father made me swear, saying, "I am about to die. Be sure to bury me in the grave which I made ready for myself": Joseph presents his request for Jacob's funeral as an exclusively individual affair, rather than a national one. This personal motif is understandable in Egypt, where the Pharaohs even during their lifetimes built pyramids for their own burials.

[6] And Pharaoh said, "Go up and bury your father, as he made you promise on oath": The oath that Jacob exacted from Joseph turned out to be completely warranted, for it helped Joseph obtain permission from Pharaoh to fulfill Jacob's wish to be buried in Canaan.

[11] This is a solemn mourning on the part of the Egyptians: The neighboring peoples see this funeral as a purely Egyptian event. Apparently, Jacob's sons were no longer very different in appearance from the Egyptians.

[12] Thus his sons did for him as he had instructed them: Joseph did not want the Egyptians to get too close to the Cave of Machpelah. He therefore held the final state ceremony at Goren ha-Atad, after which just a very modest family funeral followed. Jacob's sons simply carried the coffin containing the body of their father to the family tomb.

Chapter 57

Joseph's Old Age and Death

57.1. Joseph Will Not Retaliate Against His Brothers After His Father's Death (50:14-21)

יד וַיָּשָׁב יוֹסֵף מִצְרַיְמָה הוּא וְאֶחָיו וְכָל־הָעֹלִים אִתּוֹ
לִקְבֹּר אֶת־אָבִיו אַחֲרֵי קָבְרוֹ אֶת־אָבִיו: טו וַיִּרְאוּ אֲחֵי־
יוֹסֵף כִּי־מֵת אֲבִיהֶם וַיֹּאמְרוּ לוּ יִשְׂטְמֵנוּ יוֹסֵף וְהָשֵׁב
יָשִׁיב לָנוּ אֵת כָּל־הָרָעָה אֲשֶׁר גָּמַלְנוּ אֹתוֹ: טז וַיְצַוּוּ
אֶל־יוֹסֵף לֵאמֹר אָבִיךָ צִוָּה לִפְנֵי מוֹתוֹ לֵאמֹר: יז כֹּה־
תֹאמְרוּ לְיוֹסֵף אָנָּא שָׂא נָא פֶּשַׁע אַחֶיךָ וְחַטָּאתָם כִּי־
רָעָה גְמָלוּךָ וְעַתָּה שָׂא נָא לְפֶשַׁע עַבְדֵי אֱלֹהֵי אָבִיךָ וַיֵּבְךְּ
יוֹסֵף בְּדַבְּרָם אֵלָיו: יח וַיֵּלְכוּ גַּם־אֶחָיו וַיִּפְּלוּ לְפָנָיו
וַיֹּאמְרוּ הִנֶּנּוּ לְךָ לַעֲבָדִים: יט וַיֹּאמֶר אֲלֵהֶם יוֹסֵף
אַל־תִּירָאוּ כִּי הֲתַחַת אֱלֹהִים אָנִי: כ וְאַתֶּם חֲשַׁבְתֶּם
עָלַי רָעָה אֱלֹהִים חֲשָׁבָהּ לְטֹבָה לְמַעַן עֲשֹׂה כַּיּוֹם הַזֶּה
לְהַחֲיֹת עַם־רָב: כא וְעַתָּה אַל־תִּירָאוּ אָנֹכִי אֲכַלְכֵּל
אֶתְכֶם וְאֶת־טַפְּכֶם וַיְנַחֵם אוֹתָם וַיְדַבֵּר עַל־לִבָּם:

[14] *After burying his father, Joseph returned to Egypt, he and his brothers and all who had gone up with him to bury his father.*
[15] *When Joseph's brothers saw that their father*

was dead, they said, "What if Joseph still bears a grudge against us and pays us back for all the wrong that we did him!"

[16] So they sent this message to Joseph, "Before his death your father left this instruction:

[17] So shall you say to Joseph, 'Forgive, I urge you, the offense and guilt of your brothers who treated you so harshly.' Therefore, please forgive the offense of the servants of the God of your father." And Joseph was in tears as they spoke to him.

[18] His brothers went to him themselves, flung themselves before him, and said, "We are prepared to be your slaves."

[19] But Joseph said to them, "Have no fear! Am I a substitute for God?

[20] Besides, although you intended me harm, God intended it for good, so as to bring about the present result – the survival of many people.

[21] And so, fear not. I will sustain you and your children." Thus he reassured them, speaking kindly to them.

Only after Jacob's death do the brothers genuinely clarify their relationship, and achieve true mutual understanding.

[15] What if Joseph still bears a grudge against us and pays us back for all the wrong that we did him: While burying their father in the Cave of Machpelah, the brothers all together see Hebron, almost forty years after leaving there, and it brings back memories of their youth. However, the Midrash further reports that after his father's funeral,

Joseph went to see another important place in the Land of Israel: the pit into which he had been thrown by his brothers. This was Joseph's only opportunity to see the place where events occurred that were a critical turning point in his life. And upon seeing Joseph's actions, the brothers became frightened.

When Joseph's brothers saw that their father was dead: After his father's death, Joseph became somewhat estranged from his brothers. The Midrash adds that in the past Joseph would invite them to visit, but he now no longer did. It is quite possible that Joseph still found it difficult to have intimate dealings with the people who cast him into a pit, were prepared to kill him, and then sold him into slavery. The brothers now begin to fear that Joseph's kindly demeanor toward them is only a façade, and that he is actually planning to punish them.

[16] So they sent this message to Joseph, "Before his death your father left this instruction": The brothers, perhaps projecting their wary attitude towards Joseph onto themselves, even conceive on their own the idea that Jacob himself had asked Joseph not to harm them. But instead of telling Joseph themselves , they send someone to convey their message to him. (The Midrash reports that "they sent this message" means that they did so through one of their children.) The conflict of Joseph and his brothers had ended, but no lasting unity between them was actually established.

[17] And Joseph was in tears as they spoke to him: Joseph loves his brothers, and is therefore shocked and distressed to tears by their suspicions. Seeing that the brothers still fail to understand him, and still fear his royal status, Joseph realizes that his efforts to reeducate them have, at a deeper level, not led to any actual success.

[21] Thus he reassured them, speaking kindly to them:
While Jacob was alive, Joseph's relationship with his brothers could be considered a kind of forced existence, where they avoided open conflict only in order not to antagonize their father. When Joseph after Jacob's death would not take revenge on his brothers, and he even "reassured them, speaking kindly to them," this catches them off guard, and serves to correct them.

57.2. Joseph's Remorse (50: 22-26)

כב וַיֵּשֶׁב יוֹסֵף בְּמִצְרַיִם הוּא וּבֵית אָבִיו וַיְחִי יוֹסֵף
מֵאָה וָעֶשֶׂר שָׁנִים: כג וַיַּרְא יוֹסֵף לְאֶפְרַיִם בְּנֵי שִׁלֵּשִׁים
גַּם בְּנֵי מָכִיר בֶּן־מְנַשֶּׁה יֻלְּדוּ עַל־בִּרְכֵּי יוֹסֵף: כד וַיֹּאמֶר
יוֹסֵף אֶל־אֶחָיו אָנֹכִי מֵת וֵאלֹהִים פָּקֹד יִפְקֹד אֶתְכֶם
וְהֶעֱלָה אֶתְכֶם מִן־הָאָרֶץ הַזֹּאת אֶל־הָאָרֶץ אֲשֶׁר נִשְׁבַּע
לְאַבְרָהָם לְיִצְחָק וּלְיַעֲקֹב: כה וַיַּשְׁבַּע יוֹסֵף אֶת־בְּנֵי
יִשְׂרָאֵל לֵאמֹר פָּקֹד יִפְקֹד אֱלֹהִים אֶתְכֶם וְהַעֲלִתֶם
אֶת־עַצְמֹתַי מִזֶּה: כו וַיָּמָת יוֹסֵף בֶּן־מֵאָה וָעֶשֶׂר שָׁנִים
וַיַּחַנְטוּ אֹתוֹ וַיִּישֶׂם בָּאָרוֹן בְּמִצְרָיִם:

[22] So Joseph and his father's household remained in Egypt. Joseph lived one hundred and ten years.
[23] Joseph lived to see children of the third generation of Ephraim; the children of Machir son of Manasseh were likewise born upon Joseph's knees.
[24] At length, Joseph said to his brothers, "I am

*about to die. God will surely take notice of you
and bring you up from this land to the land that
He promised on oath to Abraham, to Isaac, and
to Jacob."
[25] So Joseph made the sons of Israel swear,
saying, "When God has taken notice of you, you
shall carry up my bones from here."
[26] Joseph died at the age of one hundred and
ten years; and he was embalmed and placed in
a coffin in Egypt.*

**[23] Joseph lived to see children of the third generation of
Ephraim; the children of Machir son of Manasseh were
likewise born upon Joseph's knees:** Seeing several generations of descendants living constructive, rewarding lives is
among the greatest blessings that any person can receive.

**[24] Joseph said to his brothers, "I am about to die. God
will surely take notice of you and bring you up from this
land to the land that He promised on oath to Abraham, to
Isaac, and to Jacob":** Joseph before his death speaks of the
Exodus from Egypt. He now understands that his ultimate
purpose is not the restructuring of Egypt, but establishing
a proper relationship with his brothers in order to build the
future Jewish people.

Joseph said to his brothers: Toward the end of his life
Joseph realizes that his extraordinary economic successes
and his fantastic career in Egypt are of only secondary
importance, while most important is the future of the Jewish people. With his last words Joseph paves the way for creating the category of *Mashiach ben Yosef*. The main thread of

human development will happen through the influence of the Jewish people, living as a single unit in their own Land, and not through the Jewish "economic messianism" of the Diaspora.

God will surely take notice of you and bring you up: It was hardly even necessary for Joseph to bring his brothers and father to Egypt. But he then arranged it such that they did not return to Canaan even after the seven years of famine had ended. And now, on the brink of death, Joseph can only rely on Divine support to feel certain that the Exodus will actually happen.

57.3. A Retrospect of Joseph's Life

Joseph is an exceptionally capable manager, who was appointed to solve a tactical problem, but mistakenly believed that his task was strategic. He fancied himself an economic messiah called upon to feed all of humanity. But in the end he saved only Egypt from starvation. And even that he was able accomplish only by relocating his family to him there.

Had it been only a matter of hunger, Joseph could have sent his family food from Egypt. He was wealthy enough to pay for that (nor did anyone demand of Joseph to account for his expenditures). Or, alternatively, he could have first introduced his family to Egyptian society merely to elevate his own status, and then devised an excuse for his father and brothers to return immediately to Canaan. But Joseph used the famine as a pretext to do what he wanted, namely, to relocate his family to Egypt, so that their presence would help him rebuild the country.

However, in wishing to preserve the nascent Jewish nation, he created a ghetto for his family on the outskirts of Egypt, for he understood that otherwise it would be impossible to prevent the Jews from intermarrying with the locals. And inevitably, the Children of Israel, already so very small in number, would have then disappeared among the Egyptians after only a few generations.

Joseph apparently believed that that is how the Chosen People was destined to be created. As he saw it, the Jews would become priests of the Almighty and conductors of the Divine light within Egypt, which would then serve as a source of illumination for all of humanity.

Paradoxically, Joseph himself combines universalism, his desire to wield influence through Egypt, with nationalism, his desire to preserve Jewish identity. But Joseph's plan failed, for the Jews were unable to influence Egypt.

Joseph's problem is that he sees only the nearest, most concrete task, and the issue he considers most central is the one that he is best able to cope with. It is therefore noteworthy that Joseph lived long enough to grasp the incorrectness of his original plan. Most reformers do not. Joseph's *teshuvah* (repentance) therefore lies in acknowledging that the efforts he made to improve Egypt, a foreign land, would have been better expended for the benefit of his own homeland.

By virtue of this repentance, Joseph paves the way for the birth of his descendant, *Mashiach ben Yoseph.*

Bible Plus

By **ISRAEL365**

Study the Bible Like Never Before

Scan to learn more

Hundreds of video courses by world renowned scholars.

Stand By Me

Hebrew Prayers for All Believers

A Three-Volume Treasury of Ancient Wisdom

Discover the transformative power of Hebrew prayer in this groundbreaking series that makes thousands of years of Jewish prayer tradition accessible to all believers.

- Volume 1: 43 essential prayers for daily life, healing, family, and gratitude
- Volume 2: Prayers for Sabbath, holidays, and spiritual growth
- Volume 3: Powerful prayers for Israel, America, and times of national crisis

Each volume features:

- Original Hebrew text
- Clear English translation
- Complete pronunciation guide
- Thoughtful commentary

Transform your prayer life with this complete collection

SCAN NOW!

Or visit
israel365store.com

Live Like David

Transform your daily spiritual practice with *Live Like David: Daily Devotional Journal,* an extraordinary three-volume masterwork that brings the timeless wisdom of King David into your daily life.

SCAN NOW!

Or visit israel365store.com